Selected Proceedings of the 14th Meeting
of the Slavic Linguistics Society

POTSDAM LINGUISTIC INVESTIGATIONS
POTSDAMER LINGUISTISCHE UNTERSUCHUNGEN
RECHERCHES LINGUISTIQUES À POTSDAM

Edited by / Herausgegeben von / Edité par

Peter Kosta, Gerda Haßler, Teodora Radeva-Bork, Lilia Schürcks, Nadine Thielemann and/und/et Vladislava Maria Warditz

Vol./Bd. 34

Zu Qualitätssicherung und Peer Review der vorliegenden Publikation

Die Qualität der in dieser Reihe erscheinenden Arbeiten wird vor der Publikation durch einen externen, von der Herausgeberschaft benannten Gutachter im Double Blind Verfahren geprüft. Dabei ist der Autor der Arbeit dem Gutachter während der Prüfung namentlich nicht bekannt; der Gutachter bleibt anonym.

Notes on the quality assurance and peer review of this publication

Prior to publication, the quality of the work published in this series is double blind reviewed by an external referee appointed by the editorship. The referee is not aware of the author's name when performing the review; the referee's name is not disclosed.

Steven L. Franks / Alan H. Timberlake /
Anna W. Wietecka (eds.)

Selected Proceedings of the 14th Meeting of the Slavic Linguistics Society

In Honor of Peter Kosta

PETER LANG

Bibliographic Information published by the Deutsche Nationalbibliothek
The Deutsche Nationalbibliothek lists this publication in the Deutsche Nationalbibliografie; detailed bibliographic data is available online at http://dnb.d-nb.de.

Library of Congress Cataloging-in-Publication Data
A CIP catalog record for this book has been applied for at the Library of Congress.

Cover illustration:
Cornelia Scheide: Untitled, 2021.
Courtesy of the artist

ISSN 1862-524X
ISBN 978-3-631-81160-3 (Print)
E-ISBN 978-3-631-86328-2 (E-PDF)
E-ISBN 978-3-631-86329-9 (EPUB)
DOI 10.3726/b18798

Peter Lang – Berlin · Bern · Bruxelles ·
New York · Oxford · Warszawa · Wien

This publication has been peer reviewed.

www.peterlang.com

Contents

List of Contributors

Vrinda Subhalaxmi Chidambaram
University of California, Riverside
vrinda@ucr.edu

Steven Franks
Indiana University, Bloomington
franks@iu.edu

Jadranka Gvozdanović
Heidelberg University
Jadranka.Gvozdanovic@slav.uni-heidelberg.de

Iliyana Krapova
Ca'Foscari University of Venice
krapova@unive.it

Alexander Letuchiy
HSE University, Moscow
alexander.letuchiy@gmail.com
Staraya Basmannaya st., 105066
Moscow

Franc Lanko Marušič
University of Nova Gorica
franc.marusic@ung.si
Center za kognitivne znanosti jezika
Univerza v Novi Gorici
Vipavska 13, Rožna Dolina
SI-5000 Nova Gorica
Slovenia

James Joshua Pennington
Concordia College
james.pennington@cord.edu

Katrin Schlund
University of Heidelberg/University of Trier, Germany
katrin.schlund@slav.uni-heidelberg.de/schlund@uni-trier.de

Tomislav Sočanac
Ca'Foscari University of Venice
tomislav.socanac@unive.it

Luka Szucsich
Humboldt University Berlin
luka.szucsich@hu-berlin.de
Department of Slavic and Hungarian Studies
Humboldt University
Unter den Linden 6
10099 Berlin
Germany

Alan Timberlake
Columbia University
at2205@columbia.edu

Beata Trawiński
Leibniz Institute for the German Language – Mannheim, Germany
trawinski@ids-mannheim.de

Mladen Uhlik
University of Ljubljana
Fran Ramovš Institute of Slovenian Language

Vladislava Warditz
University of Potsdam
warditz@uni-potsdam.de
Department of Slavic Studies / Slavic Linguistics

Jacek Witkoś
Adam Mickiewicz University
wjacek@amu.edu.pl
Faculty of English
Collegium Heliodori Święcicki
Grunwaldzka 6
60-780 Poznań
Poland

Rok Žaucer
University of Nova Gorica
rok.zaucer@ung.si
Center za kognitivne znanosti jezika
Univerza v Novi Gorici
Vipavska 13, Rožna Dolina
SI-5000 Nova Gorica
Slovenia

Andreja Žele
University of Ljubljana
Andreja.Zele@ff.uni-lj.si
Research Centre of the Slovenian Academy of Sciences and Arts

Ilse Zimmermann†
Leibniz–ZAS Berlin

Karolina Zuchewicz
Humboldt University Berlin and Leibniz ZAS Berlin
karolina.zuchewicz@gmail.com
Department of Slavic and Hungarian Studies
Humboldt University
Unter den Linden 6
10099 Berlin
Germany

Introduction

We are pleased to present this collection of papers on the occasion of the retirement of Professor Peter Kosta, longtime chair of Slavic linguistics at the Department of Slavic languages and literatures at the University of Potsdam. The volume offers a selection of papers from the 14th annual meeting of the Slavic Linguistics Society, which was held at the University of Potsdam on 11–13 September 2019. That conference, largely organized by Peter, was intended not only as an event to showcase Slavic linguistic scholarship from around the world, but also as a way to mark Peter's life-long contribution to our discipline. The papers in these pages are by his friends and colleagues, in honor and recognition of a distinguished career. We wish him success in his transition to retirement, although fully expecting him to continue along the same arc that has defined his interests over the past 40-odd years. These are inspired by but go well beyond purely Slavic topics, and include biolinguistics, generative and comparative syntax, formal semantics, and language typology and universals. The breadth and depth of Peter's intellectual pursuits can be seen in the titles on the List of Publications that follows this brief introduction, although these do not do complete justice to his relentless energy and unflagging productivity, nor do they recognize his other extensive activities as a teacher and mentor for generations of students, editor of numerous volumes, organizer of diverse meetings, and recipient of prestigious academic awards and honors.

On a more personal note, those of you who know Peter will also know that his verve can border on the frenetic, and that when he sets his mind to something it can border on the fanatical. He brings this special kind of enthusiasm and commitment to all that engages him, both in his professional and his personal life. We have already pointed out his astonishing productivity, varied research interests, and impressive service, but no tribute to Peter Kosta can fail to acknowledge his personal passions. He holds friendship and romance dear, he loves to travel and experience new cultures, and above all he is devoted to rock music. His knowledge in that area is phenomenal, his guitar skills are prodigious, his musical compositions are heartfelt, and his capacity to record songs for streaming until (or sometimes starting at!) the wee hours of the night is overwhelming. How Peter manages to do all this, and also to write and edit so much, remains a mystery even to us, his friends. Of course, he has the unflagging assistance of Monika Kruschinski, to whom we are very grateful for her help in formatting this volume, not to mention the loving support of his wife Erika.

The 15 papers in the volume embrace a range of topics. In the remainder of this introduction we describe the contributions of Vrinda Chidambaram, Steven Franks, Jadranka Gvozdanović, Iliyana Krapova and Tomislav Sočanac, Alexander Letuchiy, Lanko Marušič and Rok Žaucer, Joshua Pennington, Katrin Schlund, Luka Szucsich and Karolina Zuchewicz, Alan Timberlake, Beata Trawiński, Mladen Uhlik and Andreja Žele, Vladislava Warditz, Jacek Witkoś, and the late Ilse Zimmermann. **Chidambaram's** paper, "A Case of Parasitic Attrition: The disappearance of the degree morpheme *-ьš* in Bulgarian and Macedonian superlative adjectives," examines the historical development of degree adjectives in Bulgarian and Macedonian, which differ from other Slavic languages in forming them only through prefixation to the positive adjective and do not involve suffixation. In it, she identifies the loss of a morpheme in one context due to its disappearance in a different context as "parasitic attrition," and concludes that, although the comparative degree adjectives lost the degree suffix *-ьš* via a Jespersen-cyclic change, the loss of the same *-ьš* degree morpheme in superlatives occurred through the process of parasitic attrition. **Franks**'s "Reflexive Typology, Movement, and the Structure of NP" is concerned with reflexives in English and Slavic. The properties of these two types of reflexives are very different but are shown to follow from their distinct derivational paths. He argues that the reflexive element is always introduced in a Refl(exive)P, but that the reflexive interpretation is established differently. The English mechanism involves merging a DP with Refl and moving that DP to a higher argument position; this gives rise to reflexivity through coreferring co-arguments and causes an agreeing pronominal element to appear (e.g., *himself*). In Slavic languages it is instead Refl (e.g., *sebja*) that moves, thereby establishing a reflexive predicate. The Slavic DP-languages Bulgarian and Macedonian have an extra component, a reflexive clitic (e.g., *sebe si*), the source of which is explored, with differences between the languages attributed to Macedonian's lack of the Bulgarian DP-internal Agr(eement)P. The paper ends with a consideration of connectivity effects found in English, in light of the proposed typology. **Gvozdanović**'s paper, "'Have' + infinitive in Czech: a long multilingual history," treats the contemporary spread of 'have' + infinitive across the modal domains in Czech, where the construction is far-reaching. She establishes German equivalents with Czech-specific implementations and then discusses historical attestations of the 'have' + infinitive, showing that this construction appears before there was a significant increase in German influence. She argues that it can be ascribed to the Latin model, observing that the first attestations of modal 'have' in Old Czech occurred in texts translated from Latin. The paper by **Krapova and Sočanac**, "Factivity in South Slavic languages: Complement and relative clauses," focuses on a specific type of factive complement clauses and relative clauses in Bulgarian and Croatian. These are clauses headed by *deto* and *što*, respectively, which denote specific and presuppositional readings grounded in discourse. They argue that the factive readings associated with such clauses are triggered by these items themselves, which are analyzed as strong presupposition triggers residing in C. The broader implication of the analysis is that factivity is syntactically encoded, and should not be seen as a purely semantic or pragmatic phenomenon. **Letuchiy**'s contribution, "'Missed TAM': The lack of tense and mood marking in Russian argument conditionals – semantic and formal motivation," discusses Russian sentences with non-verbal predicates which unexpectedly remain unmarked for tense and mood. When conditional *esli* introduces an argument clause a mismatch in tense-aspect-modality (TAM) marking between main and embedded predicate can arise. The TAM form is normally the same in both clauses, but in this construction the main predicate must be a predicative (rather than a verb) and the present tense is used instead of the expected future or subjunctive. It is argued that the construction results from both semantic and formal factors, and that it is the grammatically "non-standard" head that makes a syntactically non-standard construction possible. The paper concludes with some typological observations. In "Investigation of Slovenian copular agreement" **Marušič and Žaucer** report their investigation of agreement inside simple predicative sentences. In this type of sentence both noun phrases are nominative, so in principle either could trigger agreement on the copula. They examine various types of copular constructions and show that, regardless of the type of predicative sentence, when a plural is combined with a singular it is always the plural that agrees. Similarly, when a dual is combined with a singular the dual wins out. The novel observation is that when a dual and a plural are combined, the copula can agree with either of the two noun phrases (with a preference for the one following the copula). The relevance of these findings for the recent literature on predication is discussed, and the paper ends by posing several questions for future investigation. **Pennington**'s contribution to the volume, "Today's Grammaticalization Theory is Yesterday's Grammaticalization: the BCMS Future as An(other) Strike Against the Unidirectionality Hypothesis," concerns the ordering of semantic shift and phonological reduction in the development of the South Slavic future. While advocates of grammaticization contend that semantic shift always precedes phonological reduction, this paper argues that, in the case of BCMS *hoću/ću*, phonological reduction may have actually preceded the semantic shift. The arguments are based on the negated form *neću*, which developed out of *nehoću*, through intermediate stages *ne(h)oću* and *ne(o)ću*, with long forms *nehoće* occurring in folk poetry long after the change via analogical levelling with *jesam/sam, nijesam*. **Schlund**'s paper, "On the origin of East Slavic Elemental Constructions/Adversity Impersonals. Evidence from town chronicles of the Old Rus'," addresses the longstanding debate over the origin of so-called Elemental Constructions (ECs, also known as "adversity impersonals") in East Slavic. While there are no attestations of ECs in Old Church Slavonic, they can be found in medieval chronicles of the Old Rus'. The structure of many of these early supposedly impersonal constructions is however ambiguous between personal and impersonal readings. The paper reviews these early alleged examples of ECs, some of which seem to attest an intermediate stage (with a nominative noun phrase denoting the cause and a non-agreeing neuter predicate). Importantly, they all denote instances of external, physical causation, with other kinds of causation (e.g., emotional causation) missing in both historical and contemporary ECs. In "Incrementality and (non)clausal complementation in Slavic," **Szucsich and Zuchewicz** examine the notion of incrementality in Slavic languages, where a common property of all incremental theme predicates is graduality. The assumption that incrementality is a phenomenon involving the partition of events allows them to extend the standard definition of incremental theme verbs taking nominal objects to incremental theme verbs taking clausal complements. Since 'reveal'-type predicates (e.g., 'show', 'prove', 'reveal') imply a gradual creation of a proof for a 'that'-clause, they are similar to incremental theme verbs such as 'build' or 'read'. This, they argue, is why perfective 'reveal'-type predicates induce a veridical interpretation of the embedded proposition. The paper ends with an overview of incremental relations in Finnish and English. **Timberlake**'s paper, "String Syntax," puts forward a novel understand of the workings of syntax, demonstrated through diverse properties of Slavic and other languages. It is argued that the driving mechanism of syntax is strings, or forces, that link disparate and discontinuous elements and control the interpretation of constructions. The claim is that syntactic structures cannot be reduced to or derived from a single "Ur-node" that is uniform across languages. There are thus many different types of strings, more than one of which can be attached to a single constituent. Examples of strings considered in the paper include: linearization and information (Russian), individuation and quantification (Estonian), case marking across clause boundaries (Lithuanian), and the nominative object with infinitive in Finnic (and North Russian). **Trawiński**'s contribution to the volume, "Polish *żeby* under negation," discusses two types of complement clauses in Polish introduced by the complementizer *żeby*: those with obligatory negation in the main clause and those with an obligatory negation in the embedded clause. It is argued that *żeby*-clauses with an obligatory negation in the matrix clause, licensed by epistemic verbs, can be treated in terms of negative polarity, with *żeby* defined as an *n*-word (an element that requires a negative context). Structures with *żeby*-clauses and obligatory negation in the embedded clause, licensed by predicates expressing fear (*verba timendi*), are argued to be an instance of negative complementation, with *żeby* specified as a negative complementizer. A uniform lexicalist analysis of these phenomena is proposed within the HPSG framework; it is shown to employ established tools and require no extensions or modifications of that framework. The paper by **Uhlik and Žele**, "Reflexive Possessive Pronouns in Slovene: A Contrastive Analysis with Russian," is concerned with the use of the Slovene reflexive possessive pronoun *svoj*. The properties are contrasted with those of its Russian counterpart. Various syntactic environments are considered, as well as the question of coreference between pronoun and its antecedent. Laying bare the rules governing the use of reflexive possessive pronouns sheds light on the connection between the syntactic contexts they function in and the various meanings expressed. Contrastive analysis reveals contexts in Russian that permit use of nominative *svoj*, with no overt antecedent; it is also shown that identifying the antecedent of *svoj* in Slovenian infinitival clauses depends on many factors, most prominent of which are choice of matrix verb and infinitival complement. In "Structural Variation in Heritage Russian Speakers in Germany: Language Usage or Language Change?" **Warditz** presents ongoing research into transgenerational language changes in Russian heritage speakers living in Germany. Some of the conclusions she draws about the relationship between language usage and language system changes include: (i) certain systemic tendencies can be identified by sampling individual usages from a longitudinal perspective; (ii) these tendencies differ between the first and second generations of heritage speakers; (iii) areas of potential language shift, as well as sensitivity or resistance of certain structures to change, can be identified by documenting the multiformity of contact-affected word-formation; and (iv) word-formation connects morphology, semantics, pragmatics, and lexis, and is a sensitive area in speech in both monolingual and multilingual settings. **Witkoś**'s paper, "On Some Aspects of Agree, Move and Bind in the Nominal Domain," extends his previous account of reflexive binding in Polish to cases where a reflexive element is placed in complement position within a nominal projection and its antecedent is placed either within or outside that projection. The account draws from both Agree-based and Move-inspired theories, with the addition of a competition-based element. The paper ends by presenting two kinds of empirical challenge in need of further study. **Zimmermann**'s contribution, "On Pronouns Relating to Clauses," deals with Russian anaphoric, cataphoric, interrogative, and relative pronouns relating to root and embedded clauses. The analysis takes into account the semantic flexibility and vagueness of constructions with these pronouns and includes parameters in their grammatically determined Semantic Form. These are specified at the level of Conceptual Structure and depend on the context and knowledge of the interlocutors. It is shown why embedded clauses sometimes function as modifiers and sometimes as complements. Also shown is how lexical entries of the anaphor *èto*, of the cataphoric pronoun *to* and its zero-correspondent, and of the interrogative and relative pronoun *čto* play a basic role in the correlation of their phonological, morphosyntactic, and semantic properties.

We hope that you enjoy reading this collection of new and exciting research in diverse areas of Slavic linguistics.

Steven Franks
Alan Timberlake
Anna Wietecka

Publications

Prof. Dr. phil. habil., Prof. h.c. (Russian-Armenian-University Yerevan) Peter Kosta

1982. Eine russische Kosmographie aus dem 17. Jahrhundert. Sprachwissenschaftliche Analyse mit Textedition und Faksimile. München: Sagner.
1982. N. Kul'mann: *Iz istorii russkoj grammatiki* (Petrograd 1917). Nachdruck von Peter Kosta. München: Sagner.
1982. I. Balickij: *Materialy dlja istorii slavjanskago jazykoznanija* (Kiev 1876), Nachdruck von Peter Kosta. München: Sagner.
1983. Das Weissmannsche 'Petersburger Lexikon' (1731) und das 'Lexikon trejazyčnyj' (1704) von F. P. Polikarpov. In: *Weissmanns Petersburger Lexikon von 1731* 3. München: Sagner, 5–22.
1983. Zur jüngsten Lehnwortschicht im Russischen des 17. Jahrhunderts. In: Freidhof, G., Kosta, P., Schütrumpf, M. (eds.). *Studia slavica in honorem viri doctissimi Olexa Horbatsch.* Teil 1: Beiträge zur ostslawischen Philologie (I). München: Sagner, 88–111.
1983. Freidhof, G., Kosta, P. Schütrumpf, M. (eds.). *Studia Slavica in honorem viri doctissimi Olexa Horbatsch*: Festgabe zum 65. Geburtstag. Bände I–IV, München: Sagner.
1985. [Review] Schmidt, H. Zur Textkomprimierung beim Übersetzen aus dem Russischen ins Deutsche. In: *Probleme des Übersetzungswissenschaftlichen Textvergleichs.* Leipzig 1981. In: *Russian Linguistics* 9, 133–134.
1985. Freidhof, G., Kosta, P. [Review] Hüttl-Folter, Gerta: *Die trat/ torot - Lexeme in den altrussischen Chroniken:* ein Beitrag zur Vorgeschichte der russischen Literatursprache. Wien 1983. Österreich. AdW., phil.-histor. Kl. Sitzungsberichte; 420. In: *WSlJb* 31, 193–200.
1986. [Review] Asche, H. Überlegungen zu einer Richtung innerhalb der Textlinguistik, in: Probleme des Übersetzungswissenschaftlichen Textvergleichs. Leipzig 1981. In: *Russian Linguistics* 10, 360–362.
1986. [Review] Růžička, R. Die Synthesis der Übersetzungswissenschaft: Theorie – Bewertung – Anweisung. In: *Äquivalenz bei der Translation.* Leipzig 1982. In: *Russian Linguistics* 10, 362–364.
1986. [Review] Børtnes, J. The Function of Word-weaving in the Structure of Epiphanius' Life of Saint Stephen, Bishop of Perm'. (In: Medieval Russian Culture. Berkeley 1984.) In: *Russian Linguistics* 10, 121–122.

1986. Probleme der Švejk-Übersetzungen in den west- und südslavischen Sprachen. Linguistische Studien zur Translation literarischer Texte. München: Sagner [=Doktordissertation/PhD diss. J.W. Goethe-Universität Frankfurt am Main 1985].

1986. Entsprechungstypen und Übersetzungsverfahren bei der Translation von Phraseologismen (anhand der west- und südslawischen Übersetzungen tschechischer Prosa). In; Rathmayr, R. (ed.). *Slavistische Linguistik 1985*. München: Sagner, 95–131.

1986. Tipy transpozicij i perevod xudožestvennogo teksta. In: *Probleme der russischen Gegenwartssprache und -literatur in Forschung und Lehre. Materialien des Internationalen MAPRJAL-Symposiums Marburg*, 8.–10. Oktober 1985. Hamburger Beiträge für Russischlehrer 35. Hamburg: Helmut Busse Verlag, 107–121.

1986. (ed.). S. K. Bulič: *Cerkovnoslavjanske elementy v sovremennom literaturnom i narodnom russkom jazyke*. Čast' I (Sankt Peterburg 1893), Nachdruck und Nachwort von Peter Kosta. München: Sagner.

1986. (ed.). I. Nosovič: *Slovar' belorusskago narečija* (Sankt Peterburg 1870), Nachdruck und Nachwort in zwei Bänden von G. Freidhof und P. Kosta, Teil I: A–O München: Sagner, 1984; Teil II: P–Ja München: Sagner, 1986.

1987. Das komplexe Wortspiel als Problem der Übersetzungstheorie. In: 1987. Freidhof, G., Kosta, P. (Eds): *Slavistische Linguistik 1986:* Referate des XII. Konstanzer Slavistischen Arbeitstreffens in Frankfurt/M., Riezlern vom 16.–19.09.1986. München: Sagner, 125–156.

1987. Metapher und Metonymie als Translationskategorien. In: Hentschel, G. et al. (eds.) *Sprach- und Kulturkontakte im Polnischen (Festschrift Andre de Vincenz)*, München: Sagner, 485–515.

1987. Sprachwechsel, Interferenz und Sprachmischung in Hašeks Švejk als translationslinguistisches Problem. In: Schamschula, W. (ed.): *Jaroslav Hašek 1883–1983*, Frankfurt/M.: Lang, 471–512.

1987. Freidhof, G./Kosta, P. (eds.). *Slavistische Linguistik 1986*: Referate des XII. Konstanzer Slavistischen Arbeitstreffens in Frankfurt/M./Riezlern vom 16. 19.09.1986. München: Sagner.

1988. Die literarische Übersetzung – eine Kunstgattung? Zum Problem der sogenannten 'Gattungsverschiebung' bei der Translation eines literarischen Textes. In: Harder, H.-B. et al. (eds.). *Gattungen in den slavischen Literaturen* (Festschrift Alfred Rammelmeyer), Köln: Böhlau, 259–282.

1988. Sprach- und Wortspiel in den 'Abenteuern des braven Soldaten Švejk von J. Hašek. Möglichkeiten und Grenzen der Übertragung des Polysemie-Wortspiels in den südslavischen Sprachen. In: Olesch, R. et al. (eds.).

Slavistische Studien zum 10. Internationalen Slavistenkongress, Sofia 1988, Köln: Böhlau, 83–96.

1988. Zum Einfluss des 'Umständlichen Lehrgebäudes' (1782) von J. Chr. Adelung auf die 'Rossijskaja grammatika' (1783–88) von A. A. Barsov. Anfänge der funktionalen Satzperspektive in Russland. In: Biedermann, J. et al. (eds.). *Texts and Studies on Russian Universal Grammar 1806–1812.* Linguistische, philosophische und wissenschaftsgeschichtliche Grundlagen 3. München: Sagner, 125–151.

1988. Zur Beschreibung der translatorischen Textkompression im Rahmen eines 'scenes- and frames'- Modells. In: Raecke, J. (ed.). *Slavistische Linguistik 1988.* München: Sagner, 209–232.

1988. Kosta, Peter: [Review]: Nozsiczka, A. 1988. *Die Grammatik der Negation (Am Beispiel des Deutschen und Russischen)*, Wien: 476 S. (Akad. d. Wiss., Philosophisch-historische Klasse).

1988. Kosta, *P. (ed.). Studia Indogermanica et Slavica. Festgabe für Werner Thomas zum 65. Geburtstag* (unter Mitarbeit von Gabriele Lerch, Peter Oliver). München: Sagner.

1989. Zur Translation von Mehrsprachigkeit und Interferenz im literarischen Text (J. Hašeks Švejk in slawischen und nichtslawischen Übersetzungen). In: Schmidt, H. (ed.). *Interferenz in der Translation.* Leipzig: VEB Verlag Enzyklopädie, 120–128. (Übersetzungswissenschaftliche Beiträge, 12).

1990. Zur formalen Lizensierung und inhaltlichen Determination leerer Subjekte im Russischen. In: Breu, W. (ed.). *Slavistische Linguistik 1989*: Referate des XV. Konstanzer Slavistischen Arbeitstreffens Bayreuth 18.–22.9.1989. München, 117–165.

1992. *Leere Kategorien in den nordslavischen Sprachen. Zur Analyse leerer Subjekte und Objekte in der Rektions-Bindungs-Theorie.* J. W. Goethe-Universität Frankfurt am Main: Habil-Schrift, available online: http://www.uni-potsdam.de/u/slavistik/wsw/habil/habil.htm.

1993. Bewertung und Konnotation in Milan Kunderas Werk als axiologisches und translationslinguistisches Problem. In: Gutschmidt, K. et al. (eds.). *Slavistische Studien zum 11. Internationalen Slavistenkongress, Pressburg 1993*, Köln: Böhlau, 247–271.

1995. Gliederungssignale in tschechischen umgangssprachlichen und literarischen Texten. Zeitschrift für Slawistik 40 (2), 181–201.

1995. Zur Forschungsgeschichte und Forschungssituation bezüglich der Temporalität in slavischen Sprachen. In: Jachnow, H., Wingender, M., Tafel, K. (eds.). *Temporalität und Tempus: Studien zu allgemeinen und slavischen Fragen.* Wiesbaden, 297–365.

1995. Zur Modellierung persuasiver Sprechakte. Zeitschrift für Slawistik 40 (3), 305–324.
1995. Tagungsberichte: 1. Tagung der Deutsch-Tschechischen Dobrovský-Gesellschaft in Prag: Zum Faksimile–Nachdruck der Kralitzer Bibel (1579–1594). In: Zeitschrift für Slawistik 40 (4), 455–457.
1996. Sprechakttheoretische Überlegungen zur Translation literarischer Texte aus dem Tschechischen ins Deutsche. In: Freidhof, G. et al. (eds.). *Slavische Sprachwissenschaft und Interdisziplinarität 3*. München, 103–122.
1996. Zur semantischen Struktur und illokutionären Kraft persuasiver Sprechakte. In: Girke, W. (ed.). *Slavistische Linguistik 1995*: XXI. Konstanzer Slavistisches Arbeitstreffen, Mainz 26.09.–29.09.1995. München: Sagner, 201–226.
1996. Zur Sprachsituation der Sorben/Wenden in der Niederlausitz. Bulletin der Deutschen Slavistik 2, 10–13.
1996. [Review] Zybatow, Lew N. 1995. *Russisch im Wandel*: Die russische Sprache seit der Perestroika. Wiesbaden: Harrassowitz (Slavistische Veröffentlichungen; 80). In: Zeitschrift für Slawistik 41 (3), 358–362.
1996. [Review] Jachnow, H., Mečkovskaja et. al. (eds.) 1994. *Modalität und Modus: Allgemeine Fragen und Realisierungen im Slavischen.* Wiesbaden: Harrowitz. (Slavistische Studienbücher, Neue Folge; 4). In: Zeitschrift für Slawistik 41 (3), 363–369.
1996. [Review] Eckert, E. (ed.). *Varieties of Czech. Studies in Czech.* Amsterdam: Atlanta, Georgia, 1993. In: Zeitschrift für Slawistik 41 (1), 88–96.
1996. "70 Years Existence of the Prague Linguistic Circle and 100th Anniversary of Roman Jakobson's Birthday" (Prag, 28.–30.03.1996). In: Zeitschrift für Slawistik 41 (3), 338–342.
1997. Kosta, Peter: [Review with Anette Muschner] Karlík, P.; Nekula, M.; Rusínová, Z. (eds.) *Příruční mluvnice češtiny*. Praha: Lidové noviny. 1995. In: Zeitschrift für Slawistik 42 (2), 234–245.
1997. Empty Categories, Null–Subjects and Null–Objects and How to Treat Them in the Minimalist Program. Linguistics in Potsdam 2, 7–30.
1997. Syntaktische Prinzipien und Informationsstruktur in sogenannten "nichtkonfigurationellen" Sprachen. In: Kosta, P., E. Mann (eds.). *Slavistische Linguistik 1996.* Referate des XXII. Konstanzer Slavistischen Arbeitstreffens Potsdam, 17.–20.9.1996. München: Sagner, 105–135 (Slavistische Beiträge 354).
1997. Kosta, Peter, Mann, Elke (eds.). *Slavistische Linguistik 1996.* Referate des XXII. Konstanzer Slavistischen Arbeitstreffens Potsdam, 17.–20.9.1996. München: Sagner (Slavistische Beiträge 354).

1998. Argumentation, Persuasion und der turn-taking-Mechanismus. In: Čmejrková, S., (eds.) et al. *Dialoganalyse VI/I:* Referate der 6. Arbeitstagung, Prag 1996.Tübingen: Niemeyer, 115–131 (Beiträge zur Dialogforschung Band 16).

1998. K problematice jazykových menšin za T. G. Masaryka. In: *T. G. Masaryk a situace v Čechách a na Moravě od konce XIX. století do německé okupace Československa*: sborník příspěvků z mezinárodního vědeckého kolokvia pořádaného ve dnech 31. května - 2. června 1996 v Praze ve vile Lanna, ed. Ústav T. G. Masaryka. Praha, 125–131.

1998. Über Argumentstruktur, Fokussierung und modale Satzadverbien im Tschechischen und Russischen. *Beiträge zum XII. Internationalen Slavistenkongress in Kraków 1998*. Zeitschrift für Slawistik 43 (2), 140–154.

1998. Überlegungen zum "phatischen Diskurs" (und zur phatischen Partikel 'jako') in der Konversation tschechischer Intellektueller. In: Freidhof, G. et al. (eds.). *Slavische Sprachwissenschaft und Interdisziplinarität 4:* Olexa Horbatsch zum Gedenken, München: Sagner, 109–145.

1999. Konzepte des Sprachwandels in Russland, in der UdSSR und in den GUS-Staaten. In: Jachnow, H. et al. (eds.). *Handbuch der sprachwissenschaftlichen Russistik und ihrer Grenzdisziplinen.* Wiesbaden: Harrasowitz, 924–994.

1999. Prohibitiv und Präventiv im Slavischen (Zur Grammatik, Semantik und Pragmatik des verneinten Imperativs unter besonderer Berücksichtigung des Russischen, Tschechischen und Südslavischen). In: Grünberg, K., Potthoff, W, (eds.). *ARS PHILOLOGICA*: Festschrift für Baldur Panzer zum 65. Geburtstag. Frankfurt /M. Lang, 283–294.

1999. Quantoren und Satznegation im Slavischen aus typologisch-vergleichender Sicht. In: Hansack, E.,Koschmal, W., Nübler, N. and R. Večerka (eds.). *Festschrift für Klaus Trost zum 65. Geburtstag.* München: Sagner, 171–187 (Die Welt der Slaven: Sammelband 5).

1999. Spracherwerb und Sprachwandel: Zur Erklärung von Grammatikalisier ungserscheinungen im Slavischen. In: , Girke, W. et al. (eds.). Вертоградъ многоцвѣтный: Festschrift für Helmut Jachnow. München: Sagner, 131–144 (Speciminae philologiae slavicae. Supplementband 64).

1999. Gladrow, W., Kosta, P. *Syntax und Syntaxkonzeptionen.* In: Jachnow, H. et al. (eds.). *Handbuch der sprachwissenschaftlichen RUSSISTIK und ihrer Grenzdisziplinen*, Wiesbaden: Harrasowitz, 386–424.

1999. Westslavisch Poztupimi - deutsch Potsdam: Zur Geschichte der Etymologie eines Ortsnamens. Lětopis 46 (2), 95–100.

1999. Zur Kultur- und Sprachspezifik von Karel Poláčeks Werk am Beispiel der Übersetzungprobleme von 'Bylo nás pět' und 'Muži v ofsidu'. In: Kosta, P. et al.

(eds.). *Juden und Judentum in Literatur und Film des slavischen Sprachraums:* Die geniale Epoche. Wiesbaden: Harrassowitz, 95–112.

1999. Zur Syntax und Semantik von negativen und positiven "Polaritätsanzeigern". In: Rathmayr, R. et al. (eds.). *Slavistische Linguistik 1998:* Referate des XXIV. Konstanzer Arbeitstreffens in Wien. München: Sagner, 117–136.

1999. Kosta, Peter: [Review] Hajičová, E. et al. (eds.). 1995. *Travaux du Cercle linguistique de Prague n.s. – Prague Linguistic Circle Papers.* Vol. 1. Amsterdam / Philadelphia: Benjamins, 1995. In: Zeitschrift für Slawistik 44 (3), 339–345.

1999. Kosta, P. et al. (eds.). *Juden und Judentum in Literatur und Film des slavischen Sprachraums:* Die geniale Epoche, Wiesbaden: Harrassowitz.

2000. Semiotische Überlegungen zur Máchas Máj. In: Herta Schmid et al. (eds.). *Kapitel zur Poetik Karel Hynek Máchas.* Die tschechische Romantik im europäischen Kontext. Beiträge zum Internationalen Bohemistischen Mácha–Symposium and der Universität Potsdam vom 21. bis 22. Januar 1995, 178–194 (Sammelbände. Sborniki Band 7).

2000. Zur lateinischen Dichtung des Johannes Boccatius (1569–1621). Podstupimske pśinoski k Sorabistice 1. Potsdamer Beiträge zur Sorabistik 1. Potsdam: Universitätsverlag Potsdam, 48–58.

2001. Die Tschechoslowakei seit 1918. In: Elke–Vera Kotowski, Julius H. Schoeps, and Hiltrud Wallenborn (eds.). *Handbuch zur Geschichte der Juden in Europa*, Darmstadt: WBG Bd. 1, 143–150.

2001. Negace a větná struktura v češtině. In: Hladká, Z., Karlík, P. (eds.). *Čeština. Univerzália a specifika.* Sborník konference v Brně 22.–24.11. 2000. Brno: Masarykova univerzita v Brně. 117–138.

2001. Zum Einfluss der deutschen Syntax auf die Wortstellung im Sorbischen (unter besonderer Berücksichtigung des Niedersorbischen). In: Haßler, G. (ed.). *Sprachkontakt und Sprachvergleich,* Münster: Nodus Publikationen, 2001. 107–114 (Studium Sprachwissenschaft. Beiheft 34).

2002. Klitika im Slavischen: Sind sie immer optimal? Zeitschrift für Slawistik 47 (2), 27–146.

2002. Minimalism and Free Constituent Order (in Russian as Compared to German). In: Kosta, P., Frasek, J. (eds.). *Current Approaches to Formal Slavic Linguistics..* Frankfurt/M.: Peter Lang, 253–272 (Linguistik International 9).

2002. Kosta, P. and L. Veselovská. Modularity of language system (271), Control (303 f.), Principle of full interpretation (345), Projection Principle (345), Spell Out (435 f.), Trace (442 f.), Deep structure (444 f.), Surface structure (445), Control theory (481), Bounding theory (482), Case theory (482), Theory of principles and parameters (482 f.), Government theory (484), Government and binding theory (484 f.), Theta theory (θ–Theory) (486 f.), Binding theory

(487), T-Model (490 f.), X-bar Theory (553 f.). In: Karlík, P. et al. (eds.). *Encyklopedický slovník češtiny*. Praha: Lidové Noviny.

2002. Kosta, Peter, Frasek, Jens (eds.). *Current Approaches to Formal Slavic Linguistics*. Frankfurt/M., Berlin, Bern, Bruxelles, New York, Oxford, Wien: Peter Lang. (Linguistik International. Band 9).

2003. Probleme des Sprachvergleichs in Kontaktzonen und L2-Erwerb am Beispiel der deutsch-sorbischen/wendischen Interferenzen. In: Reflexionen zur sorbischen/wendischen Sprache, Kultur und Literatur. Sorbische Sektion auf dem VIII. Deutschen Slavistentag (30.9.-3.10.2001), Potsdam. Tagungsband dieses sorbischen Panels veröffentlicht im fünften Band der Reihe Podstupimske pśinoski k Sorabistice Potsdamer Beiträge zur Sorabistik veröffentlicht. Hrsg. Peter Kosta und Madlena Norberg, Nr. 5. Universität Potsdam. Potsdam, 16–43.

2003. Syntaktische und semantische Besonderheiten von Adverb und Negation im Slavischen. Zeitschrift für Slawistik 48 (3), 377–404. [= Beitrag zum XII. Internationalen Slavistenkongress in Ljubljana, 15.-21.08.2003].

2003. The New Animacy Category in Slavic Languages: Open Questions of Syntax, Semantics and Morphology. In: *GERMANOSLAVICA*. Zeitschrift für germano-slawische Studien. Jahrgang IX (XIV), Nr. 2, 179–198.

2003. Negation and Adverbs in Czech. In: Kosta, P., Błaszczak, J., Frasek, J., Geist, L. & M. Żygis (eds.). *Investigations into Formal Slavic Linguistics:* Proceedings of the Fourth European Conference on Formal Description of Slavic Languages – FDSL 4, Potsdam, 28–30 November 2001. Frankfurt/M. Peter Lang, 601–616. (Linguistik International 10.1–2).

2003. Kosta, P., Norberg, M. Zu den tschechischen, deutschen und englischen Übersetzungen/Adaptionen der Gedichte von Mato Kosyk: einige translationslinguistische Überlegungen. In: Marti, R. (ed.). *Mato Kosyk 1853–1940*. Proceedings of the First Kosyk Conference Wjerbno/Werben 15.–18.6.2003. Edited by Roland Marti. Budyšin/Bautzen: Domowina Verlag (Spise Serbskego Instituta; 40) [On Czech, German and English Translations/ Adaptations of Mato Kosyk's Poetry – Some Translatological Considerations], 321–333.

2003. Zum Aspektgebrauch im Niedersorbischen: "Budu ten list napisaś". In: Lehmann, V., Udolph, L. (eds.). *Normen, Namen und Tendenzen in der Slavia*. Festschrift für Karl Gutschmidt zum 65. Geburtstag. München: Sagner. 369–378.

2003. Kosta, Peter, Błaszczak, Joanna, Frasek, Jens, Geist, Ljudmila & Marzena Żygis (eds.). *Investigations into Formal Slavic Linguistics*. Contributions of the Fourth European Conference on Formal Description of Slavic Languages

(FDSL IV) held at Potsdam University, November 28–30, 2001. Linguistik International. Band 10; 1/2. Frankfurt/M., Berlin, Bern, Bruxelles, New York, Oxford, Wien: Peter Lang.

2003. Lužičtí Srbové ve Výmarské republice a problém národnostních menšin v politice První Československé republiky. Internationale Konferenz zum Masaryk in Prag, 5. Dezember 2003, Masarykův ústav AV ČR.

2004. Neakuzativita (ergativita) vs. neergativita v češtině, polštině a jiných slovanských jazycích na rozhraní morfologie a syntaxe. In: Hladka Z. & Karlík, P., univerzália a specifika 5, Praha: Nakladatelství Lidové noviny. (with Jens Frasek), S. 172–194. [= Unaccusativity (Ergativity) vs. Unergativity in Czech, Polish and Some Other Slavic Languages at the Morpho-Syntactic Interface]

2004. Die historische Grammatik Arnošt Mukas und ihre Bedeutung für die Entwicklung der niedersorbischen Sprache. In: Arno Arnošt Muka – ein Sorbe und Universalgelehrter. Universitätsverlag Potsdam. (Potsdamer Beiträge zur Sorabistik Nr. 6. Herausgegeben von Peter Kosta und Madlena Norberg), 9–17.

2004. Lužictí Srbové ve výmarské republice a problém národnostních menšin v politice první Ceskoslovenské republiky [= Lusatian Serbia in the Weimar Republic and the issue of national minorities in the first Czechoslovak Republic]. In: Češi a Němci v pojetí a politice T. G. Masaryka. Sborník příspěvků mezinárodní konference. Masarykův ústav AV ČR. Praha, 217–228.

2004. Rěcno-wědomostne źěło Arnošta Muki: Swjednzenske zarjadowanje k cesći pred 150. lětami we Wulkim Wosyku narodzeneho wucenca a wótcinca. In: *Rozhlad* 11/12; Jahrgang 54. Bautzen, 403–406.

2004. Syntax ticha (VP-elipsa / gapping a IP-elipsa / sluicing) v češtině a angličtině, aneb: jak získat a teoreticky popsat něco, co není viditelné v korpusu? In: Karlík, Petr (eds.). *Korpus jako zdroj dat o češtině*. Brno: Masarykova univerzita v Brně, 11–27.

2004. [Review]: J.G. Sparwenfeld's Diary of a Journey to Russia 1684–87. Editor Ulla Birgegård; Stockholm 2002 (Slavica Suecena. Series A – Publications. Vol. 1). In: Zeitschrift für Slawistik 49.

2005. Zum Tschechenbild bei den Polen und zum Polenbild bei den Tschechen aus der Sicht der Stereotypen- und Prototypensemantik. In: Berwanger, K., Kosta, P. (eds.). *Stereotyp und Geschichtsmythos in Kunst und Sprache.* Die Kultur Ostmitteleuropas in Beiträgen zur Potsdamer Tagung, 16.–18. Januar 2003. Frankfurt/M.: Peter Lang, 51–70.

2005. Einige Bemerkungen zu den Bauernbaladen von Jaroslav Vrchlický. In: von Erdmann, E. et al. (eds.). *TUSCULUM SLAVICUM.* Festschrift für Peter

Thiergen. Zürich: Pano Verlag, 349–361. (Basler Studien zur Kulturgeschichte Osteuropas 14).

2005. Die Faszination der Stille oder wie erwirbt ein Kind leere Kategorien – unter Einbeziehung primärsprachlicher Daten aus dem Korpus "CHILDES". Zeitschrift für Slawistik 50 (4), 417–443.

2005. Direkte und indirekte Direktiva als Strategien des (Miss-)Verstehens in Dialogen tschechischer Frauen und Männer. In: van-Leeuwen-Turnovcová, J.; Richter, N. (eds.). *Mediale Welten in Tschechien nach 1989*: Genderprojektionen und Codes des Plebejismus. München: Sagner, 191–198. (Specimina Philologiae Slavicae. Band 142).

2005. Kosta, Peter: [Review]: Ja. G. Testelec: *Vvedenie v obščij sintaksis*. Moskva 2001: Rossijskij Gosudarstvennyj Gumanitarnyj Universitet. In: V*oprosy jazykoznanija* 2005, 1–6.

2005. Kosta, Peter [Review]: E.V. Raxilina: Kognitivnyj analiz predmetnyx imen: semantika i sočetaemost. In: *Russian Linguistics* 25 (3), 403–407.

2005. Katrin Berwanger/ Peter Kosta (eds.). *Stereotyp und Geschichtsmythos in Kunst und Sprache.* Die Kultur Ostmitteleuropas in Beiträgen zur Potsdamer Tagung, 16.–18. Januar 2003. Frankfurt/M. Peter Lang. (Vergleichende Studien zu den slavischen Sprachen und Literaturen. Band 11).

2006. Zur deutschen Švejk-Übersetzung von Grete Reiner (1926) und ihrem Einfluss auf die Übersetzungen in die verschiedenen slavischen Sprachen. In: *De Hašek à Brecht. Fortune de la figure de Chvéïk en Europe.* Colloque 2004: CERAAC/CESC. Textes réunis par Marie-Odile Thirouin. Institut des langues et de cultures d'Europe et d'Amérique. Université Stendhal-Grenoble 3. Les Cahiers de l'ILCEA 8, 93–107.

2006. On free word order phenomena in Czech as compared to German: Is Clause Internal Scrambling A-movement, A-Bar-Movement or is it Base Generated? Zeitschrift für Slawistik 51 (3), 306–321.

2006. Kosta, Peter [Review]: *Russistika. Slavistika. Lingvistika.* Festschrift für Werner Lehfeldt zum 60. Geburtstag. Herausgegeben von Sebastian Kempgen, Ulrich Schweier und Tilman Berger. München: Verlag Otto Sagner 2003. 533 S. (Die Welt der Slaven. Sammelbände. Sborniki. Band 19). In: *Kritikon Litterarum Jg.* 33, Heft 1/2, 29–33.

2007. Kosta, P., Schürcks, L. The focus feature revisited. In: Kosta, P., Schürcks, L. (eds.). *Linguistic Investigations into Formal Description of Slavic Languages.* Contributions of the Sixth European Conference held at Potsdam University, November 30 – December 3, 2005. 245–267. Frankfurt/M.: Peter Lang (Potsdam Linguistic Investigations 1).

2007. [Review]: Meyer, Roland: *Syntax der Ergänzungsfrage*. Empirische Untersuchungen am Russischen, Polnischen und Tschechischen. München: Sagner 2004. In: *Kritikon Litterarum*. 34 (2007), 134–143. (Slavistische Beiträge. Bd. 436).

2007. Kosta, P., Schürcks, L. (eds.). *Linguistic Investigations into Formal Description of Slavic Languages*. Contributions of the Sixth European Conference held at Potsdam University, November, 30 - December 3, 2005. Frankfurt/M.: Peter Lang. (Potsdam Linguistic Investigations 1).

2008. Sprachwandel als Diskurswandel in postkommunistischen Staaten Osteuropas (am Beispiel politischer Presse–Artikel, Reden und Interviews polnischer, russischer und tschechischer Politiker). In: Stehl, Th. (ed.), *Kenntnis und Wandel der Sprachen*: Beiträge zur Potsdamer Ehrenpromotion für Helmut Lüdtke. Tübingen: Gunter Narr Verlag, 241–263. (Tübinger Beiträge zur Linguistik. Bd. 507).

2008. Quantification of NPs/DPs in Slavic. In: Kosta, P., Weiss, D. (eds.). *Slavistische Linguistik 2006/2007*. Beiträge zum XXXII. / XXXIII. Konstanzer Slavistischen Arbeitstreffen in Boldern und Potsdam (03.09.–06.09.2007). München: Sagner, 247–266. (Slavistische Beiträge 464).

2008. A- vs. B-languages or 2nd position vs. Verb-adjacent clitics in West- und South-Slavic Languages. In: Comati, Sigrun (eds.). Bulgaristica - Studia et Argumenta. Festschrift für Ruselina Nitsolova zum 65. Geburtstag. München: Otto Sagner, 195–210.

2008. Kosta, P., Weiss, D. (eds.). *Slavistische Linguistik 2006/2007*. Referate des XXXII. Konstanzer Slavistischen Arbeitstreffens Männedorf bei Zürich, 18.–20. September 2006 und Referate des XXXIII. Konstanzer Slavistischen Arbeitstreffens Potsdam, 4.–6. September 2007. Herausgegeben von Peter Kosta und Daniel Weiss. München. (Slavistische Beiträge 464).

2009. Targets, Theory and Methods of Slavic Generative Syntax: Minimalism, Negation and Clitics. In: Kempgen, S., Kosta, P., Berger, T., Gutschmidt, K. (eds.). *Slavic Languages. Slavische Sprachen. An International Handbook of their Structure, their History and their Investigation. Ein internationales Handbuch ihrer Struktur, ihrer Geschichte und ihrer Erforschung*. Berlin, New York: Mouton de Gruyter, Volume 1, 282–316. (HSK 32.1).

2009. Satzglieder und impersonale Konstruktionen im Slavischen. In: Kempgen, S., Kosta, P., Berger, T., Gutschmidt, K. (eds.). *Slavic Languages. Slavische Sprachen. An International Handbook of their Structure, their History and their Investigation. Ein internationales Handbuch ihrer Struktur, ihrer Geschichte und ihrer Erforschung*. Berlin, New York: Mouton de Gruyter, Volume 1, 391–414. (HSK 32.1).

2009. Kosta, P., Schürcks, L. Word Order in Slavic. In: Kempgen, S., Kosta, P., Berger, T., Gutschmidt, K. (eds.). *Slavic Languages. Slavische Sprachen. An International Handbook of their Structure, their History and their Investigation. Ein internationales Handbuch ihrer Struktur, ihrer Geschichte und ihrer Erforschung*. Berlin, New York: Mouton de Gruyter, Volume 1, 654–684. (HSK 32.1).

2009. Prototypensemantik und Stereotypen. In: Kempgen, S., Kosta, P., Berger, T., Gutschmidt, K. (eds.). *Slavic Languages. Slavische Sprachen. An International Handbook of their Structure, their History and their Investigation. Ein internationales Handbuch ihrer Struktur, ihrer Geschichte und ihrer Erforschung*. Berlin, New York: Mouton de Gruyter, Volume 1, 829–848. (HSK 32.1).

2009. Kosta, P., Thielemann, N. Gesprächsanalyse. In: Kempgen, S., Kosta, P., Berger, T., Gutschmidt, K. (eds.). *Slavic Languages. Slavische Sprachen. An International Handbook of their Structure, their History and their Investigation. Ein internationales Handbuch ihrer Struktur, ihrer Geschichte und ihrer Erforschung*. Berlin, New York: Mouton de Gruyter, Volume 1, 1029–1047. (HSK 32.1).

2009. [Review]: Alexander Bierich: Russische Phraseologie des 18. Jahrhunderts. Entstehung, Semantik, Entwicklung. Frankfurt/M. Peter Lang 2005. (Heidelberger Publikationen zur Slavistik. Linguistische Reihe 16). In: *Kritikon Litterarum Jg*. 36, Heft 1/2, 44–52.

2009. [Review]: Björn Hansen / Petr Karlík (eds.). Modality in Slavonic Languages. New Perspectives. München: Verlag Otto Sagner, 2005. (Slavolinguistica 6). In: *Kritikon Litterarum Jg*. 36, Heft 1/2, 36–44.

2009. [Review]: Dönninghaus, Sabine: Die Vagheit der Sprache. Begriffsgeschichte und Funktionsbeschreibung anhand der tschechischen Wissenschaftssprache. Wiesbaden: Harrassowitz Verlag 2005. (= Slavistische Studienbücher, Neue Folge. Bd. 15). In: *Kritikon Literarum Jg*. 36, Heft 1/2, 52–60.

2009. Kempgen, S., Kosta, P., Berger, T., Gutschmidt, K. (eds.). *Slavic Languages. Slavische Sprachen. An International Handbook of their Structure, their History and their Investigation. Ein internationales Handbuch ihrer Struktur, ihrer Geschichte und ihrer Erforschung*. Berlin, New York: Mouton de Gruyter, Halbband 1 (Series HSK= Handbücher zur Sprach- und Kommunikationswissenschaft / Handbooks of Linguistics and Communication Science / [HSK 32.1]) Link: www.degruyter.de/cont/imp/mouton/detailEn.cfm

2009. Kosta, P., Jungraithmayr, H. Nachruf auf Werner Thomas *14.11.1923, † 1.1.2008 von Herrmann Jungraithmayr und Peter Kosta, in: *Sitzungsberichte* *der Wissenschaftlichen Gesellschaft an der Johann Wolfgang Goethe-Universität Frankfurt/M.* Band XLVII, Nr. 2. Franz Steiner Verlag Stuttgart, 39 (7) - 43 (11).

2010. Linguistische Universalienforschung bei Comenius oder auf der Suche nach der perfekten Universalsprache. In: Janečková, M., Alexová, J., Pospíšilová, V. (eds.). *Slovesné baroko ve středoevropském prostoru.* Praha: Nakladatelství ARSCI, 168–185.

2010. Problém jazykových menšin v Rade Evropy – mezi ochranou, revitalizací a jazykovým útlakem (na príkladu Lužických Srbu v Německu) // Krčmová, M. a kol. (eds.). *Integrace v jazycích – jazyky v integraci.* Praha: Nakladatelství Lidové noviny, 275–293.

2010. Kulturbilder und ästhetische Verarbeitung des Französischen in den letzten Romanen Milan Kunderas und ihre Wiedergabe im Polnischen, Tschechischen und Deutschen: der Versuch einer kultursemantischen und diskursanalytischen Funktionsbestimmung der interlingualen Invarianz/ Varianz. In: Krysztofiak, M. (eds.). *Probleme der Übersetzungskultur.* Frankfurt/M.: Peter Lang, 129–143. (Danziger Beiträge zur Germanistik 33).

2010. Kontrastive Analyse Tschechisch – Deutsch. In: Krumm, Hans-Jürgen; Fandrych, Christian; Hufeisen, Britta; Riemer, Claudia (eds.). *Handbuch Deutsch als Fremd- und Zweitsprache.* (Neubearbeitung). Berlin: Mouton de Gruyter, 711–719. (HSK 19).

2010. The Problem of Language Minorities in the European Council – between Protection, Revitalization and Necessity of Saving Costs: The Example of the Sorbs/Wends in Germany. In: Krčmová, M. et al. (eds.). *Languages in the Integrating World.* Lincom Europa, 3–37.

2010. Causatives and Anti-Causatives, Unaccusatives and Unergatives: Or How Big is the Contribution of the Lexicon to Syntax? In: Bičan, A. et al. (eds.). *Karlík a továrna na lingvistiku.* Prof. Petru Karlíkovi k šedesátým narozeninám. Brno: Masarykova univerzita, 230–273.

2010. [Review]: Bergmann, Anke. 2006. *Binomina im Russischen als Kategorie der komplexen Benennung.* Frankfurt/M. Peter Lang, 2006 (Berliner Slawistische Arbeiten, 29). In: *Kritikon Litterarum* 37 Heft 3/4, 208–218.

2011. Causatives and Anti-Causatives, Unaccusatives and Unergatives: Or how big is the contribution of the lexicon to syntax? In: Kosta, P., Schürcks, L. (eds.). *Formalization of Grammar in Slavic Languages.* Contributions of the Eighth International Conference on Formal Description of Slavic Languages-FDSL VIII 2009. University of Potsdam, December 2–5. Frankfurt/M. Peter Lang, 235–295. (Potsdam Linguistic Investigations 6).

2011. Modalité Epistémique et Evidentialité et sa disposition à la base déictique. In: Schlaak, C., Busse, L. (eds.). *Sprachkontakte, Sprachvariation und Sprachwandel.* Festschrift für Thomas Stehl zum 60. Geburtstag. Tübingen: Narr, 257–283.

2011. Linguistische Universalienforschung bei Comenius oder auf der Suche nach der perfekten Universalsprache. In: Hassler, G. (eds.). *Nationale und transnationale Perspektiven der Geschichte der Sprachwissenschaft.* Beiträge zur XI. Internationalen Konferenz zur Geschichte der Sprachwissenschaften (ICHoLS) - Potsdam, 28. 8.–2. 9. 2008. Juli 2011, 288–300.

2011. Konversationelle Implikaturen und indirekte Sprechakte auf dem Prüfstein. In: Kotin, M., Kotorova, E. (eds.). *Die Sprache in Aktion. Pragmatik.* Sprechakte. Diskurs. Language in Action. Pragmatics. Speech Acts. Discourse. Heidelberg: Universitätsverlag Winter, 55–69.

2012. Kosta, P., Krivochen, D. G. [Review article of the book]: Di Sciullo, A. M., Boeckx, C. (eds.). *The Biolinguistic Enterprise: New Perspectives on the Evolution and Nature of the Human Language Faculty.* Oxford: Oxford University Press. (Oxford Studies in Biolinguistics). // International Journal of Language Studies 6 (4), 154–182.

2012. Kosta, P., Krivochen, D. Some Thoughts on Language Diversity, UG and the Importance of Language Typology: Scrambling and Non-Monotonic Merge of Adjuncts and Specifiers in Czech and German. Zeitschrift für Slawistik 57 (4), 377–407.

2012. [Review]: Meškank, T. 2009. *Aussagestruktur im Sorbischen.* Untersuchungen zur Syntax und Satzsemantik. Teilband I + Teilband II. Hamburg: Verlag Dr. Kovač 2009. In: *Kritikon Litterarum* 39, Heft 1/ 2, 60–65.

2012. [Review]: Ziková, M., Dočekal, M. 2010. Slavic Languages in Formal Grammar. Proceedings of FDSL 8.5, Brno 2010. Frankfurt/M.: Peter Lang 2012. In: *Kritikon Litterarum* 39, Heft 3/ 4, 202–212.

2012. Kosta, Peter; Lieb, H.-H. [Review Reflection]. Stellungnahme zur Rezension von Thomas Daiber: Friedrich, Svetlana: *Definitheit im Russischen.* Frankfurt/M.: Peter Lang, 2009. (Potsdamer Linguistische Untersuchungen 4). In: *Kritikon Litterarum* 39, Heft 3/4, 212–221.

2013. Krivochen, D., Kosta, P. Eliminating Empty Categories: A Radically Minimalist View on their Ontology and Justification. Frankfurt/M.: Peter Lang. (Potsdam Linguistic Investigations 11).

2013. How can I lie if I am telling the truth? The unbearable lightness of the being of strong and weak modals, modal adverbs and modal particles in discourse between epistemic modality and evidentiality. In: Thielemann, N., Kosta,

P. (eds.). *Approaches to Slavic Interaction*. Amsterdam, Philadelphia: John Benjamins Publishing Company, 167–184 (Dialogue Studies 20).

2013. Mehrdeutigkeit und Humor in der Übersetzung. Zeitschrift für Slawistik 58 (3), 297–324.

2013. Early Subjects and Patterns of Agreement and Word Order in L1-Acquisition. A Radical Minimalist Perspective. In: Deutsche Beiträge zum 15. Internationalen Slavistenkongress, Minsk 2013. Herausgegeben von S. Kempgen, M. Wingender, N. Franz und M. Jakiša (Die Welt der Slaven. Sammelbände. Sborniki 50). München–Berlin–Washington/D.C. Verlag Otto Sagner, 161–174.

2013. Kosta, P., Zimmerling, A. Slavic clitics: a typology. In: *STUF – Language Typology and Universals*, Akademie Verlag 66 (2), 178–214.

2014. Kempgen, S., Kosta, P., Berger, T., Gutschmidt, K. (eds.). *Die slavischen Sprachen / The Slavic Languages – Ein internationales Handbuch zu ihrer Struktur, ihrer Geschichte und ihrer Erforschung / An International Handbook of their Structure, their History and their Investigation* Berlin, Boston: de Gruyter [HSK 32.2].

2014. Kosta, P., Zimmerling, A. Slavic Clitic Systems in a Typological Perspective. In: Schürcks, L., Giannakidou, A., Etxeberria, U. (eds.), *The Nominal Structure in Slavic and Beyond.* Berlin, Boston: de Gruyter (Studies in Generative Grammar Volume 116), 442–487.

2014. Kosta, P., Franks S., Radeva-Bork, T., Schürcks, L. (eds.). Minimalism and Beyond: Radicalizing the Interfaces. Amsterdam, Philadelphia: John Benjamins. (Series Language Faculty and Beyond 11).

2014. Kosta, P., Krivochen, D. Flavors of Movement: Revisiting the A / A' distinction. In: Kosta, P. et al. (eds.). Minimalism and Beyond: Radicalizing the Interfaces. Amsterdam, Philadelphia: John Benjamins, 236–266 (Series Language Faculty and Beyond 11).

2014. Kosta, P., Krivochen, D. G. Inner Islands and Negation: The Case of *Which*-Clauses and *As*-Clauses Revistited. In: Witkoś, J. & S. Jaworski (eds.). *New Insights into Slavic Linguistics.* Frankfurt/M. Peter Lang, 205–219. (Sprach- und Kulturkontakte in Europas Mitte. Studien zur Slawistik und Germanistik. Band 3).

2014. Kosta, P., Krivochen, D. Interfaces, Impaired Merge and the Theory of the Frustrated Mind. Czech and Slovak Linguistic Review 1, 32–75. (ed. by Peter Kosta and Michaela Zemková, Satellite Workshop of QUALICO "Informational Fundamentals of Life: Genes and Languages").

2014. [Review] 2011. Breu, W.; Piccoli, G. *Südslavisch unter romanischem Dach.* Die Moliseslaven in Geschichte und Gegenwart im Spiegel ihrer

Sprache. Teil 1: Texte gesprochener Sprache aus Acquaviva Collecroce / Breu, Walter; Piccoli, Giovanni. Südslavisch unter romanischem Dach. Die Moliseslaven in Geschichte und Gegenwart im Spiegel ihrer Sprache. Teil 2: Texte gesprochener Sprache aus Montemitro und San Felice del Molise. München: Sagner (Sagners Slavistische Sammlung, Band 32). In: *Kritikon Litterarum* Bans 41 Heft 1/2, 81–85.

2015. On the Causative/Anti-Causative Alternation as Principle of Affix Ordering in the Light of the Mirror Principle, the Lexical Integrity Principle and the Distributed Morphology. Zeitschrift für Slawistik 60 (4), 570–612.

2015. Code-switching and Code-mixing Revisited in Urban and Ethnic Styles: A Brief Sketch on Variation and Language Shift. In: Warditz, V., Kress, B. (eds.). *Multilingualism and Translation.* Studies on Slavonic and Non-Slavonic Languages in Contact. Frankfurt/M.: Peter Lang, 111–129. (Potsdam Linguistic Investigations 17).

2015. Třetí faktor "relevance" mezi sémantikou, pragmatikou a syntaxí. In: Bednaříková, B., Pittnerová, M. (eds.). *Čítanka textů z kognitivní lingvistiky II.* Univerzita Palackého v Olomouci. Filozofická fakulta. Olomouc, 57–76.

2015. Negacja a struktura zdania w języku czeskim. In: Bednaříková, B., Pittnerová, M. (eds.). *Čítanka textů z kognitivní lingvistiky II.* Univerzita Palackého v Olomouci. Filozofická fakulta. Olomouc, 287–310.

2017. "BIOLINGVISTIKA" [Biolinguistics], in: Karlík, P. et al. *Nový encyklopedický slovník češtiny online.* Praha: Lidové Noviny.

2017. "HLOUBKOVÁ STRUKTURA" (Deep Structure), in: Karlík, P. et al. *Nový encyklopedický slovník češtiny online.* Praha: Lidové Noviny.

2017. "KLITIKON" [Clitic], in: Karlík, P. et al. *Nový encyklopedický slovník češtiny online.* Praha: Lidové Noviny.

2017. "LOGICKÁ FORMA" [Logical Form], in: Karlík, P. et al. *Nový encyklopedický slovník češtiny online.* Praha: Lidové Noviny.

2017. "MODULARITA JAZYKA" [Modularity in Language], in: Karlík, P. et al. *Nový encyklopedický slovník češtiny online.* Praha: Lidové Noviny.

2017. "NEAKUZATIVNÍ SLOVESO" (neakuzativum, ergativní sloveso) [Unaccusative Verb] online, in: Karlík, P. et al. *Nový encyklopedický slovník češtiny online.* Praha: Lidové Noviny.

2017. "NEERGATIVNÍ SLOVESO" (neergativum) [Unergative Verb] online, in: Karlík, P. et al. *Nový encyklopedický slovník češtiny online.* Praha: Lidové Noviny.

2017. "OVLÁDÁNÍ" (command) online, in: Karlík, P. et al. *Nový encyklopedický slovník češtiny online.* Praha: Lidové Noviny.

2017. "POSUN α" (move α, posun alfa, move alpha)" online, in: Karlík, P. et al. *Nový encyklopedický slovník češtiny online*. Praha: Lidové Noviny.
2017. "POVRCHOVÁ STRUKTURA" (surface structure) online, in: Karlík, P. et al. *Nový encyklopedický slovník češtiny online*. Praha: Lidové Noviny.
2017. "PRÁZDNÁ KATEGORIE" (empty category), in: Karlík, P. et al. *Nový encyklopedický slovník češtiny online*. Praha: Lidové Noviny.
2017. "PRINCIP PLNÉ INTERPRETACE" online [Principle of Full Interpretation, PFI], in: Karlík, P. et al. *Nový encyklopedický slovník češtiny online*. Praha: Lidové Noviny.
2017. "PROJEKČNÍ PRINCIP" (projection principle) online, in: Karlík, P. et al. *Nový encyklopedický slovník češtiny online*. Praha: Lidové Noviny.
2017. "SPELL OUT" online, in: Karlík, P. et al. *Nový encyklopedický slovník češtiny online*. Praha: Lidové Noviny.
2017. "STOPA" (trace) online, in: Karlík, P. et al. *Nový encyklopedický slovník češtiny online*. Praha: Lidové Noviny.
2017. "T-MODEL" online, in: Karlík, P. et al. *Nový encyklopedický slovník češtiny online*. Praha: Lidové Noviny.
2017. "TEORIE OHRANIČENÍ" (bounding theory) online, in: Karlík, P. et al. *Nový encyklopedický slovník češtiny online*. Praha: Lidové Noviny.
2017. "TEORIE PÁDU" (Case Theory) online, in: Karlík, P. et al. *Nový encyklopedický slovník češtiny online*. Praha: Lidové Noviny.
2017. "TEORIE ŘÍZENÍ" (Government Theory) online, in: Karlík, P. et al. *Nový encyklopedický slovník češtiny online*. Praha: Lidové Noviny.
2017. "THETA TEORIE" (θ–/Theta-Theory), in: Karlík, P. et al. *Nový encyklopedický slovník češtiny online*. Praha: Lidové Noviny.
2017. "X-BAR TEORIE" (X-bar Theory) online, in: Karlík, P. et al. *Nový encyklopedický slovník češtiny online*. Praha: Lidové Noviny.
2017. Über das Übersetzen von Spandrels. In: Schwejk: Prager Original oder antimilitaristischer Schelm? // Sudetenland. Europäische Kulturzeitschrift Sonderheft 3, 273–278. Hrsg. Franz Adam, Peter Becher, Hansjörgen Gartner und Ursula Haas im Auftrag des Adalbert Stifter Vereins. München.
2018. Einige Anmerkungen zur Syntax von Sprache und Musik: Am Beispiel von Rekursivität und Merge bei J.S. Bach und in der Sprache. In: *Musica in Litteris*. Musikalische Geburtstagsgabe für Ludger Udolph. Dresden: Thelem Universitätsverlag und Buchhandlung GmbH und Co. KG, 57–72.
2018. Slavistische und baltistische Anteile in der Forschung und Forschungsnachfolge Franz Bopps. Historische Sprachforschung 130, 236–256.

2019. Third Position Repair, Overlaps, and Code–Switching within a Strict Turn–Taking Model. In: Thielemann, N., Richter, N. (eds.). *Urban Voices*: The Sociolinguistics, Grammar and Pragmatics of Spoken Russian. Berlin: Peter Lang, 183–191. (Potsdam Linguistic Investigations 25).

2019. [Review]: 2017. Murray, Sarah E. The Semantics of Evidentials. Oxford University Press Oxford (Oxford Studies in Semantics and Pragmatics 9). In: Journal of Pragmatics 140, 156-159.

2019. Grammatical and prosodic means of human– and animal–oriented (pre–) directives of talk–in–interaction, St. Petersburg State Polytechnical University Journal. Humanities and Social Sciences, 10 (4), 113–140.

2019. Model' "radikal'nogo minimalizma" pri izučenii sintaksičeskih javlenij (k kritike ponjatij "soglasovanie", "upravlenie", "specifikator") // Vestnik Moskovskogo gosudarstvennogo oblastnogo universiteta. Serija: Lingvistika, No 5. S. 40–55. Kosta P. Adjectival and argumental small clauses vs. Free adverbial adjuncts – a phase–based approach within the radical minimalism. In: Bulletin of Moscow Region State University. Series: Linguistics, no. 5, 40–55.

2019. Адъективные и Аргументальные Малые Клаузы в Сопоставлении со Свободными Адвербиальными Адъюнктами – Фазовый Подход в Радикальном Минимализме. In: IV Международная Научно Практическая Конференция – Русский Язык на Перекрёстке Эпох: Традиции и Инновации в Русистике 26–28 Сентября 2019 г. Сборник Научных Статей Часть 1: Pp. 21–25. Ереван Издательство РАУ 2019 Доклады Пленарного Заседания.

2020. Radeva-Bork, T., Kosta, P. (eds.). Current Developments in Slavic Linguistics. Twenty Years After (based on selected papers from FDSL 11). Berlin: Peter Lang. (Potsdam Linguistic Investigations 29).

2020. On Extraction and Clitic Climbing out of Subject-/Object-Control Clauses and Causative Clauses in Romance and Czech. In: Radeva-Bork, Teodora and Peter Kosta (eds.). *Current Developments in Slavic Linguistics*. Twenty Years After (based on selected papers from FDSL 11), 185–202. (Potsdam Linguistic Investigations 29).

2020. The Syntax of Meaning and the Meaning of Syntax: Minimal Computations and Maximal Derivations in a Label-/Phase-Driven Generative Grammar of Radical Minimalism. Berlin: Peter Lang. (Potsdam Linguistic Investigation 31).

2020. Kosta, P., Karlík, P. Die Nominalisierung von Nebensätzen im Tschechischen. Zeitschrift für Slawistik 65 (4), 479–497.

2020. Multiple modification in Slavic as compared to Romance and Germanic Languages (the proof by degree phrases and comparatives). In: Pavel Caha,

Market Ziková, and Michael Starke (eds.): Petr Karlík 70 Festschrift. https://lingbuzz.com/t/karlik/. To appear also in Rivista de Grammatica Generativa (eds. Starke, Michal and Pavel Caha).

2021. Code switching and code mixing in colloquial Russian–German casual urban styles and varieties in openings and closings. In: Nadobnik, Renata/Skorupska-Raczyńska, Elżbieta (Hrsg.): Deutsch und Polnisch im Kontakt mit anderen Sprachen. Beiträge anlässlich des Jubiläums "500 Jahre deutsch-polnische Sprachführer". Schriftenreihe Schriften zur Vergleichenden Sprachwissenschaft 33, Hamburg: Verlag Dr. Kovač, 175–194.

2021. On Comparative and Degree Scales in Czech, Russian and Polish: A Radical Minimalist Look at their Syntax, Morphology, and Semantics. In: Brehmer, B., Gattnar, A., and Perevozchikova, T. (eds.). *Von A wie Aspekt bis Z wie zdvořilost. Ein Kaleidoskop der Slavistik für Tilman Berger zum 65. Geburtstag.* Tübingen: TLP, S. 117–126.

2021. The Unified Voice Phase Hypothesis and the Nature of Parametrized Functional Heads in a Phase-Label driven Model of Radical Minimalism. In: Kosta, Peter and Katrin Schlund, eds.: *Keynotes from the International Conference on Explanation and Prediction in Linguistics (CEP): Formalist and Functionalist Approaches. Heidelberg, February 13th and 14th, 2019.* Berlin; Bern; Bruxelles etc.: Peter Lang, 149–212. (Potsdam Linguistic Investigations vol. 33).

2021. Kosta, P., Schlund, K. (eds.). *Keynotes from the International Conference on Explanation and Prediction in Linguistics (CEP): Formalist and Functionalist Approaches. Heidelberg, February 13th and 14th, 2019.* Berlin; Bern; Bruxelles, etc.: Peter Lang. (Potsdam Linguistic Investigations vol. 33).

2021. Iskakova, G. Z., Kosta, P., Berdibay, S., Raushan, K. and Kabykenovich, S.A. (2021). Ways To Express the Author's Modality in Kazakh, Kyrgyz and English Fiction Works. *Homeros.* 4 (2), 97–117.

2021. Iskakova, G. Z., Kosta, P. Көркем Мәтіннің Модалділік Аспектісі: Ә. Кекілбаев Пен Ш. Айтматов Шығармаларының Негізінде. Модальный аспект художественного текста: на материале произведений А. Кекильбаева и Ч. Айтматова. In: Ш. Уәлиханов атындағы КУ хабаршысы. Филология сериясы. No 2, 2021, 23–31.

[forthcoming]. Schlund, K., Kosta, P. (eds.). *Exploring the Impersonal Domain: Empirical and Theoretical Perspectives on Slavic languages.* Special Issue of *Journal of Slavic Linguistics.*

[forthcoming]. On Time – The Incremental Compositionality of Temporality and Aspectuality. In: Warditz, Vladislava (ed.). *Russian Grammar: System – Language Usage – Language Variation* (Fifth International Symposium) – Русская грамматика: Система – узус – языковое варьирование. University of Potsdam, Germany, September 22–25, 2021. Berlin, etc.: Peter Lang. (Potsdam Linguistic Investigations).

[forthcoming]. Globalizace vs. regionalizace, přepînánî kódu a mîšenî kódu, kreolizace vs. pidžinizace jako forma změn v městských řečových stylech. *Bohemica Olomucensis.*

Vrinda Subhalaxmi Chidambaram

A Case of *Parasitic Attrition*: The Disappearance of the Degree Morpheme -*ъš* in Bulgarian and Macedonian Superlative Adjectives

Abstract In this paper, I consider two distinct types of historical morphological change; one is the familiar Jespersen-cycle type of change (in which one morpheme gradually replaces another as a result of their fluctuations in semantic strength[1]) and the other involves the loss of a morpheme in one context due to its disappearance in an entirely different context. I refer to this second type of change as "parasitic attrition." Specifically, I examine the historical development of Bulgarian and Macedonian degree adjectives, which unlike those in other Slavic languages, are formed only through prefixation to the positive adjective and do not include suffixation. Using evidence from the *Trojanska Priča*, I argue that while Bulgarian and Macedonian (hereafter, Bg and Mac) comparative degree adjectives lost the degree suffix -*ъš* via a Jespersen-cyclic change, the loss of the same -*ъš* degree morpheme in superlatives occurred via parasitic attrition.

Keywords: Degree Adjectives, Morphology, Bulgarian, Macedonian, Diachronic

1. Introduction

The majority of Slavic languages form degree adjectives through a combination of prefixation and suffixation. In Slovene, for example, the comparative adjective is derived by merging the suffix –*š* to the positive adjective. The superlative degree adjective is then built on the comparative adjectival stem by merging the prefix *naj*-, as illustrated in (1).

(1)	lep –	lep-*š*-i	– *naj*-lep-*š*-i	
	beautiful	beautiful-CMPR-NOM.SG.MASC.	– SUP-beautiful-CMPR-NOM.SG.MASC.	
	'beautiful'	– 'more beautiful'	– 'most beautiful'	(Slovene)

In contrast to all other Slavic languages, Modern Bulgarian and Macedonian express degree on adjectives through prefixation alone, as illustrated in (2).

(2)	ubav	*po*-ubav	*naj*-ubav	
	beautiful	CMPR-beautiful	-SUP-beautiful	
	'beautiful'	'more beautiful'	-'most beautiful'	(Macedonian)

This difference between Bg and Mac and the other Slavic languages raises two questions: How did the comparative degree prefix *po*- arise and what happened to the degree adjectival suffix?

To explore potential answers to these questions, I will consider the historical development of Bulgarian and Macedonian degree adjectives.

2. Old Bulgarian Degree Adjectives

2.1. Comparatives

Early Bulgarian/Macedonian texts are replete with examples involving *-ьj/-ьš* as the sole comparative degree affix.[2]

(3)	svoi	bo	oči	nikomuže	ne	lŭžete.	ašte	i	te	sę	drugoici
	own	for	eyes	to-no one	NEG	lie.	If	and	they	REFL	occasionally
	blaznite,	nŭ	obače	te	izvestĭnei-**ši**	jeste	inogo.				
	err	but	still	they	reliable-CMPR	are	other				

'One's own eyes will not lie. And if they occasionally err, still they are more reliable than those of another.'
(*The Hexameron of John the Exarch*, late 9th-early 10th century AD. Ed. Butler 1996: 128)

In these Old Bulgarian texts, *po*- does not appear at all in comparative degree constructions, indicating that the comparative prefix is a relatively recent innovation.

2.2. Superlatives

A careful study of Bulgarian/Macedonian literature reveals an extensive transformation of the expression of superlative degree, but unfortunately the intermediate steps of this change are poorly documented. In the earliest Old Bulgarian texts, which date from around the mid-9th century AD, we find that superlative degree is marked by the prefix *prě*- (spelled either прѣ- or пре-). By far most adjectives bearing this prefix are interpreted as absolute superlatives (which are interpreted as intensified adjectives and do not permit a comparison class), but there are examples in which such adjectives are unambiguously relative superlatives (whose interpretations require a comparison class). Below are examples of both absolute and relative superlatives using the *prě-* prefix from Saint Constantine-Cyril's Sermon on the Translation of the Relics of Saint Clement of Rome (late 9th or early 10th century, Ed. Butler 1996: 2). This text itself is a translation of Constantine-Cyril's original Greek sermon into Slavonic; the translation is likely to have been done some time between 863 and 927 AD (Butler 1996: 7).

(4) Absolute Superlative

vŭsię	namĭ	s[vę]taę	**prě**-slavnaa	glava	**prě**-slovuštago	Klimenta.
shone	us	holy	**SUP**-glorified	head	**SUP**-renowned-GEN	Kliment-GEN

'there shone to us the holy and most glorified head of the most renowned Kliment'

(Ed. Butler 1996: 14)

(5) Relative Superlative

o	**prě**-slovęi	**prě**-slavne	predo	vsemi	i nado vsemi	Klimente.
oh	**SUP**-renowned$_{VOC.}$	**SUP**-glorified$_{VOC.}$	before	all and	above all	Kliment$_{VOC.}$

"Oh, you, Kliment, who are most renowned and most glorified above and before all!"

(Ed. Butler 1996: 20)

Because the usage is ambiguous, *prě-* used in the first of these examples could be mistaken for an enclitic intensifier, simply meaning 'exceedingly'. However, we see from the second example that the effect of affixing *prě-* to the adjective is indeed to select a unique entity from a set to indicate that this single entity exceeds all others within that set with respect to some specific attribute. This is precisely the function of a relative superlative degree modifier. Thus, it is evident that the prefix *prě-* was indeed being used in the 9th and 10th centuries as a true (i.e., relative) superlative morpheme.

It is, however, worth noting that the surviving documents from this period show that adjectives prefixed with *prě-* were nearly always used to express an absolute superlative meaning. And in fact the direction that this prefix subsequently took may indeed be a modification of these absolute superlative semantics. In other words, over time, the meaning of the *prě-* adjectival affix transformed from 'exceedingly' to 'excessively', the latter of which is the contemporary meaning of this morpheme.[3]

3. Medieval Development of Degree Adjectival Morphology

Although the meaning of this *prě-* morpheme may have already shifted by the late 14th and early 15th centuries, much of the documentation that we have from that period is linguistically conservative and follows the conventions of Old Church Slavonic and Old Bulgarian.[4] For example, we have the works of Grigorij Camblak, a nobleman from the capital of Tarnovo. Camblak was born in the early 14th century. He moved to Serbia where he became an Abbott and subsequently moved to Kyiv, where he attained the position of Metropolitan of Kyiv (Fine 1994: 444). Given his ecclesiastical vocation as well as his education as a member of the Bulgarian nobility, it is no surprise that his writing is stylistically and linguistically conservative, bearing all the features of Old Church Slavonic.

(6)	podviže	burę	prŭvyę	veliča-**jš**-ǫ	že	i	ljute-**jš**-ǫ
	raised	storm	first	great-CMPR-ACC	even	and	furious-CMPR-ACC

'He raised a storm, even greater and more furious than the first.'

(Camblak, *Eulogy for St. Euthymius*, 14th century; Ed. Kałužniacki 1971: 52)

This excerpt includes two instances of comparative adjectives, both marked with the *–ъš* comparativizing suffix. And unsurprisingly, within the same text we also find the archaic form of the superlative, which is the positive form of the adjective additionally marked with the *prě-* prefix:

(7)	I	cr[ŭ]kovĭ	vŭzdvižet	vŭ	slavǫ	**prě**-svętěj	trojci
	and	church	will-raise-up	in	glory	SUP-holy	trinity

'and he will raise up the Church for the glory of most holy Trinity'

(Camblak, *Eulogy for St. Euthymius*, 14th century; Ed. Kałužniacki 1971: 52)

Camblak's writing exhibits an adherence to Church Slavonic conventions, which can be attributed to his social and professional status. There are, however, indications that at the time of Camblak's writing, the vulgate was generally transforming, and in particular, new morphemes had been introduced.

3.1. The Emergence of the *naj-* Prefix

There is little consensus about the origin of the affix *naj-*; scholars agree that it somehow replaced the *prě-* prefix, but how it came to be the superlativizing prefix remains a mystery.[5] Although largely absent from Old Church Slavonic texts, *naj-* prefixation suddenly it emerged as the unique formulation of superlative degree adjectives. It is certainly conceivable that it developed via a process akin to the Jespersen Cycle, by which the meaning of one affix (in this case, *prě-*) is weakened and requires the introduction of a new affix (*naj-*).

What is known is that the modern superlative prefix *naj-* has fully replaced the previous superlativizing prefix *prě-*. The question is how this exchange transpired. As noted earlier, *prě-* underwent a crucial semantic shift. Although it had the potential to be used as both a relative and absolute superlative, it came to be used exclusively in the absolute sense as an intensifier rather than a superlative marker. Thus, the language was left in need of a way to express the relative superlative meaning. It is not unreasonable to postulate that it was at this stage that the *–ъj/–ъš* suffix was borrowed from the comparative onto the superlative in order to denote the existence of a comparison class, thus creating a true relative superlative that is distinguishable from an absolute superlative. It is crucial to note that this process entails an essential transformation of the basic semantics of *–ъj/–ъš* from indicating a comparative adjective to denoting a comparison class.

Another important fact to note is that an excessive degree adjective cannot be combined with a comparison class. In terms of compositional semantics, an expression such as "this donut is too sweet than the other pastries" is nonsensical, because an excessive degree morpheme, unlike a comparative or relative superlative degree morpheme, does not select for a comparison class. Indeed, in modern Slavic languages where the *pre-* prefix has come to be the excessive degree marker, it cannot be combined (morphologically or syntactically) with any marker of or reference to a comparison class. This point is illustrated by Slovak in (8):

(8) a. prevysok-ý
pre-visok-ý
too-tall-NOM.SG.MASC.

b. vyš-š-í
tall-COMP.CLASS-NOM.SG.MASC.
tall-er

c. *pre-vyš-š-í
too-tall-COMP.CLASS.-NOM.SG.MASC.
too-taller (i.e., 'too much taller')

d. *pre-vysoký ako ona
too-tall-NOM.SG.MASC. than she
*too tall than her (Slovak)

Eventually, as the meaning of *prě-* as an excessive (rather than a superlative) morpheme crystallized (and thus became incompatible with the comparison-class-denoting suffix *–ьj/–ьš*), *naj-* was introduced to replace it and attached to the comparative degree adjectival stem. Thus, we derive the superlative form found in many modern Slavic languages of *naj-*+comparative.

(9) lep – *lepši* – naj*lepši*
beautiful – more beautiful – most beautiful

And indeed, even in Medieval Bulgarian/Macedonian texts, we find that *naj-* co-occurs with the comparative degree suffix *-ьš*.

(10) poveždi mene nai-lep-**š**-ǫ
pronounce $\text{me}_{\text{ACC.}}$ SUP-beautiful-**COMP**-acc
'pronounce me [as] the most beautiful'
(*Trojanska Priča*, 1345, insert of the *Manasses Chronicle*. Vat.slav.2: 10)3.2.

4. *PO-*, *NAJ-*, AND *–ЬJ/–ЬŠ* IN THE *TROJANSKA PRIČA*

Example (10) given above comes from a document that deserves special attention with respect to the question of the development of degree adjectives in Bulgarian/Macedonian. This text was the Trojanska Priča, the Story of Troy, which was placed as an insert into the Manasses Chronicle.[6] Written circa 1345 AD, approximately concurrent with Camblak's writing, the Trojanska Priča reveals a great deal about the state of degree adjectives in spoken Bulgarian/Macedonian at the time. What stands out most conspicuously is the extensive variability in the expression of degree adjectives; it appears to have been written at a point in history when nearly all of the combinatorial possibilities for forming comparative and superlative degree adjectives were simultaneously available.

If we count only comparative and superlative adjectives, we find in the *Trojanska Priča* a total of 26 tokens (11 superlative and 15 comparative). By excluding repetitions, we find 21 types (see Appendix A for full glosses of all the degree adjective types in the *Trojanska Priča*). This is noteworthy in and of itself: of 26 tokens, we have only 5 instances of repeated forms. This is particularly surprising given that many of the types have the same intended readings (e.g., many would be translated 'most beautiful' or 'more beautiful'). This illustrates the extent of variability in the expression of degree adjectives in the *Trojanska Priča*. We can suggest either that the author of the *Trojanska Priča* is hopelessly confused, or, the more likely scenario, that he is using all the lexical variations available to him to compose a more pleasing translation (see the appendix for a full morphemic breakdown of the 6 superlative types and 15 comparative types found in the *Trojanska Priča*).

By running a simple analysis of these types and breaking them into component morphemes, we can determine the frequency of the degree prefixes *po-* and *naj-* and the frequency of the *-ьš* suffix. We can also examine the combinations of the affixes (summarized also in Tabs. 1 and 2).

SUPERLATIVES:
- CONTAIN *NAJ-*: 6/6 = 100 %
  - CONTAIN ONLY *NAJ-*: 2/6 = 33.33 %
- CONTAIN-*ЬŠ*: 4/6 = 66.67 %
  - CONTAIN ONLY-*ЬŠ*: 0/6 = 0 %
- CONTAIN NEITHER MORPHEME: 0/6 = 0 %
- CONTAIN BOTH MORPHEMES = 4/6 = 66.67 %

COMPARATIVES:
- CONTAIN *PO-*: 10/15 = 66.67 %
  - CONTAIN ONLY *PO-*: 8/15 = 53.33 %
- CONTAIN -*ЬŠ*: 5/15 = 33.33 %
  - CONTAIN ONLY -*ЬŠ*: 3/15 = 20 %
- CONTAIN NEITHER MORPHEME: 2/15 (analytic forms) = 13.33 %
- CONTAIN BOTH MORPHEMES: 2/15 = 13.33

4.1. Comparative Adjektives in the *Trojanska Priča*

Although the sample size of comparative expressions is small (only 15 types total), we can nevertheless observe some interesting tendencies in the data, which are highly suggestive of a Jespersen-cyclic change.

The original Jespersen-cycle change referred to patterns of emerging and vanishing negation morphology (Jespersen 1917). Jespersen noted that an existing negative morpheme may weaken, thereby precipitating the introduction of a new negative morpheme. This new morpheme starts out as simply a reinforcing negative particle but gradually, the original negative morpheme becomes obsolete and the newly introduced negative particle eventually assumes the negative meaning entirely.

A clear and well-known example of this type of change comes from French.

(11)	Je **ne** regrette	→ Je ne regrette	→ Je ne regrette pas	→ Je regrette pas
	I NEG regret	→ I NEG$_{(WEAK)}$ regret	→ I NEG$_{(WEAK)}$ regret NEG$_{(WEAK)}$	→ I regret (NEG)
	'I don't regret'			

Example (11) illustrates the chronological development of negation morphology in French. The negative morpheme *ne* is intially strong but weakens over time, which creates a need for a new morpheme that can reinforce the negative semantics. For this reason, *pas* is introduced. For some time the two morphemes coexist in this way, cumulatively conveying the negative semantics. Over time, however, the original negative morpheme, *ne*, has continued to weaken and the negative morpheme *pas* has continued to strengthen. Consequently in contemporary French, we find increasingly frequent examples of negative constructions that include only *pas*.

The distribution of *po-* and -*ъš* is highly suggestive of a Jespersen-cyclic change in comparative morphology in Medieval Bulgarian/Macedonian. Consider the data as presented in the table below.

	-*ъš*	no -*ъš*	*Sum*
po-	**(2)**	**8**	*10*
no *po-*	**3**	**2** (*periphrasis*)	*5*
Sum	*5*	*10*	*15*

po- appears most of the time (in 2/3 cases)

-*ъš* mostly does not appear (1/3 of the time only)

Tab. 1: Comparative adjectival morphology in the *Trojanska Priča*

From this table, we see that there is near complementarity of distribution between the morphemes *po-* and *-ъš*. Furthermore, it appears that by this time *po-* was already the more common marker of comparative degree and the *-ъš* affix is already declining. The former occurs in 2/3 of comparative adjectives and the latter occurs in 1/3. The overlap, i.e., number of instances in which both morphemes appear, is small (2/15 or 13.33 %). The low-frequency of overlap of the two morphemes is precisely what one would expect to see in the middle of Jespersen-cycle type change. In other words, at the time the *Trojanska Priča* was written, the use of *po-* as the sole comparative-degree marking morpheme was on the rise as the use of *-ъš* was simultaneously declining. Although the sample size is small, what we can surmise from these data is that *po-* is replacing *-ъš* as the comparativizing affix. This replacement of one morpheme by another is Jespersen-cyclic change.

What we find in the expression of superlative degree adjectives, on the other hand, paints a rather different picture of morphological change.

4.2. Superlative Adjectives in the *Trojanska Priča*

Tab. 2 shows the distribution of degree adjectival morphology on superlative adjectives in the Trojanska Priča. Again, the sample size is quite small, but the data nevertheless indicate a markedly distinct pattern from what we have observed for comparatives.

	-ъš	no *-ъš*	*Sum*
naj-	**4**	**2**	*6*
no *naj-*	**0**	**0**	*0*
Sum	*4*	*2*	*6*

naj- always occurs

-ъš appears most of the time (in 2/3 cases)

Tab. 2: Superlative adjectival morphology in the *Trojanska Priča*

In contrast to comparatives, most of the examples of superlative degree adjectives include the degree suffix *-ъš*. And more strikingly – and more convincingly indicative of a difference from the comparative *po-* –, the prefix *naj-* is invariably present. The prevalence of *-ъš* and ubiquity of *naj-* results in a fair degree of overlap between the two morphemes across tokens (i.e., twice as many as in comparatives despite the smaller sample).

The occurrence of *naj-* in all superlative forms indicates that this prefix has already fully assumed the role of the superlative degree marker. This contrasts with the emergence of the *po-* comparative marker, which exhibits a gradual strengthening simultaneous with and contingent upon the weakening of the *-ъš* morpheme. The superlative adjective pattern suggests that, rather than replacing one morpheme with another (as we see in comparatives), superlatives in Bulgarian/Macedonian simply lose the *-ъš* morpheme and its function is fully assumed by the already-present *naj-* prefix. The question that persists is why the *-ъš* morpheme is lost in superlatives.

At the moment the *Trojanska Priča* was written, 2/3 of superlative adjectives still contained *-ъš*. But as noted, 100 % of superlative tokens contain *naj-*. This is significant, because rather than indicating a Jespersen-cycle type replacement, it points to a different variety of historical morphological change, namely a kind of *parisitic attrition.*

A *parasitic attrition* may be defined as the loss of a morpheme in one context as a result of the loss of the same morpheme in another, distinct context.

In other words, the eventual loss of the *-ъš* morpheme in superlative degree adjectives in Bg/Mac may have been parasitic on the attrition of *-ъš* in the more-common comparative form. This attrition is enabled (or perhaps even licensed) by the presence of *naj-*, a morpheme that independently bears the semantics of superlative degree.

Parasitic attrition likely reflects a change in the lexicon; i.e., it is a change that must be mediated by the lexicon. If the lexical entry for a morpheme loses semantic value (and retains only its phonological and syntactic features), then this will affect its appearance in a range of contexts. Certainly, there are semantically weak/bleached elements that remain in the lexicon and are productive, but a semantically null element (that serves no syntactic purpose either) will not survive long. For this reason, the *-ъš* morpheme became obsolete in Bg/Mac superlatives; it lost its function as a comparison class marker in the comparative due to the introduction of *po-*. This Jespersen-cyclic change affected the lexical entry for *-ъš*; its comparison-class-denoting semantics were diminished and eventually erased. As a result, the affix was dropped in the superlative, as well.

5. Conclusion

The (admittedly sparse) data we find that offer a glimpse into the state of degree adjective morphology in medieval Bulgarian/Macedonian paint two different pictures of morphological change: one for comparative adjectives and another for superlative degree adjectives. Comparative degree adjectives underwent a Jespersen-cycle type change, resulting in the replacement of the –ьš suffix by the *po-* prefix. Although there is a similar resulting structure for Bg/Mac superlatives (namely, the inclusion of a prefix and the loss of an affix), it appears to have been derived through a different kind of diachronic change. The prefix *naj-* was introduced into the medieval Bg/Mac lexicon as a superlative degree marker; it never underwent a process of semantic strengthening in the way that *po-* did. The subsequent loss of the –ьš morpheme in the superlative was related to its semantic weakening / bleaching in the context of the comparative degree adjective. In essence, the lexical item -ьš had weakened, and this weakening / semantic bleaching was a lexical change (i.e., independent of morphological context). Having lost its semantic strength as a comparison class marker, it began to disappear from superlative degree adjectives as well. I have referred to this process as parasitic attrition.

Appendix A: Gloss of All Degree Adjectives in the Trojanska Priča

	SUPERLATIVES	COMPARATIVES
1	Наилѣпшѫѧ nailěpšǫę nai-lěp-š-ǫę SUP-beautiful-DEG-ACC$_{LF}$	Полѣпшаа polěpšaa po-lěp-š-aa CMPR-beautiful-DEG- NOM$_{LF}$
2	Наилѣпа nailěpa nai-lěp-a SUP-beautiful-NOM$_{SF}$	Лѣпшаа lěpšaa lěp-š-aa beautiful-DEG- NOM$_{LF}$
3	Наилѣпшаа nailěpšaa nai-lěp-š-aa SUP-beautiful-DEG-NOM$_{LF}$	Побогатъ pobogatŭ po-bogat-ŭ CMPR-wealthy-NOM$_{SF}$

	SUPERLATIVES	COMPARATIVES
4	Наилѣпѣиша nailěpěiša nai-lěp-ě-iš-a SUP-beautiful-ě-DEG-NOM$_{SF}$	Полѣпшѫѧ polěpšǫę po-lěp-š-ǫę CMPR-beautiful-DEF- NOM$_{LF}$
5	Наимъдръ naimŭdrŭ nai-mŭdr-ŭ SUP-wise-NOM$_{SF}$	Храбрѣиша xrabrěiša xrabr-ě-iš-a brave-ě-DEG-NOM$_{SF}$
6	Наилѣпша nailěpša nai-lěp-š-a SUP-beautiful-DEG-NOM$_{SF}$	храбыи паче вьсѣх гръкь xrabryi pače vĭsěx grŭkĭ brave more all$_{GEN.PL.}$ Greeks$_{GEN.PL.}$ more brave than all Greeks
7		**Подоброго** **podobrogo** **po-dobr-ogo** **CMPR-good-GEN$_{LF}$**
8		Похрабєръ poxraberŭ po-xraber-ŭ CMPR-brave- NOM$_{SF}$
9		Подобръ podobrŭ po-dobr-ŭ CMPR-good- NOM$_{SF}$
10		Поскоро poskoro po-skoro CMPR-soon
11		Почьстно počĭstno po-čĭst-n-o CMPR-honor-able-ADV

	SUPERLATIVES	COMPARATIVES
12		Меншего menšego men-š-ego small-DEG-GEN$_{LF}$
13		помного pomnogo po-mnogo CMPR-many
14		Подобрѣ podobrě po-dobr-ě CMPR-good-ADV
15		вѧще кривъ vęšte krivŭ vęšte kriv-ŭ more guilty-NOM$_{SF}$

Notes

1 The concept of semantic strength will be addressed more fully in the body of this paper; however, a simple definition of semantic strength is the expressive potency of a morpheme (i.e., a morpheme's ability to convey a particular meaning). As Jespersen (1917) noted, we find examples of cyclic patterns of semantic weakening / bleaching and semantic strengthening across languages; in this paper, we will explore one such example from Medieval Bulgarian.
2 *–ьj/–ьš* is an allomorphic pair.
3 In contemporary Macedonian, *premnogu* is an excessive adverbial intensifier meaning 'too much', as in (i):

i.	премногу	сладок
	pre-mnogu	sladok
	too-much	sweet
	'too sweet'	

In most other Slavic languages, e.g., Slovene, *pre-* was simply adopted as an adjective-selecting affix. In these languages, too, the prefix adds to the adjective the excessive meaning:

ii.	To	pecivo	je	res	pre-sladko!
	That	pastry	is	truly	too-sweet

'That pastry is really too sweet!'

4 It should be noted that very little textual documentation survives from the Medieval Period of Bulgarian/Macedonian literature. This is largely due to the Ottoman occupation of this region, which lasted 500 years beginning with the fall of the Second Bulgarian Empire in the late 14th century (Petkov: xi). Therefore, the linguistic developments that led from Old Bulgarian/Macedonian to Modern Bulgarian and Modern Macedonian are largely unrecorded.

5 One convincing account of the morphological development and structure of *naj-* can be found in Wandl (2019).

6 *The Manasses Chronicle* is a Medieval Bulgarian translation of a Greek Chronicle written by Constantine of Manasses. It is unclear whether the translator of the *Trojanska Priča*, which was placed as an insert into the *Manasses Chronicle*, was the same as the translator of the rest of the Chronicle. From the repeated use of the root *lep* (as opposed to *xub*) to mean 'beautiful', it seems likely that the *Trojanska Priča* was translated by someone from an eastern region of the 2nd Bulgarian Empire, in modern day North Macedonia.

Bibliography

Bobaljik, Jonathan. 2012. *Universals in Comparative Morphology*. Cambridge, MA: The MIT Press.

Butler, Thomas. 1996. *Monumenta Bulgarica: A Bilingual Anthology of Bulgarian Texts from the 9th to the 19th Centuries*. Ann Arbor: Michigan Slavic Publications.

Dujchev, Ivan. 1943. *Iz starata balgarska knizhnina*. Vol. 2. Sofia, Bulgaria: Xemus Publishers.

Fine, John van Antwerp. 1994. *The Late Medieval Balkans: A Critical Survey from the Late Twelfth Century to the Ottoman Conquest*. Ann Arbor: University of Michigan Press.

Friedman, Victor A. 2002. *Macedonian*. Munich: Lincom Europa.

Jespersen, Otto. 1917. *Negation in English and Other Languages*. Copenhagen: Høst.

Kałużniacki, Emil. 1901. *Aus der panegyrischen Litteratur der Südslaven*, 28–60. London: Varorium Reprints.

LUNT, HORACE. 1955. *Old Church Slavonic Grammar*. The Hague, The Netherlands: Mouton.

PETKOV, KIRIL. 2008. *The Voices of Medieval Bulgaria, Seventh-Fifteenth Century: The Records of a Bygone Culture*. Leiden, The Netherlands: Brill.

Trojanska Pritča. 1345. *The Manasses Chronicle*. MS, Vat.slav.2, 103–146. Vatican City: Biblioteca Apostolica Vaticana.

Steven Franks

Reflexive Typology, Movement, and the Structure of NP*

Abstract It is argued that, although the reflexive element is always introduced in ReflP, there are distinct ways to establish the reflexive interpretation. The English mechanism involves merging a DP with Refl and moving that DP to a higher argument position, which gives rise to reflexivity through coreferring co-arguments and causes an agreeing pronominal element to appear (e.g., ***him**self*). The Slavic mechanism does not involve any phrase merging with Refl; instead Refl (e.g., *sebja*) moves to *v*, rendering *v*P a reflexive predicate. The Slavic DP-languages, Bulgarian and Macedonian, also have a reflexive clitic in their anaphoric expressions (e.g., *sebe* ***si***). The source of this element is explored, and differences between the languages are attributed to Macedonian's lack of the Bulgarian DP-internal AgrP.

Keywords: Reflexives, Anaphora, Movement, DPs, Multiattachment, English, Bulgarian

1. Introduction

This paper considers superficially different reflexive constructions in English and Slavic. Although the anaphoric element is always introduced in a ReflP contained within the nominal domain, I argue for distinct paths towards the creation of the reflexive interpretation. One mechanism, instantiated by English, involves merging a DP with the Refl head and then moving that DP to a higher argument position (typically subject, but also object or indirect object). This gives rise to reflexivity through coreferring co-arguments. I show how one consequence of this movement is the appearance of a pronominal element that agrees with the moved DP in phi-features. The other mechanism does not involve any phrase merging with Refl, so that Refl itself must move to *v*, thereby establishing that *v*P as a reflexive predicate (so that the subject binds an internal argument). This is what happens in Slavic languages that lack DPs, such as Polish or Russian. The properties of these two types of reflexives are very different, but can be made to follow from their distinct derivational paths. With this in mind, I then look at Bulgarian and Macedonian, which can have an oblique/dative *si* clitic in their anaphoric expressions, and speculate about the source of this element. Differences between Bg and Mac are, in part, attributed to the lack of the Bg AgrP projection in otherwise comparable Mac DPs. Finally, I point to the extremely obscure nature of the sort of binding connectivity effects found in English.

2. English: Putting the *Him* in *Himself*

Franks (2015a) suggests that English reflexives of the *himself* type can be derived along the lines of the multiattachment model of movement put forward in Franks (2014, 2017). This paper elaborates on that proposal and explores how English differs from reflexive systems found in Slavic. Further details can be found in chapter 3 of Franks (2020).

2.1. Background: Hornstein's Movement Theory of Control (MTC) Approach

Hornstein (2001: chapter 5) proposed that in a sentence such as *John likes himself*, *John* first merges with *self*, where it receives the object theta-role (presumably, Theme), then moves to SpecVP, where it gets the subject theta-role (presumably, Experiencer), and finally moves to SpecIP for case purposes. He first provides the "underlying phrase marker" in (1), and then offers the derivation sketched in (2):

(1) [$_{IP}$ John I [$_{VP}$ John [likes [[John] self]]]]

(2) [$_{IP}$ John I [self [$_{VP}$ John [likes [[John] self]]]]] ⇒ John likes ~~John~~ self
−nom −acc +nom +nom +acc ⇒ John likes **him**self

The idea is that the role of *self* is to check the accusative case of *likes* (for Hornstein only in the covert interface level of logical form, LF, although this detail is immaterial); *self* is thus "generated as having accusative," Hornstein argues, "while the D/NP it is adjoined to carries nominative." The question, of course, is why the output of (2) is not the otherwise expected **John likes self*. Hornstein (p. 161) contends that "the pronoun is inserted after the copy is deleted to provide morphological support for the bound morpheme 'self'," and the pronoun is accusative because it "agrees in case with the adjunct it supports." However, in light of perfectly well-formed English phrases in which *self* can stand on its own, such as *the inner self* or *my other self*, as well as the lack of clarity about why the pronominal form that appears is, in particular, accusative *him* (but see Section

2.4 below), I offer a variant of Hornstein's system that derives *him* in a different way. The basic idea is to capitalize on intermediate movement effects as analyzed in Franks (2017).

2.2. Multiattachment Analysis Background

My analysis of intermediate *wen* 'whom' in colloquial German (3) and dialectal (4) involves directly associating the *wh*-word's interrogative feature with the matrix C but "entangling" with the intermediate C head in accessing the *wh*-phrase in order to pronounce it in SpecCP. This results in the spelling out of phi-features on that head, here *wen*, as diagrammed in (5) and (6):

(3)	[$_{CP}$ **Wen**	glaubt	Hans [$_{CP}$ ***wen*** [$_{TP}$	Jakob ~~wen~~	gesehen	hat]]]?	
	whom$_{ACC}$	believes	Hans whom$_{ACC}$	Jakob whom	seen	has	

'Whom does Hans believe (whom) Jakob saw?'

(4)	[$_{CP}$ **Welchen**	**Mann**	denkst	du	[$_{CP}$ ***wen*/*welchen**	***Mann***
	which$_{ACC}$	man	think	you	who$_{ACC}$/which$_{ACC}$	man
	[$_{TP}$ er	~~welchen~~	~~Mann~~	kennt]]]?		
	he	which$_{ACC}$	man	knows		

'Which man do you think (whom) he knows?'

(5)

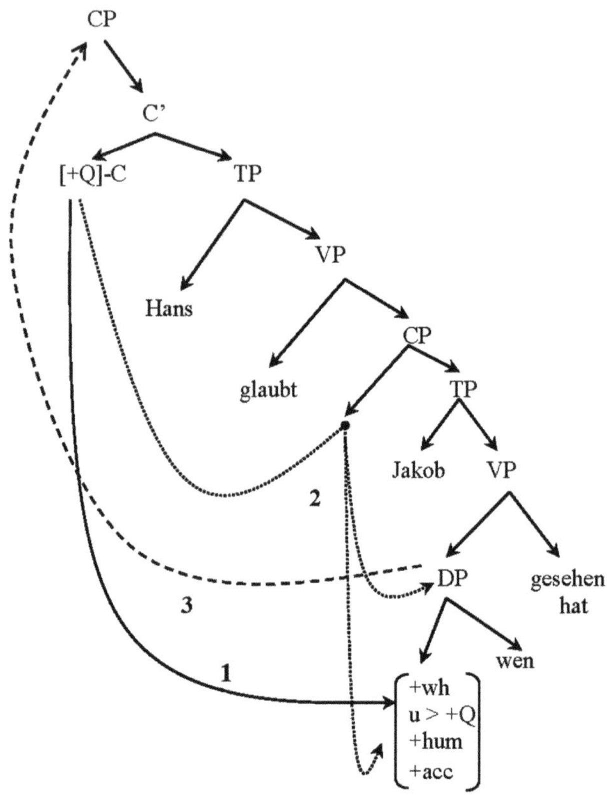
CP
C'
[+Q]-C
TP
Hans
VP
glaubt
CP
TP
Jakob
VP
DP
gesehen
hat
wen
+wh
u > +Q
+hum
+acc
1
2
3

(6)

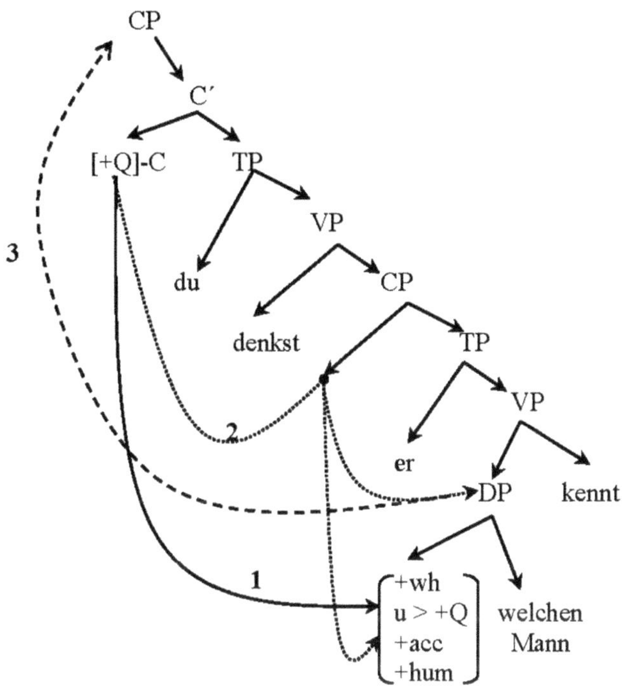

How to interpret these diagrams is discussed in detail in Franks (2014, 2017), but the basic idea is that in the syntax a feature probes down (labelled "1") and gives its value to some unvalued head (here [Q], on C). Spell-Out later tries to access the lexical material associated with that head (labelled "2") in order ultimately to move that material as close as possible (labelled "3").[1] If in the search process a similar head is encountered, this can cause the phi-features of the target element to become associated with that head. This is the source of "intermediate landing-site" effects, such as the *wen* in (3) and (4), which are traditionally attributed to successive-cyclic movement, but are derived in the multiattachment system without literally moving through any intermediate specifier positions. In this approach all such effects are head effects, there being no intermediate phrasal/specifier positions since there is no successive-cyclic movement.

2.3. Adaption to English Reflexives

A similar account is proposed for English reflexives. Assuming the initial structure in (7), the Refl head *self* merges with a DP which then associates with T for nominative case, as in (8):

(7) [$_{DP1}$ D [$_{ReflP}$ self [$_{DP2}$ the man]]]

(8) [$_{TP}$ [$_{DP2}$ **The man**] [Case(nom)]-T likes [$_{DP1}$ ***him*** [$_{ReflP}$ self [$_{DP2}$ ~~the man~~]]]].

That is, in the course of Spell-Out, the phi-features of *the man* are realized on the intermediate D head as *him*. The intuitive idea is that we want DP$_2$, *the man* in (9), to move out of DP$_1$ (hence it is stricken through) and for *him*, as a consequence, to arise in D$_1$ (hence it is in parentheses).

(9)

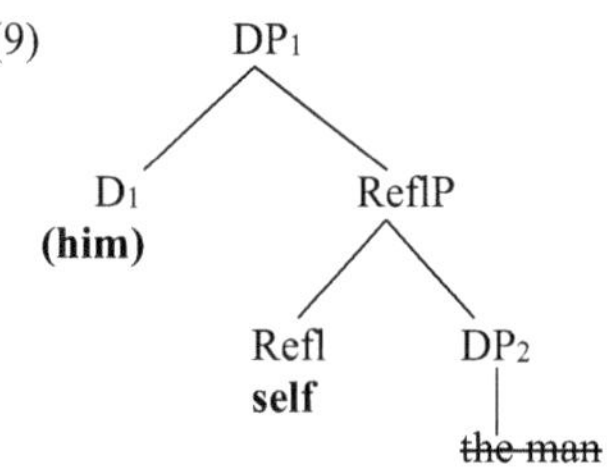

The containing DP$_1$ is valued as OBJ(ective), i.e., accusative, and the case feature of DP$_2$, *the man*, will eventually be valued as NOM(inative). Adapting Hornstein's MTC approach, we could say that the R-expression *the man* moves to the position in which the external theta-role is discharged. In (1) Hornstein employed VP, but we can update this and use *v*P instead. For me, however, this is simple association of features, in this instance those of theta-roles. This derivation is schematized in (10). The theta-role features associated with *v* become associated with *the man*, as shown by the solid line in (10). Since my model does not countenance intermediate movement, *the man* does not literally pass through Spec*v*P (even though it is attached to *v* for theta-role purposes), and since we know that *the man* ultimately ends up in SpecTP, we can use NOM to obtain the desired result of eventual movement to SpecTP. In sum, *the man* receives some valuation from above DP$_1$, in this instance NOM case from T (Step 1, the solid line) and, subsequent to this, in the process of Spell-Out to PF (the overt interface level of phonetic form), it moves out of that DP to be as close as possible to T (thereby creating SpecTP). But the crucial step is Step 2 (the dotted line). In the course of searching for DP_2, T will encounter and become entangled with D_1, the result of which being that, just as the phi-features of *welchen Mann* are realized on the intermediate C in (5), the phi-features of *the man* are realized on the intermediate D in (10). The only crucial difference here is that DP_1, as the direct object of the verb *likes*, has an independent source for case,[2] namely OBJ, hence is unlike the CP in (5).

There are two key points to bear in mind about Step 2, which is the search for lexical material containing the feature valued by Step 1, the initial probe. First, it checks the content of all intervening similar heads in its downwards search, so that, just as C intervenes in the German *wh*-copying construction, D interevenes here. Second, only heads are examined and can become entangled, which is why all so-called intermediate movement effects are head effects, a point developed at length in Franks (2014, 2017).

(10)

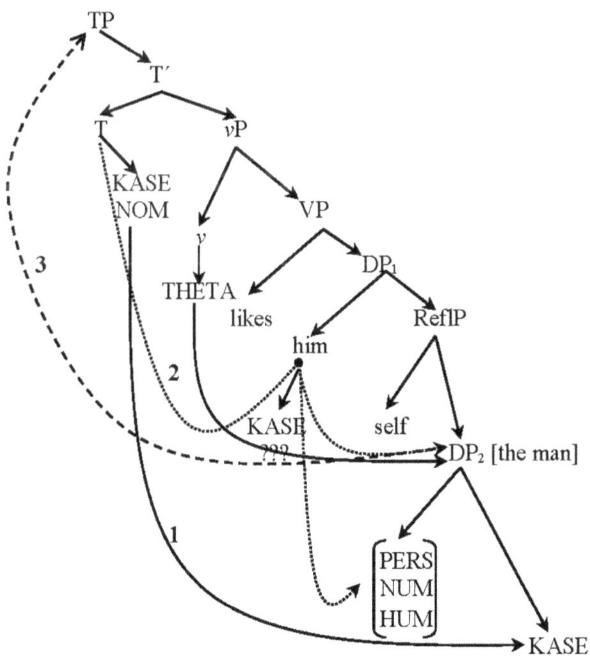

Although the diagram in (10) is complicated, the idea for the source of *him* in *himself* is not: assuming a structure as in (7)/(9), D_1 is realized as *him* as a consequence of extraction of DP_2, i.e., masculine singular *the man*, out of DP_1. This approach can be implemented regardless of one's view of the actual mechanics of movement; it could even involve standard Spec-head agreement if, under the traditional phase-based/successive-cyclic movement approach, DP_2 passed through $SpecDP_1$. Under such a view we would have something like (11):

(11)

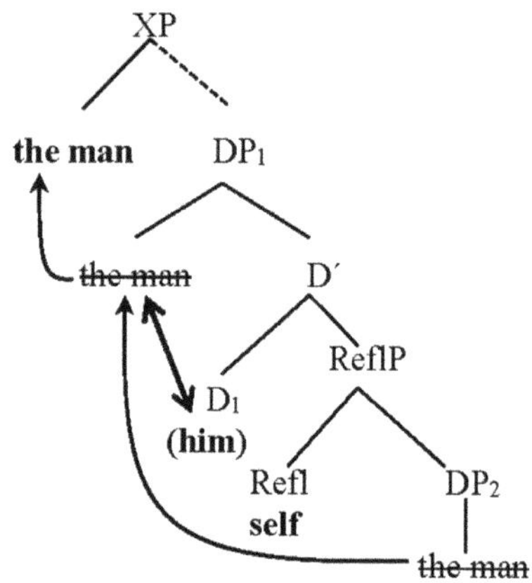

To summarize, for me *him* arises because whatever feature of X in (11) that is the cause of *the man*'s movement (e.g., the NOM of T in the scenario in (10)) searches for the DP with the feature it has valued (e.g., in (10), the KASE of DP_2) and becomes entangled with D_1. It is this entanglement with the intervening D head that associates the masculine singular phi-features of DP_2 *the man* with D_1.[3]

2.4. Excursus on Case

One piece of the puzzle intentionally left vague concerns the case of *him* in (10). Recall that Hornstein regards this as accusative (my OBJ), claiming that it somehow agrees with *self*, which is presumably the nominal head of the complement to *likes* in his (1). But the facts are considerably more complicated, the problem being that several mechanisms compete to value the case of D_1. First, as reflected by the form *him*, it could be OBJ since this is the case of the maximal projection DP_1. Another plausible possibility is that it is what one might call

POSS(essive), namely, the pronominal form used for possession, comparable to the Saxon genitive in *–s* that occupies D and therefore occurs after full phrases in SpecDP. Even the normative reflexives in (12) embody this confusion, when compared with the POSS and OBJ forms in (13a) and (13b), respectively:

(12)	**my**self [=POSS]	**our**selves [=POSS]
	yourself [=POSS]	**your**selves [=POSS]
	himself/**her**self/ **it**self [=OBJ]	**them**selves [=OBJ]

(13)	a.	**my** (body)	**our** (bodies)
		your (body)	**your** (bodies)
		his/**her/its** (body)	their (bodies)
	b.	(likes) me	(likes) us
		(likes) you	(likes) you
		(likes) **him/her/it**	(likes) **them**

Here we see that the synchronic form of the pronominal piece of the reflexives in (12) actually corresponds best to the POSS form in (13a) rather than to the OBJ form in (13b) for all first and second person pronouns, and it is only in the third person that it resembles OBJ case.[4] Even here there are some possible confounds, first because *her* in *herself* is syncretic OBJ-POSS,[5] and second because colloquial variants exhibit much confusion. POSS-like third person forms such as *hisself* and *theirself/theirselves* are common in spoken English, and there is of course British dialectal *meself*, which looks like OBJ but could be a spelling that goes back to a pronunciation related to an earlier dative or accusative.

As van Gelderen's (2000) superb examination of the history of the English reflexive amply reveals, the diachronic data are extremely complex and messy, and always have been. Apparently, in the Old English of *Beowulf* pronouns (mostly dative, but also accusative) were used reflexively and *self* was an adjective. Interestingly, even then there was a person difference in that when modifying first or second person pronouns *self* had indefinite inflection, whereas when modifying a third person pronoun it had definite inflection (van Gelderen 2000: 31). The adjective, she proposes, subsequently became the head of the phrase; she has it reanalyzed as D, while I assign it to its own category, Refl. Either way, this leaves the pronoun also to be reanalyzed, with ensuing confusion in case. She also argues (p. 106) that this change took place later with first and second person reflexives than with third person ones, adding to the confusion. Moreover, to the extent that the forms in (12) can sometimes occur in NOM positions, even in Modern English, this shows that they are not unequivocally OBJ. A related observation made by van Gelderen (2000: 106–107) is that if one forces a speaker to use a first or second person reflexive pronoun as a sentential subject and to select a verbal ending, it is third person that wins. We thus find *has* rather than *have* in (14):

(14) Myself has/*have done that already. (cf. *I have* … VERSUS *He has* …)

This agreement reveals that, although the *my* part of *myself* is clearly first person singular, the entire expression cannot be – even though it presumably bears the NOM case of T. I conclude that various factors compete to determine the case of the pronominal piece of the English reflexive pronoun. In my structure this is as it should be. The phi-features are unequivocal, spread as they are from the DP_2 which merges with *self* and then moves/attaches above it. But the case features are not so easily pinned down.

3. Slavic Reflexives

To make an English reflexive the DP associate of the Refl head must move. In Slavic, on the other hand, it is the Refl head which creates a reflexive predicate, through association with *v*. This is an old idea for head (or "simplex") reflexives, going back to Pica (1987), and can explain why Slavic simplex reflexives such as Polish *siebie*, Russian *sebja*, or BCMS *sebe* are subject-oriented and long-distance.[6] My innovation in this paper is that reflexivization can be implemented *either* by moving Refl *or* by moving its associate DP. The former, which is what happens in Slavic, creates a reflexive predicate, in the spirit of Reinhart and Reuland (1993), while the latter establishes two coreferential coarguments, as we have just seen for English.

3.1. Most of Slavic

For languages like Russian, Polish, or BCMS, Refl(P) is non-branching, as opposed to the English structure in (7) in which *self* merges with a DP. Instead, we have just the following:[7]

(15) $[_{DP}$ D $[_{ReflP}$ siebie/sebja/sebe]]

In Franks (2020), I argue that Refl is eventually associated with *v*, converting *v*P into a reflexive predicate, which is why, unlike English *self*, Slavic reflexives are subject-oriented; cf. footnote 6. But more can be speculated about its morphology, something I attempt below.

On the one hand, throughout Slavic, the reflexive pronoun is paradigmatically uniform with the first and second person (singular) pronouns, e.g., for the accusative in Polish, Russian, and BCMS, *mnie/ciebie*, *menja/tebja*, and *mene/tebe*, respectively (and similarly for other cases). Since the latter surely are not contained within ReflP, their parallel nature must come from other shared structure. But on the other hand, they cannot just be heads, because these tonic forms need to be distinguished from their clitic variants, at least for BCMS and, to a lesser extent, Polish.[8] The Slavic pronominal clitics, I argue in Franks (2017, 2020, and elsewhere), are essentially case markers; their morphology dictates that third person clitics are simple K(ase) heads, while first and second are presumably D, taking that to be the locus of person features, as I conclude in Franks (2017: chapter 2). If we therefore treat the full forms as amalgams of D and N,[9] we might have something like (16a) for the singular personal pronouns, and the reflexive forms could be very similar, as in (16b):[10]

(16) a.

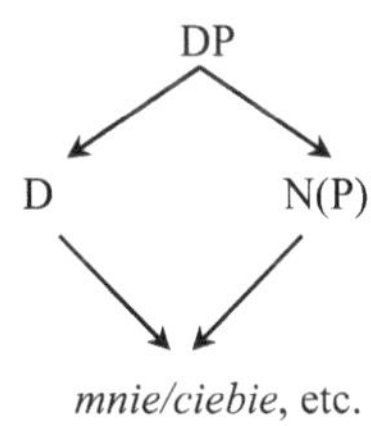

b.

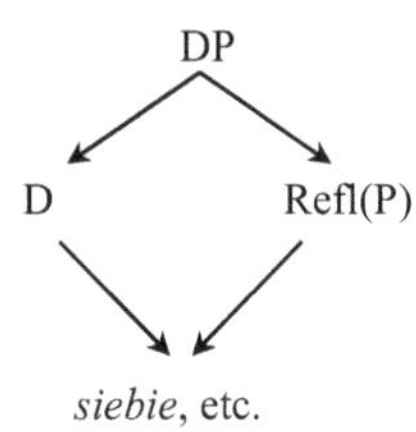

Putting aside the complexity of the extra *si* in Bg and Mac (to be discussed in Sections 3.2–3.4), reflexives are morphologically comparable throughout Slavic. That is, the same reflexive form, abstractly, *seb*–, is used even by Russian, which most likely has a smaller nominal domain than BCMS or Polish since it lacks pronominal clitics, and Bg, which surely has a larger nominal domain since it not only has pronominal clitics (hence, KP) but, as we shall see below, also admits OBL(ique) clitics internal to DP (hence, AgrP). I conclude that all such forms are created in essentially the same way across Slavic, and therefore avail themselves of common pieces of structure, tentatively, DP and ReflP, as in (16b).

Moreover, returning to questions of interpretation, unlike English reflexives in *–self*, Slavic *seb–* is invariably subject-oriented. This implies, as mentioned in footnote 6, that it moves to (or becomes multiattached to) some head position from which it is exclusively associated with the subject. In my account, the position with which Refl becomes associated is *v*, since in the standard minimalist architecture *v* is the verbal head that introduces the external argument of the clause (internal arguments being under VP). In doing so, Refl converts *v*P into a reflexive predicate, in that some internal argument must be coreferential with the subject. Also, with some debate about judgments and preferences, *seb–* is a long-distance anaphor in that it can be bound in larger domains than English reflexives in *–self* can, hence the movement/multiattachment may under certain conditions be extended further up the tree. Reflexives in *seb–* are not pronounced in *v* (or T, in systems that place simplex reflexives there), but rather appear in the same position(s) as comparable nominal phrases. The reason, I contend, is because they have an internal branching structure, hence, unlike clitic variants (e.g., *się*, *se*, etc.), cannot be realized in PF in a head position; in this regard, it is similar to why *welchen Mann* in (4) cannot be pronounced in C. A lower copy/occurrence must therefore be realized, in whatever position(s) phrasal arguments normally are;[11] for PF pronunciation of lower copies more generally, and of clitics especially, see Franks (2017). Abstracting away from details, this is schematized for Polish in (17); see also Witkoś (this volume) and references therein:

(17)	Magda	[$_{vP}$ ~~siebie~~+**zobaczyła**	[$_{VP}$	~~zobaczyła~~ [$_{DP}$	**siebie** [$_{Refl(P)}$	~~siebie~~]]]]
	Magda	self saw		saw	self	self
	'Magda saw herself.'					

In sum, there are two distinct processes for obtaining a reflexive interpretation. In English it arises by associating a single expression with two argument positions, whereas in most Slavic languages reflexivity arises by making the predicate itself reflexive. The former implies moving a referring expression (i.e., a DP) while the latter implies moving a reflexive-marking element (i.e., Refl).

3.2. Bulgarian *sebe si*

As noted, Bulgarian and Macedonian are more complex. In this and the following section I take Bg as a point of departure. A vast amount has been written about anaphora in Bg and here I just scrape the surface.[12] In (18), from Schürcks (2003: 77 and ff.), we see some representative examples, with Schürcks's judgments for the Bg and my judgments for the English sentences:

(18) a. Ivan$_1$ razkazva na doktora$_2$ [istorii za **sebe si**$_{1/*2}$].
'Ivan$_1$ tells the doctor$_2$ [stories about **himself**$_{1/2}$].'

b. Ivan$_1$ pročete [Petrovata$_2$ statija za **sebe si**$_{1/2}$].
'Ivan$_1$ read [Peter's$_2$ article about **himself**$_{?*1/2}$].'

c. Ivan$_1$ popita bašta$_2$ si za [Petrovata$_3$ statija za **sebe si**$_{1/*2/3}$].
'Ivan$_1$ asked his father$_2$ about [Peter$_3$'s article about **himself**$_{*1/*2/3}$].'

These raise two kinds of issues about Bg *sebe si*, one syntactic/interpretative and the other morphological. While here I will be more concerned with its morphological properties, in earlier work I explored its syntactic/interpretative properties, which are as follows: in (18a) *sebe si* exhibits subject-orientation; in (18b) it exhibits long-distance binding (over the nominal's subject *Petrovata*); and (18c) combines both of these properties. This range of interpretations is just like *seb–* without the *si* morpheme elsewhere in Slavic, and as such contrasts with the English sentences in (18). The interpretative facts indicate that Bg *sebe si* – PF appearances to the contrary – functions as a head rather than a phrase. As discussed in Franks (2013a), *sebe si* by all available diagnostics behaves as if simplex for binding purposes, demonstrating the irrelevance of its complex morphological structure on the PF–side. My conclusion is that in LF *sebe si* has to be simplex, regardless of PF phrasal structure.

Turning to its morphological properties, the main oddity is the (historically dative) OBL(ique) clitic *si*, which in Bg is obligatory. The account makes the obvious move of relating this *si* to the OBL clitic which is pervasive in Bg DPs, where it can have argument functions in addition to its core possessive one. Representative examples are in (19); see Franks (2020: section 5.2) for further details:

(19) a. xubavoto **ni** staro selo
beautiful$_{DEF}$ we$_{OBL}$ old village
'our beautiful old village'

b.	opisanieto	**mu**	(na	prirodata/	na	poeta)
	description$_{DEF}$	he$_{OBL}$	of	nature$_{DEF}$/	of	poet$_{DEF}$

‘the description of nature’ OR ‘the poet’s description’

I take the clitic to instantiate Agr(eement) in the nominal domain, where clitics are K heads and Agr licenses case. That is, for Bg, I posit an AgrP intervening between KP and DP, as in (20):[13]

(20) $[_{KP}$ K $[_{AgrP}$ Agr $[_{DP}$ D [… $[_{NP}$ … N …]]]]]

The nominal domain Agr values OBL, and thus gives rise to the *si* clitic, again through entanglement. In Bg this *si* obligatorily supports OBJ *sebe*, as shown in (21) and (22).[14]

(21) $[_{vP}$ ~~sebe~~+*v* … $[_{KP}$ **sebe** $[_{AgrP}$ *si* $[_{DP}$ D $[_{Refl(P)}$ ~~sebe~~]]]]]

This structure opens up the possibility of an account of *si* that exploits the same mechanism as used to obtain the pronominal piece in English reflexives. The proposal is that, in searching (Step 2) from K for the element (Refl) containing the feature provided to it (by Step 1), presumably KASE, Agr is encountered along the way, and the anaphoric and reflexive features of *sebe* become entangled with Agr, roughly as in (22).[15] The intuitive idea is thus to treat the *si* in Bg *sebe si* as arising in a way comparable to the *him* of English *himself*, except that in Bg it is the Refl part *sebe* which moves whereas in English it is Refl’s associate, its DP sister, which does. This means entanglement is with different heads (Agr vs. D), and different sorts of grammatical features (anaphoric/reflexive vs. pronominal/phi-feature) are spun off.

(22)

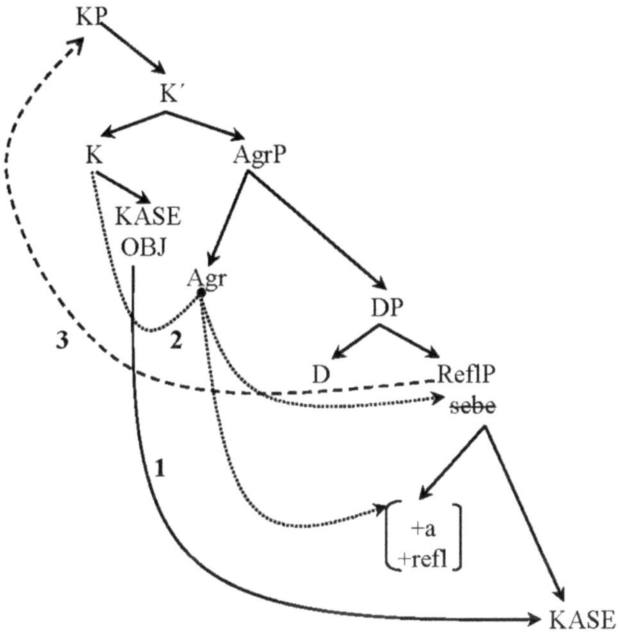

The difference between this and (10), which shows how *him* is created by entangling the phi-features of *the man* with D_1, is simply that: (i) the features that become attached to an intervening head are the anaphoric ones of *sebe,* not the pronominal ones associated with some R-expression, and (ii) the locus of that entanglement – giving rise to *si* when the feature bundle is sent to Spell–Out – is Agr, not D. Of course, the morphological cases of *sebe* and *si* look different: *sebe* reflects the case of KP, which is OBJ, whereas *si* instantiates the case of Agr, which (in the nominal domain, at least) is invariably OBL. However, just as in the derivation of English *himself,* this discrepancy in case does not matter; what is crucial is that the elements share intrinsic features. In sum, if this analysis is on the right track, it means that the obligatoriness of *si* in *sebe si* in Bg is comparable to the obligatoriness of *him* in *himself* in English.

3.3. Bulgarian *nego si*

Bg also has a colloquial anaphor *nego si* 'him self' (similarly, *neja si* 'her self', *tjax si* 'them self', etc.), which, as in (23), superficially resembles English *himself*:[16]

(23) Ivan$_1$ popita [Petâr$_2$ za **nego si**$_{1/2}$].
'Ivan asked Peter about **himself**$_{1/2}$.'

While, as I discuss in Franks (2013b, 2020), Bg *nego si* behaves very differently from English *himself*, for purposes of this paper the crucial point is that the provenance of *si* in (23) cannot be through any kind of entanglement of reflexive features from *sebe* because there is no *sebe* to start with. I thus offer a different account, relating *si* to the general possessive seen in (19a) or, for its reflexive instantiation, (24):

(24) Marija pročete [knigata **si**].
'Maria read her (own) book.'

Unlike a possessed noun, tonic *nego* is created derivationally, roughly as in (25):

(25)

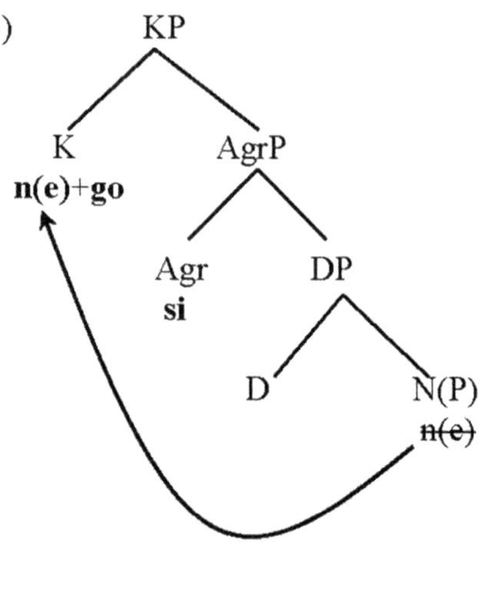

The leading idea here is that *nego* 'him' in Bg (and in Mac, as well as other languages, e.g., BCMS *njega*) consists of a K part (tantamount to the pronominal clitic, a case marker), preceded by a nominal part. This is what gives it internal structure, so that it does not move as a clitic, although details of the derivation are glossed over in (25).[17]

3.4. Macedonian

With this background, let us finally consider Macedonian reflexives. The following is representative:

(26) Go zede so **sebe(si)**.
'(S)he took it with herself/himself.'

Mac differs from Bg in some crucial respects, most important of which are: (i) in Mac *si* is optional with *sebe*, with which it is written together, hence *sebe(si)*, and (ii) Mac completely lacks the *nego si* reflexive of colloquial Bg. This latter gap is expected because Mac in general also lacks the DP-internal OBL clitic construction of Bg (19) or (24). In Franks (2015b, 2020) I argue at length that Mac differs from Bg in not countenancing a DP-internal AgrP projection, a difference which explains, inter alia, the absence of OBL (both possessive and argumental) clitics in the DP-domain.

This raises however the question of why we ever get *si* with *sebe* in Mac at all. There must be some other source than an independent Agr node, an inevitable conclusion since some OBL clitics do persist in Mac, in particular, with intrinsically definite (i.e., unarticulated) kinship terms, e.g., *majka(*ta) mi* 'my mother'. One idea is that the clitic actually originates in the definite head D, rather than Agr, which is why in Mac it is in (more or less) complementary distribution with the article. But there has to be a different account for *si* in *sebe(si)*. My idea is that this *si* reflects the optional fissioning off of reflexive features from *sebe*. What this means is that the *si* in Mac *sebe(si)* is generated in a completely different way than the obligatory *si* with Bg *sebe si*. Note that this same mechanism is presumably also available in Bg possessive reflexives, as in (27), where – unlike with Bg *sebe si* but like *si* in Mac relexives – this *si* is optional and adds emphasis:

(27) Marija pročete [svojata (**si**) kniga].
'Maria read her (own) book.'

The proposal is thus that *si* in Mac reflexives is not comparable to the obligatory *si* of argumental reflexives like *sebe si* in Bg (18) or to the Agr/possessive *si* of *nego si* in (23). It is instead like the *si* of Bg (27), which occurs optionally with Bg reflexive possessive adjectives. If so, there should be a pragmatic contrast between having *si* or not. While this proposal requires more careful investigation, speakers of Mac report a preference for *sebesi* in (28a), although *sebe* on its own, as in (28b), is also perfectly grammatical:

(28) a. **Sebesi** Ivan se razbira.
'Ivan understands himself.'
b. **Sebe** Ivan se razbira.

Apparently, the addition of *si* has a focusing effect, which supports the fronting of the direct object.[18]

4. Why Intermediate Binding Is so Marked

Let us lastly return to English reflexives and consider the cross-linguistically extremely rare phenomenon of intermediate binding, as in (29), where *Mary* can bind *herself* even though *Mary* neither c-commands the surface position of *herself* nor is sufficiently local to the initial merge position of *herself* (the intervening subject *Bill* being closer):

(29) a. **Which picture of *herself*** did *Mary* say [$_{\text{CP}}$ that Bill bought ~~which picture of herself~~]?
b. **Which picture of *herself*** did John tell *Mary* [$_{\text{CP}}$ that Bill bought ~~which picture of herself~~]?

This sort of "connectivity" effect, in which a fronted reflexive can be bound by a referring expression that is not in its original clause, has been well-known since Barss (1986) but remains poorly understood. The traditional approach, typically considered an argument for successive-cyclic movement, is to determine the reference of *herself* at the point when the *wh*-phrase putatively passes through an intermediate SpecCP. Even putting aside my arguments that there is no such operation, all intermediate effects being the result of entanglement with intervening like heads under Step 2, this cannot be the case because long-distance binding is universally subject-oriented. Thus, (30) – in which the reflexive actually is in SpecCP – contrasts with (29b):

(30) John told *Mary* [$_{\text{CP}}$ **which picture of *her*/?**herself*** Bill bought ~~which picture of her/herself~~].

Traditional successive-cyclic approaches to the connectivity effects in (29) aside, what is of interest here is that, to the best of my knowledge, such a possibility is unknown in Slavic (or most other languages). The fact that it is so unusual implies that mainstream attempts to derive it from standard binding theories are misguided. Instead, I contend that intermediate binding results from an unlikely confluence of multiple factors. First, one needs a language with DPs. Second, it has to be a language in which the reflexive interpretation results from merging a DP with the Refl head, as in English (7), and then moving that DP to an A-position, as in (8) or (9), rather than having a bare reflexivizing Refl, as in Slavic, since in such languages it is Refl rather than the associate that moves. Third, the language has to have overt *wh*-movement, as in English, and, finally – again as in English – that movement must pied-pipe the reflexive. My point here is thus that the connectivity effect seen in (29) is an extreme outlier, something the theory predicts but which can only happen when a set of unlikely circumstances all come together.

5. Conclusion

My main argument has been for two competing ways to establish a reflexive interpretation. The first involves merging a DP phrase with Refl and then moving that DP, as in English, giving rise to reflexivity through coreferring co-arguments. This can have the consequence of producing a pronominal element that agrees with the moved DP in phi-features; this is the *him* of *himself*. The second is when no phrase merges with Refl, but rather Refl itself moves, as in Polish or Russian, associating with *v* and giving rise to a reflexive predicate. The properties of these two types of reflexives are very different, but can be made to follow from their distinct derivational paths. With this in mind, I then looked at Bulgarian and Macedonian, which have an OBL clitic *si* in their anaphoric expressions, and speculated about the source of this element. Differences between Bg and Mac were, in part, attributed to the lack of the Bg AgrP projection in otherwise comparable Mac DPs. Finally, I pointed to the extremely obscure nature of the sort of binding connectivity effects found in English.

Notes

* This paper, which updates and corrects proposals in Franks (2020: chapter 3), is dedicated to my friend and colleague Peter Kosta.

1 In (5) and (6) this movement creates SpecKP, since the DP *wen/welchen Mann* is a phrase hence cannot be realized in C, a head position.

2 My account of English reflexives differs from Hornstein's in that, since *himself* in (7) actually consists of two DPs, there is no reason here to reject the Theta-Criterion: DP_1 receives the Theme role from *likes* and DP_2 receives the Experiencer role. Whether or not this is an advantage remains to be seen, but see footnote 7 for one possibility.

3 Under the standard minimalist model of movement, as depicted in (11), phase-theory would force DP_2 to move through $SpecDP_1$, and agreement in phi-features could arise at that point. My assumption of ReflP allows this more traditional derivation to comply with the antilocality restriction on movement.
4 To quote van Gelderen (2000: 107): "There is another difference between first and second person reflexives on the one hand and third person ones on the other related to Case: the former have genitive pronouns and the latter have accusative forms. This difference is well-known but not well accounted for. One could argue that since 'him' has a deictic function, it is a demonstrative inflected for Case. First and second person might have been seen as adjectives to the nominal *self* head. More likely is that *himself* grammaticalized in Late Old English before *self* was a noun, but that *myself* and *thyself* grammaticalize after."
5 On the basis of pronunciation, *itself* could conceivably also be analyzed as containing POSS *its* rather than OBJ-NOM *it*.
6 Most implementations exploit the idea that the anaphor can move either as a phrase or as a head (cf., e.g., Pica 1987, Battistella 1989, or Cole and May 1994), and when it moves as a head subject-orientation is forced because it goes to I(NFL), or to T (in later accounts), or to *v* (in mine), to which it multiattaches; Progovac (1992) presents an interesting variant according to which the binding domain is determined by the phrasal or head status of the antecedent. Under all such approaches, the syntax includes some mechanism that allows an anaphor's morphology to exert direct impact on its choice of an antecedent, although in Franks (2013a) I argue that such accounts are best understood in terms of the LF rather than PF structure of the anaphor, since LF is where interpretation is defined. This is why reciprocals are never subject-oriented and must be locally bound: they have two logical pieces, a distributor and a reciprocator, hence necessarily function as phrasal in LF.
7 Jacek Witkoś (p.c.) raises the important question of why Refl merges with DP in English but not in Slavic. Since Merge is driven by the needs of whatever projects – for example, a V merges with its arguments to discharge theta-roles – the question of what is satisfied in (7) by merging *self* with a referential expression is far from trivial. Presumably *self* has no other recourse; for some reason it cannot move as simplex reflexives do. One thing it does, however, accomplish is to give rise to two distinct DPs, each of which can bear its own theta-role.
8 In Polish the clitics behave more like weak pronouns than canonical clitics, in that they display certain properties typical of phrases, such as greater freedom of placement and relative order, and they can even coordinate; there is also some morphological confusion with the tonic forms.

9 The representations in (16) put aside technical questions of how *mnie/ciebie/siebie*, etc. are derived; the relevant process could involve syntactic head movement and/or morphological merger (which restructures adjacent nodes), possibly followed by morphological fusion (which combines the features of merged nodes).

10 Following argumentation in Franks (2016, 2017, 2020), the clitic versions are non-branching – K heads for third person, D for first and second, and Refl for reflexives. While this requires more careful fleshing out, there are clear cross-linguistic implications any viable account must address: the existence of shared forms implies shared structures, and the absence of comparable forms implies the absence of comparable structures.

11 Pronounced copies are given in boldface, silent ones stricken through. The structure ignores various aspects of the derivation, such as that the accusative object *siebie* would actually move out of VP, to the specifier of whatever functional category licenses its case (e.g., AgrP or AspP).

12 See for example the various works by Schürcks listed in the references, or my 2013 papers, both also originally SLS presentations.

13 Under the traditional successive-cyclic approach to movement, *sebe* could pass through SpecAgrP and *si* could arise at that point through Spec-head agreement, as depicted in (11) for English *himself*. Also, AgrP could be low, right above *n*P/NP, as suggested for other reasons by Rudin (2021).

14 I put D in SpecKP to express the idea that definiteness features are associated with KP, and also to capture the similarity between *sebe* and *mene/tebe,* although these presumably just involve N-to-D movement hence do not require such a complicated structure.

15 K is determined to be OBJ by its role in the clause, this being the case valued on direct objects (and objects of Ps) by clausal Agr (and Agr associated with PPs), hence *sebe*. The Agr inside the nominal domain is always OBL, hence *si*.

16 This form and its distribution is described in a series of works by Schürcks (2003, 2006, 2008, 2018); I put forward an analysis in Franks (2013b, 2020) based on her judgments.

17 For example, movement of N directly to K would violate the Head Movement Constraint (HMC), so if this is head movement it would have to apply stepwise, i.e., N to D, [N+D] to Agr, and then [N+D] excorporating to adjoin to K (otherwise *si* would intervene between *ne* and *go*). It strikes me, however, that once N moves to (or undergoes merger with) D and subsequently fuses with it, as suggested in footnote 9 for tonic pronouns, DP can have its case valued by K (Step 1 in my system) and then move to it (Steps 2 and 3). This would, inter alia, circumvent the HMC, since technically DP would be in SpecKP.

18 A final suggestive fact that this use of *si* is more advanced in terms of grammaticalization in Mac than Bg, and that it reflects fissioning off of features, is orthographic: in Mac it is written together with its host, e.g., *sebesi* and *svojasi*.

Bibliography

Barss, Andy. 1986. *Chains and Anaphoric Dependence.* Doctoral dissertation, Massachusetts Institute of Technology.

Battistella, Edwin. 1989. Chinese Reflexivization: A Movement to INFL Approach. *Linguistics* 27: 987–1012.

Cole, Peter, and Li-May Sung. 1994. Head Movement and Long-distance Reflexives. *Linguistic Inquiry* 25(3): 355–406.

Franks, Steven. 2013a. Binding and Morphology Revisited. *Current Issues in Slavic Linguistics*, ed. by Irina Kor Chahine. Amsterdam: John Benjamins, 25–42.

Franks, Steven. 2013b. Bulgarian NEGO SI is a Balkan Anaphor. *Linguistique Balkanique* 52(2/3): 3–28.

Franks, Steven. 2014. Multiattachment Syntax, "Movement" Effects, and Spell-Out. *Minimalism and Beyond: Radicalizing the Interfaces*, ed. by Peter Kosta, Steven Franks, Teodora Radeva-Bork, and Lilia Schürcks. Amsterdam: John Benjamins, 195–235.

Franks, Steven. 2015a. Less Movement is More Minimalist Movement. *Florida Linguistics Papers* 2. Available online at: http://journals.fcla.edu/floridalinguisticspapers/issue/view/4123.

Franks, Steven. 2015b. Speculations on DP-Structure: Macedonian Versus Bulgarian. *Formal Approaches to Slavic Linguistics: The First Berkeley Meeting*, ed. by Małgorzata Szajbel-Keck, Roslyn Burns, and Darya Kavitskaya. Ann Arbor: Michigan Slavic Publications, 56–76.

Franks, Steven. 2016. Clitics are/become Minimal(ist). *Formal Studies in Slovenian Syntax. In Honor of Janez Orešnik*, ed. by Franc Marušič and Rok Žaucer. Amsterdam: John Benjamins, 91–127.

Franks, Steven. 2017. *Syntax and Spell-Out in Slavic.* Bloomington: Slavica.

Franks, Steven. 2020. *Microvariation in the South Slavic Noun Phrase.* Bloomington: Slavica.

Hornstein, Norbert. 2001. *Move! A Minimalist Theory of Construal.* Oxford: Blackwell.

Pica, Pierre. 1987. On the Nature of the Reflexivization Cycle. *Proceedings of the North East Linguistics Society* 17(2): 483–500.

Progovac, Ljiljana. 1992. Long-distance Reflexives without Movement. *Linguistic Inquiry* 23(4): 671–680.

Reinhart, Tanya, and Eric Reuland. 1993. Reflexivity. *Linguistic Inquiry* 24(4): 657–720.

RUDIN, CATHERINE. 2021. Demonstratives and Definiteness: Multiple Determination in Balkan Slavic. *Advances in Formal Slavic Linguistics 2018*, ed. by Andreas Blümel, Jovana Gajić, Ljudmila Geist, Uwe Junghanns, and Hagen Pitsch. Berlin: Language Science Press, 305–38.

SCHÜRCKS, LILIA. 2003. *Binding and Bulgarian.* Doctoral dissertation, Rijksuniversiteit Groningen.

SCHÜRCKS, LILIA. 2006. Binding and Point of View in Bulgarian. *Zeitschrift für Slawistik* 51: 386–405.

SCHÜRCKS, LILIA. 2008. *Binding and Discourse: Where Syntax and Pragmatics Meet.* Frankfurt am Main: Peter Lang.

SCHÜRCKS, LILIA. 2018. Binding and Labeling in Bulgarian. *Katerino Mome: Studies in Bulgarian Morphosyntax in Honor of Catherine Rudin*, ed. by Steven Franks, Vrinda Chidambaram, Brian Joseph, and Iliyana Krapova. Bloomington: Slavica, 251–70.

VAN GELDEREN, ELLY. 2000. *A History of English Reflexive Pronouns.* Amsterdam: John Benjamins.

WITKOŚ, JACEK. This Volume. On Some Aspects of Agree, Move and Bind in the Nominal Domain.

Jadranka Gvozdanović

'Have' + Infinitive in Czech: A Long Multilingual History

Abstract The first part of the paper discusses the contemporary spread of 'have' + infinitive across the modal domains in Czech, significantly more far-reaching than in the other western and south-western Slavic languages. German equivalents with Czech-specific implementations can be established. The second part of the paper discusses historical attestations of the 'have' + infinitive construction, showing that this construction appears before a significant increase of the German influence and can be ascribed to the Latin model. The paper ends with general implications of the presented analyses.

Keywords: Modality, Deontic, Epistemic, Czech, German, Latin

1. Introduction

Modality, in a nutshell conceptualizing either possibility or necessity, either at objective (predication-denotational) or subjective (speaker-evaluative) levels, was only rudimentary in Proto-Slavic (with modal infinitives and 'can' and 'will' verbs) and developed into an elaborate system only since the Middle Ages. Medieval religious texts incorporated influences of the languages of the Bible, Old Testament Greek and Latin, on indigenous Slavic linguistic traditions. The interplay of these traditions can be assumed to have laid the basis for much of later Slavic creativity and functional extension in modal domains, also in contact situations.

Studies of modality in Slavic frequently point to language contacts as sources of modality, especially in areas where long-lasting contacts have been attested, such as the outer west of Slavic with Germanic and subsequently Old High German. For the contemporary languages, especially studies by Berger (2008, 2014) about German influences on Czech, Weiss (1987) about Polish modality in comparison with other West Slavic languages and with German, Hansen (2000) about German influences on Slavic in the realm of deontic modality (especially Slavic correlates of German *müssen* 'must'), and Weiss (2009) critically evaluating German influences on Polish, should be mentioned.

Berger carefully distinguishes different degrees of likelihood that a language element results from contact: (1) clear contact, (2) motivating contact but independent development, (3) areal phenomena, (4) general developments, and

(5) exclusion of any German influence; Berger discusses modal auxiliaries in Czech as belonging to the first group. However, differences exist even among closely related Slavic languages, and Polish seems to belong primarily to the second group. This can be concluded from the works of Weiss (e.g., 2009: 138), who compares the use of German *sollen* with Polish *mieć* 'have/ should' and points to differences, e.g., in conditional clauses, in which Polish requires a conjunction and a conditional verbal form, in contrast to mere past *Konjunktiv* of *sollen* in German. Concerning past (intended) unrealized action, Weiss (1987: 139 f.) points out that Polish distinguishes between *powinno się* 'should', used for indirect instigation, usually by the speaker, and *mieć* + infinitive, used for direct instigation, usually by a participant in the narrated situation (who may coincide with the speaker). This distinction is in the author's view neutralized in Czech.

Martínek (2020) discusses modal conditional clauses with *mít* 'have', which normally necessitate a conjunction and a conditional marker in Czech conditional clauses, but not so in German, and points out that conjunction-less uses, similar to German, seem possible in contemporary spoken Czech (i.e. *měl bych…*, German *sollte ich…*), but assumes that this is unacceptable for a certain part of contemporary Czech speakers.

Given all the aforementioned findings, the modal uses of 'have', especially in Czech, require further investigation, both in the sense of modality and of principles of language contact.

2. *Mít* 'have' + Infinitive in Contemporary Czech

The oldest modal auxiliaries in Slavic conceptualized the agent/ experiencer as the source of modality (who 'can', 'will', or 'is able to'). Since the Middle Ages, the newer types of modality in Slavic conceptualize externally instigated modality. An external instigator may be the speaker, another person, a causing event or a general norm (cf. Grepl 1973 concerning his contemporary Czech, partly also Adamec 1974, Buřáňová 1979). Šipková (1985) discussed Czech *mít* 'have' in comparison with its English equivalents mainly based on meaning explications; this comparison showed the striking richness of Czech modal uses of *mít*, especially in the colloquial language. I shall use her examples, but classify the variants of Czech modal *mít* in terms of more general modal categories.

First of all, let me remark that possessive and modal *mít* 'have' exhibit an essential semantic similarity and modal 'have' may be viewed as a derived variant of the same relational predicate. 'Have' is a relational verb expressing an asymmetrical relation between a controlling entity (agent of possessive 'have', instigator of modal 'have') and a(n actually or virtually) controlled entity (the possessed goal of 'have', the instigated predicate or state of affairs of modal 'have'). In a partly similar way, Weiss (2009: 136) speaks about an actual and a virtual communicative act, the latter either reported or anticipated. Czech is especially interesting for exhibiting an impressive variety of modal readings and meanings attached to 'have (to)' due to far-reaching extensions of the deontic meaning into other modal domains. The following examples show that the basic difference is in the instigator relative to the state of affairs.

(1)	Máš	jít	k	děkanovi.
	Have-2SG.PRES	go-INF	to	dean-DAT.SG

'You are to go to the Dean('s office).'

(2)	Kdy	tam	mám	(máš, má)	jít?
	When	there	have-1SG.PRES	(2SG.PRES, 3SG.PRES)	go-INF

'When should I (should you, should he) go there?'

(3)	Měl	bys	mu	pomoci.
	Have-APP.M	be-2SG.COND	he-DAT.SG	help-INF

'You should have helped him.'

(4)	Neměl	jsi	mu	to	říkat.
	Not-have-APP.M	be-2SG.PRES	he-DAT.SG	that	tell-INF

'You should not have told him that.'

(5)	Petr	má	jet	zítra	do	Prahy.
	P.	have-3SG.PRES	travel	tomorrow	to	Prague

'Peter has to travel tomorrow to Prague.'

(6)

Mám	se	mu	omluvit?
Have-1SG.PRES	REFL	he-DAT.SG	apologize-INF

'Do I have to apologize to him?'

(7)

Definice	má	být	jasná.
Definition-NOM.SG	have-3SG.PRES	be-INF	clear

'The definition has to be clear.'

(8)

Zítra	má	pršet.
Tomorrow	have-3SG.PRES	rain-INF

'It is supposed to rain tomorrow.'

(9)

Má	to	být	zajímavý	film.
Have-3SG.PRES	that	be-INF	interesting	movie-NOM.SG

'It is supposed to be an interesting movie.'

(10)

Uklouzl	jsem	a	měl	jsem	spadnout.
Slip-APP.M	be-1SG.PRES	and	have-APP.M	be-1SG.PRES	fall-INF

'I slipped and nearly fell.'

Examples (1)–(4) illustrate an external instigator, in (1), (3) and (4) equalling the speaker. Example (5) is ambiguous between an external and an internal instigator (Petr can either be forced or impose the necessity on himself). Example (6) is ambiguous between an external instigator and the norm of behavior as an instigator. In example (7), the instigator is understood as a general norm. Example (8) is ambiguous between a norm as instigator (the meteorological situation) and an evaluator asserting the state of affairs. Example (9) clearly expresses the report of external evaluator(s). Finally, example (10) is interesting because the conditioning event is mentioned, but its influence did not lead to the realization of the main event. Indeed, literary Czech would use here *dív* 'almost', but spoken Czech uses modal *mít* in such situations, in the past tense, to express that a past situation threatened to occur, but did not materialize.

These examples illustrate the fact that modal 'have' in Czech is extended from deontic to epistemic to counterfactual modality, and contextual evidentiality illustrated by (9). Moreover, we can now understand how this extension could have happened: by way of extending the instigator of deontic modality from concrete to general deontic to becoming an evaluator of states of affairs not directly accessible to him, or counterfactual.

In fact, there is still a missing link in this chain – the hypothetical use. Martínek (2020: 186 f.) discusses especially attestations of this use from the 19th c., which now seem peripheral in Czech, such as (11).

(11)	Kdybych	ti	měl	psát,	co	dělam,
	If-would-1SG	you-DAT	have-APP	write-INF	what	do-1SG.PRES
	co	pracuju,	nepopsal	bych	tím	
	what	work-1SG.PRES	not-write-APP	would-1SG	this-INSTR	
	mnoho	papíru.				
	much	paper-GEN				

'If I had to write you about what I am doing, what I am working on, I would not fill many sheets of paper in doing so.' (Gabler Vilém, cited from Martínek 2020)

Polish has the same type of construction (Hansen 2009: 176; Weiss 2009: 138).

(12)	Gdyby	posiedzenie	miało	trwać	dłużej,
	If-would	meeting	have-APP	last-INF	longer
	musiałbym	zadzwonić	do domu.		
	must-would-1SG	call	to home		

'If the meeting would have to last longer, I would be obliged to call home.'

In fact, the Polish uses of modal *mieć* (Weiss 1987, 2009; Hansen 2009) are parallel to Czech (1–9) and (11), but not to (10). Consider example (13) illustrating an intended, but unrealized past action in Polish (Weiss 2009: 138), the future-in-the-past derived from the general deontic use in Polish illustrated by (14) and the epistemic use (possibly an evidential reading) illustrated by (15), mentioned in Hansen (2009: 174 f.).

(13)	Właśnie	miałem	wyjść,	gdy	zadzwoniłeś.	
	Just	have-1SG.PRT	out-go-INF	where	call-2SG.PRT	

‘I was (just) about to go, when you called.’

(14)	Miał	jeszcze	wiele	przecierpieć,	zanim	wyzdrowiał.
	Have-3SG.PRT	still	much	suffer-INF	before	recover-3SG.PRT

‘He still had to suffer a lot before he recovered.’

(15)	Pożar	miał	być	spowodowany	przez	nieuwagę.
	Fire-NOM	have-3SG.APP	be-INF	caused-PPP	by	carelessness-ACC

‘The fire was (apparently) caused by carelessness.’

It is also in the light of this comparative West Slavic evidence that we can reconstruct the development of modal (readings and subsequently) meanings of *mít* in Czech as a process by which the original deontic meaning became transferable to other modal domains. Two different processes underlie these possible developments: either the temporal implicature of future realization becomes part of the meaning, or the instigator (usually the speaker) becomes an evaluator of the (epistemic) likelihood or evidentiality of the presumed state of affairs on the propositional level.

(16) Reconstructed development of modal variants of ‘have’ in Czech

```
                     / (temporal) > future
concrete deontic >   general deontic > probabilistic
                     \ (evaluator) epistemic > hypothetical > counterfactual.
```

By this reconstruction of the development, general deontic modality develops into probabilistic modality of a likely development, and further bifurcates into two paths: one time-dependent, the other evaluator-dependent. Evaluator-dependent modality scopes over the entire state of affairs with its propositional value, evaluating its likelihood or evidence. This so-called subjective modality differs from so-called objective modality of possibility or necessity, which essentially scopes over the predicate. These details were not discussed by Bybee et al. (1994: 195), who assumed that epistemic modality develops from agent-oriented modality.

Czech exhibits all the reconstructed stages, and Polish exhibits them all except the counterfactual one. In most instances, the German equivalent of Czech and Polish modal 'have/ should' is *sollen*, e.g. the epistemic use such as German *das soll ein guter Film sein* 'this is apparently a good movie' lit. 'this should be a good movie', or the hypothetical use in the past *Konjunktiv* of *sollen*, e.g. (German translation of example 12) *sollte die Sitzung länger dauern, müsste ich zu Hause anrufen* 'should the meeting last longer, (then) I would have to call home.' However, the counterfactual example (10) has an equivalent in the German past *Konjunktiv II* of the main verb (without *sollen*), i.e. *ich rutschte aus und* <u>*wäre (fast) gefallen*</u> 'I slipped and almost fell'. The German *Konjunktiv* is used for epistemic, hypothetical, and counterfactual modalities. Given contact of Czech and German since the Middle Ages, it seems quite likely that the Czech modal 'have' extended its modal domain to counterfactuality by following the model of the German *Konjunktiv*.

3. Modal 'have' in Czech History

In addition to the already existing modal auxiliary verbs *moci* 'can' and *chtieti* 'will', Old Czech developed *drbiti* 'may', *musiti/musieti* 'must' and *jmieti* 'have (to)' as well. *Drbiti* and *musiti/musieti* correspond in form and meaning to Middle High German *durfen* and *müezen, jmieti* is the equivalent of German *soln* (Berger 2014: 193). Porák (1967: 31–35) assumed that the modal 'have' developed from constructions like *nejmáš dáti* 'you do not have to give/should not give', Němec (1979: 15) and Vykypěl (2010: 132) assumed a transformation from *jest mi jíti* 'I have to go' to *jmám jíti* 'I have to go'. Berger (2014: 193) does not reject the assumptions of Němec and Vykypěl, but points to the influence of German on the development of other constructions with 'have', particularly the resultative construction (with 'have' and the past passive participle) in Czech.

In order to understand this development, we must trace the origin of modal 'have' in the oldest Czech texts.

The first attestations of this construction start in the 14th ct. There are no attestations in *Alexandreida* or *Mastičkář*, the *Dalimil chronicle* (early 14th ct) has one example (*nebo jmám o Darynkovi mluviti* 'or I have to speak about Darynko'). Systematic use of modal 'have' starts in the 1360s, specifically in *Desatero kázanie božie* 'The Ten Commandments', illustrated by the following example.

(17)

A	proto	buoh	nad	ní	pomstil,	že	ji	ve	psí tvář
And	for-that	God	on	her	revenge-APP	that	her	in	dog's face

proměnil;	i	jmá	tiem	psem	veždy	býti,
turn-APP	and	have-3SG.PRES	these-DAT	dogs-DAT	always	be-INF

nikdy	nemohúci	zbýti.
never	not-able	change

'And for that God took revenge on her, so that he turned her into a dog's face, and these dogs have to be forever, never able to change.'

Život Krista Pána 'The Life of our Master Jesus Christ' ms. A 1360/1380 (a text of 61303 tokens on 75v foils) contains 28 examples of modal 'have', the majority in the third person singular present. Most frequent are examples of general deontic and probabilistic meanings, as illustrated by (18).

(18)

Zajisté	toto	jest	prorok,	jenžto	jmá	na	tento
Truly	this	is	prophet,	who	have-3SG.PRES	on	this

svět	přijíti.
world	come-INF

'Truly this is the prophet who has/is to come on this world.'

Such examples lead to the conclusion that the first attestations of modal 'have' in Czech did not follow the full development path that would be expected starting from concrete deontic meanings. Moreover, the first examples are found in religious texts of the middle of the 14th ct., whereas the first Bible in Czech followed in the second half of the 14th ct., and the first Bible in the German language was based on the Czech Bible and written in Prague between 1390 and 1400 (the so-called *Wenzeslavsbibel*, preserved in the National Library in Vienna, Cod. 2759). In the 14th ct., the model for religious texts clearly came from Latin, not from German.

Classical Latin had a construction of *habere* + gerundive that could have a reading of a possibility or necessity, depending on the context. As shown by Pinkster (1987: 207), starting with Cicero's writing in 80 BC, *habere* could combine with the infinitive; by the second half of the 2nd century AD (in Tertullian's writings), *habere* + infinitive could be used in epistemic (like *posse* 'can') and deontic meanings (like *debere* 'must'). By the second half of the 3rd century

AD, *habere* could be used as a future auxiliary. Hertzenberg's (2012) diachronic analysis of Latin texts shows that in Classical Latin *habere* + infinitive was used to express (the agent's) ability or capacity (or will/plan, we should add), in the Post-Classical period it was additionally used for obligation and possibly permission, and in the later, Christian period to express ability/capacity, obligation, permission, general deontic possibility and necessity, or future. We can see that Latin went through most of the development process of modal 'have'. It seems plausible to hypothesize that Old Czech took it over as an already developed system directly from Latin.

In addition, the Old Church Slavic tradition was strongly present in the Czech lands (the Emmaus monastery was an important center of Old Church Slavic scribal activity) and the oldest religious texts in Czech contain phrases and clauses known from the Old Church Slavic Gospel texts. Indeed, Old Church Slavic, itself influenced by Old Testament Greek (i.e., OT Greek) and to a lesser extent Latin, already had modal 'have' constructions (with deontic and future readings), but predominantly negated. For example, *Codex Marianus* from the 11th ct. (usually taken as the basis for the reconstruction of Gospels) had 57 modal 'have' constructions, of which 41 were negated (71.9 %), whereas *Život Krista Pána* had 28 examples of modal 'have' and only three of them were negated (i.e. 10.7 %). Altogether the Old Church Slavic tradition had an influence, but Latin influence was decisive in the period of the formation of the Czech language in the 14th century, at least in the still prevalent genre of religious texts.

This leads to the following reconstruction of the development of modal 'have' in Czech.

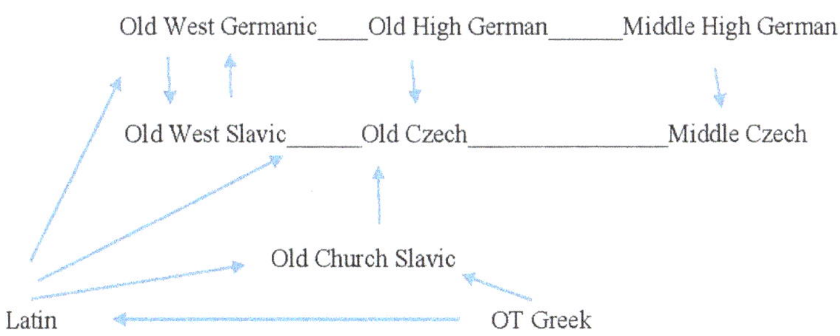

Needless to say, German was influenced by Latin as well. Both Czech and German continued this heritage and developed hypothetical meanings, expressed by means of the *Konjunktiv* of *sollen* in German and the conditional of modal 'have' in Czech. The most advanced stage, that of counterfactual 'have', was in all likelihood shaped under German influence, but in a Czech-specific way (by using the past tense).

4. Conclusion

The extraordinary functional productivity of the modal 'have' in Czech resulted from a complex interplay of foreign influences and inherent functional capacities. This investigation has argued that the first attestations of modal 'have' in Old Czech occurred in texts translated from Latin texts which reflected an already advanced state of development of this modal up to the epistemic stage. Only the subsequent development, characteristic of the spoken language, was influenced by German in the bilingual situation which developed throughout the second millennium AD.

The semantic and functional investigation has shown that the Czech development was unidirectional from deontic to probabilistic and (by implicature) to temporally subsequent, or to epistemic > hypothetical > counterfactual on the evaluative cline. This process hinged crucially on implicature becoming part of the meaning, and the instigator becoming an evaluator of likelihood and evidentiality on the propositional level. The hypothesized order based on synchronic Czech appeared to have a diagnostic value for the reconstruction of the development of this modal construction in a historical perspective.

Abbreviations

ACC	accusative
APP	active past participle
COND	conditional
DAT	dative
GEN	genitive
INF	infinitive
INST	instrumental
PL	plural
PRES	present
PRT	preterite
REFL	reflexive
SG	singular

Bibliography

Adamec, Petr. 1974. *Muset* nebo *mít*? [Must or have to?] *Konfrontační studium ruské a české gramatiky a slovní zásoby*, 133–52.

Berger, Tilman. 2008. Deutsche Einflüsse auf das grammatische System des Tschechischen. *Studien zur historischen Grammatik des Tschechischen. Bohemistische Beiträge zur Kontaktlinguistik*, ed. by Tilman Berger, 57–69. München: Lincom.

Berger, Tilman. 2014. The convergence of Czech and German between the years 900 and 1500. *Congruence and Contact-induced Langage Change*, ed. by Juliane Besters-Dilger, Cynthia Dermarkar, Stefan Pfänder, and Achim Rebus, 184–98. Berlin; Boston: Walter de Gruyter.

Buřáňová, E. 1979. Vztah mezi pravdepodobnostní, dispoziční a zaměrovou modalitou [The relation between probability modality, modality of disposition and intentional modality], *Slovo a slovesnost* 2. 98–101.

Bybee, Joan; Revere Perkins; and William Pagliuca. 1994. *The Evolution of Grammar: Tense, Aspect and Modality in the Languages of the World.* Chicago: University of Chicago Press.

Grepl, Miroslav. 1973. K podstatě modálnosti [On the essence of modality], *Otázky slovanské syntaxe* III, 23–38. Brno: Universita J.E. Purkyně.

Hansen, Björn. 2000. The German modal verb *müssen* and the Slavonic languages –reconstruction of a success story. *Scando-Slavica* 46. 77–92.

Hansen, Björn. 2009. The hypothetical use of Polish '*mieć* plus Infinitive' revisited. *Von grammatischen Kategorien und sprachlichen Weltbildern – Die Slavia von der Sprachgeschichte bis zur Politsprache. Festschrift für Daniel Weiss zum 60. Geburtstag*, ed. by Tilman Berger, 173–81. München: Sagner.

Hertzenberg, Anne Johanne. 2012. The use and development of *habere* plus infinitive: An LFG approach. *Historical Linguistics 2009, Selected Papers of the 19th International Conference on Historical Linguistics, Nijmegen, 10–14. August 2009*, ed. by Ans van Kemenade and Nynke de Haas, 373–98. Amsterdam: Benjamins.

Martínek, František. 2020. Remarks on the development of the Czech modality system in contact with German. *Areal Convergence in Eastern Central European Languages and Beyond*, ed. by Luka Szucsich, Agnes Kim, and Uliana Yazhinova, 177–206. Berlin: Peter Lang.

Němec, Igor. 1979. Staročeské *jmieti* a novočeské *míti*. *Listy filologické* 102, 12–17.

Pinkster, Harm. 1987. The strategy and chronology of the development of future and perfect tenses in Latin. *Historical development of auxiliaries*, ed. by Martin Harris and Paolo Ramat, 185–93. Berlin: Mouton de Gruyter.

Porák, Jaroslav. 1967. *Vývoj infinitivních vět v češtině* [Development of infinitive clauses in Czech]. Praha: Univerzita Karlova.

Šipková, Milena. 1985. The English equivalents of the Czech modal verb *mít*. *Sborník prací Filozofické fakulty Brněnské Univerzity, Studia Minora Facultatis Philosophicae Universitatis Brunensis 7 – Brno Studies in English* 16. 109–21.

Vykypěl, Bohumil. 2010. Slavonic-Baltic addenda to the *World Lexicon of Grammaticalization*. *Jazykovedný časopis* 61. 131–44.

Weiss, Daniel. 1987. Polsko-niemieckie paralele w zakresie czasownikow modalnych (na tle innych języków zachodniosłowiańskich) [Polish-German parallels in the realm of modal verbs (based on other West Slavic languages)]. *Sprach- und Kulturkontakte im Polnischen,* ed. by Gerd Hentschel, Gustav Ineichen, and Alek Pohl, 131–56. Munchen: Sagner.

Weiss, Daniel. 2009. Mögliche Argumentationen zum Nachweis von Calques am Beispiel der polnischen Modalverben. *Von Zuständen, Dynamik und Veränderung bei Pygmäen und Giganten,* ed. by Lenka Scholze and Björn Wiemer, 129–53. Bochum: Brockmeyer.

Sources

Codex Marianus

http://www.helsinki.fi/slaavilaiset/ccmh/MAR.TXT

Corpus of Old Czech texts, Czech Academy of Sciences

https://korpus.vokabular.ujc.cas.cz/view?ctxattrs=word&attr_vmode=mouseover&pagesize=40&refs=%3Ddoc.zkratkaPramene%2C%3Dfolio.cislo%2C%3Dkniha.zkratka%2C%3Dkapitola.cislo%2C%3Dvers.cislo&q=~SqnIcmIqFf5s&viewmode=kwic&attrs=word&corpname=STB-1.1.13.1&attr_allpos=all&fromp=3

Iliyana Krapova and Tomislav Sočanac

Factivity in South Slavic Languages: Complement and Relative Clauses

Abstract Our paper focuses on a special class of factive complement clauses and relative clauses in Bulgarian and Croatian, embedded under the item *deto* in the former and *što* in the latter language. These clauses differ from others in that they denote specific and presuppositional readings grounded in discourse. We account for these distinctive properties by claiming that both *deto/što* complements and *deto/što* relatives are embedded under a C-head containing a [+anaphoric] feature which agrees with a higher definite nominal head. The broader implication of our analysis is that factivity/presuppositionhood is encoded in syntax and hence should not be seen as a purely semantic or pragmatic phenomenon.*

Keywords: Factivity, Presupposition, Complement Clauses, Relative Clauses, Bulgarian, Croatian

1. Introduction

Ever since the seminal work in Kiparsky and Kiparsky (1970), there has been a rich and growing literature dealing with the subject of factivity. Authors studying this area mostly tended to focus on so-called factive predicates and their clausal complements,[1] which exhibit a series of semantic and syntactic differences with respect to their non-factive counterparts. Observe, for instance, the contrast between (1) and (2).

(1) a. John thinks that Mary left, but she did not leave.
    b. John said that Mary left, but she did not leave.

(2) a. John knows that Mary left, # but she did not leave.
    b. John regrets that Mary left, # but she did not leave.

* The research conducted by Tomislav Sočanac at Ca'Foscari, which partly contributed to the present paper, was supported by the Swiss National Science Foundation. We would also like to thank Guglielmo Cinque, Marija Bradaš, Ivana Koleva and Maria Schnitter for their help in sorting out the data and their theoretical implications.

The complements in (1), selected by non-factive predicates such as *think* or *say*, can be contradicted by the speaker, whereas such contradicting continuations are infelicitous when applied to clauses embedded under factive predicates such as *know* or *regret* (hence the # sign in [2]). This contrast has typically been accounted for in the literature via the notion of *presuppositionhood* (Karttunen 1971, 1973, Heim 1992 etc.): factive predicates introduce a presupposition in their complement, meaning that the embedded proposition is assumed to be true by both the subject and the speaker, hence it cannot be contradicted, whereas non-factive predicates do not introduce such a presuppositional reading.

Our paper will focus on factivity in South Slavic languages, specifically Bulgarian (Bg) and Croatian (Cr),[2] where this issue has not yet been sufficiently studied in the literature, particularly from a formal perspective. Factive complements in Bg and Cr share the pattern observed with their English counterparts in (2), i.e. their truth cannot be contradicted by the speaker, as shown in (4) below. Another distinctive property that such complements exhibit in Bg and Cr (which is not typically observed on a cross-linguistic level) is that they can be embedded under a special subordinator (*deto* 'that-fact.' in Bg and *što* 'that-fact.' in Cr) which is different from the one used to introduce non-factive declarative complements (*če* 'that' in Bg and *da* 'that' in Cr).[3] Observe the contrast in (3–4).

(3) a. Ivan kazva če Marija e pristignala, no tja ošte ne e tuk. (Bg)
I. says that M. has arrived but she still not is here
'Ivan says that Marija has arrived but she is still not here.'

b. Ivan misli da je Marija stigla, ali ona još ni-je stigla. (Cr)
I. thinks that has M. arrived, but she yet not-has arrived
'Ivan thinks that Marija arrived, but she has not yet arrived.'

(4) a. Ivan sǎžaljava **deto** Marija si e zaminala
I. regrets that.FACT. M. REFL. has left
(# no tja e ošte tuk). (Bg)
but she is still here
'Ivan regrets that Marija left (#but she is still here).'

b. Ivan je sretan **što** je Marija stigla (# ali ona još ni-je stigla). (Cr)
I. is happy that.FACT. has M. arrived, but she yet not-has arrived
'Ivan is happy that Marija arrived (#but she has not yet arrived).'

In (4) we can observe the main distinctive properties of factive complements in Bg and Cr: (i) like their English counterparts in (2), they cannot be contradicted (i.e. the contradicting continuations signaling speaker disagreement are equally infelicitous); (ii) unlike their English counterparts, they are embedded under special factive complementizers.

Note, moreover, that the complementizers *deto/što* in (4) cannot be selected by all predicates that are typically labeled as factives (or semi-factives) in the literature.[4] These complementizers are typically only selected by factive predicates that express a certain emotional state or reaction on the part of the subject (e.g. *regret, be happy, be surprised* etc.), such as those we observed in (4) (Bibović 1971, Mønnesland 1972, Browne 1986 etc.). These predicates are usually labeled as *factive emotives* in the literature (Kiparsky and Kiparsky 1970, Giannakidou 2006, Baunaz and Puskas 2014, Djärv, Schwarz and Zehr 2016 etc.). On the other hand, factive-type predicates that do not express this additional emotive dimension (e.g. *know, realize, find out* etc.) cannot select factive complementizers in Bg and Cr (with few rare exceptions that we do not discuss here), hence the grammaticality contrasts below.

(5)	a.	Ivan	znae,	**če**	/	* **deto**	Marija	e	pristigla.		(Bg)
		I.	knows	that	/	that.FACT.	M.	has	arrived		
		'Ivan knows that Marija has arrived.'									
	b.	Marko	je	shvatio	**da** /	* **što**	ga	je	Petar	prevario.	(Cr)
		M.	has	realized	that /	that.FACT.	him.CL.	has	P.	swindled	
		'Marko realized that Petar swindled him.'									

The contrast between (4) and (5) (among other data) leads us to argue in Krapova and Sočanac (in preparation) that 'true factive' predicates in South Slavic only comprise factive emotives, as in (4), whereas cognitive-type factive verbs, as in (5), are better defined as 'semi-factives', in accordance with the distinction proposed in Karttunen (1971). In this paper we will only be focusing on true factive predicates.

An additional context where Bg *deto* and Cr *što* can be used involves relative clauses. Both Bg and Cr feature two types of relativizers: a variant one (*kojto* in Bg and *koji* in Cr,[5] meaning 'who, which') and an invariant one, which shares the same form as the complementizers we observed in (4) (i.e. Bg *deto* and Cr *što*, 'that') (van der Auwera and Kučanda 1985, Browne 1986, Rudin 1986, Krapova 2010, Franks and Rudin 2015, Baunaz and Lander 2017).[6] We can observe these two types of relativizers being used in the same contexts in (6).

(6)	a.	Srešn-ax	čovek-a,	kojto	/	deto	e	napisal	tazi	kniga.		(Bg)
		met-1.SG.	man-the	who	/	that	has	written	this	book		
	b.	Upoznao	s-am	čovjeka	koji /		što	je	napisao	ovu	knjigu.	(Cr)
		met	have-1.SG.	man	who /		that	has	written	this	book	
		'I met the man who has written this book.'										

The main question that will be addressed in this paper is whether the complementizers in (4) and the homophonous relativizers in (6) can be considered as the same items from a syntactic point of view or whether they should be analyzed as different formal items.

Before we address this question, we will first provide, in Section 2, a brief introductory exposé on factivity and presuppositions, which will establish the background for the analysis that will be developed later on. In Section 3 we will look at the relevant data pertaining to *deto/što* complements and relatives, which will allow us to observe a number of common patterns that they exhibit. Section 4 will then provide a syntactic analysis of such clauses which will account for these shared patterns. Finally, in Section 5 we summarize and conclude the paper.

2. Factivity and Presupposition

Factivity has been a somewhat thorny issue in the literature of the past few decades, and there is little agreement as to how factivity is encoded from language to language, or whether it even exists as a linguistic phenomenon. Thus, some authors suggested that factive interpretations are encoded in syntax (e.g. Kiparsky and Kiparsky 1970), others argued that factivity should be seen more as a pragmatic phenomenon (e.g. Simons 2007), while still others claimed that factivity is not a property of natural language at all (Hazlett 2010). The analysis that we will develop later on will argue in favor of the view that factivity is indeed a linguistic phenomenon and that it is encoded in syntax (at least in the languages we are dealing with here).

When it comes to the semantic contrasts we observed between complements in (1–4), the standard view in the literature is that factive predicates introduce a presupposition of truth in relation to their embedded complement, whereas non-factive ones do not (Karttunen 1971, Heim 1992, Simons 2007, Egrè 2008 etc.). There is also a rather complex debate in the semantic and pragmatic literature on the nature and definition of presuppositions (going all the way back to Frege [1948] and Strawson [1950]), which we will not be entering into within the present paper. Here we will assume a relatively simple view in this context, which is broadly agreed upon in the literature, that presuppositions are background assumptions which are part of the common ground and taken to be true by the participants in the discourse (Strawson 1964, Stalnaker 1974 etc.). This explains, among other things, why presuppositional complements selected by factive predicates cannot have their truth cancelled by the speaker, as we observed in the previous section.

The idea that factive predicates introduce a presupposition in their embedded complement can also account for a series of additional semantic contrasts that they exhibit with respect to their non-factive counterparts. For instance, in non-veridical contexts (e.g. in questions or negated sentences),[7] the presupposition of truth is still preserved in complements to factive predicates, whereas this is not the case with non-factive clauses, as shown in (7–8) below.[8]

(7) a.

Misl-iš	/	tvărd-iš	li, če	Marija	si	e	vzela	izpit-a?	(Bg)
believe-2.SG.	/	claim-2.SG.	Q that	M.	REFL.	has	taken	exam-the	

'Do you believe/claim that Marija has passed the exam?'

//>> no presupposition, i.e. Marija may or may have not passed the exam'

b.

Săžaljav-aš	li,	deto	Marija	ne	uspja	da	si	vzeme	izpit-a?
regret-2.SG.	Q	that.FACT.	M.	not	managed	to	REFL.	take	exam-the

'Do you regret that Marija did not manage to pass the exam?'

>> presupposition 'Marija did not pass the exam'

(8) a.

Ivan	ne	vjeruje	/	tvrdi	da	je	Marija	otišla.	(Cr)
I.	not	believes	/	claims	that	has	M.	left	

'Ivan does not believe/claim that Marija left.'

//>> no presupposition, i.e. Marija may or may not have left

b.

Ivan	ne	žali	što	je	Marija	otišla.
I.	not	regrets	that.FACT.	has	M.	left

'Ivan does not regret that Marija left.'

>> presupposition 'Marija left'

The examples in (7b/8b) are akin to those already observed in (2) and (4) from a semantic point of view: they all feature factive presuppositional clauses that cannot have their truth value cancelled, neither by the speaker, nor in non-veridical contexts such as negated clauses or questions. As such, they warrant a separate analysis.

3. Factive Complements and Relatives in Bg and Cr: Shared Patterns

In this section, we will introduce the relevant data pertaining to *deto/što* complements and relatives in Bg and Cr, whereas in Section 4 we will put forward an analysis that will account for the patterns we observe here. The first observation that needs to be made is that factive predicates in Bg and Cr can introduce their embedded complements both under a factive complementizer (as we already saw in [4], for instance), but also under a non-factive one (i.e. Bg *če* and Cr *da*), as shown below.

(9) a.	Ivan	săžaljava,	**deto**	/	**če**	tja	ne	e	v	grad-a	sega.	(Bg)
	I.	regrets	that.FACT.	/	that	she	not	is	in	town-the	now	

'Ivan regrets that she is not in town now.'

b.	Ivan-u	je	drago	**što**	/	**da**	je	prošao	ispit.	(Cr)
	I.-DAT.	is	glad	that.FACT.	/	that	has	passed	exam	

'Ivan is glad that he passed the exam.'

In this sense, Bg and Cr differ from a language such as Greek, which also contains a factive complementizer (*pu*) but which requires the use of this complementizer in factive contexts such as those in (9) (Roussou 2010).[9] Here we will not attempt to account for this cross-linguistic difference, since we are mainly interested in South Slavic data.

The contrasts in (9) are not trivial because complementizer choice can have an impact on the interpretation of the embedded clause, specifically when it comes to its presuppositional status. Even though complements selected by factive predicates such as those in (9) are typically presupposed to be true regardless of the subordinator under which they are introduced (as a function of the lexical semantics of the matrix predicate), this is not always the case. Provided one constructs the right context, the truth of such complements can be cancelled. One such context is given in the examples (10–11) below, i.e. the context of 'false belief', where the speaker's knowledge, indicated by the evaluative adverb *wrongly*, contradicts the main subject's mental belief that the embedded proposition *p* is true. This results in the cancellation of the presuppositional status of *p* (Oedipus is dead) in spite of the presence of the factive verb *regret* (see also the discussion in Egrè 2008).[10] This, however, is possible only if *p* is introduced by the non-factive complementizers (*če/da*); if instead the factive ones (*deto/što*) are used, the example becomes infelicitous.[11]

(10) a.

Edip	pogrešno	misleše,	če	e	nanesăl	smărtonosen	udar,	i
E.	wrongly	believed	that	has	inflicted	deadly	strike,	and
săžaljavaše,	**če**	e	ubil	strannik-a.				(Bg)
regretted	that	has	killed	stranger-the				

b.

# Edip	pogrešno	misleše,	če	e	nanesăl	smărtonosen	udar,	i
E.	wrongly	believed	that	has	inflicted	deadly	strike	and
săžaljavaše,	**deto**	e	ubil	strannik-a.				
regretted	that.FACT.	has	killed	stranger-the				

'Oedipus wrongly believed that he had inflicted a deadly strike, and regretted that he killed the stranger.'

(11) a.

Ivan	pogrešno	vjeruje	da	se	Marija	već	udala,	i	žao	mu
I.	wrongly	believes	that	REFL.	M.	already	married	and	sorry	him.CL.
je	**da**	je	ušla	u	brak	s	tim	tipom.	(Cr)	
is	that	has	entered	in	marriage	with	that	guy		

b.

# Ivan	pogrešno	vjeruje	da	se	Marija	već	udala,	i	žao	mu	je
I.	wrongly	believes	that	REFL.	M.	already	married	and	sorry	himCL.	is
što	je	ušla	u	brak	s	tim	tipom.				
that.FACT.	has	entered	in	marriage	with	that	guy				

'Ivan wrongly believes that Marija got married, and is sorry that she entered into marriage with that guy.'

What the data in (10–11) show us is that the truth-presuppositional interpretation associated with this type of factive complement is not crucially triggered by the factive predicate per se, but rather by the factive complementizer embedded under such predicates. In other words, we can say that the factive predicate functions as a *weak presupposition trigger* (i.e. the presupposition that it projects can be cancelled in certain contexts), whereas factive complementizers *deto* and *što* function as *strong presupposition triggers* (presuppositional reading associated with the embedded complements cannot be cancelled if the latter are introduced by these subordinators).[12] This is the first piece of evidence that shows us, more broadly, that factivity in Bg and Cr is encoded within syntax, and should not be seen as a purely semantic or pragmatic phenomenon.

Let us now turn our attention to relative clauses. As we already saw in (6), repeated in (12), relative clauses in Bg and Cr can be introduced both under a variant relativizer (Bg *kojto*; Cr *koji*) and under an invariant one, which shares the same overt form as the factive complementizers we discussed before (i.e. Bg *deto* and Cr *što*). Thus the optionality in (12) below can be seen as somewhat analogous to the one we observed in (9).

(12)	a.	Srešn-ax	čovek-a,	kojto	/	deto	e	napisal	tazi	kniga.		(Bg)
		met-1.SG.	man-the	who	/	that	has	written	this	book		
	b.	Upoznao	s-am	čovjeka	koji	/	što	je	napisao	ovu	knjigu.	(Cr)
		met	have-1.SG.	man	who	/	that	has	written	this	book	
		'I met the man who has written this book.'										

The main question that we will address in the remainder of the paper is whether *deto/što* complementizers and *deto/što* relativizers can be analyzed on a common basis, or whether they should be seen as different formal items.

The first piece of data which suggests that a common analysis may be warranted in this context has to do with the semantic status of *deto/što* complements and relatives. As we saw in (10–11), *deto/što* complementizers trigger a presuppositional reading of the embedded complement which cannot be cancelled in context (i.e. they function as strong presupposition triggers). A similar pattern seems to be at play in *deto/što* relatives as well. Let us focus, first of all, on the relative clauses in Cr, where the semantic contrast resulting from the use of the variant vs invariant relativizer (i.e. *koji* vs *što*, respectively) can be observed more clearly.

(13)	a.	Ne-ma	čovjeka	**koji**	je	pametniji	od	tebe.	(Cr)
		no-has	man	who	is	smarter	than	you	
		'There is no man who is smarter than you.'							
	b.	Ne-ma	čovjeka	**što**	je	pametniji	od	tebe.	
		no-has	man	that	is	smarter	than	you	
		'The man that is smarter than you is not present.'							

Once again, the contrast in (13a/b) is not trivial, because the use of one or the other relativizer brings about different interpretations (as can be observed from the English translations beneath the examples). The difference with respect to factive complements we looked at in (10–11) is that the interpretative contrasts in question no longer involve truth-presuppositional vs non-presuppositional readings but rather existential vs non-existential readings. In the case of the variant relativizer in (13a), the default interpretation that is strongly preferred in this context is one of universal quantification which under negation gives a non-existential reading, i.e. 'Nobody is smarter than you'.[13] However, the interpretation changes when the relative is embedded under the invariant *što* in (13b). In this case, the quantificational reading is no longer universal but existential, and this existential reading is preserved under negation as well: 'The man that is smarter than you is not present (but he exists).'

Bg presents a somewhat more complex picture in this context, and needs to be discussed in a bit more detail. First of all, unlike Cr, Bg contains definite articles, which can further contribute to the interpretation of the head of the relative clause (e.g. *čovek* 'a man' vs *čovek-a* 'man-the = the man'). In Cr, a noun like *čovjek* 'man' is inherently ambiguous between a definite/specific ('the man') and an indefinite/non-specific reading ('a man'), and one of the ways to disambiguate between the two readings is through the use of the variant vs invariant relativizers, as we saw in (13). In Bg, on the other hand, the specific reading of the type we observed in (13b) can only be achieved if the head noun is accompanied by the definite article, as in (14) below.[14]

(14) a. Nj-ama go čovek-a kojto znae kak da opravi mivka-ta. (Bg)
no-has him.CL man-the who knows how to fix sink-the
'The man who knows how to fix this sink does not exist/is not available/present.'

b. Nj-ama go čovek-a deto znae kak da opravi mivka-ta.
no-has him.CL man-the that knows how to fix sink-the
'The (only) man who knows how to fix this sink is not available/present.'

These constructions feature the negative existential *ima* 'there is' (like their Cr counterparts in [13]) combined with a definite noun marked accusative by the clitic. Similarly to Cr, the choice of relativizer affects the interpretation in Bg as well: the *deto*-relative makes reference to a fixed/ specific individual whose existence is presupposed and, as a consequence, what is being denied is the individual's current availability, so (14b) is a kind of locative structure in which exact location can be left implicit (note that the locatee/theme argument doesn't need to be previously introduced since the sentence can be uttered out of the blue). We propose that this specificity effect is directly related to the invariant relativizer. The variant relativizer, on the other hand, is ambiguous between a specific and a non-specific reading, so it can be used when the speaker does not have in mind a particular referent (in fact, the number of referents can potentially be bigger than one) or even if the speaker believes such a referent to be non-existent, as illustrated in (15), where the use of *deto* is unacceptable:

(15)	Čovek-ăt, *	deto /	kojto	znae	kak	da	opravi	mivka-ta	mi	ošte
	man-the	that	which	knows	how	to	fix	sink-the	my	yet
	ne	se	e	rodil.						
	not	REFL.	is	born						

'The man who knows to fix my sink has not been born yet.'

At first glance, it would seem that the difference between Cr, where the variant relativizer *koji* appearing in negative environments of the type exemplified in (13) gives rise to non-specific/non-existential readings, and Bg, where both specific and non-specific readings are possible, depends on the overt definite morphology of the head noun, that is the fact that the head noun in Bg relatives can be accompanied by a definite article. However, even though definites are usually taken to be also specific, numerous studies (see e.g. von Heusinger 2002) have shown that specificity is a separate discourse category which cross-cuts that of grammatical definiteness. As is well-known since Quine (1960/2015), definites can also be used non-referentially much like non-specific indefinites. Bg is not an exception, as illustrated by the generic reading in (16b) which is obligatorily definite:

(16)	a.	Ivan	zagubi	portmone-to.							(Bg)
		I.	lost	purse-the							

'Ivan lost the purse.' ➔ specific

b.	Portmone-to	trjabva	da se pălni	s	pari	ot	vreme	na	vreme.
	purse-the	must	to be filled	with	money	from	time	to	time

'A purse/purses must be filled with money from time to time.' ➔ non-specific

A more likely explanation for the semantic contrast observed between Cr and Bg in (13a/14a) (namely the fact that koji-relatives in Cr are more conducive to non-specific readings than their kojto-counterparts in Bg), lies in the morphological make-up of the variant relativizers in these two languages (see Franks and Rudin [2015], Franks [2021] for a more detailed analysis in this context). The variant relativizer in Bg contains the morpheme –*to* (i.e. *koj-to*) whereas this is not the case in Cr (*koji*). If this –*to* is the same type of morpheme as the one contained within the invariant relativizers that bring about specific readings (i.e. Bg *de-to* and Cr *š-to*), then it can be seen as a marker of specificity in its own right.[15] The specificity effect thus does not depend on the definite marking of the head noun (as is obvious from the Cr example in [13b]) but, in the case of the variant relativizer *kojto* in particular, there is likely some type of agreement relationship that is established between the definiteness feature +D of the head noun and the specificity morpheme –*to* within the relativizer (in the absence of the definite article, the variant relativizer *kojto* cannot bring about specific readings, as we will see shortly). Thus, we can postulate that +D heads may combine with the variant relativizer, giving rise to specific readings, while +/-D heads combine with the variant relativizer producing non-specific readings.[16]

The prediction stemming from this observation is that those relative clauses which force a generic/non-specific reading of the head noun should not allow for the use of the invariant *deto/što* relativizers. One example of this type of relative clause are free relatives, as in (17), which involve aggressively non-specific readings. As expected, such clauses only allow for the use of the variant relativizer, while disallowing the use of the invariant one.

(17)	Toz,	kojto / *	deto	padne	v	boj	za	svoboda,	toj	ne	umira.	(Bg)
	that-one	who /	that	falls	in	battle	for	freedom,	he	not	dies	

'Whoever falls in battle for freedom will not die.'

(from the poem "Hadži Dimităr" by Hristo Botev, a Bulgarian 18th c. poet)

The data we observed so far thus lead us to a two-fold conclusion: (i) the invariant relativizers *deto* and *što* bring about similar semantic contributions in both Bg and Cr, which can be described in terms of specificity/existence; (ii) these semantic contributions are already encoded in syntax, through the use of the invariant relativizers in question, which leaves no interpretative ambiguities, as we observed in (13b/14b). One can thus note a broad parallel between *deto/što* relativizers, on the one hand, and *deto/što* complementizers, on the other, in that they bring about meaningful contributions to the interpretation of the clause already at the level of syntax. In the discussion that follows, we will look more closely at some other parallels that can be observed between *deto/što* complements and relatives in Bg and Cr.

Note, first of all, the Bg relatives in (18), which differ from those we previously observed in (14) in that the head noun is no longer accompanied by the definite article but appears in its bare form.

(18)	a.	Nj-ama	čovek	kojto	te	obič-a	poveče	ot	men.	(Bg)
		no-has	man	who	you	love-3.SG.	more	than	me	
		'There is nobody who loves you more than me.'								
	b.	Nj-ama	čovek	deto	te	obič-a	poveče	ot	men.	
		no-has	man	that	you	love-3.SG.	more	than	me	
		'None of the men loves you more than me.'								

Given the absence of the definite article on the head noun, the relative clauses in question can no longer refer to a specific individual, as was the case in (14). Nevertheless, one can still observe a semantic contrast between *kojto* and *deto* relatives in terms of non(specific) readings, but the contrast in question now concerns sets of individuals. In the *kojto*-relative in (18a), there is no specific-set reading and the interpretation is one of non-existence (similar to what we observed in the Cr example in [13a], for instance): 'Nobody loves you more than me.' In the *deto*-relative in (18b), on the other hand, the head noun scopes over a specific/presupposed set of individuals (an existentially presupposed set) which are known to both discourse participants (part of their common ground) and it is claimed that no member of the set loves you as much as I do (the sentence does not presuppose the existence of such people outside of the set). Thus we may conclude that the *deto*-relative always induces a specific interpretation whether the head noun is definite (as in 14b) or indefinite (as in 18b).

A similar semantic contrast in terms of specific vs non-specific set readings emerges both in Bg and in Cr when relative clauses are used in quantificational contexts that involve distributive interpretations, as in (19).[17]

(19)	a.	Nito	edin	čovek	ne	e	prodal	kuče-to,	koeto	e	kupil.	(Bg)
		not	one	man	not	has	sold	dog-the	which	has	bought	
	b.	Nito	edin	čovek	ne	e	prodal	kuče-to,	deto	e	kupil.	
		not	one	man	not	has	sold	dog-the	that	has	bought	
	c.	Niti	jedan	čovjek	ni-je	prodao	psa	koga	je	kupio.		(Cr)
		not	one	man	not-has	sold	dog	which	has	bought		

d. Niti jedan čovjek ni-je prodao psa što ga je kupio.[18]
not one man not-has sold dog that CL.ACC. has bought
'No man sold the dog he bought.'

These examples have in common two things: (a) neither is true in a scenario in which all the men bought more than one dog; (b) neither is true in a scenario in which no man bought any dog. They differ, however, in the following way: (19a/c) are true in a scenario in which, out of all the men that bought one dog in general (non-specific set of men that bought one dog), none of them sold the dog, with the value of the embedded subject varying with the individuals quantified over; (19b/d), on the other hand, are true in a scenario in which some men bought exactly one dog and none of them sold the dog. In other words, the interpretation of (19b/d) is that there exists a set of men and a set of dogs and that each man from the set of men bought exactly one dog from the set of dogs. Hence we observe the same type of specific-set reading both with *deto*-relatives in Bg and with *što*-relatives in Cr in this context.

This brings us to a clear semantic parallel between *deto/što* relativizers, on the one hand, and *deto/što* factive complementizers, on the other, because all of these items seem to interact with quantifiers in a similar way, bringing about specific-set readings. Note the following examples involving factive complements in Bg and Cr.

(20) a. Nito edin student ne se radva, če e kăsmetlija. (Bg)
not one student no REFL. is-happy that is fortunate
b. Nito edin student ne se radva, deto e kăsmetlija.
not one student no REFL. is-happy that.FACT. is fortunate
'No student is happy that he is fortunate.'

(21) a. Niti jed-nom student-u ni-je drago da je privilegiran. (Cr)
not one-DAT. student-DAT. not-is glad that is privileged
b. Niti jed-nom student-u ni-je drago što je privilegiran.
not one-DAT. student-DAT. not-is glad that.FACT. is privileged
'No student is glad that he is privileged.'

The semantic contrast between (20a/21a), on the one hand, and (20b/21b), on the other, is subtle but important for the argument we are presenting here. When the embedded complement is introduced under the default declarative complementizer (i.e. *če* in [20a] and *da* in [21a]), the reading is universal: 'as a general statement, students never appreciate how fortunate/privileged they are' (this does not imply any specific student or group of students). When the complement clause is embedded under the factive complementizer *deto* or *što*, however, the quantification is no longer universal but existential, referring to a specific set of individuals. Thus the examples in (20b/21b) can be paraphrased as: 'Out of these students, not a single one appreciates how fortunate/privileged he is.' In this case there is a presupposed set of students that the embedded subject quantifies over, similarly to the case with *deto* or *što* relatives in (18) and (19).

The data we observed in this section thus show us that *deto/što* complements and relatives exhibit common semantic patterns in that they bring about specific and presuppositional readings. In the following section, we will provide a formal analysis that will account for these shared patterns, as well as for some additional pieces of data, of a more syntactic nature, that were not yet discussed (with regards to island effects in particular).

4. Syntactic Analysis: *deto/što* Complements and Relatives as Definite Constituents

From a semantic point of view, both *deto/što* complements and relatives can be analyzed through the prism of presuppositionhood: *deto/što* complements involve a presupposition of truth, whereas *deto/što* relatives involve a presupposition of existence. This nuanced difference is due to the fact that complements of this type denote propositions (i.e. the proposition denoted by the embedded clause is presupposed to be true), whereas relatives of this type denote individuals (i.e. the individual/s *x* modified by the relative clause is presupposed to exist). Nevertheless, the deeper semantic property that both of these types of clauses share is that they involve specific readings. Here we will propose that the underlying reason for this lies in the common formal features contained within the structures associated with *deto/što* complements and relatives.

In this context, we will adopt a version of the standard analysis that was proposed by Kiparsky and Kiparsky (1970) (K&K) in relation to factive complements. The original claim by K&K was that complements introduced under factives contain an additional nominal projection on top of the embedded clause, unlike non-factive complements.

(22) a. [V [NP [S]]] ➔ factives
b. [V [S]] ➔ non-factives

This allowed K&K, for instance, to account for the fact that factive predicates of this type allow for the insertion of an additional noun phrase on top of the embedded complement, which is generally disallowed in non-factives.

(23) a. I regret (**the fact**) that Henry arrived late.
b. I think/claim (***the fact**) that Henry allowed late.

Within the contemporary minimalist framework, the nominal projection on top of the embedded CP is recast as DP:

(24) [V [DP [NP]] [CP]]]

Given the analysis in (22/24), the grammaticality contrast in (23) is to be expected.

However, full nominal constituents such as 'the fact' cannot combine with factives like *regret* in Bg and Cr (even if one might expect such a configuration to be possible as a sort of noun clause complement, as in Cinque and Krapova [2016], the examples in [25] show that this is not the case).

(25) a. Ivan săžaljava za (*fakt-a), deto ne mož-e da dojd-e. (Bg)
I. regrets for (fact-the) that.FACT. not can-3.SG. to come-3.SG.
b. Ivan žali (*činjenicu) što ne mo-že do-ći. (Cr)
I. regrets (fact) that.FACT. no can-3.SG. come-INF.
'Ivan regrets (the fact) that he cannot come.'

Nevertheless, these complements can be headed by a light pronominal element (*tova* in Bg and *to* in Cr, meaning 'it, that'), as shown below.[19]

(26)	a.	Ivan	săžaljava	za	**tova**	deto	Marija	si	e	zaminala.			(Bg)
		I.	is-sorry	for	it	that.FACT.	M.	REFL.	has	left			
		'Ivan is sorry because of the fact that Marija left.'											
	b.	Marko	je	zabrinut	zbog	**to-ga**	što	Jana	još	ni-je	stigla.		(Cr)
		M.	is	worried	because	it-GEN.	that.FACT.	J.	still	not-has	arrived		
		'Marko is worried because of the fact that Jana still hasn't arrived.'											

Let us therefore suggest that the structure in (24) applies to Bg and Cr as well, the only difference being that the D-head in these languages hosts the clausal nominalizers/light pronominals in (26) but not full noun phrases (25).[20]

This analysis can also explain why factive complements bring about syntactic island effects in Bg and Cr (27b/28b), whereas non-factive clauses typically do not (27a/28a).

(27)	a.	Kăde	misl-iš	če	Ivan	e	otišăl__?	(Bg)
		where	think-2.SG.	that	I.	has	gone	
		'Where do you think that Ivan has gone?'						
	b.	* Kăde	săžaljava-š	deto	Ivan	e	otišăl__?	
		where	regret-2.SG.	that.FACT.	I.	has	gone	
		'*Where do you regret that Ivan has gone?'						

(28)	a.	Gdje	misl-iš	da	je	Ivan	otišao__ ?	(Cr)
		where	think-2.SG.	that	has	I.	gone	
	b.	?* Gdje	žal-iš	što	je	Ivan	otišao__?	
		where	regret-2.SG.	that. FACT.	has	I.	gone	

The grammaticality contrasts in (27–28) are expected if we assume that factive complements in (27b/28b) contain a nominal projection on top of CP, which presents an additional syntactic barrier to wh-extraction, and which is not present within non-factive complements in (27a/28a). This D-head can either be overt (as in [26]) or silent (as in [27b/28b]).

The D-head, which we claim contains the +Definiteness feature, then further embeds the C-head which functions similarly as strong determiners in the sense of Schwartz (2019), bringing about anaphoric reference to a specific and/or familiar antecedent (either a proposition in the case of factive complements or individual/s in the case of *deto/što* relatives).

(29) [D+definiteness [CP C +anaphoric]]
To/tova deto/što

The agreement relation between D and C in (29) encodes the specific/presuppositional reading that we observed both with *deto/što* complements and with *deto/što* relatives in Bg and Cr. The only difference between factive complements and relatives in this context is a syntactic one, i.e. the fact that the latter are headed by a full nominal DP/NP, whereas the former are headed by a light D/N.[21]

5. Conclusion

In this paper, we have focused on a specific type of complement and relative clauses in Bg and Cr, headed by the items *deto* and *što*. We were able to determine that the factive (specific/presuppositional) readings associated with such clauses are crucially triggered by these items themselves, which were thus analyzed as strong presupposition triggers. From a syntactic perspective, *deto/što* were analyzed as inserted under a C-head encoding anaphoric reference which agrees with a higher D-head containing the [+Def] feature. The C-head containing *deto/što* is where factive/presuppositional readings are crucially encoded (the higher D-head in (29) is likely present with a broader set of predicates, not all which involve a presupposition of truth, such as discourse-linked negative predicates like *deny* or *doubt*, which we do not discuss here). We thus agree with Kratzer (2006) that factivity resides in C, and we showed that a version of her analysis applies to South Slavic as well. Factivity in this sense is syntactically encoded, and hence it should not be seen as a purely semantic or pragmatic phenomenon.

Notes

1 See (among others) Karttunen (1971), Klein (1975), Haegeman (2006), Basse (2007), De Cuba (2007) etc.
2 We name the language as Croatian, as opposed to BCMS, because Croatian is the native language of one of the coauthors of the paper and the examples given are written in standard Croatian of the *ijekavian* variety.
3 Factive predicates such as those in (4) can actually select both the factive complementizers we observe in (4) as well as the non-factive complementizers we observe in (3), thus differing from their counterparts in some other languages which also feature factive complementizers, such as Greek, where there is no such optionality (Roussou 2010).

4 See Karttunen (1971), Hooper and Thompson (1973) or Simons (2007), among others, for a more comprehensive discussion (which we will not develop here in detail) on which groups of predicates can be considered as 'true factives' as opposed to 'semi-factives' and non-factives.

5 Cr also contains the variant relativizer *tko* 'who', which is used specifically when the head of the relative is human. The present paper will only focus on the variant relativizer *koji*, and the differences that the latter exhibits with respect to the invariant *što*.

6 Note that the invariant relativizer *što* in Cr is used less productively than its Bg counterpart, for grammatical reasons that are beyond the scope of this paper. Nevertheless, most speakers that were consulted agree that the use of the invariant relativizer is possible in the examples given in the paper (although they generally prefer the variant one).

7 See Zwart (1995), Giannakidou (1998, 2009) or Egrè (2008) for more on the notion of (non)veridicality.

8 This has to do with the phenomenon known as *presupposition projection* (Langendoen and Savin 1971, Karttunen 1973, Heim 1992 etc.): in effect, the presupposition denoted by factive complements in (7b/8b) *projects* outside the scope of the non-veridical operators in these examples and the presuppositional reading is therefore preserved in these types of environments.

9 As shown in the example below, complements to factive emotives in Greek must be introduced under the factive complementizer *pu*, whereas the use of the default declarative complementizer (*oti)* in this context results in ungrammaticality.

(i)	Xero-me	**pu**	/ * **oti**	o	Janis	elise	to	provlima.	(Gr)
	glad-1.SG.	that.FACT.	/	that the	J.	solved	the	problem	

'I'm glad that Janis solved the problem.'

(Roussou 2010)

10 From the semantic point of view, the speaker's intervention in the examples (10–11) produces a similar result as in the examples (1) or (3), for instance, which involved contradicting continuations by the speaker: in both cases, the speaker cancels the truth value of the embedded clause and hence its presuppositional status as well. Nevertheless, the use of contradicting continuations after clausal complements embedded under factive-emotive predicates (as in [2] or [4], for instance) would produce an infelicitous result regardless of the type of complementizer we have (i.e. factive or non-factive). This further demonstrates that the factive predicate per se largely contributes to the presuppositional reading of the embedded clause. Nevertheless, the data of the

type exemplified in (10–11) show us that factive complementizers function as stronger presupposition triggers.

11 Example (10) is adapted from Klein (1975) and the one in (11) is adapted from Baunaz (2017).

12 The distinction between strong and weak presupposition triggers we propose is similar to the one between *hard* and *soft* presupposition triggers put forward in Abusch (2002, 2010). The difference is that Abusch applied this distinction to different factive-type predicates themselves, analyzing cognitive factives as soft triggers and emotive factives as hard triggers.

13 The existential reading in (13a) is not impossible but it is strongly contextually marked, and can only obtain if we construct a context where the head of the relative, *čovjek* 'man', unambiguously refers to a specific individual previously mentioned in the discourse. With the *što*-relative in (13b), on the other hand, only the existential/specific reading obtains.

14 In the absence of the definite article, we can still observe a contrast between the specific vs non-specific readings of the head noun in Bg *deto* vs *kojto* relatives, respectively, the difference being that the specific readings in such contexts no longer involve single individuals but rather specific sets of individuals. See (18) and the discussion that follows.

15 *To* is the neuter form of the definite article. We understand specificity as referring to the unique status of the referent with respect to the overall information of the discourse participants (perhaps involving some notion of 'weak familiarity' [Craige 2003] rather than 'strong familiarity' in the sense of Heim [1992], i.e. that the entity in question is presupposed to exist although it may not have been introduced in previous discourse [D-linked]). In this sense, uniqueness can also be understood as the speaker's intent to refer to a specific referential set which he/she has in mind and which is familiar also to the hearer or entailed by way of accommodation (Craige 2003). The set can consist of a single referent (singleton set) or of a specific number of referents. We return to this issue shortly.

16 A distinction between weak and strong determiners also comes to mind. From that point of view, the *-to* of *deto/što* is a strong determiner (i.e. anaphoric, in terms of Schwartz [2019], with respect to a head noun which must be specific), while the *-to* of *koj-to* is a weak one (i.e. one that signals uniqueness and may show up also with non-specific heads), and can only denote specific readings when conjoined with the definite article in Bg. It is very probable that even though *deto* retains the morpheme -to, it has lost the ability to express the ambiguity associated with the definite determiner in the *kojto* paradigm. In other words, *-to* is fixed to its default meaning of signaling uniqueness. Here we will not further pursue this line of analysis: the most relevant observation in the context of our paper is that the invariant relativizers *deto/što* unambiguously bring about specific readings in both Bg and Cr.

17 See Elbourne (2018) for a general discussion and original examples after which (19) and (20) have been adapted.
18 The example (19d) is grammatical only if the relative clause contains a resumptive pronoun that co-refers with the head of the relative (the accusative clitic *ga* in this case). As noted by van der Auwera and Kučanda (1985), the resumptive pronoun is obligatory when the invariant relativizer appears under a direct object which is animate, as is the case here. We will not discuss this in further detail here.
19 We can also note in (26) that the light pronominals heading the factive complements are, in turn, preceded by prepositions (Bg *za* 'for' and Cr *zbog* 'because of' in this case). This has led authors such as Krapova (2010) or Roussou (2020) to suggest that factives of this type are actually PP (oblique) complements (i.e. the matrix verb selects the P-head, which in turn embeds the pronominal item in D, which then embeds the CP complement). Here we will not develop this analysis in more detail, but will instead remain focused on the part of the structure embedded below this higher P.
20 We are not committed to the exact syntactic label of the nominal head in question- what is more relevant is its underlying feature content resulting in the semantic effects we observed. Bošković (2005, 2008) argued that Cr (as other languages lacking articles) does not project DPs at all. Bošković's view can be accommodated by simply claiming that the nominal head on top of CP in factives corresponds to D in Bg and to N in Cr (with the same underlying feature content as in [29], however). In fact, such an analysis could be used to account for some nuance syntactic differences between Bg and Cr factives that were not discussed in this paper, such as the fact that the island effects in Bg are stronger in this context.
21 This can also explain why the island effects in *deto/što* relatives are much more pronounced than those in *deto/što* complements, even in Bg where they both bring about a strong island constraint.

Bibliography

ABUSCH, DORIT. 2002. Lexical alternatives as a source of pragmatic presupposition. *Natural Language Semantics (SALT)* 12, ed. by Brendan Jackson, 1–19. Ithaca, NY: Cornell University.

ABUSCH, DORIT. 2010. Presupposition triggering from alternatives. *Journal of Semantics* 27. 37–80.

BASSE, GALLEN. 2007. A Phase-Based Approach to Factivity. MA Thesis. University of Washington.

BAUNAZ, LENA, and GENOVEVA PUSKAS. 2014. The selection of French mood. *Variation within and across Romance Languages: Selected Papers from the 41th*

Linguistic Symposium on Romance Languages, ed. by Marie-Hélène Côté and Eric Mathieu. Ottawa: John Benjamins.

Baunaz, Lena. 2017. Embedding verbs and subjunctive mood: The emotive factor. *Selected Papers from the 44th Linguistic Symposium on Romance Languages*, ed. by David Heap, Irtziri Moreno-Villamar, Sílvia Perpiñan, and Adriana SotoCorominas. London, Ontario: John Benjamins, 9–31.

Baunaz, Lena, and Eric Lander. 2017. Syncretisms with the nominal complementizer. *Studia Linguistica* 71. 1–34.

Bibović, Ljiljana. 1971. Some remarks on the factive and non-factive complements in English and Serbo-Croatian. *The Yugoslav Serbo-Croatian-English Contrastive Project. Studies 3*, ed. by Rudolf Filipović, 37–48. Zagreb: Institute of Linguistics.

Bošković, Željko. 2005. On the locality of left branch extraction and the structure of NP. *Studia Linguistica* 59(1). 1–45. https://onlinelibrary.wiley.com/toc/14679582/2005/59/1. DOI:10.1111/j.1467-9582.2005.00118.x

Bošković, Željko. 2008. What will you have, DP or NP?. In *Proceedings of NELS* 37, 101–14. Amherst, MA: GLSA.

Browne, Wayles. 1986. Relative clauses in Serbo-Croatian in comparison with English. *Institute of Linguistics*. University of Zagreb.

Cinque, Guglielmo, and Iliyana Krapova. 2016. On noun clausal "complements" and their non-unitary nature. *Annali di Ca'Foscari, Serie Occidentale* 50. 77–108.

Craige, Roberts. 2003. Uniqueness in definite noun phrases. *Linguistics and Philosophy* 26(3). 287–350.

de Cuba, Carlos F. 2007. *On (non)factivity, clausal complementation, and the CP-field*. PhD dissertation. Stony Brook University.

Djärv, Kajsa; Florian Schwarz; and Jérémy Zehr. 2016. Cognitive vs. emotive factives: An experimental differentiation. In *Proceedings of Sinn und Bedeutung* 21, ed. by Chris Cummins, Caroline Heycock, Brian Rabern, Hannah Rohde, and Robert Truswell. Edinburgh: Edinburgh University, 367–85.

Egrè, Paul. 2008. Question-embedding and factivity. *Grazer Philosophische Studien* 77(1). 85–125.

Elbourne, Paul. 2018. Definite descriptions and negative existential quantifiers. *Philosophical Studies* 175. 1597–1612.

Franks, Steven, and Catherine Rudin. 2015. Invariant *-to* in Bulgarian. *Studies in Accentology and Slavic Linguistics in Honor of Ronald F. Feldstein*, ed. by Edna Andrews, George Fowler, Steven Franks, and Miriam Shrager, 99–136. Bloomington, IN: Slavica.

Franks, Steven. 2021. *Microvariation in the South Slavic Noun Phrase*. Slavica.

Frege, Gottlob. 1948. Sense and reference. *Philosophical Review* 57(3). 207–30.

Giannakidou, Anastasia. 1998. *Polarity Sensitivity as (Non)veridical Dependency*. Amsterdam/Philadelphia: John Benjamins.

Giannakidou, Anastasia. 2006. *Only*, emotive factive verbs, and the dual nature of polarity dependency. *Language* 82(3). 575–603.

Giannakidou, Anastasia. 2009. The dependency of the subjunctive revisited: Temporal semantics and polarity. *Lingua* 119. 1883–1908.

Haegeman, Liliane. 2006. Conditionals, factives and the left periphery. *Lingua* 116(10). 1651–69.

Hazlett, Allan. 2010. The myth of factive verbs. *Philos. Phenomenol. Res.* 80(3). 497–522.

Heim, Irene. 1992. Presupposition projection and the semantics of attitude verbs. *Journal of Semantics* 9. 183–221.

Hooper, Joan, and Sandra Thompson. 1973. On the applicability of root transformations. *Linguistic Inquiry* 4(4). 465–97.

Karttunen, Lauri. 1971. Some observations on factivity. *Papers in Linguistics* 4(1). 55–69.

Karttunen, Lauri. 1973. Presuppositions and compound sentences. *Linguistic Inquiry* 4(2). 169–93.

Kiparsky, Carol, and Paul Kiparsky. 1970. Fact. *Progress in Linguistics*, ed. by Manfred Bierwisch and Karl Erich Heidolph, 143–173. The Hague: Mouton.

Klein, Ewan. 1975. Two sorts of factive predicate. *Pragmatic Microfiche* 1.1. Frames B5–C14.

Krapova, Iliyana. 2010. Bulgarian relative and factive clauses with the invariant complementizer *deto*. *Lingua* 12. 1240–72.

Krapova, Iliyana, and Tomislav Sočanac. In preparation. Complementizer selection and the syntax of factivity in Bulgarian and Serbian/Croatian. *Studia Linguistica*.

Kratzer, Angelika. 2006. Decomposing attitude verbs. *Unpublished Ms, UMass Amherst*.

Langendoen, Terence D., and Harris B. Savin. 1971. The projection problem for presuppositions. *Studies in Linguistic Semantics*, ed. by Charles J. Filmore and Terence D. Langendoen, 373–88. New York: Holt, Rinehart and Winston.

Mønnesland, Svein. 1972. Semantic factors in the syntax of nominal subordinate clauses in Serbo-Croatian. *Scando-Slavica* 18. 145–57.

QUINE, WILLARD VAN ORMAN. 1960/2015. *Word and object*. New edition, with a foreword by Patricia Churchland, Cambridge, MA.: MIT Press.

ROUSSOU, ANNA. 2010. Selecting complementizers. *Lingua* 120. 582–603.

ROUSSOU, ANNA. 2020. Complement clauses: Case and argumenthood. *Studies in Honor of M. Rita Manzini*, ed. by Ludovico Franco and Paolo Lorusso. Mouton de Gruyter: Berlin.

RUDIN, CATHERINE. 1986. *Aspects of Bulgarian Syntax: Complementizers and Wh- Constructions*. Columbus, OH: Slavica Publishers.

SCHWARZ, FLORIAN. 2019. Weak vs. strong definite articles: Meaning and form across languages. In *Definiteness Across Languages*, ed. by Ana Aguilar-Guevara, Julia Pozas Loyo and Violeta Vázquez-Rojas Maldonado, 1–37. Berlin: Language Science Press.

SIMONS, MANDY. 2007. Observations on embedding verbs, evidentiality, and presupposition. *Lingua* 117. 1034–56.

STALNAKER, ROBERT C. 1974. Pragmatic presupposition. *Semantics and Philosophy*, ed. by Milton Munitz and Peter Unger, 197–213. New York: New York University Press.

STRAWSON, PETER FREDERICK. 1950. On referring. *Mind* 59(235). 320–44.

STRAWSON, PETER FREDERICK. 1964. Intention and convention in speech acts. *Philosophical Review* 73. 439–60.

VAN DER AUWERA, JOHAN, and DUBRAVKO KUČANDA. 1985. Serbo-Croatian *što*: Pronoun or conjunction. *Linguistics* 23. 917–62.

VON HEUSINGER, KARL. 2002. Specificity and definiteness in sentence and discourse. *Journal of Semantics* 19(3). 245–74.

ZWART, FRANS. 1995. Nonveridical contexts. *Linguistic Analysis* 25(3–4). 286–312.

Alexander Letuchiy

'Missed TAM': The Lack of Tense and Mood Marking in Russian Argument Conditionals – Semantic and Formal Motivation

Abstract The present paper discusses cases when Russian sentences with non-verbal predicates (so-called predicatives) unexpectedly remain unmarked for tense and mood (termed below as 'missed TAM'). When the conditional marker *esli* 'if' introduces an argument clause, a mismatch of tense-aspect-modality marking can be observed between the main and the embedded predicate. Standardly, the TAM form is the same in both clauses. By contrast, in the construction under analysis, the main predicate is a predicative, and the unmarked present tense is used instead of the expected future or subjunctive. This is impossible for constructions with a verbal head.

The occurrence of the construction results both from semantic and formal factors. Semantically, 'missed TAM' is observed with evaluation predicates, e.g. 'it is good'. This follows from the semantics of evaluation: a situation can be evaluated as 'good' even if it has not taken place. Formally, with predicatives tense is expressed periphrastically in all forms except the present tense form, where the tense value remains unmarked. Thus, the use of present tense follows the economy principle: the phrase without a copula is shorter. This is not the case with verbs, where all tenses, except the analytical future, are expressed inside the verb form.*

Keywords: Conditional Clauses, Tense, Russian Language, Predicatives, Non-Verbal Heads, Zero Verb

1. Introduction

Russian, like many languages, has numerous strategies for coding argument clauses (on their behaviour in Russian, see Knyazev 2009, Letuchiy 2012, among others). In my paper, I focus on argument clauses introduced by the marker *esli* 'if'. Although this marker primarily codes conditional adjunct clauses (1), it is also used as a complementizer (2):

* This research is supported by the grant from the RFBR № 17-29-09154. I am grateful to Pavel Rudnev, Laura Janda, Tore Nesset, Alexander Berdichevsky, Svetlana Sokolova and other colleagues from the Arctic University of Tromsø for their valuable feedback.

(1)	Esli	ona	pried-et	ja	s	nej	pogovorj-u.
	if	she.NOM[1]	come-FUT.3SG	I.NOM	with	she.INS	talk-FUT.1SG

‘If she comes, I will talk to her.’ (real condition).

(2)	Mam-u	rasstro-it	esli	tebja	vygonj-at.
	mother-SG.ACC	upset-PRS.3SG	if	you.ACC	fire-FUT.3PL[2]

‘It will upset your mother if you are fired.’

The paper focuses on non-standard tense and mood marking in constructions where *esli* introduces complement clauses. Sometimes the main clause remains unmarked for tense and mood: no future marker is used, even if the embedded clause is marked for future or subjunctive (I call these cases ‘missed TAM’). This happens if the matrix predicate is not a verb, but a predicative, as in (3):

(3)	a.	Stranno	esli	by	my	tuda	sejčas	poexa-l-i.
		strange	if	SUBJ	we.NOM	there	now	go-PST-PL

‘It will be strange (lit. ‘it is strange’) if we go there now.’

	b.	Stranno	esli	my	tuda	sejčas	poed-em.
		strange	if	we.NOM	there	now	go-FUT.1PL

‘It will be strange (lit. ‘it is strange’) if we go there now.’

For instance, in (3a), the embedded clause is marked for subjunctive mood, and in (3b) for indicative future tense, while the main clause lacks a lexical verb in both examples. In the main clauses of (3a) and (3b), nothing marks irreality and future reference, respectively. In other words, I analyze contexts where:

(i) The embedded clause includes a predicate marked for future or subjunctive.
(ii) The matrix clause does not include an overt verb form.
(iii) The embedded clause is introduced by the marker *esli* ‘if’ in its complementizer use and, thus, described as possibly unreal.

Note that normally, the lack of a lexical verb is interpreted as an expression of present tense in Russian. This means that in (3a) and (3b), the main clause is in present, while the embedded one is in an unreal mood and future, respectively.

The standard variant with future marking is also possible in all these cases – cf. (4) and (5), where the tense and mood is marked periphrastically with a form of *byt'* 'be':

(4)	By-l-o	by	stranno	esli	by	my	tuda
	be-PST-N	IRR	strange	if	SUBJ	we.NOM	there
	sejčas	poexa-l-i.					
	now	go-PST-PL					

'It will be strange (lit. 'it is strange') if we go there now.'

(5)	Bud-et	stranno	esli	my	tuda	sejčas	poed-em.
	be-FUT.3SG	strange	if	we.NOM	there	now	go-FUT.1PL

'It will be strange if we go there now.'

Note that the phenomenon of missing tense and mood markers is only attested in structures with *esli* argument clauses, which are addressed in detail in Section 2.3 (cases when a conditional clause, marked with a usual conditional marker, is an argument of the matrix predicate).

Missed TAM is unavailable in constructions like 'If Peter comes, I will talk to him', where the conditional clause 'If Peter comes' is an adjunct. It does not fill any valency slot of the main verb 'talk'.

The paper is organized as follows. Section 2 presents a general overview of tense marking in embedded clauses in Russian, as well as predicatives and their special features. Section 3 is central for the paper, it describes the phenomenon of 'missed TAM' on the head predicate, its lexical distribution across complement-taking predicates and predicates which do not license tense and mood omission. In Section 4, explanations are given, while Section 5 describes a typological parallel from Kabardian (East Circassian).

Most examples of the 'missed TAM' strategy come from the Russian National Corpus, some examples are taken from Google search in Russian texts.

2. General Information

2.1. Tense Marking in Embedded Clauses in Russian

In Russian, tense marking opposes argument vs. adjunct clauses (see Barentsen (1995), Khrakovskij (ed.) (2009), Khomitsevich (2007), for analysis). In argument clauses, tense is usually marked relatively to the time of the event, designated by the main clause. The choice of tense form shows the temporal localization of the event with respect to the main event:

(7)	My	zna-l-i	čto	on	skoro	pried-et.
	we	know-PST-PL	COMP	he.NOM	soon	arrive-FUT.3SG

'We knew that he would come soon.'

In (7), the speaker means that the person he mentions was supposed to arrive soon after the reference point when everyone was waiting for him. We do not know how this arrival is localized with respect to the speech act.

In adjunct clauses, tense is mostly marked absolutely. The tense form choice is anchored to the speech act.

(8)	My	priexa-l-i	kogda	vs-e	side-l-i
	we.nom	come-PST-PL	when	everyone-NOM	sit-PST-PL
	za	stol-om.			
	at	table-SG.INS			

'We came when everyone was sitting at the table.'

In (8), both situations, the subjects' arrival and someone's eating precede the moment of speech, and this is what the past forms in the main clause (*priexali* '(we) arrived') and in the dependent clause (*sideli* '(they) sat') mark.

Conditional constructions have a special place among adjunct clauses. As in many languages of the world, in Russian one finds two strategies for marking verbs in conditional constructions (see Athanasiadou & Dirven (1997), Khrakovskij (ed.) (2005)). The first one is reserved for real clauses. It employs indicative forms in both clauses (see (9)) which describe the localization of both situations.

(9)	Esli	ona	pried-et	ja	s	nej	pogovorj-u.
	if	she.NOM	come-FUT.3SG	I.NOM	with	she.INS	talk-FUT.1SG

'If she comes, I will talk to her.' (real condition).

The second strategy is used for counterfactual and unreal clauses. In both parts of this construction, subjunctive forms are used, as in (10). The subjunctive form includes two components: a past tense form (as *priexala* 'came' and *pogovoril* 'talked' in (10)) and the subjunctive marker *by*.

(10)	Esli	by	ona	priexa-l-a	
	if	IRR	she.NOM	come-PST-SG.F	
	ja	by	s	nej	pogovori-l-Ø.
	I.NOM	IRR	with	she.INS	talk-PST-SG.M
	(i)	'If she came, I would talk to her.' (unreal condition).			
	(ii)	'If she had come, I would have talked to her' (counterfactual condition).			

These two patterns can potentially be mixed, but this happens rather rarely in standard language. Most native speakers of Russian reject examples like (11) (with a subjunctive form in the main clause and future indicative in the embedded one) as ungrammatical.

(11)	*Esli	ona	pried-et	Petj-a	by	s	nej	pogovori-l-Ø.
	if	she.NOM	come-PRS.3SGF	Petja-SG.NOM	IRR	with	she.INS	talk-PST-SG.M
	Intended: 'If she comes, Petja would talk to her.'							

It has been mentioned that the conditional marker *esli* 'if' can introduce argument clauses, too. In this case, the two main patterns of marking are inherited from adjunct clauses with *esli*: either both clauses are marked for the same indicative tense (12) or for subjunctive (13).

(12)	Menja	udiv-it	esli	èt-a	komand-a	vyigra-et.
	I.ACC	surprise-PRS.3SG	if	this-F.SG.NOM	team-SG.NOM	win-FUT.3SG
	'It will surprise me if this team wins.'					

(13)

Menja	by	udivi-l-o	ėsli	by	èt-a	komand-a
I.ACC	IRR	surprise-PST-SG.N	if	IRR	this-F.SG.NOM	team-SG.NOM
vyigra-l-a.						
win-PST-SG.F						

'It would surprise me if this team won.'

As with adjunct conditional clause, mixed strategies are impossible for most speakers of standard language. Note that this fact is not universal: Tynan and Lavin (1997, 126–127), as well as some other studies, show that in English, the general ban on future forms in the protasis can be violated under certain conditions.

2.2. Tense in Real Conditional Clauses

While TAM marking under the 'unreal' strategy shows no variation (both parts contain subjunctive forms), a special comment is required on the tense marking in the real conditional construction. In principle, there is no rule saying that the tense should be identical. For instance, in (14), the tense forms are different, present in the main clause and future in the embedded one:

(14)

Esli	u	tebja	vyjd-et	knig-a
if	at	you.GEN	go.out-FUT.3SG	book-SG.NOM
ja	ee	točno	xoč-u	kupi-t'.
I.NOM	she.ACC	surely	want-PRS.1SG	buy-INF

'If you publish a book, I surely want (to get) it.'

However, the general tendency is that the tense forms are the same. In particular, this concerns argument conditionals, where the matrix and the embedded verb are mainly marked for the same tense. This follows naturally from their semantics.

Esli-taking predicates mainly belong to the emotion and evaluation class. Moreover, since these predicates are factive (see Section 2.4), it is presupposed that the stimulus situation has already occurred by the moment when the emotion occurs. As I will show in 2.3–2.4, if *esli* is used, it introduces a possible world, where the stimulus situation occurs and causes the occurrence of emotion or evaluation of the situation. If the stimulus situation only has to occur in future, it is obvious that the emotion and / or evaluation itself will also occur in future: if Peter only plans to come tomorrow, the emotional state 'be glad with Peter's coming' could not have occurred before Peter's coming and / or before the speech act.

Since tense forms usually coincide in real conditional clauses, examples like (3b) should be described as non-standard: the future tense in the embedded clause does not correspond to the present tense in the matrix one (as noted before, the absence of lexical verb is normally interpreted as a present tense expression).

2.3. Special Properties of Argument Conditionals

Argument conditionals possess several properties which show their special nature. See Quer 1999, Schwabe 2015, Letuchiy 2015 for further details. It covers cases when the embedded conditional clause occupies a valency slot of the main predicate.

For instance, if a conditional occupies a valency slot of the verb, it can only be situated **after**, and not **before,** the verb:[3]

(15)	*Esli	èt-a	komand-a	vyigra-et,	menja	udiv-it.
	if	this-F.SG.NOM	team-SG.NOM	win-FUT.3SG	I.ACC	surprise-FUT.3SG

Intended: 'It will surprise me if this team wins.'

Schwabe (2015) and her colleagues propose that the structure with a pronoun, as in (15'), is parallel to the argument use in (12): in her account, in both cases the conditional clause is an adjunct, the difference being that in (12), the subject pronoun is omitted. However, this logic is unable to explain the unacceptability of (15) without a pronoun.

(15')	Esli	èt-a	komand-a	vyigra-et,
	if	this-F.SG.NOM	team-SG.NOM	win-FUT.3SG
	menja	èt-o	udiv-it.	
	I.ACC	this-NOM	surprise-FUT.3SG	

Intended: 'It will surprise me if this team wins.'

Of course, we can consider that a special restriction requires the pronoun to be used in postposed main clauses. However, it seems more natural and simple to suppose that (15) and (15') simply belong to different types of complex sentences: in the former, the conditional clause is an argument, while in the latter, the argument place is occupied by the pronoun, and the conditional clause has the function of an adjunct.

Finally, argument conditionals, contrary to regular adjunct conditional clauses can only contain the conditional subordinator *esli*. Other synonymous markers, such as *v slučae esli* 'in the case if' or *koli* and *eželi* 'if' are impossible or stylistically poor in this context:

(16)	*Menja	udiv-it	v	sluča-e	esli	/	koli
	I.ACC	surprise-FUT.3SG	in	case-SG.LOC	if	/	if
	èt-a	komand-a	vyigra-et.				
	this-F.SG.NOM	team-SG.NOM	win-FUT.3SG				

Intended: 'It will surprise me if this team wins.'

The non-standard syntactic properties of argument conditionals are also accompanied with very special semantic properties. This type of clauses is compatible with factive predicates in terms of Kiparsky and Kiparsky (1971). In other words, the use of these lexemes can only be semantically acceptable if the embedded situation has taken place. Otherwise the construction will be meaningless. For instance, we can only say that *It is good that Peter came* if Peter really came. Otherwise, the utterance (as well as another sentence, *It is not good that Peter came*) cannot be understood at all.

However, the use of the argument conditional makes the situation with factivity more complicated (see Quer (1999), Letuchiy (2015)). It is not obvious whether the predicate *be glad* is factive or not in utterances like *Peter will be glad if you come*. On the one hand, this utterance does not require that the embedded clause *if you come* is true – the speaker does not know whether the addressee will really come or not.

On the other hand, as argued by Letuchiy (2015), the predicate *be glad* does not change its meaning in utterances with *if*. As in typical predications with *that*-like complementizers, *be glad* denotes a property which can only be assigned to a situation which has taken place. We can argue that the complementizer *if* does not make the matrix predicate non-factive. It just creates a possible world, in which the addressee really comes to Peter. In this world, the predicate *be glad* is factive and compatible with an event which will take place in the future.

2.4. Predicatives and their Special Properties

The tense marking tendencies, mentioned in 2.2, are violated in constructions where the predicate position is not occupied by a single verb form. To be more precise, the predicate includes an adjective and a copula verb (the latter is zero in the present indicative, as in (17), and lexically expressed in other contexts, as in (18)). The indicative form does not include an explicit verb (usually this absence of a verb is interpreted as a zero copula), while all other contexts require lexical forms of *byt'*.

(17)	Mne	neinteresno	zdes'	side-t'.	
	I.DAT	not.interesting	here	sit-INF	
	'It is not interesting for me to sit here.'				
(18)	Mne	by-l-o	neinteresno	zdes'	side-t'.
	I.DAT	be-PST-SG.N	not.interesting	here	sit-INF
	'It was not interesting for me to sit here.'				

This type of use of adjective / adverbs in the predicate position without a head noun is called 'predicatives' in the Russian grammatical tradition. In this use, the adjective, lacking a head noun, are syntactically connected with an embedded clause (an infinitive construction in (17) and (18)).

The list of predicatives that can be used in the 'missed TAM', construction includes *ploxo* '(it is) bad', *xorošo* 'good / well', *stranno* '(it is) strange', *objasnimo* '(it is) explicable', *ponjatno* 'understandable', *otlično* 'great, very nice', *prekrasno* 'great, very nice' and, perhaps, some other lexemes. In other words, the phenomenon under analysis is far from being productive.

3. Cases of Missed TAM

3.1. Description of the Phenomenon

The phenomenon I call 'missed TAM' is observed in structures where the matrix predicate position is occupied by a predicative. These units can head a canonical structure with no missed TAM:

(19)	Bylo	by	stranno	esli	by	ty	obradova-l-a-s'.
	be-PST-SG.N	IRR	strange	if	IRR	you.NOM	be.glad-PST-SG.F-REFL
	'It would be strange if you were glad.'						

In (19), the TAM properties marked on the copula verb 'be' follow the general rule: the copula *bylo (by)* is marked for subjunctive, just as the embedded verb *obradovalas' by* 'you (F) would be glad.'

However, there also exist two non-standard constructions, illustrating the phenomenon, which is termed 'missed TAM' here. The first one occurs in real conditional constructions. It is possible to use *esli* in examples like (20) without any tense marking on the matrix predicate, though the verb in the embedded clause is marked for future. In (21), as well, a zero auxiliary / copula manifests itself with a predicative, though the embedded clause contains a future tense form:

(20)	Stranno	esli	ty	obradu-eš'-sja.
	strange	if	you.NOM	be.glad-FUT.2SG-REFL

'It will be (lit. 'is') strange if you are glad.'

(21)	Xorošo	esli	vy	sume-ete	prodela-t'	vsj-o
	good	if	you(PL).NOM	can-FUT.2PL	do-INF	all-N.SG.ACC
	èt-o	v	prisutstvi-i	professor-a.		
	it-SG.ACC	in	presence-SG.GEN	professor-SG.GEN		

'It will be (lit. 'is') good if you manage to do all of this in the presence of the professor.' [Yu.O. Dombrovskij. Obez'jana prixodit za svoim čerepom. Part 2 (1943–1958)].

The second subtype occurs in unreal conditional constructions. Along with the canonical structure (22), we observe here another one with a missed TAM, where no TAM value is marked on the predicative (23):

(22)	Bylo	by	stranno	esli	by	ty	obradova-l-a-s'.
	be-PST-SG.N	IRR	strange	if	IRR	you.NOM	be.glad-PST-SG.F-REFL

'It would be (lit. 'is') strange if you were glad.'

(23)	Stranno	esli	by	ty	obradova-l-a-s'.
	strange	if	IRR	you.NOM	be.glad-PST-SG.F-REFL

'It would be (lit. 'is') strange if you were glad.'

Example (23) shows a mixed strategy which is not expected to be possible in conditional constructions. The whole sentence has an unreal meaning, but this fact is marked only in the embedded verb form and is left unexpressed in the main clause with a predicative. Example (23) is in a sense less standard than (20) and (21), since the restriction on conditional marking, which is violated here, is in general more strict than the tendency to have the same tense marking in the two parts of the real conditional construction. Below are given additional examples from the Russian National Corpus:

(24)

Soglasi-te-s'	stranno	esli	by	ja
agree.IMV-PL-REFL	strange	if	IRR	I.NOM

sta-l-Ø	zanima-t'-sja	rossijsk-im	prokat-om.
become-PST-SG.M	occupy.oneself-INF-REFL	Russian-M.SG.INS	distribution-SG.INS

'Can't you agree that it would be strange (lit. 'it is strange') if I began to work with the Russian film distribution.' ["Izvestija" newspaper, 2013.05.18] (subjunctive is missing).

(25)

Neploxo	esli	OON	prim-et
not.bad	if	United.Nations.SG.NOM	approve-FUT-3SG

nov-yj	document-Ø.
new-M.SG.ACC	document-SG.ACC

'It won't be bad if the United Nations approves a new document.' [Izvestija newspaper, 2003.02.19] (future is missing).

The two types of conditional constructions are not equally tolerant to missed TAM. The phenomenon is not marginal for the real type and somewhat rare with the unreal type.

3.2. Combinability of 'missed TAM' with Other Contexts

In this section, I analyze some constructions, functionally or formally similar to the ones analyzed before, for (in)ability to contain 'missed TAM'. I show that the phenomenon is incompatible with verbal heads taking argument conditionals and with adjunct clauses, and with the default complementizer *čto*, no missed TAM in the proper sense is found.

Verbal Heads with Argument Conditional Clauses: No 'missed TAM'

The missed TAM never occurs in constructions with a verbal matrix predicate. This is why (26) and (27) are ungrammatical in the meaning under analysis:

(26)	#Mam-a	serd-it-sja	esli	my	opozda-em.
	mother-SG.NOM	get.angry-PRS.3SG-REFL	if	we.NOM	be.late-FUT.1PL

Intended: 'Mother gets angry if we are late' (lit. 'Mother is angry if we will be late'). (only in the repeated action meaning 'mother is always angry if we are late').

(27)	*Menja	udivlja-et	esli	èt-a	komand-a	pobed-it.
	I.ACC	surprise-PRS.3SG	if	this-F.SG.NOM	team-SG.NOM	win-FUT.3S

Intended: 'It will surprise me if this team wins.' (lit. 'It surprises me if this team will win').

The difference between verbal vs. non-verbal (predicative) heads shows that the type of head is relevant for the TAM marking. In other words, the morphological type of the head is linked to the syntactic features of the construction. This fact seems to be of typological relevance: though non-verbal predicates have recently become the subject of linguistic research (see, for instance, Roy 2013), mostly their clause-internal syntax is discussed. By contrast, special properties that non-verbal heads demonstrate in complex sentences are mostly ignored (for instance, one finds almost no mention of these constructions in special volumes by Athanasiadou & Dirven 1997 and Khrakovskij 2005).

Adjunct Conditional Clauses: No 'missed TAM'

It has been said above that 'missed TAM' cases are observed in argument conditional clauses. By contrast, the usual type of conditionals when they are in the adjunct position follows the standard pattern. For instance, in (28), the future tense marking on the main predicate cannot be changed to the alternative zero present tense marking, hence the almost full ungrammaticality of (29)

(28)	Esli	ja	pried-u,	èto	bud-et	ploxo.
	if	I.NOM	come-FUT.1SG	this-NOM	be-FUT.3SG	bad

'If I come, it will be bad.'

(29)

??Esli	ja	pried-u,	èto	ploxo.
if	I.NOM	come-FUT.1SG	this-NOM	bad

Intended: 'If I come, it will be bad.' (lit. 'If I come, it is bad').

Real Complement Clauses with čto*: No Real 'missed TAM'*

Argument conditional clauses alternate with real clauses, marked mainly by the complementizer *čto*. With the same verbs, such as predicates of emotion (*radovat'* 'rejoice') and knowledge (*znat'* 'know'), both *esli* and *čto* can be used.

Along with *esli*, predicatives allow the use of *čto* (mainly if the situation is realized, as in (30)):

(30)

Stranno	čto	ty	opozda-l-Ø.
strange	COMP	you.NOM	be.late-PST-SG.M

'It is strange that you were late.'

It may seem that in example (32), contrary to (31), the 'missed TAM' occurs. The embedded event may take place in future, yet, the main evaluation predicate 'strange' is unmarked for tense explicitly (and, thus, refers to present).

(31)

Bud-et	stranno	čto	ty	ne	priexa-l-Ø.
be.FUT-FUT.3SG	strange	COMP	you.NOM	NEG	arrive-PST-SG.M

'It will be strange that you won't come.'

(32)

Stranno	čto	ty	ne	pried-eš.
strange	COMP	you.NOM	NEG	arrive-FUT.2SG

'It is strange that you won't come.'

However, it turns out that the behavior of *čto*-clauses does not correspond to the behavior of *esli*-clauses in 'missed TAM' constructions. Example, (33) shows that emotional predicates are compatible with *čto*-constructions where the main predicate is in present tense.

(33) Mam-u ogorča-et čto ty ne pried-eš'.
mother-SG.ACC upset-PRS.3SG COMP you.NOM NEG arrive-FUT.2SG
'It upsets my mother that you won't come.'

In fact, example (33) also shows that verbal predicates in structures with the default complementizers show quasi-'missed TAM' strategy, rather than the real missed TAM. The reason of present tense marking in (32) and (33) is simply the fact that the embedded clause does not denote an event in the proper sense. It is rather understood as a piece of information (see Boye 2012 on the semantic types of situations in dependent clauses):

(34) 'The information that you won't come surprises my mother.'

Thus, it is natural to say that in sentences with the default complementizer *čto*, no 'missed TAM' is observed.

3.3. The Class of Predicatives Allowing 'missed TAM'

It has been shown that the 'missed TAM' phenomenon occurs in a rather narrow class of cases: only with predicatives as heads and only with conditional clauses in an argument position (recall that constructions with the default complementizer do not fall under the 'missed TAM' notion due to their different behavior). There are however, more restrictions. Only some semantic groups of predicatives (mainly evaluation predicates) occur in missed TAM constructions. With other groups (e.g., emotion, physical perception and so on) this strategy is unacceptable (cf. *prijatno* 'pleasant' in (35) or *xolodno* 'cold' in (36)).

(35) #Tebe xolodno esli ty ne naden-eš' pal'to.
you.DAT cold if you.NOM NEG put.on-FUT.2SG coat.SG.ACC
Intended: 'You will be cold if you don't put on your coat.'

(36) #Mne prijatno esli vy pozvon-ite.
I.DAT pleasant if you(PL).NOM call-FUT.2PL
Intended: 'It will be pleasant for me if you call.'

4. Tentative Explanation

4.1. Why Only Evaluation Predicatives?

In this section, I propose a possible explanation for the 'missed TAM' phenomenon and account for the distribution of this marking strategy. The questions are (1) why the phenomenon is observed at all and (2) why it covers such a narrow group of matrix predicates (only predicatives and mainly with meanings of the evaluation type).

The Nature of Evaluation: The Generalized Status and Relevance for the Speech Act Time

At first glance, the explanation seems to lie in the meaning of predicatives. I have demonstrated above that evaluation predicatives are most likely to show the missed TAM strategy. This results from the 'generalized', 'stative' nature of evaluation. If a person evaluates a situation in a particular way, this characterization is usually applicable to the situation as such, as an abstract concept. A situation can be characterized as 'strange', 'good' or 'bad' regardless of whether it has or has not taken place – the evaluation is relevant for the speech act time

However, this explanation alone turns out to be too simplistic to account for the whole range of facts. First, if evaluation is applicable to situations of any temporal localization and even to unreal ones, the distribution of 'missed TAM' across condition types remains unexplained. It has been mentioned that the strategy is found more often with real condition than with unreal ones.

This question can be answered in the following way: only the restriction on the combination of indicative and subjunctive forms really belongs to the grammatical domain, as proved by Khrakovskij (2009), Russkaja grammatika (1980), etc. (the identity restriction on tense form, as already mentioned, is semantic rather than grammatical). This is why even in constructions like (3a), the general grammatical marginality of verbal indicative + subjunctive constructions demotes the acceptability rating of constructions with predicatives. A 'mismatch' between the two parts creates unacceptable or highly colloquial structures, which are never accepted by speakers, though sometimes used in colloquial speech. In this sense, sentences like (23) violate a strong tendency to have subjunctive in both clauses (see Dobrushina 2012, 2016 for details). Restrictions on tense forms of the real conditional construction are tendencies, rather than rules, and (20) does not create a structure that is highly atypical of Russian.

Second, the selective behavior of 'missed TAM' with semantic types of predicatives is not explained either. The claim about the nature of the evaluation can also be applied to emotional meanings. For instance, all situations could theoretically be divided into those which are pleasant to the experiencer and those which are unpleasant to him. It turns out that examples (35) and (36) are different in the relevant respect. Of course, in (35), the experiencer cannot have the physical sensation *xolodno* 'be cold' if the situation has not taken place. However, (36) could in principle be interpreted as in (37):

(37) 'The hypothetical situation that you call is pleasant to me'.

I think that the hypothetical (36), interpreted as (37) is in fact impossible because the emotional predicative *prijatno* 'pleasant', as well as other emotional predicates, requires an experiencer. Since the situation in (36) has not occurred and has not been perceived by the experiencer, it cannot be described in present as 'pleasant'. To conclude, although the tense or mood mismatch in examples like (35) and (36) seems to be marginal, it is not the case in fact for evaluation predicatives. The peculiar property of the evaluation group of meanings is that evaluation is compatible with any situation, irrespectively of its reality status and temporal location.

However, the semantic explanation does not cover the whole situation. For instance, in this way we cannot account for the fact that the 'missed TAM' strategy is only possible with a predicative in the main clause. This fact shows that our explanation requires a formal component, along with the semantic one. This part of analysis will be described in 4.2.

4.2. Non-Semantic Motivation? 'Missed TAM' and Part of Speech

Earlier I have shown that the 'missed TAM' strategy rests on a solid semantic footing. However, this explanation does not account for the fact that the phenomenon occurs only with predicatives. This is why I want to find a formal part of explanation.

For instance, dependent clauses in the 'missed TAM' construction cannot be referred to by the pronoun *ėto*, the main device of sentence anaphora. While example (38), with the standard future tense, is compatible with *ėto*, in (39), with the 'missed TAM' strategy, pronominalizaiton sounds strange, according to my intuition (see Padučeva 1985 on the use of *ėto* as a sentential anaphora marker):

(38)	Bud-et	stranno	esli	on	opozda-et. –
	be.FUT-FUT.3SG	strange	if	he.NOM	be.late-FUT.3SG
	Da	èt-o	bud-et	stranno.	
	yes	this-NOM	be-FUT.3SG	strange	

'It will be strange if he is late. – Yes, it will be strange'.

(39)	?Stranno	esli	on	opozda-et.	–	Da	èt-o	stranno.
	strange	if	he.NOM	be.late-FUT.3SG		yes	this-NOM	strange

Intended: 'It is strange if he is late (in future). – Yes, it is strange'.

In other words, tense omission on a predicative is only possible if the future tense is expressed in the embedded clasue. In a sense, the two predicates 'share' the tense form: the interpretation of the predicative, used without an overt auxiliary / copula, is based on the verb form interpretation.[4]

Of course, the same is impossible if both the main and the embedded predicates are verbs. Tense is always expressed on indicative verb forms. Thus, if the main verb here was marked for present (instead of future), it would have a present tense marking and it could not be assigned a future interpretation from the embedded verb. Therefore, the 'missed TAM' interpretation crucially depends on the formal type of the matrix predicate (predicative vs. verb). We can say that the 'missed TAM' is possible because a predicative has no lexically / morphologically expressed tense value and can get a tense interpretation from the embedded verb.

This explanation agrees with the fact that the 'missed TAM' interpretation is only compatible with argument, and not adjunct conditional clauses. Argument clauses are more tightly linked with their main clause than adjunct clauses (see, for instance, Noonan 2007 and other parts of the same volume for details). This is why it is easier for the predicative to inherit tense from an argument clause than from an adjunct one.

This explanation also accounts for the strangeness of example (39). Since the embedded clause of the first part is referred to by the pronoun in the second part, the matrix predicate *stranno* does not have any embedded verbal predicate to share with it its tense value.

4.3. Tense with Predicatives: The General Corpus Perspective

As shown above, the missed TAM phenomenon has to do with the semantic classes of predicatives, rather than with the part of speech distinction. It should be noted, though, that tense marking with predicatives differs from that observed with verbs also in another respect.

This difference is statistical, rather than grammatical. The Russian National Corpus (only the corpus of disambiguated texts was searched) shows that verbs show up in a non-present tense much more frequently than predicatives (see Tab. 1). Note that only imperfective verbs (e.g., *idti* 'go') were searched, since they are semantically closer to predicatives than perfective ones (e.g., *prijti* 'come').

Tab. 1. Tense features with verbs of imperfective aspect and with predicatives (indicative) (all figures are based on the subcorpus of Russian National Corpus where the grammatical homonymy is disambiguated).[a]

	Verbs	Predicatives
Total (imperfective indicative, excluding *byt'* 'be')	353 130	42 433
Present	181 375 (51,4 %)	35 936 (84,7 %)
future (imperfective)	4655 (1,3 %)	732 (1,7 %)[5]
past (imperfective) (not including subjunctive)	164 536 (46,6 %)	5323 (12,5 %)
subjunctive (imperfective)	2553 (0,7 %)	442 (1 %)

a The search was conducted in May 2018. For verbs, the figures designate the number of each tense form in the corpus (e.g., present tense forms, perfect past forms, and so on). For predicatives, the procedure was different, since they do not require any verb form for present tense expression. First, I counted explicit tense forms of the auxiliary verb / copula *byt'* 'be', compatible with predicatives: the future tense 3SG form *budet,* the past tense singular neuter form *bylo*, and the subjunctive singular neuter form *bylo by* the condition being that they have to be separated from the predicative by no more than one word. Then the present tense figures were counted as a difference between the number of predicatives in the corpus and the number of non-present tenses. Of course, this method of counting for predicatives may lead to a mistake in the per cent of the present form (= form with a zero copula), because an explicit form of *byt'* be' can be separated from the predicative with more than one word. The real number of present tense forms may be less than 84,7 % because in some contexts the form of the verb *byt'*, linked to the predicative, is separated from it by more than one word. However, these contexts do not seem to be statistically significant: for instance, the corpus search finds only 777 examples where there are two words between *byt'* and a predicative. Forms of the verb *byt'* were not counted in the 'verbal' part of Tab. 1, because this particular verb cannot be unequivocally classified as imperfective or perfective.

As the table shows, for predicatives, the present tense is the most frequent, while for verbs, the past tense is almost as frequent as the present tense. This difference cannot be explained by the fact that verb forms often denote sequences of events, referred to in past: events which follow each other are most typically designated by perfective verbs, which we do not count here.

The data from Tab. 1 can be explained if one recalls that with predicatives, tense is expressed by a separate word (the copula verb *byt'* 'be'). Perhaps, the infrequency of past tense results from the economy principle: the language system tends to avoid the use of an extra word together with the predicative itself. At the same time, it must be explained why future in the construction with predicatives has about the same frequency as imperfective future with verbs.

In any case, the economy-based explanation is rather speculative and cannot account for the whole data, unless accompanied by other semantic and syntactic explanations, proposed in Sections 4.1 and 4.2 above. However, the general statistics is useful in that it confirms a tendency, which has been pointed out for the construction with argument conditionals: the tense value tends to be omitted / remain unexpressed with predicatives, while this is not typically the case for verbs.

5. Typological Parallels

The 'missed TAM' phenomenon might seem to be an isolated syntactic rarity. To demonstrate that it is not the case, I will show data from Kuban Kabardian which are to a large extent parallel to the Russian data.

Kabardian is a language of the Circassian (West Caucasian) family. This group also includes Adyghe, very close to Kabardian, and Abkhaz and Abaza, close to each other and strongly different from Adyghe and Kabardian. Both Kabardian and Adyghe are represented by multiple dialects, which, given the spatial proximity of the speakers, creates a situation, close to the classical dialect continuum. The data of both idioms under analysis were collected in the Adyghea republic of Russia during my participation in joint field trips by HSE University and Russian State University for Humanities.

Kabardian (as well as its closest relative Adyghe) is a polysynthetic language with many typologically rare features, which include absence of an obvious borderline between nouns and verbs; marking multiple participants of the situation in the verb form, where an agent, a patient ("direct object") and several in direct objects can be cross-referenced; a rich system of valency increasing devices, including causative, locative, instrumental, benefactive, malefactive, etc.; high freedom of zero expression of verb arguments, which make it possible to list Adyghe and Kabardian among pro-drop languages.

While in Russian, predicatives and verbs are easily differentiated, in Kabardian, no predicative class can be distinguished. Although properties like 'it is bad' or 'it is good' are coded by words which can behave like canonical adjectives in other languages, in the predicative position, they show verb like behavior: e.g., they show TAM marking and person and number agreement. In (40), the standard construction is shown, where the tense value is expressed.

(40)	ʔjejə-ne	mə	pojezd-əm	wə-q̇e-č̣'erəxʷə-nə-r.
	bad-FUT	this	train-OBL	2SG.ABS-DIR-be.late-POT-ABS

'It will be bad if you don't catch this train.'

In (40), the word *ʔjejə-ne* 'it will be bad' contains the typical future marker *-ne*, which is applied here to the adjective *ʔjej* 'bad'. The embedded clause includes a nonfinite predicate in the masdar form meaning 'if we are late'.

As in Russian, in Kabardian the 'missed TAM' strategy can also be used in structures with argument conditional clauses, as in (41) where the main adjectival predicate 'bad' is unmarked (= is in the present tense form), though the situation is situated in future. (41) represents the real condition type and is usually accepted by native speakers. The same strategy is more problematic with unreal conditional clauses than in real ones, also similarly to Russian – most native speakers do not allow it.

(41)	ʔjejə	mə	pojezd-əm	wə-q̇e-č̣'erəxʷə-nə-r.
	bad	this	train-OBL	2SG.ABS-DIR-be.late-POT-ABS

'It will be bad if you don't catch this train.'

It should be noted that the 'missed TAM' strategy in Kabardian does not seem to be a Russian influence. In general, strategies of tense marking in embedded clauses, including conditional clauses, in Kabardian are not affected by Russian impact.

6. Conclusions

In this article, I have shown that in argument conditional clauses, a special phenomenon is observed: I have called it 'missed TAM'. Even if the argument clause with *esli* introduces a situation located in the future or irreal situation, the matrix predicate can lack future or subjunctive tense marking, though this construction is less frequent than the standard one. Only the embedded argument clause is marked for future or subjunctive.

I have claimed that the phenomenon is observed in cases where the matrix predicate is a predicative (plus a zero copula), but never in sentences with a canonical verbal head. This can be motivated purely on semantic grounds. In Russian, predicatives often express meanings of the evaluation group, while these meanings are not characteristic of verbs. Emotional meanings, by contrast, are often expressed by verbs, but they are incompatible with the 'missed TAM' phenomenon. Emotional meanings presuppose direct impact of the event on someone's feelings, which is only possible if the event has already taken place or will take place for sure.

On the other hand, the data analyzed in the article cannot be entirely explained by this semantic analysis. The fact that the 'missed TAM' strategy is more characteristic for predicatives than for verbs seems to result from the fact that verbs express tense synthetically, while with predicatives, tense meaning is only expressed in the copula form. This 'analytic' type of tense expression is easier to omit than the canonical morphological tense. Moreover, the omission of tense marking with predicatives can result from the economy principle, while with verbs, present is no more 'economic' than past and (perfective) future.

However, this kind of explanation is only valid for languages where the distinction between verbs and predicatives (and other non-verbal heads) is applicable. In Kabardian, for instance, where adjective-like heads can get verbal TAM and other markers, the 'missed TAM' strategy also seems to be allowed.

Another syntactic explanation is that predicatives, which can lack a tense or mood marker, can share their tense value with the embedded verb. The same is impossible for verbal heads, which always bear a tense marker. This tense / mood sharing is of particular typological and theoretical interest, because the case when TAM meanings are expressed within the main clause (and remain unexpressed in the embedded one) seems to be much more widespread or at least better studied. The phenomenon under analysis is an exception of this tendency.

Both in Russian and in Kabardian, the 'missed TAM' strategy is more problematic with unreal conditional clauses than with real ones. The reason is that the unreal construction in Russian and Kabardian (as well as in many other languages) employs special TAM forms which are mainly possible in combination with each other. Tense omission in the main clause would lead to a TAM mismatch between the two clauses. In real conditional constructions, similarity of TAM marking in the two clauses is a tendency, rather than a strict grammatical principle.

The main point of my paper is that the grammatical rules of conditional construction formation can be violated if the main predicate is not a verb. The fact that the head is grammatically 'non-standard' makes a syntactically non-standard construction possible. This conclusion is also of typological importance. The behavior of structures with non-canonical predicates in conditional, temporal and other types of complex clauses can be a parameter of cross-linguistic variation. If non-canonical predicates (e.g., copular constructions) behave in a non-standard way, as in Russian, this may show that the morphological features of the predicates are relevant for its syntactic behavior. This conclusion requires to be checked for validity on the data of other languages and language groups.

Notes

1 Abbreviations:
1,2,3 – 1st, 2nd, 3rd person
ABS – absolutive, cross-reference marker of absolutive argument
ACC – accusative
COMP – complementizer
COND – conditional
DIR – directional preverb
ERG – cross-reference marker of ergative agent
FUT – future
IPF - imperfect
INS - instrumental
IRR – irrealis
NOM – nominative
PLSQP – pluperfect
POT – potential / unreal form
PRS – present tense
PST – past tense

2 Given that the inflectional endings in future are the same as in present, the gloss "PRS" is sometimes used for both tenses. However, I use the gloss "FUT" for future tense forms (in the perfective aspect) just to make the glossing clearer.

3 This word order restriction is not typical for Russian. Other types of embedded clauses mainly have free ordering, though they are subject to some tendencies, described by Diessel (2015) in typological perspective.

4 Note that structures like (3) are usually described as containing a zero copula / auxiliary. An interesting question is why the tense value of this copula (e.g., the present tense) can be ignored in missed TAM constructions. The preliminary answer is that structures the zero copula (contrary to their analogues with overt copula forms) are, in general, able to accommodate to grammatical values of other clauses (see Letuchiy 2015a for argumentation).

5 Since **imperfective future** is periphrastic in Russian (it is marked by the indicative form of the verb *byt'* 'be', e.g. *bud-et* (be.FUT-3SG)), I counted here examples where the form of the verb *byt'* is located immediately before or after the imperfective form / the predicative or is only separated from it by one word. Another periphrastic form is **subjunctive**: as mentioned before, it contains of the particle *by* and a past tense form. With predicatives, subjunctive is marked by the combination of the particle *by*, a past tense form of the verb *byt'* 'be' and a predicative. For verbs, I searched for subjunctive as a context in which the particle *by* either immediately precedes or follows a past tense form or is located before a past tense form and is separated from it by one word (if the particle follows the verb, it tends not to be separated from the verb form). For predicatives, I searched for a combination of the particle *by* and a past tense form of *byt'* (in any linear order) which is either siutated immediately before or after a predicative or is separated by one word from the predicative.

Bibliography

Athanasiadou, Angeliki, and René Dirven (eds.). 1997. *On Conditionals Again* (Current issues in linguistic theory 143). Amsterdam and Philadelphia: John Benjamins.

Barentsen, Adrian. 1995. Shifting points of orientation in Modern Russian. Tense selection in 'reported perception'. *Reported Speech: Form and Functions of the Verb*, ed. by Theo Janssen and Wim van der Wurff, 15–55. Amsterdam and Philadelphia: John Benjamins.

Boye, Kasper. 2012. *Epistemic Meaning: A Crosslinguistic and Functional-Cognitive Study*. Berlin, New York: Mouton de Gruyter.

Diessel, Holger. 2015. Competing motivations for the ordering of main and adverbial clauses. *Linguistics* 43.3. 449–70.

Dobrushina, Nina R. 2012. Soslagatel'noe naklonenie. Online.

Dobrushina, Nina R. 2016. *Russkoe soslagatel'noe naklonenie: opyt issledovanija grammatičeskoj semantiki*. Prague: Artmedia Company.

Khomitsevich, Olga. 2007. *Dependencies across Phases. From Sequence of Tense to Restrictions on Movement*. Utrecht: University of Utrecht, Ph.D. dissertation.

KHRAKOVSKIJ, VIKTOR S. (ed.). 2005. *Typology of Conditional Constructions*. (LINCOM studies in theoretical linguistics 25). München: LINCOM Europa.

KHRAKOVSKIJ, VIKTOR S. (ed.). 2009. *Tipologija taksisnyx konstrukcij* [Typology of Taxis Constructions]. Znak: Moscow.

KIPARSKY, PAUL, and CAROL KIPARSKY. 1971. Fact. *Semantics: An Interdisciplinary Reader*, ed. by Leon Jakobovits and Danny Steinberg, 345–369. Cambridge: Cambridge University Press.

KNJAZEV, MIKHAIL YU. 2009. *Predikatnye aktanty s mestoimeniem* to *v russkom jazyke: Grammatičeskij status i osobennosti upotreblenija* [Complement clauses with the pronoun *to* in Russian: Grammatical status and contexts of use]. BA thesis. Saint-Petersburg: Saint Petersburg University.

LETUCHIY, ALEXANDER B. 2012. O nekotoryx svojstvax sentencial'nyx aktantov v russkom jazyke. [On some properties of complement clauses in Russian]. *Voprosy jazykoznanija* 5. 57–87.

LETUCHIY, ALEXANDER B. 2015. Factivity and unreal contexts: The Russian case. *Donvm Semanticum. Opera lingvistica et logica in honorem Barbarae Partee a discipvlis amicisqve Rossicis oblate*, ed. by Ekaterina V. Rakhilina et al., 158–179. Moscow: Jazyki slavjanskoj kul'tury.

LETUCHIY, ALEXANDER B. 2015a. Russian zero copulas and lexical verbs: Similar or different? *Lingue e linguaggio* XIV.2. 233–49.

NOONAN, MICHAEL. 2007. Complementation. *Language Typology and Syntactic Description 2: Complex Constructions*, ed. by Timothy Shopen, 52–150. Cambridge: Cambridge University Press.

PADUČEVA, ELENA V. 1985. *Vyskazyvanie i ego sootnesennost' s dejstvitel'nost'ju* [Utterance and its correspondence with the reality]. Moscow: Nauka.

QUER, JOSEP. 1999. Non-Logical if. *Current Issues in Romance Languages. Selected Papers from the 29th Linguistic Symposium on Romance Languages, Ann Arbor, 8–11 April 1999*, ed. by Teresa Satterfield, Christina Tortora, and Diana Cresti, 241–55. Amsterdam and Philadelphia: John Benjamins.

ROY, ISABELLE. 2013. *Non-Verbal Predication. Copular Sentences at the Syntax-Semantics Interface*. Oxford: Oxford University Press.

SCHLENKER, PHILIPPE. 2003. A plea for monsters. *Linguistics & Philosophy* 26. 29–120.

SCHWABE, KERSTIN. 2015. On the licensing of argument conditionals. *Logic, Language and Computation, 10th International Tbilisi Symposium TbiLLC 2013*, ed. by Martin Aher, Emil Jerabek, Daniel Hole, and Clemens Kupke, 1–20. Berlin, Heidelberg: Springer Verlag.

Švedova, Natalia Yu. 1980. *Russkaja grammatika* [A grammar of Russian]. Moscow: Nauka.

Tynan, John, and Eva Delgado Lavin. 1997. Mood, tense, and the interpretation of conditionals. *On Conditionals Again* (Current issues in linguistic theory 143), ed. by Angeliki Athanasiadou and René Dirven, 115–144. Amsterdam, Philadelphia: John Benjamins.

Franc Lanko Marušič and Rok Žaucer

Investigation of Slovenian Copular Agreement

Abstract This paper reports on a detailed investigation of agreement inside simple predicative sentences. In this type of sentence, both noun phrases are in the nominative, so in principle either one can trigger agreement on the copular verb. We examine various types of copular constructions and show that regardless of the type of predicative sentence, when a plural is combined with a singular, it is always the plural that agrees. Similarly, when a dual is combined with a singular, the dual wins out. But when we combine a dual and a plural, the copula can agree with either of the two noun phrases, with a preference for the noun phrase following the copula. We discuss the relevance of these findings for the recent literature on predication.*

Keywords: Slovenian, Syntax, Copular Clauses, Number Agreement

1. Introduction

An old observation about copular number agreement in Slovenian, which goes back at least to Breznik (1934), holds that the copular verb in Slovenian agrees with the plural nominal rather than with what appears to be the surface subject, (1). The most influential reference grammar of Slovenian (Toporišič 2000:609) describes this as follows: "The subject has no influence on predicate agreement when the predicate noun is in the plural or the dual" (our translation), giving (2) and (3) as examples. Toporišič (2000) also gives (4), which combines a plural noun phrase with a noun phrase coordinating two singular nouns but does not comment on this single example or on the generality of its pattern. He also makes no claim as to what happens when a dual and a plural noun phrase are combined.

(1)	Smrt	so	vrata	v	nebesa.	(Breznik 1934:p. 217)
	death.SG	AUX.PL	door.PL	to	heaven	
	'Death is the doors to heaven.'					

* We would like to thank the audience of the SLS 2019 at the University of Potsdam, Potsdam, Germany for comments and discussion, and Steven Franks for comments on an earlier version of this paper. This work was partially supported by Slovenian Research Agency/ARRS grants P6-0382 and N6-0113.

(2) To mesto so Brežice. (Toporišič 2000:p. 609)
this town.SG AUX.PL Brežice.PL
'This town is Brežice.'

(3) Ta par sta Rodinova ljubimca. (Toporišič 2000:p. 609)
this couple.SG AUX.DU Rodin's.DU lover.DU
'This couple is Rodin's lovers.'

(4) Starši sta oče in mati. (Toporišič 2000:p. 609)
parents AUX.DU father and mother
'Parents are a father and a mother.'

A further set of illustrating examples of this type is in (5) below.

(5) a. Ta vas so Ponikve.
this village.SG AUX.PL Ponikve.PL
'This village is Ponikve.'

b. To pobočje so Lašte.
this slope.SG AUX.PL Lašte.PL
'This slope is Lašte.'

c. Ta risanka sta Lolek in Bolek.
this cartoon.SG AUX.DU Lolek.SG and Bolek.SG
'This cartoon is Bolek and Lolek.'

Breznik (1934) and Toporišič (2000) do not attempt to provide an explanation, they just describe the facts. Even from a descriptive perspective, however, there is room for improvement. First, the discussions in Breznik (1934) and Toporišič (2000) include examples of only a subset of the different types of predicative clauses that have been described in the literature. And secondly, they only mention two combinations of non-matching-number noun phrases, failing to mention what happens when a dual and a plural noun phrase are combined.

In this paper we explore these structures a bit more systematically, determine what the relation between dual and plural noun phrases in copular structures is, and see if Slovenian copular agreement can tell us something about copular constructions more generally. Note that certain aspects of copular-clause agreement patterns have received a lot of attention in the literature (agreement with NP1, NP2, etc.), see den Dikken and O'Neill (2017), Heycock (2012), etc. But these discussions seem irrelevant for the pattern described so far since the shared observation from the traditional Slovenian literature was simply: the plural and the dual always win out over the singular.

2. Copular Clauses

Different types of copular clauses [hereafter CC] that involve two noun phrases have been identified. Typically CCs are divided into: identificational CCs [ICC], as in (6a), predicational CCs [PCC], as in (6b), specificational CCs [SCC], as in (6c), and equative CCs [ECC], as in (6d), see Higgins (2015), den Dikken and O'Neill (2017), etc.

(6) a. This is X. → ICC
b. X is my favorite Y. → PCC
c. My favorite Y is X. → SCC
d. X is Y. → ECC

This classification has been questioned, among others, by den Dikken (2006), Mikkelsen (2005), Heycock (2012). For the most part these alternative views have proposed to reduce the four categories into a smaller set of categories by merging various types of CC together. Den Dikken (2006), for example, collapses SCCs and ECCs.

CCs that have the shape *A is B* are typically composed of a subject and a predication, where it is not always obvious which of the two noun phrases is the subject and which one is the predication. If we can identify which of the two noun phrases is the subject, it may be possible to make a further division on the basis of the definiteness or other similar properties of the subject noun phrase and of the predicate noun phrase. We will not, however, spend much time discussing the classification; we will simply adopt it in order to present the Slovenian agreement facts.

2.1. Plural Agreement in Copular Clauses

As explained in Section 1, whenever one of the noun phrases in a CC is plural and the other singular, the copula agrees with the plural noun phrase. This is true of ICCs, i.e. CCs of the type given in (7).

(7) This is X_{PL}. ICC

Example (8) demonstrates this for ICCs with definite NPs, example (9) for ICCs with indefinite NPs and example (10) for ICCs with a personal pronoun.

(8)	To	(mesto)	{*je	/	so}	Brežice.
	this.SG	town.SG	AUX.SG		AUX.PL	Brežice.PL

'This is Brežice.'

(9)	a.	To	{*je	/	so}	ene	hlače.
		this.SG	AUX.SG		AUX.PL	some	pants.PL

'This is some pair of pants.'

b.	Ta	kos	obleke	{ *je	/	so}	ene	hlače.
	this.SG	piece.SG	clothing.GEN.SG	AUX.SG		AUX.PL	some	pants.PL

'This piece of clothing is some pair of pants.'

(10)	To	{* je	/ so}	oni.
	this.SG	AUX.SG	AUX.PL	they.PL

'This is them.'

The distribution of the syntactic roles of the two noun phrases is irrelevant to this patterning, so that reversing the syntactic roles of the plural and the singular noun phrases has no effect on agreement, which is still plural. This is shown in (12)–(14), which all represent the format given in (11).

(11) These Y_{PL} are X_{SG}. ICC

(12)

Tile	hribi	{* je	/ so}	Martuljkova	skupina.
this.PL	mountains.PL	AUX.SG	AUX.PL	Martuljek.SG	group.SG

'These mountains are the Martuljek group.'

(13)

Martuljkova	skupina	{* je	/ so}	tile	hribi.
Martuljek.SG	group.SG	AUX.SG	AUX.PL	this.PL	mountains.PL

'The Martuljek group is these mountains.'

(14)

Tile	kamni	{* je	/ so}	ena	stara	hiša.
this.PL	rock.PL	AUX.SG	AUX.PL	one.SG	old.SG	house.SG

'These rocks are an old house.'

The next type of CCs we look at are PCCs, i.e. CCs with the shape from (15) below.

(15) X_{PL} are my favorite $NOUN_{SG}$. PCC

In this type, too, agreement on the copula is always with the plural noun phrase, regardless of the definiteness of the subject noun phrase. Example (16) demonstrates this for definite, and (17) for indefinite subjects.

(16)

Brežice	{* je	/ so}	moje	najljubše	mesto.
Brežice.PL	AUX.SG	AUX.PL	my.SG	favorite.SG	town.SG

'Brežice is my favorite town.'

(17)

Hlače	{* je	/ so}	moje	najljubše	oblačilo.
pants.PL	AUX.SG	AUX.PL	my.SG	favorite.SG	clothing.SG

'Pants are my favorite piece of clothing.'

If the syntactic roles of the plural and the singular noun phrases are reversed, as in (18), the plural still wins out, as shown in (19)–(20).

(18) X_{SG} are my favorite NOUN_{PL}. PCC

(19)

Martuljkova	skupina	{* je	/ so}	moji	najljubši	hribi.
Martuljek.SG	group.SG	AUX.SG	AUX.PL	my.PL	favorite.PL	mountain.PL

'The Martuljek group are my favorite mountains.'

(20)

Nočna	mora	{* je	/ so}	moje	najljubše	sanje.
night.SG	nightmare.SG	AUX.SG	AUX.PL	my.PL	favorite.PL	dream.PL

'A nightmare is my favorite dream.'

Moving on to the next type of CCs, we present examples of the type from (21a) and (21b) below, i.e., SCCs.

(21) a. My favorite NOUN_{SG} are X_{PL}. SCC
b. My favorite NOUN_{PL} are X_{SG}.

In this type of construction, a plural noun phrase in any syntactic role forces the agreement on the copular verb to be plural, as demonstrated in the set of examples from (22) through (25). Note that this is true regardless of the position / syntactic role of the plural noun phrase and regardless of its definiteness. In (22) it is the second noun phrase that is in the plural, and it is a definite noun phrase; in (23) the plural is on an indefinite noun phrase in the second position; and in (24)–(25), it is the first noun phrase that is in the plural (whereas the second noun phrase is singular definite and singular indefinite, respectively).

(22)

Moje	najljubše	mesto	{* je	/ so}	Jesenice.
my.SG	favorite.SG	town.SG	AUX.SG	AUX.PL	Jesenice.PL

'My favorite town is Jesenice.'

(23)

Moja	najljubša	obleka	{* je	/ so}	hlače.
my.SG	favorite.SG	clothing.SG	AUX.SG	AUX.PL	pants.PL

'My favorite clothing is pants.'

(24)

Moji	najljubši	hribi	{* je	/ so}	Martuljkova	skupina.
my.PL	favorite.PL	mountain.PL	AUX.SG	AUX.PL	Martuljek.SG	group.SG

'My favorite mountains are the Martuljek group.'

(25)

Moje	najljubše	sanje	{* je	/ so}	nočna	mora.
my.PL	favorite.PL	dream.PL	AUX.SG	AUX.PL	night.SG	nightmare.SG

'My favorite dream is a nightmare.'

Turning to the last type of CCs, we present ECCs, i.e. the CC type in (26).

(26) a. X_{SG} are Y_{PL}. ECC
b. X_{PL} are Y_{SG}.

On a par with the other types of CCs presented above, ECCs also exhibit plural agreement on the copula regardless of the relative order of the singular and the plural noun phrase, as demonstrated in (27) and (28).

(27) a.

Topničarji	{* je	/ so}	Arsenal.
Gunners.PL	AUX.SG	AUX.PL	Arsenal.SG

'The Gunners are Arsenal.'

b.

Arsenal	{* je	/ so}	Topničarji.
Arsenal.SG	AUX.SG	AUX.PL	Gunners.PL

'Arsenal is the Gunners.'

(28) *Context: At a costume party three people are dressed up as a single person (or vice versa).*

a.

Oni	{* je	/ so}	on.
They.PL	AUX.SG	AUX.PL	he.SG

'They are him.'

b.

On	{* je	/ so}	oni.
he.SG	AUX.SG	AUX.PL	they.SG

'He is they.'

To briefly recapitulate, this section showed, echoing previous literature, that in CCs that combine a plural noun phrase and a singular noun phrase, agreement is always plural. We systematically demonstrated for all four types of CCs typically posited in the literature that this holds irrespectively of the distribution of the syntactic roles / relative order of the singular and the plural noun phrase, as well as of characteristics such as definiteness, or the common noun / pronoun distinction.

A Note on Personal Pronouns

Note that personal pronouns behave differently, which is why we have avoided examples where a personal pronoun cooccurs with a noun phrase in a copular clause. In short there is a preference for agreement with the pronoun in the construction, but this preference is not absolute. Firstly, first and second person pronouns always win regardless of number, (29)–(30). Between first and second person, in an ECC, whichever comes first (whichever is in the subject position) is the one that will win, (31).

(29) a. Jaz {sem / * so} možgani te operacije. PCC
I AUX.1P.SG AUX.3P.PL brains.PL this operation
'I am the brains of this operation.'

b. Možgani te operacije {sem / * so} jaz. SCC
brains.PL this operation AUX.1P.SG AUX.3P.PL I
'The brains of this operation is me.'

(30) a. Ti {si / * so} možgani naše ekipe. PCC
you.SG AUX.2P.SG AUX.3P.PL brains.PL this operation
'You are the brains of our team.'

b. Možgani naše ekipe {si / * so} ti. SCC
brains.PL our team AUX.2P.SG AUX.3P.PL you.SG
'The brains of our team is you.'

(31)	a.	Jaz	{sem	/ * si}	ti.	ECC
		I	AUX.1P.SG	AUX.2P.SG	you.SG	
		'I am you.'				
	b.	Ti	{* sem	/ si}	jaz.	ECC
		you.SG	AUX.1P.SG	AUX.2P.SG	I.	
		'You are me.'				

The situation with third person pronouns is slightly more complicated, which may be partially related to reasons that will become clear in Section 4. In PCCs and SCCs, when a plural personal pronoun is used the plural wins out, (32), which is in accordance with the claim we just presented about the advantage of personal pronouns in the determination of agreement.

(32)	a.	Oni	{* je	/ so}	moja	najljubša	ekipa.	PCC
		they.PL	AUX.SG	AUX.PL	my.SG	favorite.SG	team.SG	
		'They are my favorite team.'						
	b.	Moja	najljubša	ekipa	{* je	/ so}	oni.	SCC
		my.SG	favorite.SG	team.SG	AUX.SG	AUX.PL	they.PL	
		'My favorite team is them.'						

But when the personal pronoun is third person singular, it is not the pronoun that wins, as shown in (33).

(33)	a.	Pazi	na	Zidana!	On	{* je	/ so}	možgani	te	ekipe.	PCC
		watch	on	Zidane	he.SG	AUX.SG	AUX.PL	brain.PL	this	team	
		'Watch Zidane! He is the brains of this team.'									
	b.	Pazi	na	Zidana!	Možgani	te	ekipe	{* je	/ so}	on.	SCC
		watch	on	Zidan	brain.PL	this	team	AUX.SG	AUX.PL	he.SG	
		'Watch Zidane! The brains of this team is him.'									

Even ICCs, such as (34), behave alike. While third person plural pronouns win, third person singular pronouns do not, (35).

(34)	a.	Verjameš	v	vesoljce?	Tista	pikica	{* je	/ so}	oni.	ICC
		believe	in	aliens.PL	that	dot.SG	AUX.SG	AUX.PL	they.PL	
		'Do you believe in aliens? That dot is them.'								

b. Verjameš v vesoljce? Oni {* je / so} tista pikica. ICC
believe in aliens.PL they.PL AUX.SG AUX.PL that dot.SG
'Do you believe in aliens? They are that dot.'

(35) a. Poznaš Vidovo mamo? Tele čačke {* je / so} ona. ICC
know Vid's mom this.PL scribble.PL AUX.SG AUX.PL she.SG
'Do you know Vid's mom? These scribbles are her.'

b. Poznaš Vidovo mamo? Ona {?? je / so} tele čačke. ICC
know Vid's mom she.SG AUX.SG AUX.PL this.PL scribble.PL
'Do you know Vid's mom? She is these scribbles.'

A similar situation holds for ECC, except that judgments are less sharp in these cases. A third person plural pronoun wins when combined with a singular noun phrase, (36), but when a singular third person pronoun is used with a plural noun phrase, both auxiliaries seem possible, (37).

(36) a. Vidite te ljudi? Oni {* je / so} Valter. ECC
see these people.PL they.PL AUX.SG AUX.PL Valter.SG
'Do you see these people? They are Valter.'

b. Vidite te ljudi? Valter {* je / so} oni.
see these people.PL Valter.SG AUX.SG AUX.PL they.PL
'Do you see these people? Valter is them.'

(37) a Poznaš Dalija? On {? je /? so} nadrealisti. ECC
know Dali he.SG AUX.SG AUX.PL surrealists.PL
'Do you know Dali? He is the surrealists.'

b. Poznaš Dalija? Nadrealisti {* je /? so} on.
know Dali surrealists.PL AUX.SG AUX.PL he.SG
'Do you know Dali? He is the surrealists.'

In what follows, we will only use copular clauses with two noun phrases or copular clauses with two third person pronouns, in order to avoid a possible interference of person.

2.2. Dual Agreement in Copular Clauses

Just like with combinations of a plural and a singular noun phrase in CCs, combinations of a dual and a singular noun phrase can also generally be said to trigger non-singular agreement on the copula. This is shown in (38) for ICCs, in (39)–(40) for PCCs, in (41)–(42) for SCCs, and in (43)–(44) for ECCs.

(38)	To	{* je	/ sta}	onadva /	Rodinova	ljubimca	/ dvojčka.		ICC
	this.SG	AUX.SG	AUX.DU	they.DU	Rodin's	lovers.DU	twins.DU		
	'This is them / Rodin's lovers / twins.'								

(39)	Ribi	{?* je	/ sta}	moje	najljubše	znamenje.	PCC
	fish.DU	AUX.SG	AUX.DU	my.SG	favorite.SG	sign.SG	
	'The Pisces is my favorite zodiac sign.'						

(40)	Rodinova	ljubimca	{?* je	/ sta}	moj	najljubši	kip.	PCC
	Rodin's	lovers.DU	AUX.SG	AUX.DU	my.SG	favorite.SG	statue.SG	
	'Rodin's lovers is my favorite statue.'							

(41)	Moje	najljubše	znamenje	{?* je	/ sta}	ribi.	SCC
	my.SG	favorite.SG	sign.SG	AUX.SG	AUX.DU	fish.DU	
	'My favorite sign is the Pisces.'						

(42) Moj najljubši kip {?* je / sta} Rodinova ljubimca. SCC
my.SG favorite.SG statue.SG AUX.SG AUX.DU Rodin's lovers.DU
'My favorite statue are Rodin's lovers.'

(43) a. Dvojčka {* je / sta} WTC. ECC
twins.DU AUX.SG AUX.DU WTC.SG
'The Twin Towers are the WTC.'

b. WTC {* je / sta} dvojčka. ECC
WTC.SG AUX.SG AUX.DU twins.DU
'The WTC are the Twin Towers.'

(44) *Context: At a costume party two people are dressed up as a single person (or vice versa).*

a. Onadva {* je / sta} on. ECC
They.DU AUX.SG AUX.DU he.SG
'They are him.'

b. On {* je / sta} onadva. ECC
he.DU AUX.SG AUX.DU they.SG
'He is they.'

The dual unequivocally wins out in ICCs and ECCs. In PCCs and SCCs, our judgments on combinations of a singular and a dual noun phrase are somewhat less straightforward (as indicated in (39) through (42)); even in these cases, however, the dual still seems more natural to us. Furthermore, while the singular may be less clearly impossible in these cases, the perfect acceptability of the dual is always undisputed.

2.3. [Dual] is [Plural] / [Plural] is [Dual]

While the judgments for the two combinations presented above, i.e., [Singular] is [Plural] and [Singular] is [Dual], are fairly clear, the two combinations involving a dual noun phrase and a plural noun phrase are far less obvious. To set the stage, we start off by presenting some examples for which the judgments seem rather clear. These data suggest that at least at first sight, neither the dual nor the plural can be said to clearly take precedence over the other number. In ECCs it seems that it is the dual that takes precedence over the plural, (45)–(46).

(45) *Context: 'Two Spikes' and '(Three) White Heads' are alternative names for the same mountain (e.g. a mountain that is seen as two spikes from one valley and as three peaks from another valley).*

a.

Dve	špici	{sta	/? so}	(Tri)	Bele	glave.	ECC
two	spikes.DU	AUX.DU	AUX.PL	three	white.PL	heads.PL	

'The Two Spikes are the (Three) White Heads.'

b.

(Tri)	Bele	glave	{sta	/?? so}	Dve	špici.
three	white.PL	heads.PL	AUX.DU	AUX.PL	two	spikes.DU

'The (Three) White Heads are the Two Spikes.'

(46) *Context: Suppose that two physics experiments observed a similar event but interpreted it differently, e.g., LHC interpreted it as two pions, while Belle interpreted it as four mesons.*

a.

LHC-jeva	piona	{sta	/? so}	Bellovi	mezoni.	ECC
LHC's	pion.DU	AUX.DU	AUX.PL	Bell's	meson.PL	

'LHC's pions are Bell's mesons.'

b.

Bellovi	mezoni	{sta	/?* so}	LHC-jeva	piona.
Bell's	meson.PL	AUX.DU	AUX.PL	LHC's	pion.DU

'Bell's mesons are LHC's pions.'

Since there seems to be a preference for agreement with pronouns, as shown in Section 2.1., we would expect a plural pronoun to require plural agreement and a dual pronoun to require dual agreement, so we need to look at cases where pronouns are used on both sides of the copula. When both a dual and a plural pronoun are used, as in (47), judgments become less clear. It seems that for some speakers it is the relative position of the two pronouns that may be the decisive factor, for others the phi-features of the pronouns, e.g., with first person pronouns possibly attracting agreement more than third person pronouns.[1]

(47) *Context: At a costume party two people are dressed up as three people (or vice versa).*

a. Onadva {??sta /?so} oni. ECC
they.DU AUX.DU AUX.PL they.PL
'The two of them are them.'

b. Oni {sta /??so} onadva. ECC
they.PL AUX.DU AUX.PL they.DU
'They are the two of them.'

In line with the relatively greater difficulty of determining the winning pattern of agreement, as demonstrated above, the split between acceptable and unacceptable versions is rather unclear, too. While in many cases the dual-agreement version seems better, the plural-agreement version does not seem completely ungrammatical either, e.g., (48)–(50).

(48) Ti dve stvari {sta /??so} Rodinovi Calaijski meščani. ICC
these two things.DU AUX.DU AUX.PL Rodin's.PL Calais.PL burghers.PL
'These two things are Rodin's Burghers of Calais.'

(49) Ta dva kovančka {bosta /??bojo} snežakove oči. ICC
these two coin.DU AUX.DU AUX.PL snowman's.PL eye.PL
'These two coins will be snowman's eyes.'

(50) Te tri stvari {sta /??so} Rodinova ljubimca. ICC
these three things.PL AUX.DU AUX.PL Rodin's.DU lovers.DU
'These three things are Rodin's lovers.'

Similarly, our judgments for the lone plural-dual example from Toporišič (2000), i.e., for (4) above, repeated here as (51), are also not very clear-cut. Plural agreement is certainly possible, but depending on other factors, such as the position of the copula relative to the two noun phrases, one or the other agreement can be prefered.

(51) Starši sta oče in mati. (= example (4))
parents.PL AUX.DU father.SG and mother.SG
'Parents are a father and a mother.' (Toporišič 2000:p. 609)

(52) Starši so oče in mati.
parents.PL AUX.PL father.SG and mother.SG
'Parents are a father and a mother.'

In order to address the questions left open by these murky judgments, we set up an online experiment testing agreement in copular clauses. The methodology and results of this experiment will be presented in the following sections.

3. Experiment

3.1. Methodology

The experiment was carried out online using the Ibex Farm tool (Drummond 2011). The experiment consisted of 30 test examples grouped in 5 conditions, with an additional 30 fillers (which were test items for a different experiment) and 8 practice examples. The 30 target items were interspersed with the 30 fillers.

For every test example, subjects were asked to fill the gap by selecting, from the given three options, the auxiliary they found most appropriate for a particular copular sentence. For all examples, the list they had to choose from consisted of the singular, the dual and the plural forms of the present-tense auxiliary, which were always presented all at the same time and always in the same order: *je – sta – so* "is – are.DU – are.PL".

The conditions we tested were as given in (53)–(57). As reported above, there does not seem to be any real difference in number agreement between ICCs, PCCs, SCCs, and ECCs, which is why we did not differentiate between the four types of constructions in our experiment. All examples were ICCs, in which one of the noun phrases started with a demonstrative.[2] Additionally, having a demonstrative in the first or the second noun phrase was also incorporated in the experiment as a variable, such that approximately half of the sentences had the demonstrative in the first noun phrase and the other half in the second noun phrase.[3]

(53) SINGULAR copula PLURAL

Petrovo	kosilo	___	tista	kurja	bedrca	v	pečici.
Peter's	lunch.SG		this	chicken	legs.PL	in	oven

'Peter's lunch are these two chicken legs in the oven.'

(54) SINGULAR copula DUAL

Tale	kupček	kamenja	___	zadnja	kipa	lokalnega	kiparja.
this	pile.SG	stone		last	figure.DU	local	sculptor

'This pile of stones are the last two figures of a local sculptor.'

(55) DUAL copula SINGULAR

Tista	dva	pomečkana	lista	___	naša	kupoprodajna	pogodba.
this	two	crushed	papers.DU		our	selling	contract.SG

'These two crushed papers are our selling contract.'

(56) DUAL copula PLURAL

Ta	dva	polkroga	___	tvoji	možgani.
this	two	half-circles.DU		your	brains.PL

'These two half-circles are your brains.'

(57) PLURAL copula DUAL

Vse	knjige	iz	naše	knjižnice	___	ta	dva	kupa	papirja.
all	books.PL	from	our	library		this	two	piles.DU	paper

'All books from our library are these two piles of paper.'

Note that in the singular–plural combination we only tested the SINGULAR copula PLURAL condition. As we demonstrated in Section 2.1 above, the singular–plural combination generally seems clear and thus not in need of additional experimental verification. Therefore, we decided to include one of the orders for this combination (i.e., the SINGULAR copula PLURAL condition) in the experiment as a control condition, and to leave the other condition for this combination (i.e., the PLURAL copula SINGULAR condition) out of the experiment in order to keep the number of test items and hence the size of the experiment managable for the subjects.

3.2. Participants

The experiment was posted online on the KSEnJa website (https://sites.google.com/view/ksenja) and then advertised through social media. Twenty-five participants completed the experiment. Four participants were excluded because they self-reported coming from an area where the local dialect is a predominantly non-dual variety of Slovenian.[4]

3.3. Results

The results of our experiment are in Tab. 1. We ran a number of tests on the data. First we wanted to know whether the presence of the demonstrative in one of the two noun phrases had any effect on the type of agreement (i.e., on whether the chosen agreement was with the noun phrase containg the demonstrative or not). We fitted a linear mixed model to predict this interaction. The model included Subject and Item as random effects. Standardized parameters were obtained by fitting the model on a standardized version of the dataset. The model's total explanatory power is substantial (conditional R2 = 0.58) and the part related to the fixed effects alone (marginal R2) is of 5.56e–05. Within this model, the effect of having the demonstrative is not significant (beta = 7.32e–03, SE = 0.10, std. beta = 0.02, p = 0.943). For the remainder of the analysis we are treating the two conditions (having the demonstrative in the first noun phrase, having the demonstrative in the second noun phrase) as a single condition.

Given what we concluded about copular clauses combining a plural and a singular noun phrase in Section 2.1 above and as explained in Section 3.1, we used the condition SG copula PL (as in example (53)) as a control condition. Our judgments, as well as judgments less systematically reported in previous literature, indicate that the agreement options in this condition are clear: plural agreement seems to be the only possibility. As shown in Tab. 1 our experimental setting yielded over 95 % of plural in this condition, 0 % of dual and under 5 % of singular. Given that the singular seems impossible in this condition, we assume that these 5 % of singular responses are essentially errors, possibly a type of attraction error in the sense of Bock and Miller (1991).[5]

Tab. 1: Summary of the results of our agreement experiment. The shaded cells either have 0 % or else their response is so low that we consider it an error, possibly an attraction error.

	Singular	Dual	Plural
SG copula PL	4.76 %	0.00 %	95.24 %
SG copula DU	7.94 %	92.06 %	0.00 %
DU copula SG	5.56 %	93.65 %	0.79 %
PL copula DU	0.00 %	63.49 %	36.51 %
DU copula PL	0.79 %	26.98 %	72.22 %

A similar amount of singular responses were recorded also in the two conditions with dual and singular noun phrases – SG copula DU and DU copula SG. In both cases the predominantly selected form of the copula was the dual *sta*, in both cases over 92 %, but some singular responses were also recorded. A Welch two sample t-test shows that the amount of singular in these two conditions is not different from the amount of singular in condition SG copula PL, where we assumed the singular to be a type of (attraction) error (comparing amounts of the singular in SG copula DU and SG copula PL: $t = -0.9325$, $df = 38.826$, p-value = 0.3568; comparing amounts of the singular in DU copula SG and SG copula PL: $t = -0.2132$, $df = 39.987$, p-value = 0.8323).

Given the similarity of these effects, we assume that in these two conditions the singular should also be seen as a type of (attraction) error. This means, in turn, that we can conclude that dual agreement is the only option for copular clauses combining a dual and a singular noun phrase, much like what we had explained to be the case for copular clauses combining a plural and a singular noun phrase.

Tab. 2: Results of the two conditions with dual and plural noun phrases.

	Dual	Plural
PL copula DU	63.49 % ≈ 2/3	36.51 % ≈ 1/3
DU copula PL	26.98 % ≈ 1/3	72.22 % ≈ 2/3

Performing a Welch two sample t-test on the other results, we see that the dual and the plural responses in the DU copula PL condition and the PL copula DU condition (percentages are given in Table 2), respectively, are significantly different from the assumed attraction error (dual in DU copula PL vs. singular in SG copula DU: t = 2.6487, df = 24.039, p-value = 0.01405), while they are not significantly different from each other (t = -1.0186, df = 39.785, p-value = 0.3146). The same is true if we compare dual responses in the PL copula DU condition with plural responses in the DU copula PL condition (t = 0.94186, df = 39.87, p-value = 0.3519); statistically speaking, there is no difference between the two results.

3.4. Discussion

In support of claims from the previous literature, our study confirms that the plural and the dual always win out over the singular, regardless of the type of copular construction; we corroborated these claims with an additional, more systematic set of introspection-based data, and we also provided experimental data for one of the orders of the singular-plural combination and for both orders of the singular-dual combination.

A possible explanation for why the plural and the dual would consistently win out over the singular is relative markedness. Formally speaking, the plural and the dual are generally viewed as more marked than the singular, so the fact that in singular-plural and singular-dual combinations agreement is plural and dual, respectively, can be attributed to the higher markedness of these number values. If we extend such a formal markedness-based explanation to the dual-plural combination, we presumably predict that the dual will win out over the plural given that the dual is typically considered more marked than the plural (e.g. Greenberg 1963, Nevins 2011). This prediction does not seem to be borne out, however, given that the dual-plural combination did not yield a clear winner. (Note that not having a clear winner also means that it cannot simply be the case that the relative markedness was determined incorrectly and that it is in fact the plural that is more marked; if that was the case, then the plural should consistently win out over the dual, but our results show a situation without a clear winner.)

Another possible approach that could be seen in the context of markedness is couched in the semantics of the singular, dual and plural. It has been claimed that the plural is actually semantically number-neutral and can as such sometimes be used for any number (Sauerland 2003, 2008: among others). This is reflected in the Sauerland (2003)-based example in (58), which is false even if Lina has one child (cf. also Martí 2020), as well as in the fact that the question from (59a) can also be answered with the singular, as in (59b) (Marušič and Žaucer 2021).

(58) Lina nima otrok.
Lina NEG-has child.GEN.PL
'Lina doesn't have children.'

(59) a. Ali ima Črt otroke?
Q has Črt child.ACC.PL
'Does Črt have children?'
b. Ja, ima enega.
yes has one
'Yes, he has one.'

Similarly, the dual has been claimed to be semantically less restricted than the singular, essentially meaning 'one or two' and therefore able to also cover reference to singular items, whereas the singular is said to be narrower and thus not able to cover reference to dual sets (Dvořák and Sauerland 2006, Sauerland 2008). With respect to the agreement patterns that our study identified, this approach correctly predicts that the dual and the plural will strictly win out over the singular. However, the prediction that this approach makes with respect to the dual-plural combinations is not quite borne out: the prediction of this approach would be that the plural will strictly win out over the dual, but the results of our study do not identify either the plural or the dual as a clear winner.

4. The Bigger Picture

Our data show that in Slovenian copular constructions agreement is neither strictly with NP1 nor strictly with NP2, but that it is rather sensitive to the featural specifications of the two noun phrases.

All the examples we have seen above were with mixed-numbered noun phrases. We were not explicit about this above (nor did our experiment test for this), but undisputedly, when the two noun phrases are both singular, the copula is also singular, and no other form of the copula is possible, as shown in (60).[6] Similarly, copular clauses with two dual noun phrases can only have dual agreement, and copular clauses with two plural noun phrases can only have plural agreement.

(60)	Ta	avto	{je	/ * sta	/ * so}	Petrin	fičko.
	this	car.SG	AUX.SG	AUX.DU	AUX.PL	Petra's.SG	fičko.SG

'This car is Petra's fičko.'

Leaving such simple copular clauses with same-numbered noun phrases aside, let us start the discussion by restricting ourselves to copular constructions with non-pronominal mixed-numbered noun phrases. The fact that if a non-singular noun phrase exists the copula agrees with the non-singular noun phrase can be modeled if we assume that the probe is looking for a feature in both directions and if we assume that number features are privative (an assumption shared also by Preminger 2014, Franks 2020, among others), that is, if singular means the absence of [plural]/[dual]. With these two assumptions, the first part falls out naturally. Sample derivations are sketched in (61).

(61) Sample derivations

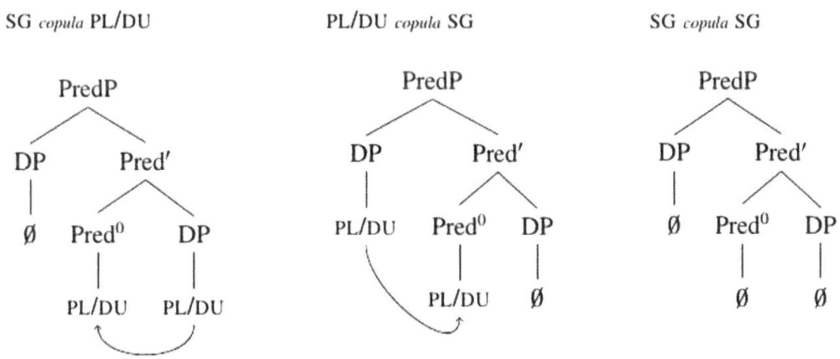

As explained above, agreement patterns are different when a copular clause contains a pronominal. Pronouns have person features on top of the number features that the auxiliary probes for. Person features probe first, and once an Agree relation is established between the auxiliary probe and the goal, all features need to be valuated on the probe. So even though NP1 has no number feature in (62) (partially repeated from (30)) it still controls agreement on the copula.

(62) Ti si možgani naše ekipe.
you.SG AUX.2P.SG brains.PL our team
'You are the brains of our team.'

This is not true, however, of third person singular pronouns. Assuming phi-features are privative (as, e.g., in Preminger 2014), third person singular pronouns have neither any number nor any person features, so they cannot control agreement. As shown in Section 2.1.1, when a third person singular pronoun is coupled with a plural noun phrase, the copula is in the plural.

Such an account and the presented derivations explain why singular agreement never surfaces when a non-singular noun phrase is present; however, this does not explain the situation we observed above in copular clauses that combine a dual and a plural noun phrase. We saw that in such cases the copula can agree with either of the two noun phrases and that there is an asymmetry in the sense that agreement with NP2 is more likely than agreement with NP1.

At this point we do not have a clear answer about what happens there. It appears that various factors might play a role in these cases, and the situation is clearly complex, so in what follows we only mention one possible factor as a speculation for what one could consider looking at in future work.

4.1. Enclitic vs. Proclitic

The Slovenian copula is a clitic realized as an element of the second-position clitic cluster, and one factor that might affect agreement patterns has to do with two different options for how the copular clitic can be pronounced. The pronounciation of Slovenian second-position clitics varies between procliticization and encliticization (cf. Bošković 2001), with procliticization perhaps being the default option (Orešnik 1984). When pronounced proclitically, the auxiliary is part of the same prosodic word as the plural noun phrase *tvoji možgani* "your brains" in example (63) (based on (56) above); in this case, plural agreement seems preferred. Similarly, if the auxiliary is pronounced as a proclitic in (64) (based on (57) above) it is pronounced in the same prosodic word as the dual noun phrase *ta dva kupa papirja* "these two piles of paper".

But if the auxiliary is pronounced as an enclitic, dual agreement may be preferred in (63) and plural agreement in (64). Variation in agreement could thus perhaps reduce to variation in the pronunciation of the auxiliary clitic, and moreover, if procliticization is indeed the default realization for Slovenian clitics, as suggested by Orešnik (1984), then the greater likelihood for the copula to agree with the second NP might also follow simply from properties of Slovenian cliticization.

(63) Ta dva polkroga {sta / so} tvoji možgani.
this two half-circles.DU AUX.DU AUX.PL your brains.PL
'These two half-circles are your brains.'

(64) Vse knjige iz naše knjižnice {sta / so} ta dva kupa papirja.
all books.PL from our library AUX.DU AUX.PL this two piles.DU paper
'All books from our library are these two piles of paper.'

On a more general note, if procliticization vs. encliticization of the copula turned out to be the main factor behind agreement patterns in copular clauses with a dual and a plural NP, this would mean that agreement is sensitive to prosodic structure, which would further suggest that agreement (or at least a part of the entire process) happens after spell-out to PF (cf. Marušič, Nevins, and Badecker 2015).

4.2. 5&Ups

Just like many (if not all) other Slavic languages, Slovenian has another type of noun phrases triggering specific agreement: certain quantifiers and all noun phrases with a numeral higher than 5 (henceforth 5&Ups) trigger (default) neuter singular agreement, see (65).

(65) a. Pet otrok je igralo nogomet.
five child.M.GEN.PL AUX.SG played.N.SG football
'Five children played football.'

b. Šest punc je streljalo z lokom.
six girl.F.GEN.PL AUX.SG shot.N.SG with bow
'Six girls shot bows.'

c. Deset telet je ležalo v senci.
ten calf.N.GEN.PL AUX.SG lain.N.SG in shade
'Ten calves lay in the shade.'

The emergence of default neuter singular agreement is typically analyzed as a lack of feature specifications at the DP level (cf. Marušič & Nevins 2010). On the basis of what we said above, the prediction for copular clauses seems to be that 5&Ups should behave like singulars. The existing literature does not mention cases where 5&Ups participate in copular clauses, and since our experiment did not contain any such examples either, this section will just briefly present a few such examples and report our judgments.

Given that both singular noun phrases and 5&Ups trigger singular agreement, combining a 5&Up with a singular noun phrase should, straightforwardly, result in singular agreement as the only option. This is indeed what we find, as shown in (66).

(66) a. To je (mojih) deset miši.
this AUX.SG my.GEN.PL ten mouse.GEN.PL
'These are (my) ten mice.'

b. Pet jajc je moj najljubši zajtrk.
five eggs AUX.SG my.SG favorite.SG breakfast.SG
'Five eggs is my favorite breakfast.'

c. Moj najljubši zajtrk je pet kuhanih jajčk.
my.SG favorite.SG breakfast.SG AUX.SG five boiled eggs
'My favorite breakfast is five boiled eggs.'

On the other hand, our story above about the privativity of number features and the functioning of probe seems to predict that in a copular construction combining a 5&Up with a plural noun phrase, the copula should be strictly plural. Example (67) shows that whereas our judgments do confirm this prediction to some extent, they are not as categorical as one would expect (*the Four Brave Men* is the group nickname of the first ascenders of Mount Triglav).

(67) a. Teh osem rok {* je / so} štirje srčni možje.
these eight hands AUX.SG AUX.PL four brave men.PL
'These eight hands are the Four Brave Men.'

b. Štirje srčni možje {?? je / ? so} teh osem rok.
four brave men.PL AUX.SG AUX.PL these eight hands
'The Four Brave Men are these eight hands.'

When we combine a 5&Up with a dual noun phrase, our story above would again predict that the dual will win out, and as shown in (68), this is indeed what we find.

(68)	a.	The	dvajset	prstkov	{* je	/ sta}	sosedova	otroka.
		these	twenty	fingers	AUX.SG	AUX.DU	neighbor's	children.DU
		'These twenty fingers are the neighbor's children.'						
	b.	Sosedova	otroka	{* je	/ sta}	teh	dvajset	prstkov.
		neighbor's	children.DU	AUX.SG	AUX.PL	these	twenty	fingers
		'The neighbor's children are these twenty fingers.'						

Regarding the lack of a clear difference between the two options in (67), note that this perhaps need not be unexpected if we take into consideration the fact that regardless of some common characteristics, simple singular noun phrases and 5&Ups also have their differences. For example, unlike simple singular noun phrases, 5&Ups do not agree in gender. 5&Ups lack features, which is why agreement with them simply fails. When conjoined, two simple singular noun phrases yield dual agreement, but two conjoined 5&Ups do not. So it may well be wrong to simply expect that whatever holds of simple singular noun phrases in copular constructions should also be true for 5&Ups.

Suppose the Agree operation is first attempted with the first or the second noun phrase. If Agree determines that both noun phrases have at least one phi-feature and that it could therefore agree with either one of them, it proceeds, following the procedure explained above. But if one of the two noun phrases is a 5&Up, Agree determines that it cannot agree with either of the two noun phrases, and (in some cases) fails. In case it fails, agreement is established with the second noun phrase, following the same logic as we outlined above for dual/plural combinations.

5. Conclusion

When none of the arguments of a Slovenian copular clause is a personal pronoun, the plural and the dual will both win out over the singular, as shown again in (69). This is probably only indirectly related to the fact that the dual and the plural are more marked than the singular. That is, it is not the relative markedness of the number features that determines agreement, but rather the fact that (in a system where features are privative) the unmarked singular does not have any number features which the auxiliary probe could target. As a result the auxiliary agrees with the only available feature in the structure.

(69) a. Ta dva kosa kruha {* je / sta} Petrova košta.
these two pieces.DU bread AUX.SG AUX.DU Peter's meal.SG
'These two slices of bread are Peter's meal.'

b. Petrova košta {* je / sta} ta dva kosa kruha.
Peter's meal.SG AUX.SG AUX.DU these two pieces.DU bread
'Peter's meal are these two slices of bread.'

c. Ti trije kosi kruha {* je / so} Petrova košta.
these three pieces.PL bread AUX.SG AUX.PL Peter's meal.SG
'These three slices of bread are Peter's meal.'

d. Petrova košta {* je / so} ti trije kosi kruha.
Peter's meal.SG AUX.SG AUX.PL these two pieces.PL bread
'Peter's meal are these three slices of bread.'

In a copular clause that combines the dual and the plural, however, the situation is not as straightforward and the data are less clear. Our judgments for this combination are given in (70), where the dual seems to have some edge over the plural.

(70) a. Ta dva obroka {sta / so} vse Petrove današnje košte.
these two meal.DU AUX.DU AUX.PL all Peter's today's meal.PL
'These two meals are all of Peter's meals of today.'

b. Vse Petrove današnje košte {sta /?* so} ta dva obroka.
all Peter's today's meal.PL AUX.DU AUX.PL these two meal.DU
'All of Peter's meals of today are these two meals.'

Not fully in line with our judgments, the results of our experiment show that there is some preference for the second noun phrase over the first one. We did not provide a definitive answer as to why this should be, but we speculated that it could perhaps be related to the default attachment of the Slovenian auxiliary as a proclitic (rather than an enclitic) and the resulting greater relative proximity of the second noun as the noun phrase to which the auxiliary cliticizes.

We finish by posing two questions about factors that might also be involved in the realization of agreement in copular clauses with a dual and a plural NP. First, do copular clauses combining a dual NP and a plural NP show any interpretational difference depending of whether agreement is dual or plural, such as a preference for distributive or collective reading of one or the other noun phrase? An interpretational difference we have observed but cannot say anything more about here is the difference between interpreting a (definite) noun phrase as a refering expression vs. interpreting it as a predicate (basically something like "being like X"). Second, what happens when one of the two noun phrases is a coordination? We have some examples that involve coordination in our paper, but things would clearly need to be looked at more systematically. We leave these questions aside for future work.

Notes

1 Note that if one of the noun phrases is realized by a dropped pronoun/pro, that one always wins.

(i) *Context: Look there's Tone and Slavka.*

Očitno	pro.DU	{ sta	/ * so }	oni.
apparently		AUX.DU	AUX.PL	they.PL

'Apparently they.DU are them.PL.'

(ii) *Context: Look there's Tone, Peter, and Slavka.*

Očitno	pro.PL	{ * sta	/ so }	onadva.
Apparently		AUX.DU	AUX.PL	they.DU

'Apparently they.PL are them.DU.'

There is a further complication which we cannot really go into. Copular clauses with a silent pronoun seem very restricted, and examples combining an inanimate silent pronoun with a noun phrase that is of different number appear to be simply impossible.

(iii) *Context: Do you see that object in the corner?*

Še	vedno	pro.SG	{ * je	/ * so }	moje	najljubše	sanke.
still	always		AUX.SG	AUX.SG	my	favorite	sled.PL

'That is still my favorite sled.'

2 We should acknowledge that one aspect of the classification of our examples is not entirely clear to us. As they all contained two definite noun phrases, they could be seen as ECCs, but given that one of these definite noun phrases was a noun phrase with a demonstrative, these constructions appear to be comparable to ICCs.
3 The original design of the experiment had the position of the demonstrative as a controlled variable – demonstrative in the first position vs. demonstrative in the second position, which would roughly correspond to the distinction between PCC and SCC, but due to a flaw in the design of the experiment, subjects were not shown the same number of the two types of sentences in each condition. Nevertheless, we were able to learn from the data that there is no difference between the two types of clauses in terms of agreement.
4 Slovenian dialects differ substantially in the extent of the presence of dual morphology. See Jakop (2008) for a detailed study of the presence of dual across dialects or Marušič, Žaucer, Plesničar, Razboršek, Sullivan, and Barner (2016) for a comprehensive map of the distribution and the extent of dual marking in Slovenian dialects.
5 Attraction errors are caused by the proximity of a noun phrase with a different number specification. So it is not something the grammar would produce, but something a production model could explain.
6 *Fičko* was the nickname of a popular small car produced in Yugoslavia between the sixties and the eighties.

Bibliography

Bock, Kathryn, and Carol Miller. 1991. Broken agreement. *Cognitive Psychology* 23.45–93.

Bošković, Željko. 2001. *On the Nature of the Syntax-Phonology Interface: Cliticization and Related Phenomena*. Amsterdam: Elsevier.

Breznik, Anton. 1934. *Slovenska slovnica za srednje šole. Četrta, pomnožena izdaja* [Slovenian Grammar for Highschools]. Celje: Družba sv. Mohorja.

den Dikken, Marcel. 2006. *Relators and Linkers*. Cambridge, MA: MIT Press.

den Dikken, Marcel, and Teresa O'Neill. 2017. Copular constructions in syntax. *Oxford Research Encyclopedia of Linguistics*. Oxford: Oxford University Press.

Drummond, Alex. 2011. Ibexfarm. Online: http://spellout.net/ibexfarm/ (Accessed: 24.8.2021)

Dvořák, Boštjan, and Uli Sauerland. 2006. The semantics of the Slovenian dual. *Proceedings of FASL 14*, ed. by Hana Filip, James Lavine, Steven Franks, and Mila Tasseva-Kurktchieva, 98–112. Ann Arbor: Michigan Slavic Publications.

Franks, Steven. 2020. *Microvariation in the South Slavic Noun Phrase*. Bloomington, IN: Slavica.

Greenberg, Joseph. 1963. Some universals of grammar with particular reference to the order of meaningful elements. *Universals of Language*, ed. by Joseph Greenberg, 73–113. Cambridge, MA: MIT Press.

Heycock, Caroline. 2012. Specification, equation, and agreement in copular sentences. *Canadian Journal of Linguistics/Revue canadienne de linguistique* 57(2). 209–40.

Higgins, Francis Roger. 2015. *The Pseudo-Cleft Construction in English*. London and New York: Routledge.

Jakop, Tjaša. 2008. *The Dual in Slovene Dialects*. Bochum: Universitätsverlag Brockmeyer.

Martí, Luisa. 2020. Inclusive plurals and the theory of number. *Linguistic Inquiry* 51. 37–74.

Marušič, Franc, and Andrew Nevins. 2010. Two types of neuter. closest-conjunct agreement in the presence of 5andUps. *Formal Approaches to Slavic Linguistics: The Second Cornell Meeting 2009*, ed. by Wayles Browne, Adam Cooper, Alison Fisher, Esra Kesici, Nikola Predolac, and Draga Zec, 301–17. Ann Arbor: Michigan Slavic Publications.

Marušič, Franc, and Rok Žaucer. 2021. Dual in Slovenian. *The Oxford Handbook of Grammatical Number*, ed. by Patricia Cabredo Hofherr and Jenny Doetjes. Oxford: Oxford University Press.

Marušič, Franc; Andrew Nevins; and William Badecker. 2015. The grammars of conjunction agreement in Slovenian. *Syntax* 18(1). 39–77. doi: 10.1111/synt.12025.

Marušič, Franc; Rok Žaucer; Vesna Plesničar; Tina Razboršek; Jessica Sullivan; and David Barner. 2016. Does grammatical structure speed number word learning?: Evidence from learners of dual and non-dual dialects of Slovenian. *Plos ONE* 11(8). e0159208.

Mikkelsen, Line. 2005. *Copular Clauses: Specification, Predication and Equation*. Amsterdam: John Benjamins Publishing.

Nevins, Andrew. 2011. Marked targets versus marked triggers and impoverishment of the dual. *Linguistic Inquiry* 42(3). 413–44.

Orešnik, Janez. 1984. Slovenske breznaglasnice se vedejo predvsem kot proklitike. *Jezik in slovstvo* 29. 129.

Preminger, Omer. 2014. *Agreement and its Failures*. Cambridge, MA: MIT Press.

Sauerland, Uli. 2003. A new semantics for number. *Proceedings of SALT 13*, ed. by Robert B. Young and Yuping Zhou, 258–75. Ithaca, NY: Cornell Linguistics Club.

Sauerland, Uli. 2008. On the semantic markedness of phi-features. In *Phi Theory: Phi-Features across Modules and Interfaces*, ed. by Daniel Harbour, David Adger, and Susana Béjar, 57–82. Oxford: Oxford University Press.

Toporišič, Jože. 2000. *Slovenska slovnica* [Slovenian Grammar]. Maribor: Založba Obzorja.

James Joshua Pennington

Today's Grammaticalization Theory is Yesterday's Grammaticalization: The BCMS Future as an(other) Strike against the Unidirectionality Hypothesis

Abstract This paper joins Campbell (2001), Campbell & Janda (2001), Joseph (2001, 2003, 2004, 2011), Norde (2009, 2011), and Willis (2007, 2017) in their calls to delegitimize grammaticalization theory (GT) as "pseudo-" historical linguistics. Specifically, I challenge statements made by proponents of GT, namely Kuteva (2001), Haspelmath (2011), and Wiemer (2011), that the South Slavic future developing from PSl **xъtěti* 'want', represents an instantiation of grammaticalization. While the Bulgarian and Macedonian future appears to obey the basic tenets of GT, including undergoing semantic bleaching and phonetic reduction along a unidirectional cline to zero (Givón 1979: 209; Haspelmath 1999; Heine 2003: 579), Štokavian (the dialect basis for modern literary BCMS) does not, as it has continued the volitional meaning of **xъtěti* alongside the auxiliated future, which comprises both reduced (clitic) and long forms. Furthermore, evidence from comparative Slavic and BCMS diachrony clearly indicate that the phonetic reduction of **xъtěti* (whether by ablaut or regular phonetic processes) preceded the semantic bleaching, a direct contradiction of GT. In addition, the auxiliation of **xъtěti* may have been calqued on the Balkan Sprachbund model (Joseph 1983, 2011), leading to the restructuring of full and reduced forms of **xъtěti* as clitics, likely in analogy to *biti* (Pennington 2007; Kapović pc). Finally, discomfort with the functional and semantic ambiguity of *hteti* is evidenced in Western Štokavian, as speakers have innovated a metatony towards disambiguating the 'volitional' *hteti* from the 'future' (Kapović 2018: 277).*

Keywords: Grammaticalization Theory, Auxiliation, Phonetic Reduction, Historical linguistics, Štokavian, Comparative Slavic

* I would like to thank Ronelle Alexander, Matthew C. Curtis, Andriy Danilenko, Steven Franks, Brian D. Joseph, and Alan Timberlake, for their helpful comments on previous drafts of this paper, which was presented in its initial form *way* back at the 2nd Slavic Linguistics Society Conference in Berlin, Germany in 2007. That is where I first met the venerable Peter Kosta, the honoree of this volume, who held an unforgettable post-conference party at his home in Potsdam, where we jammed out on his guitars and drank good Bavarian beer.

"What's wrong with grammaticalization?"
-Lyle Campbell

"What is not but could be if?"
-Silver Jews

1. Introduction

In Late Common Slavic (as deduced from OCS [Nandriş 1959: 157; Večerka 1993: 174–85]), four verbs could be used in compound future tense formations: *xъtěti* 'to want', *načęti/vъčęti* 'to begin', *byti* 'to be', and *iměti*[1] 'to have' + infinitive. From these four possibilities, Central and Eastern South Slavic developed a future tense out of **xъtěti* (BCMS *hteti,* sporadically /x/ > /h/ from lenition) 'to want', similar to the English future tense formation from *will*, which also developed out of an earlier volitional meaning and acquired clitic status, attaching to a prosodic host (e.g. *I'll*, *John'll*, etc.). Although volitional constructions with *will* in English are rare, they are still productive, e.g. *I willed the ball into the basket*; *I willed myself to finish the pizza*; *God willed it to be*, etc. However, these constructions have a desiderative agency that is lacking with the neutral *want*. Unlike English (and like earlier stages of Greek (Joseph 2011)), BCMS *hteti* retains both volitional meaning and future (Belić 1962, 1969), which is a critical factor in the discussion about whether or not the *hteti* future is "grammaticalized" (Wiemer 2011; Haspelmath 2011: 7). But more on this shortly.

Tab. 1: Future formation in South Slavic literary languages

South Slavic Language	(IMPF) 'I will read/(be) reading'	(PF) 'I will read (and finish reading)'
Slovenian	*Jaz bom čítal*	*Jaz bom prečítal*
Bulgarian	*Az šte čita*	*Az šte pročita*
Mac.	*Jas ḱe čitam*	*Jas ḱe pročitam*
BCMS	*Ja ću čitati* and inverted *Čitaću* (Croatian *Čitat ću*)	*Ja ću pročitati* and inverted *Pročitaću* (Croatian *Pročitat ću*)

The "odd man out", so to speak, in Tab. 1 is Slovenian (and related Croatian Kajkavian), which forms its future with the verb 'to be' + *l*-participle. However, this can be reconciled based on Slovenian's development from an earlier shared dialect continuum with Proto-West Slavic (Greenberg's [2000: 41] "Pannonian Slavic"[2]). All other South Slavic languages form the future tense with a reduced form of the verb 'to want', which is a characteristic feature of the Balkan Sprachbund (see Joseph's seminal 1983 book; for the typological perspective, see Hengeveld 2011). Yet, while all of the traditionally Balkan languages (save Gheg Albanian and literary and colloquial variants of Romanian) have an invariant future particle, BCMS has a fully inflected clitic: *ću, ćeš, će, ćemo, ćete, će*, and is often considered peripherally Balkan because of this along with its rich nominal morphology and lack of post-posed articles. Kotova (1977: 244) notes that Bulgarian, like BCMS, once had inflected auxiliary forms: "(Bulgarian) writers of the 19th and early 20th cc. used forms of the future with the inflected auxiliary verb šte and the infinitival form… e.g., *pisaštem*, instead of *šte pišem*" (my translation – JJP). The BCS Torlak dialects have an invariant future, but on the other hand they lack most cases and have post-posed articles (like Bulgarian and Macedonian), and there is argument over whether the Torlak dialects should even be considered part of the BCMS family (Browne 2002[1993]: 382).[3] Dialectological disputes aside, Wiemer (2011) implies that the South Slavic 'want' future is essentially predictable, with a singular trajectory, by including it on his list of examples of grammaticalization in Slavic. I argue here that South Slavic-internal variation cannot lead to such an assumption. Moreover, as part of a larger argument against grammaticalization theory, generally, I demonstrate that the 'be' (*byti*) future presents the same problems. But before moving on to the diachronic details, let us first pause here to outline the differences between grammaticalization and grammaticalization theory.

2. Grammaticalization Studies vs. Grammaticalization "Theory"

During the 1990s, historical linguistics saw a surge in research on so-called grammaticalization theory (GT), known earlier unassumingly as "grammaticalization studies". But over the past three decades, the proponents of GT have only grown more assertive in their claims to universal predictive power for the pathway of all words. Considered by many to be one of the co-founders of GT, Heine (1993: 124) boldly asserts that "[g]rammaticalization studies are not only a means of relating present language states to past situations, rather by proposing generalizations on past development they also allow us to predict future developments." Another GT co-founder Traugott (2003: 614; inter alios) attempts to legitimize GT by appropriating Meillet's (1912: 131) statement that grammaticalization entails: "the passage of an autonomous word into a grammatical element … the attribution of grammatical character to a previously autonomous word" [my translation – JJP]. Yet, Meillet's statement was made nearly a century before the rise of grammaticalization theory, and less > more grammatical has never been disputed among the leading practitioners of historical linguists as a *potential* pathway in the evolution of a word (see Kuryłowicz 1975 (1965); Lehman 1985). So, what did we miss all these years?

One of the key claims often made by GT adherents is that the process is unidirectional (e.g. Haspelmath 1999: 1062) or "essentially unidirectional" (Heine and Kuteva 2002: 8), beginning with the semantic bleaching of a lexeme: essentially, a change from more > less semantic weight that triggers a type of decay. This "desemanticization", as it is called (Heine 2003: 579), is considered the first stage in a lexeme's metamorphosis along a unidirectional cline into a "gram" from less to more grammatical function, **always precipitating phonetic reduction** and eventual disappearance of the gram from the surface structure of language. This process is often illustrated with reference to Givón's cline (1979: 209):[4]

(1) Discourse > Syntax > Morphology > Morphophonemics > Zero

Another widely held position by GT proponents is that grammaticalization is irreversible (Herring 1991: 253; Haspelmath 2004: 22). Likewise, Heine and Kuteva (2007: 32) state: "[grammaticalization is] the development from lexical to grammatical forms, and **from grammatical to even more grammatical**" [my emphasis – JJP], placing the emphasis here on both irreversibility (cannot return to a less grammatical state) and unidirectionality (lexeme > grammeme).

Campbell (2001: 114) is one of the first (in a special edition of *Language Sciences* entitled "Grammaticalization: A Critical Assessment") to lay formal challenge to the claims of GT, arguing that "grammaticalization does not have any independent status of its own, but rather is derivative of other kinds of language change". He presents well-known counter-examples to the purported inevitability of (1) above, including: English possessive *-s*, which developed into a ModE phrasal clitic from the OE genitive affix (i.e. a reversal: morphology > syntax); or German *haben*,[5] which retains its past participial usage in Modern German, yet has not undergone reduction[6] (for a similar case, see below on the Slavic future from **bytĭ*). Joseph's (2001) *Language Sciences* article also takes GT to task, specifically the position popularized by Hopper and Traugott (1993: 128–9) that "to date there is no evidence that grammatical items arise full-fledged, that is, can be innovated without a prior lexical history". According to Joseph (2001), the diachrony of the Greek weak pronoun *tos* is an outright contradiction of Hopper and Traugott's claim, given that it was a result of an easily traceable analogical change and not reduction from a strong form pronoun, as GT would erroneously predict. It *arose* as a weak form *ex nihilo*.

Furthermore, Norde (2009, 2012) presents a typology of counter-examples to the GT unidirectionality cline,[7] representing a counter-theory aptly named *degrammaticalization* (term first used in Lehmann 1995 [1982]: 16), involving three types of developments: (a) degrammation (aka syntactic lexicalization, e.g. OCS *něčĭto* 'something' > Bulgarian *nešto* 'thing' (pronoun > noun) (Willis 2007)); (b) deinflectionalisation (e.g. the Swedish masc. sg. adjectival suffix *-er*, which has developed into a derivational suffix denoting humans, e.g. *en slarver* 'a messy person' (< *slarv* 'messy') (Norde 2009: 179–81)); and (c) debonding, which entails the change bound morpheme > free morpheme (e.g. Irish *muid* (1pl. verb suffix > 1pl. personal pronoun 'we') (Doyle 2002)). English *-ish* is probably the most well-known example of debonding, even resulting in a new entry in the OED, as noted by Willis (2017: 36):

(2) 'Trust Davie Morrow.' 'You know him?' 'Ish. He's a regular across the road.' (Colin Bateman, Cycle of violence vi.94, 1995) (OED s.v. ish, adv.)
[Willis's ex. 10]

All the examples presented above are indisputable (and carefully chosen) counters to the unidirectionality hypothesis that GT so delicately balances upon. Yet, Campbell opines, that the very definition of the theory is designed to intrinsically cast aside any counter-examples as irrelevant (Janda's "walking North", shared in Joseph 2011):

> [...] because grammaticalization is defined as changes of *lexical* > *grammatical*, or *grammatical* > *more grammatical*, any change not going in this direction can be considered as outside of grammaticalization, and therefore, **unidirectionality becomes not an empirical hypothesis that can be tested, but an artifact of the definition itself.** [my emphasis – JJP]

Take, for example, Wiemer (2011: 2), who seems to reveal the overall GT strategy: "Cases of incipient or 'halfway' proceeded grammaticalization on all levels [in Slavic – JJP] mentioned are numerous; for lack of space they will, however, be omitted."[8] However, the Slavic 'be' auxiliary (*bytĭ), which is clearly not in its infancy, is discussed in detail in Wiemer's sketch, and while it appears in reduced form in Slovenian and Kajkavian (e.g. 1sg. *bom* < *bodem* < PSl *bǫ̋dǫ),[9] it does not in West and East Slavic. How then can GT explain the "resistance" to reduction in East Slavic? ... It cannot.

Such bet hedging does not inspire confidence in any theory, especially when considering the positions of leading GT proponents such as Haspelmath (2004: 23) and Heine et al. (1991: 52) who have dismissed counter-examples such that are found in degrammaticalization as too rare to be statistically relevant.

Others like Ramat (1998: 123) simply choose to ignore counterexamples for the sake of the "conceptual clarity" of GT. Clearly miffed by the attitude of GT proponents to counterexamples, Campbell (2001: 126) invokes the old Marie Antionette cake adage in light of Haspelmath (1998: 80), whose position he characterizes as "denying the existence of such counterexamples and asserting that they exist but are of no relevance" (echoed in Joseph 2011: 5).

Outside Campbell's (2001) understandably acerbic take (see also Campbell & Janda 2001; Joseph 2001, 2004) and the vital work of Norde (2009, 2011) and Willis (2017) on degrammaticalization, Joseph (2011) may be the most valuable direct critiques of GT to date, specifically because it is embedded within the over 800-page *Oxford Handbook of Grammaticalization* (OHG) (Narrog & Heine 2011). Joseph's nine-page chapter is easy to overlook in the massive, mostly pro-GT volume. Nonetheless, its inclusion (along with Norde's article entitled 'Degrammaticalization') is an acknowledgement that not all linguists are on board with GT (and perhaps to save face, given that Joseph & Janda's *Handbook of Historical Linguistics Vol. 1* gives ample room for grammaticalizationists to present their case). Despite making GT a pet peeve of his over the years,[10] Joseph more graciously argues here that grammaticalization is not entirely devoid of utility but emphasizes firmly that it is *not a process* but rather a clustering of various different processes that produce *an outcome* (in the spirit of Campbell 2001 and Campbell & Janda 2001). In addition, he notes that there are many examples of semantic bleaching without phonetic reduction (e.g. Rus hortative *davaj(-te)* 'Let's', deriving from the verb *davat'* 'to give' (2011: 2)). With characteristic precision, Joseph exposes serious flaws in GT thinking by illustrating the development of the Greek future:

> To take one concrete example, is the development of [Greek] *thelō hina* X 'I want that X' to [omitting several stages here - JJP] *tha X* […] by regular sound change, some by analogy, some perhaps with other motivations? Is each of these several developments an instance of 'grammaticalization', even though some, e.g. the degemination in *thenna* > *thena*, are fully regular and widely instantiated outside of this collocation? Or is the whole set of developments taken together a single instance of 'grammaticalization'? If so, since languages can stop at any point, there is nothing deterministic about this particular sequence of changes—Greek got along just fine for several decades (or more) with unreduced *thelō hina* for future, and with unreduced *theli na*, etc. **Since nothing impels the collocation on to the next stage, how would we know when a suitable endpoint has been reached that justifies the label 'grammaticalization'?** [my emphasis – JJP]

The statement in bold above, especially, poses a formidable challenge to Wiemer's (2011: 2) notion of "incipient" change.

Further, I continue the skepticism of the anti-GT scholars cited above by objecting to Wiemer's (2011) inclusion of the BCMS future in his list of Slavic grammaticalized constructions, especially given that it appears to have become a stock example of the unidirectionality cline. For example, Haspelmath (2011: 7; in the OHG) claims: "In Serbian, the future-tense marker […] was recently grammaticalized from an auxiliary meaning 'want.'" I take issue with most of this statement, including the notion that the *hteti* future was "grammaticalized", the characterization of the auxiliation[11] of *hteti* as "recent", and the description of this feature as uniquely "Serbian", given that there are four standard languages: Bosnian, Croatian, Montenegrin, and Serbian. Let us now dive into the details.

3. Chewing on the BCMS Future Tense

The first attested usage of clitic forms of **hъteti* 'to want' in any of the BCMS standards is found in a 12th century Old Serbian document (in the *Monumenta Serbica* [MS]), luckily in both the affirmative and negative (in the same sentence!):

(3) XII. 1100–1200 (MS: 7)

Commune Popovo litteras mittit ad comitem et commune Ragusii de conventu

"A letter from courteous Popovo sent to the Prince and general public of Dubrovnik concerning the delegation" [my translation – JJP].

… да ви бисте рекли да се станемо на нои странѣ Рѣке да не кемо (и)ти к вам на онȣ странȣ, дѣ ни нѣ закон, дѣ ви Радославȣ давьше рȣкȣ, тере га везасте, да ако кемо правомȣ станькȣ, ȣ ки д'н', дȣрьдевь дьнь …

"…*if you had said for us to stand on this side of the river, we won't go to you to the other side where there is no law, where you shook hands with Radoslav, and then took and bound him up, but if we go we will (go) to a just delegation, on another day, St. George's Day …*" [my translation – JJP].

As we see with the underlined forms above, *hteti* appears in its reduced (clitic) form and in the future usage. By no stretch can this be considered "recent", as Haspelmath (2011: 7) matter-of-factly states.[12] This is especially evident when considering that the first syllable is reconstructed with a reduced vowel (represented by a jer in OCS and ORus forms below) in some forms (e.g. infinitive), as illustrated in Vasmer's Etymological Dictionary:

(4) ORus. хотѣти, **хътѣти**, OCS хотѣти, хоштѫ and **хътѣти**, Gk. θέλειν, βούλεσθαι (Ostrom., Klots., Supr.; see Dil's. Aksl. Gr. 93), Bulg. ща (from ***хъштѫ**), SCr. хѝтjети, хо̏ħу, ħу, Sln. hotéti, hǒčem, OCz. **chtieti**, **chcu**, Cz. **chtíti, chci, Slo. chc(i)et**', Pol. **chcieć, chcę,** USor. **chcyć, chcu,** LSor. **kśeś** …

If we include Daničić's (ARj: v. 3, 655) note about the existence of Russian dialectal хтѣти, then we see a complete syncope (in the proper phonetic context) of the word-initial vowel /o/ (whether by ablaut or other process) in all branches of Slavic, giving the phonetic reduction of the first syllable of **xъtěti* a terminus post quem of Late Common Slavic, *before* any of the Slavic languages developed a future auxiliary from **xъtěti*.[13] Even more alarming for GT, BCMS continues the volitional meaning of *hteti* (e.g. *Hoću psa* 'I want a dog') alongside the future,[14] unlike Bulgarian and Macedonian, which lost the volitional **xъšte* and replaced it with *iskam* and *saka*, respectively. *hteti* can even be used with verbal complements in the volitional sense, e.g. *Hoćeš li spavati sad*? which can mean both "Will you go to bed now? and "Do you want to go to bed now?"[15]

In light of these facts from BCMS, Kuteva's (2001: 125–8) analysis of the Bulgarian future (ex. 5 below, adapted from Wiemer 2011: 4), which has the same starting point as the BCMS future (Proto-South Slavic), should be considered misleading:

(5) "Grammaticalization" stages of the Bulgarian future

1. autonomous lexeme *xъtěti*: present tense 3.SG *xъšte* → volition, only animate subjects >
2. *xъšte* + infinitive: loss of volitional meaning → intention → future (prediction) >
3. *šta* + infinitive >
4. *šta* + shortened infinitive > *šta* + *da*.COMP + finite verb / inanimate subjects become possible >
5. *šte* + finite verb (any subjects).

By carefully ordering the loss of volitional meaning before the phonetic reduction (a conclusion based on unreliable data from Old/Middle Bulgarian literary documents[16]), Kuteva is able to imply that the semantic bleaching is what triggered the reduction, hitting a homerun once more for GT. But replay shows that this one actually wraps around the foulpole, as Kuteva does not discuss the related changes in BCMS which do not obey this evolution, especially given that the volitional meaning in BCMS continues up until the present day. Furthermore, if Kuteva were to analyze the BCMS situation, she would run into problematic phonological issues to consider, namely the regular outcome of /x/ > /h/ > /ø in South Slavic and prosody, which has a major impact on the evolution of word forms in BCMS.

First, on /x/ > /h/ > ø: Matasović (2008: 172) notes that /x/ had already begun to be elided in all positions from 1600 (although not evenly for all Štokavian dialects). This entails that /x/ would have been susceptible to lenition under the right phonetic conditions, and especially colloquially, reduced to ø. As demonstrated above, we already have full clitic forms from the 12th century in BCMS. Now, onto prosody.

The negative forms of *hteti* offer incredible insight when factoring in BCMS historical prosody. Specifically, the phonetic conditions for phonological reduction are automatic, as the already prone to syncope /ho./ is wedged between two stable syllables, the prefix *ne-* and the present tense theme vowel *-e* for the 3rd. sg. *nehoće* > *neće*, for example. Thus, I propose that, as an orthotonic group, *nehȍće* would have been susceptible to elision (through stress retraction and vowel contraction) in allegro speech conditions, ultimately succumbing to a metatony induced by the neo-Štokavian stress retraction:[17]

(6) *ne hȍće* > ***nè(h)oće*** > *nè(o)će* > *nèćé* > *nêće* (bold form showing retraction from medial short vowel, yielding the neo-acute, aka Stang-Ivšić's law;[18] the final form shows regular metatony of rising pitch in initial syllables to falling after the retraction[19])

Moreover, a distinction in the 3rd pl. negated forms of *hteti* – *néćē* 'they don't want' vs. *nêćē* 'they won't' exists in some Western Štokavian dialects (Kapović 2018: 277), the difference being the long rising (indicating volition) or long falling (indicating future) negative prefix, respectively. This is crucial, given that there can be only one phonologically regular pathway (following the central Neogrammarian tenet) to contracted *nêćē* < *ne hȍćē* (with a long fall). This secondary outcome may reflect the incursion of metalinguistic awareness of speakers, i.e. (dialect mixing notwithstanding) speakers innovated a rising intonation on the volitional *ne hteti* to distinguish the otherwise homophonous volitional verb from its future tense counterpart.

Additional perspective is gained by considering BCMS within the context of the Balkan Sprachbund. Matasović (2008: 287) and Joseph (1983, 2011) explore the possibility that the **xъtěti* future was calqued in South Slavic on the model of Greek and Albanian (as a characteristic Balkan Sprachbund feature),[20] and thus the development of clitics from existing reduced forms of *xъtěti* would necessarily pattern according to the existing system of clitics, namely via analogy to the verb *biti* (e.g. *jesam* ~ *sam*, etc.; Pennington 2007; pc Kapović).[21] Bulgarian did not undergo prosodic developments that would have saved /ho./ from elision, i.e. the neo-Štokavian retraction in BCMS "rescued" affirmative forms of *hteti* from elision, leaving intact the surface phonological appearance of long vs. short forms. /ho./ in negated forms was doomed to obliteration in BCMS it seems from the outset. In modern BCS **ne hoće* is ungrammatical (although it is acceptable in Montenegrin[22]). However, this does not mean that negated forms do not occur. In fact, they are quite common in Serbian folk poetry:

(7) From *Srpske narodne pesme* (Serbian Folk Songs) (Karadžić 1845)
13. Opet to, ali drugčije. (iz Crne gore).
Koliko se brata uželjela,
Od zmije se odvojit' ne hoće
"No matter how much she missed her brother,
she will not separate herself from the snake."

hoće here functions as the strong form for the negative future *neće*. Yet, given the 3/2, 2/3 trochaic metric scheme (ex. 8) of the Serbian *deseterac* ("ten syllable poetry"), the long form here provides the necessary stressed syllable in the final trochee (which appears to explain the majority of full form *hteti* negatives found in Serbian folk poetry):

(8) \` - \` - \` - // \` - \` -
\` - \` - // \` - \` - \` -
[…]
\` - \` - // \` - \` *ne hȍće*

Thus, while the negative may have continued in the full form in unmarked usage dialectally (that may be the case for the current Montenegrin usage), it is clear that in Serbian folk poetry, the full form is restored analogically to fulfill poetic meter (a demonstrably marked usage).

4. Conclusion

Diachronically speaking, BCMS (like Macedonian and Bulgarian) developed its future from the Late Common Slavic verb **xъtěti*, which exhibits auxiliated reduced forms. Some proponents of GT (Kuteva 2001; Wiemer 2011) claim that this parallel development in Bulgarian is a clear-cut case of grammaticalization. However, they overlook critical details from Late Common Slavic phonology, which point to an initial syllable already undergoing some degree of phonetic erosion (whether this occurred by ablaut or due to accentological developments is irrelevant). Moreover, unlike Bulgarian and Macedonian, the sister(s) BCMS underwent a leftward stress retraction in the 15th century, resulting in a restoration of initial stress for all affirmative forms of the verb *hteti*, thereby blocking any further erosion of *hteti* (as evidenced across all of Slavic, and especially in Macedonian *ḱe* and Bulgarian *šte*). Naturally, one might expect the medial syllable in negative *hteti* constructions to also be restored by the same mechanism, but they are not. Therefore, I propose the only phonologically regular solution possible, i.e. that the neo-Štokavian retraction applied to orthotonic *nehteti* groups regularly just as it did throughout the language, except the stress shifted off of the medial syllable (or was already positioned on the negative prefix). The lack of stress on the medial syllable /ho./ would have accelerated the phonetic reduction in the negative. Eventually, speakers used the negative *neće* as a model to create the affirmative counterpart *će* via simple four-part analogy (and modeled after *biti*). There is probably no way of telling whether *hteti* was integrated into the clitic system (as a 2nd position element like pronominal clitics and clitic forms of *biti*) before or after its auxiliation as a future, but the process may have been accelerated (through calquing) via the participation of Central and Eastern South Slavic in the Balkan Sprachbund. Furthermore, in a future study, analysis of BCMS native speakers' preferences for either *hteti* 'to want' or *željeti* 'to desire' could reveal tendencies similar to Bulgarian and Macedonian, which lost the verb **da hъšte* and replaced it with *iskam* and *saka*, respectively. Evidence from Western Štokavian demonstrates that speakers have tinkered with the prosody to achieve a similar affect, inducing a metatony to eliminate the semantic and functional ambiguity caused by homophony.

Now, let us turn our attention back to GT (but not rehash the review provided in Section 2). One major irony in the mission of GT proponents to legitimize their field can be illustrated by the three main existential stages of a "linguistic expression", as adumbrated by Heine (2003: 579):

(i) There is a linguistic expression A that is recruited for grammaticalization.
(ii) This expression acquires a second use pattern, B, with the effect that there is ambiguity between A and B.
(iii) Finally, A is lost, that is, there is now only B.

While this pattern ostensibly describes the development of the future in Bulgarian and Macedonian but not BCMS, what would happen if "grammaticalization" stood in for "A" and "grammaticalization theory" for "B"? Here, one can imagine Givon's (1971) famous dictum rephrased accordingly: "Today's grammaticalization theory is yesterday's grammaticalization".

Notes

1 Although the Ukrainian synthetic 'have' future, e.g. *pysaty-mu* 'I shall write,' *pysaty-meš* 'you will write' on the surface appears to be a good contact-induced (with Romance) grammaticalization (as suggested by Dahl [2000: 317]), Danylenko (2011) demonstrates that it is in-fact Slavic internal, being derived from LCS *jĭmati* 'to take', remarkably forming a typological parallelism with Hungarian and Chinese instead.
2 This also includes BCMS "Future 2" (attested from the 13th century; Matasović 2008: 286–7); with the *l*-participle (see Piper et al. 2005: 442), also from Pannonian Slavic (see Matasović 2008: 286–7) or later dialect mixing.
3 See Friedman & Joseph (2021, Chapter 1) on their reasoning for classifying non-Torlak BCMS as peripheral Balkan.
4 The extreme version of this is Hopper's (1987) "emergent grammar", which states that "there is . . . no 'grammar', but only grammaticalization – movements towards structure" (148; as cited in Joseph 2004: 46–7).
5 This example, as Campbell notes (2001: 121), is used by Heine (1993: 109), himself, which astonishingly did not deter him from developing his GT ideas further.
6 According to Bybee (2002; 2011) "[…] frequency of use is a major factor in phonetic reduction in grammaticalization." This is a clear statement that phonetic reduction and grammaticalization are mutually exclusive. However, GT proponents often talk about grammaticalization being incomplete without phonetic reduction, e.g. "Phonetic erosion thus represents the final stage of the process, and is not a sine qua non for grammaticalization to occur" (Lamiroy and de Mulder 2011). Such conflicting statements on the position of phonetic reduction within grammaticalization are all too common in the GT literature.
7 While discussing Norde (2009), Willis (2017) is also fair in pointing out what is *not* degrammaticalization: e.g. so-called "zero derivation", where we see a category shift from an NP or PP to a VP (e.g. *to dog (someone), to down (a beer)*, both which represent lexical conversion and shift neither to more or

less grammatical); metalinguistic upgrading such as German *zig* meaning 'umpteen'; and retraction, where what appears to be a reversal in the grammaticalization cline, actually represent the loss of a form, e.g. OE *man* developing from noun > pronoun > noun, where the pronominal usage was lost, leaving only the original nominal counterpart (although relic pronominal usage can be seen scattered across English, e.g. *A man's gotta do what a man's gotta* do'; *man* here is functionally equivalent here to the indefinite pronoun *one*). These processes belong to the realm of lexicalization rather than grammaticalization.

8 Another prediction from Wiemer (ibid.): "Only colloquial Upper Sorbian (CUS) has developed both definite and indefinite articles, Molise Slavic (MSL) only has an indefinite article, Bulgarian only a definite one, as does Macedonian, where eden 'one' has **not yet** developed into a fully-fledged indefinite article." [my emphasis]

9 Kapović 2018: 271.

10 I can attest to this first-hand, as his PhD advisee at the Ohio State University (which Joseph [2011: 1] also makes clear at the outset: "it's no secret […]").

11 In my view, this is a much more informative term than the vague "grammaticalization" (cf. also "syntagmaticization", "morphologization", etc.).

12 To be fair, this statement is not a mortal sin, so to speak, on Haspelmath's part; however, it demonstrates how widely cited authors can unintentionally create an academic confirmation bias that may proliferate detrimental assumptions about a language, making later correction by specialists of those languages (my intention here) more challenging.

13 All sorts of odd spellings of reduced *hteti* can be found in Daničić (1874), MS, and the ARj, but it is difficult to discern the level of phonetic accuracy reflected because of the often arbitrary scribal habits characteristic of medieval South Slavic manuscripts. I single out one specific form noted by Daničić (1874: 260) in a letter dated by Miklosich between 1273–1314 (Miklosich 1858: 69): хкю (1sg.), which is potentially indicative that the present tense was influenced by the zero-grade of the infinitive and l-participle. Regarding the odd spelling of хкю, see Pennington (2012) on the orthography of the *Miroslav Gospel* and potential scriptorium with this characteristically odd jotated *u* usage.

14 As late as the 14th century we can see long forms of *hteti* still being used as the future auxiliary, but this could already be focus usage: *I što hoće sudije kome da sude, svaku presudu da upisuju* … "And what sentences will the judges hand down to each, registering the sentences …" (Dushanov zakonik, Prizrenski rukopis, "181. (183). O parničaru pred carem." [Miklosich 1858]).

15 Several native speakers of BCMS (including Kapović, pc) have informed me of their unease with the semantic and functional ambiguity arising in examples like these.

16 Scatton (2002: 188) observes: "The penetration of vernacular features into the written language was impeded for a number of reasons, most importantly conservative scribal attitudes and various orthographic reforms which artificially normalized scribal practices during Middle Bulgarian." See also Ivanova-Mirčeva and Xaralampiev (1999) for a detailed discussion of the earliest vernacular Bulgarian texts.

17 Brozović and Ivić (1988: 17–18) give a *terminus post quem* of the 15th century for the stress retraction based on the change /l/ ➔ /o/, which they claim is attested from 1400 in the form *seóba*, having undergone the following changes: *selbá* > *seobá* > *seóba* (not *séoba*).

18 The neo-acute forms are preserved, as expected, in Čakavian dialects, e.g. (Langston 2006: 236).

19 Garde 1976; Kortlandt 1978: 69; Derksen 1996: 29.

20 The Štokavian dialects appear to mirror exactly the development of the Greek future, as detailed by Joseph (2001): [...] reduction may have been a fast speech phenomenon, since it also affected at least some forms of the independent verb 'wants' (in present-day Greek, for instance, the second person singular of (nonfuture) *élis* 'you want' is commonly reduced to *és* and reductions with other persons and numbers may be possible as well), but it gained currency most generally with only the future marker."

21 It is worth mentioning that Čakavian has *Ćeš?* "Will you?". However, this is a recent contraction of *Ići ćeš*? 'Will you go?' and not to be considered the clitic form appearing in strong position (pc Kapović).

22 For example, in *Gorski Vijenac* (1847), the quintessential "Montenegrin" text, *ne hoće* occurs only once, as opposed to 21 times for *neće*. However, the lone instance: *Knez Bajko je sjetan, i Vuk Mandušić; oni dva* ***ne hoće*** *ništa da pričaju* 'Prince Bajko is sad, as is Vuk Mandušić; the two of them do not want to talk at all' [my translation – JJP], is from Njegoš's own speech as he addresses his readers with stage directions. This suggests that by the 19th century, uncontracted *ne hoće* had become the standard in Montenegrin. This reversal (from expected *neće*), as it were, is a real mystery, and a future study should aim to solve it thorough corpus analysis.

Bibliography

ARj = *Rječnik hrvatskoga ili srpskoga jezika*, sv. 1–97 [dijelovi I–XXIII]. JAZU. Zagreb 1881–1976.

Belić, Aleksandar. 1962. *Istorija srpskohrvatskog jezika / Predavanja*. Aleksandra Belića Beograd: Naučna Knjiga.

Belić, Aleksandar. 1969. *Osnovi istorije srpskohrvatskog jezika*. Beograd: Naučna knjiga.

Browne, Wayles. 2002 [1993]. Serbo-Croat. *The Slavonic Languages,* ed. by Bernard Comrie and Greville G. Corbett, 306–87. New York: Routledge.

Brozović, Dalibor, and Pavle Ivić. 1988. Srpskohrvatski/hrvatskosrpski, hrvatski ili srpski Zagreb: Jugoslavenski leksikografski zavod "Miroslav Krleža".

Bybee, Joan. 2011. Usage-based theory and grammaticalization. *The Oxford Handbook of Grammaticalization*, ed. by Bernd Heine and Heiko Narrog. Oxford Handbooks Online.

Campbell, Lyle. 2001. What's wrong with grammaticalization? *Language Sciences* (special issue, Grammaticalization: A Critical Assessment, ed. by L. Campbell) 23.2–3: 113–61.

Campbell, Lyle, and Richard Janda. 2001. *Language Sciences* (special issue, Grammaticalization: A Critical Assessment, ed. L. Campbell) 23. 2–3: 93–112.

Comrie, Bernard, and Greville G. Corbett (eds.). 1993 [2002]. *The Slavonic Languages*. Routledge. London.

Dahl, Östen. 2000. The grammar of future time reference in European languages. *Tense and Aspect in the Languages of Europe*, ed. by Östen Dahl, 309–328. Berlin, New York: Mouton de Gruyter.

Daničić, Duro. 1874. Istorija oblika srpskoga ili hrvatskoga jezika do svršetka XVII vijeka. [Nachdr. d. Ausg.] Biograd.

Danylenko, Andrii. 2011. Is there any inflectional future in East Slavic? A case of Ukrainian against Romance reopened. *Grammaticalization in Slavic Languages: From Areal and Typological Perspectives*, ed. by Motoki Nomachi, 147–77. Sapporo.

Derksen R. 1996. *Metatony in Baltic.* [= Leiden Studies in Indo-European 6]. Amsterdam, Atlanta.

Doyle, Aidan. 2002. Yesterday's affixes as today's clitics. *New Reflections on Grammaticalization*, ed. by Ilse Wischer and Gabriele Diewald, 67–81. Amsterdam: John Benjamins.

Friedman, Victor A., and Brian D. Joseph. 2021. *The Balkan Languages.* Cambridge: Cambridge University Press.

Garde, Paul. 1976. *Histoire de l'accentuation slave. Tome I–II. Collection de manuels de l'Institut d'etudes slaves.* Paris.

Givón, Talmy. 1971. Historical syntax and synchronic morphology: An archaeologist's field trip. *Chicago Linguistic Society* 7. 394–415.

Givón, Talmy. 1979. *On Understanding Grammar*. New York: Academic Press

Greenberg, Marc. 2000. *A Historical Phonology of the Slovene Language.* Heidelberg: Universitätsverlag Carl Winter.

HASPELMATH, MARTIN. 1999. Why is grammaticalization irreversible? *Linguistics* 37. 1043–68.

HASPELMATH, MARTIN. 2004. On directionality in language change with particular reference to grammaticalization. In *Up and down the cline: The nature of grammaticalization*, eds. Olga Fischer, Muriel Norde and Harry Perridon, 17–44. Amsterdam: Benjamins.

HASPELMATH, MARTIN. 2011. The gradual coalescence into 'words' in grammaticalization. *The Oxford Handbook of Grammaticalization*, ed. by Bernd Heine and Heiko Narrog. Oxford Handbooks Online.

HEINE, BERND. 1993. *Auxiliaries: Cognitive Forces and Grammaticalization.* Oxford: Oxford University Press.

HEINE, BERND. 2003. Grammaticalization. *The Handbook of Historical Linguistics*, ed. by Brian D. Joseph, and Richard D. Janda, 573–601. Malden, MA: Blackwell.

HEINE, BERND, and TANIA KUTEVA. 2002. *World Lexicon of Grammaticalization.* Cambridge: Cambridge University Press.

HEINE, BERND, and TANIA KUTEVA. 2007. *The Genesis of Grammar: A Reconstruction* Oxford: Oxford University Press.

HEINE, BERND, CLAUDI, ULRIKE, and HÜNNEMEYER, FRIEDERIKE. 1991. *Grammaticalization: A conceptual framework.* Chicago: Chicago University Press.

HENGEVELD, KEES. 2011. The grammaticalization of tense and aspect. *The Oxford Handbook of Grammaticalization*, ed. by Bernd Heine and Heiko Narrog. Oxford Handbooks Online.

HERRING, SUSAN C. 1991. The grammaticalization of rhetorical questions in Tamil. *Approaches to Grammaticalization*, Vol. 1, ed. by Elisabeth Traugott and Bernd Heine, 253–84. Amsterdam: John Benjamins.

Hopper, Paul. 1987. Emergent grammar. In: Proceedings of the thirteenth annual meeting of the Berkeley Linguistics Society: General session and parasession on grammar and cognition (ed. Aske J, Beery N, Michaelis L, et al.), 14–16 February, vol. 13, pp. 139–157. Berkeley, CA: Berkeley Linguistics Society. Available at: http://linguistics.berkeley.edu/bls/previous_proceedings/bls13.pdf

IVANOVA-MIRČEVA, DORA, and IVAN XARALAMPIEV. 1999. *Istorija na bŭlgarskija ezik.* Veliko Trnovo: Faber.

JOSEPH, BRIAN D. 1983. *The Synchrony and Diachrony of the Balkan Infinitive.* Cambridge: Cambridge University Press.

JOSEPH, BRIAN D. 2001. Is there such a thing as "grammaticalization"? *Language Sciences* (special issue, *Grammaticalization: A Critical Assessment,* ed. by L. Campbell) 23. 2–3: 163–86.

JOSEPH, BRIAN D. 2004. Rescuing traditional (historical) linguistics from grammaticalization theory. *Up and Down the Cline – The Nature of Grammaticalization*, ed. by Olga Fischer, Muriel Norde, and Harry Perridon, 45–71. Amsterdam: Benjamins.

JOSEPH, BRIAN. D. 2011. Grammaticalization: A general critique. *The Oxford Handbook of Grammaticalization*, ed. by Bernd Heine and Heiko Narrog. Oxford Handbooks Online.

KAPOVIĆ, MATE. 2018. Povijest glagolske akcentuacije u štokavskom (i šire). *Rasprave. Časopis Instituta za hrvatski jezik i jezikoslovlje* 44(1). 159–285.

KARADŽIĆ, VUK STEFANOVIĆ (ed.). *Srpske narodne pesme*. Available online at: https://www.rastko.rs/knjizevnost/usmena/vkaradzic-pesme_II.html. Accessed online on May 21, 2019.

KORTLANDT, FREDERIK. 1978. A History of Slavic Accentuation. A Review of Paul Garde, 'Histoire de l'accentuation slave'. *Lingua* 44. 67–91.

KOTOVA, N.V. 1977. *Bolgarskij jazyk (The Bulgarian language). Slavjanskie jazyki: Oćerki grammatiki zapadnoslavjanskich i južnoslavjanskich jazykov*, ed. by A.G. Širokova and V.P. Gudkova, 216–58. Moscow: MGU Publishing.

KURYŁOWICZ, JERZY. 1975[1965]. The evolution of grammatical categories. *Esquisses Linguistiques* 2. 38–54. (Diogenes 1965: 55–71.)

KUTEVA, TANIA A. 2001. *Auxiliation: An Enquiry into the Nature of Grammaticalization*. Oxford: Oxford University Press.

LANGSTON, KEITH. 2006. *Čakavian Prosody. The Accentual Patterns of the Čakavian Dialects of Croatian*. Slavica. Bloomington. [prijevod: Čakavska prozodija. Naglasni sustavi čakavskih govora. Matica hrvatska. Zagreb. 2015]

LEHMANN, CHRISTIAN. 1985. Grammaticalization: Synchronic variation and diachronic \ change. *Lingua e stile* 20. 303–18.

LEHMANN, CHRISTIAN (1995[1982]). *Thoughts on Grammaticalization*. Munich: Lincom Europa (revision of *Thoughts on Grammaticalization: A Programmatic Sketch*, 1 (1982), Arbeiten des Kölner Universalienprojekts 49).

MATASOVIC, RANKO. 2008. *Poredbenopovijesna gramatika hrvatskoga jezika*. (Biblioteka Theoria.) Zagreb: Matica Hrvatska.

MIKLOSICH, FRANK (ed.). 1964[1858]. *Monumenta Serbica Spectantia Historiam Serbiae, Bosnae, Ragusii*. Vienna: Apud Guilelmum Braumüller.

NANDRIS, Grigore, 1959. *Old Church Slavonic Grammar*. London: University of London, The Athlone Press.

NORDE, MURIEL. 2009. *Degrammaticalization*. Oxford: Oxford University Press.

NORDE, MURIEL. 2011. Degrammaticalization. *The Oxford Handbook of Grammaticalization*, ed. by Bernd Heine and Heiko Narrog. Oxford Handbooks Online.

PENNINGTON, JAMES J. 2007. Chewing on the BCS Future. Paper presented at the 2007 Slavic Linguistics Society Conference. Berlin, Germany.

PENNINGTON, JAMES J. 2012. If the U fits: An orthographic anomaly in the Miroslav Gospel. *Palaeoslavica: International Journal for the Study of Slavic Medieval Literature, History, Language and Ethnology* 20. 1, 277–90.

PETROVIĆ-NJEGOŠ, PETAR II. 1847. *Gorski vijenac*. Vienna. Available online at: http://www.institut-genocid.unsa.ba/pdf/GORSKI%20VIJENAC.pdf. Accessed online on May 1, 2019.

PIPER, PREDRAG, ANTONIĆ, IVANA, RUŽIĆ, VLADISLAVA, TANASIĆ, SRETO, POPOVIĆ, LJUDMILA I TOŠOVIĆ, BRANKO. 2005. *Sintaksa savremenoga srpskog jezika*. Beograd: Matica srpska.

RAMAT, ANNA G. 1998. "Testing the boundaries of grammaticalization." In The Limits of Grammaticalization, Ramat, Anna G., and Hopper, Paul J. (eds.), Amsterdam, The Netherlands: John Benjamins Publ., pp. 107–127.

SCATTON, ERNEST. 2002[1993]. Bulgarian. *The Slavonic Languages*, ed. by Bernard Comrie and Greville G. Corbett (eds.), 188–248. New York: Routledge.

SHIROKOVA, A. G., and V. P GUDKOVA (eds.). 1977. *Slavjanskie jazyki*. Moscow.

VEČERKA, RADOSLAV. 1993. *Altkirchenslavische (altbulgarische) Syntax II: Die innere Satzstruktur.* Freiburg: Weiher.

WIEMER, BJÖRN. 2011. Grammaticalization in the Slavic languages. *The Oxford Handbook of Grammaticalization*, ed. by Bernd Heine and Heiko Narrog. Oxford Handbooks Online.

WILLIS, DAVID. 2007. Syntactic lexicalization as a new type of degrammaticalization. *Linguistics* 45. 271–310.

WILLIS, DAVID. 2017. Chapter 2: Degrammaticalization. *The Cambridge Handbook of Historical Syntax*, ed. by Adam Ledgeway and Ian Roberts, 28–48. Cambridge: Cambridge University Press.

Katrin Schlund

On the Origin of East Slavic Elemental Constructions/Adversity Impersonals. Evidence from Town Chronicles of Old Rus'

Abstract There is a longstanding debate about the origin of Elemental Constructions / Adversity Impersonals in East Slavic (e.g., Russian: *mašinu oprokinulo vzryvom* – 'the car was turned over by a blast'). While there appear to be no attestations of Elemental Constructions (ECs) in Old Church Slavonic (Mrazek 1964: 169), they can be found already in medieval town chronicles of Old Rus' (Hofmann 1934; Georgieva 1978). However, the structure of many of these early, supposedly impersonal constructions is actually ambiguous; it is possible to derive both personal and impersonal readings. The present paper reviews some alleged early instances of ECs critically and discusses alternative analyses. It also presents the oldest unambiguous cases attested in old East Slavic town chronicles.

Keywords: Transitive Impersonals, Elemental Constructions, Adversity Impersonals, Old Russian, Old East Slavic

1. Introduction

The label Elemental Construction (EC) is used here to denote an impersonal construction that has become famous for its textbook examples, as illustrated in (1) and (2):

(1)	Vetrom	sorvalo	kryši.
	wind-INST[1]	ripped_off-PST.N	roofs-ACC.PL

'The wind ripped off the roofs.' or 'The roofs were ripped off by the wind.'

(2)	Soldata	ranilo	pulej.
	soldier-ACC.SG	wounded-PST.N	bullet-INST

'The soldier was wounded by a bullet.' or 'A bullet wounded the soldier.'

These constructions cannot be translated directly into English but have to be rendered as personal sentences, either active or passive, as indicated. The two most common labels for this construction, namely "Elemental Construction" and "Adversity Impersonal", relate to its characteristic semantics: ECs typically express events caused by elemental forces of nature, and such events often have an adverse effect on humans and / or their property.[2] These constructions are special in that they consist of an otherwise personal transitive verb in impersonal use and allow for the optional expression of a cause by an instrumental phrase. While most contemporary contributions about ECs focus on modern Russian and other modern Slavic languages[3] (e.g., Mustajoki & Kopotev 2005; Junghanns, Lenertová, Fehrmann 2017; Schlund 2020), some studies also discuss the origin and diachronic development of ECs (e.g., Georgieva 1978; Kwon 2010). However, examples are often cited without reference to their broader context, which is why their syntactic structure is often difficult to determine. Section 2 focuses on the presentation of natural disasters in the two oldest town chronicles of the medieval Rus', the Primary Chronicle and the Novgorod First Chronicle. Section 2 reviews some of the oldest examples circulating in the literature. Section 3 presents the first unambiguous instances.

2. Non-Evidence of ECs in the Oldest Sources

The two oldest chronicles of medieval Rus' are the so-called Primary Chronicle (Ru: *Povest' vremennyx let*) dating to 1377, and the oldest redaction of the Novgorod First Chronicle, the Synodal Manuscript (Ru: *Sinodal'nyj spisok*), dating to the middle of the 13th century.

Georgieva (1978: 233) discusses the structure of one passage in the Primary Chronicle with respect to a possible impersonal interpretation:

(3) tišině sušti i morju ukrotivšjusja, abьe burja s větrom vъsta, i volnamъ velikymъ vъstavšim zasobь, i

bezъbožnyx	rusi	korablja	smjate,		
godless-GEN	Rus-GEN	boats-ACC	confused-3SG.AOR		
i	kъ	beregu	privěrže,	i	izbi
and	towards	shore	threw-3SG.AOR	and	broke_up-3SG.AOR
ja					
them-ACC					

jako malu ixъ ot takovyja bědy izbyti i vъsvojasi vъzvratišasja

(PVL, year 6374 [866])[4]

'[t]he weather had been still and the sea calm, when a storm of wind came up, and when great waves straightway rose, confusing the boats of the godless Russes, it threw them upon the shore [...] and broke them up, so that few escaped such destruction and returned to their native land'

(translation slightly adapted from Cross and Sherbowitz-Wetzor 1953: 60)

The modern Russian translation uses ECs in the respective passage:

(4) Byla v èto vremja tišina i more bylo spokojno, no tut vnezapno podnjalas' burja s vetrom, i vstali ogromnye volny,

i	**razmetalo**	**korabli**	**bezbožnoj**	**Rusi**,	
and	confused-PRF.N	ships-ACC	godless-GEN	Rus'-GEN	
pribilo	**ix**	**k**	**beregu,**	**i**	**perelomalo,**
threw-PRF.N	them-ACC	to	shore	and	broke_up-PRF.N

tak čto nemnogim iz nix udalos' spastis' ot ètoj bedy i vernut'sja domoj[5]

Translation as in (3)

The structure of the historical example is, however, not clear. As the predicates *smjate*, *privěrže* and *izbi* occur in the aorist, it is impossible to determine whether or not they agree with the nominative phrase *burja* preceding at some distance. In the modern Russian translation, on the other hand, the impersonal structure is clear because the past tense (which evolved from a perfect to an overall past tense) is marked for gender.

The language of the Novgorod First Chronicle is less sublime and more colloquial than the language of the Primary Chronicle. There are numerous references to forces of nature in the Novgorod First Chronicle. Examples (5) and (6) are illustrative cases in point:

(5)

vъ	to	že	lěto	gromъ	bystь
in	that	same	year	thunder-NOM	was-3SG.AOR
strašьnъ	zělo	i	mъlnija		
terrible-NOM	very	and	lightning-NOM		

(NFChr, *Sinodal'nyj spisok*, year 6695 [1187])

'the same year there was terrible thunder and lightning'

(Michell and Forbes 1914: 33)

(6)	gromъ	bystь	po	zautrenii
	thunder-NOM	was-3SG.AOR	after	morning_service

(NFChr, *Sinodal'nyj spisok*, year 6722 [1214])
'there was thunder after morning service'
(Michell and Forbes 1914: 52)

These are common syntactic structures also in Old Church Slavonic. The predicate may remain in the singular even when the subject is a conjoined noun phrase, which is indicative of a volatile status of the structure fluctuating between impersonal and personal syntax. Impersonals with verbs other than the copula are also available, but less frequent. Example (7) is a case in point:

(7)	vъ	nebesi	pogremě	vъ	časъ	1	v	nošči
	in	sky	thundered-3SG.AOR	in	hour	1	in	night

(PVL, year 6618 [1110])
'there was thunder in the sky at one at night' Lit.: 'it thundered'

When forces of nature function as the cause of an event, they are typically realized as transitive subjects, and not as ECs, as in (8) through (11):

(8)	mostъ	snese	voda	na	Volxově
	bridge-M.ACC	carried-3SG.AOR	water-NOM	on	Volxov
	velikyj				
	big-M.ACC				

(NFChr, *Sinodal'nyj spisok*, year 6759 [1251])
'the water carried away the large bridge over the Volxov'
(Michell and Forbes 1914: 93)

(9)	bystь	dъžgь	sъ	gradomъ,	ijunja	vъ
	was-3SG.AOR	rain-NOM	with	hail	June	on
	27,	vъ	nedělju,	i	zažьže	gromъ
	27	on	Sunday	and	set_fire-3SG.AOR	thunder-NOM

cerkovь	svjatyja	Bogorodicja
church- ACC	holy	Mother_of_God

(NFChr, *Sinodal'nyj spisok*, year 6656 [1148])

'there was rain with hail on June 27, a Sunday; and thunder set fire to the Church of the Holy Mother of God [...]'

(Michell and Forbes 1914: 19)

(10)

na	osěnь	ubi	vsju	jar
on	autum	killed-3SG.AOR	all-ACC	corn-ACC
morozъ				
frost-NOM				

(NFChr, *Sinodal'nyj spisok*, year 6669 [1161])

'in the autumn frost killed all the spring corn'

(Michell and Forbes 1914: 23)

(11)

privlece	korablь	kъ	steně	gradьněi	větrъ
drew_up-3SG.AOR	ships-ACC	to	wall	town-ADJ	wind-NOM

(NFChr, *Sinodal'nyj spisok*, year 6712 [1204])

'the wind drew the ships up to the town wall'

(Michell and Forbes 1914: 46)

Passive constructions are also available in such contexts, but they are less frequent than the personal transitive constructions above:

(12)

edinъ	otъ	dьjakъ	zaraženъ	bystь	otъ	groma
one	of	chanters	struck-PST.PTCP.PASS	was-3SG.AOR	from	thunder

(NSChr, year 6625 [1117])

'one of the chanters, a clerk, was struck by the thunder'

(Michell and Forbes 1914: 9)

Georgieva (1978: 233 f.) interprets the following example from the Synodal Manuscript as an instance of an EC:

(13)

i	by	voda	velika	velьmi	vъ	Volxově
and	was	water:NOM	big:NOM	very	in	Volkhov
i	svjudě,	**seno**	**i**	**drъva**	**raznese**	
and	everywhere,	hay:ACC	and	wood:ACC	carried_away-3SG.AOR	

(NFChr, *Sinodal'nyj spisok*, year 6651 [1143])

'and the water was very high in the Volkhov [river] and everywhere, it carried abroad hay and wood'

(Michell and Forbes 1914: 18)

Georgieva (1978: 233) classifies example 13 and others (see Section 3) as clearly impersonal: "*iz-za nevozmožnosti otyskat' ix predikativnuju svjaz' s podležaščim, kotoraja otražala by ob"ektivnye javlenija*" [because of the impossibility of finding their predicative link with the subject that would reflect objective phenomena–KS], although what Georgieva means by "objective phenomena" is somewhat enigmatic. In any case, the predicative link between the subject *voda* and its predicate *raznese* is actually quite clear and straightforward. After all, there is no reason to assume that the nominative noun phrase *voda* does *not* function as the transitive subject of the entire phrase, and example (13) is thus no different from examples (8) through (11) above. The German translation of the respective passage given by Dietze (1971: 61) also supports this analysis:

(14)

im	Volchov	und	überall	gab	es			
in	Volkhov	and	everywhere	gave-3SG	it-EXPL[6]			
Hochwasser$_1$,	das$_1$	das	Heu	und	Brennholz	mit	sich	fortriß
water$_1$	which$_1$	the	hay	and	woods	with	REFL	carried_away

[…]

'and in the Volkhov [river] and everywhere, there was very high water which carried away the hay and wood'

As indicated by the subscript characters, Dietze analyzes the water as the subject of both clauses and even emphasizes this by using a disambiguating relative clause.[7]

Finally, it must be pointed out that paratactic syntax and distance between a subject and its predicate as seen in many of the above examples is paramount also in cases with animate subjects, where there is no doubt that they also function as the subjects of subsequent clauses. Example (15) illustrates this:

(15)	toi	že	oseni	knjazь	Vitovtъ	Litovskii	vzja
	that	same	autum	duke-NOM	Vitovt	Lithuanian	took-3SG.AOR
	gradъ	Smoleneskъ	i	naměstnikъ	svoi	posada	
	town-ACC	Smolensk	and	lieutenant-ACC	his	placed-3SG.AOR	

(NFChr, *Sinodal'nyj spisok*, year 1395)

'the same autumn *Knyaz* [italics in original] Vitovt of Lithuania took the town of Smolensk and placed his lieutenant there'

(Michell and Forbes 1914: 167)

There is thus no compelling evidence of ECs in the Synodal Manuscript of the Novgorod First Chronicle.

3. Contentious Instances of ECs

Georgieva (1978: 232 f.) further assumes that "*dostatočno jasen bezličnyj xarakter nekotoryx postroenij i s aoristnymi formami*" [the impersonal nature of a number of structures with the aorist is quite clear–KS] for constructions appearing in other medieval town chronicles of Old Rus'. She substantiates her claim with the following example taken from the chronicle of Suzdal' (*Suzdal'skaja letopis'*) from the end of the 15th century (which also includes the Primary Chronicle):

(16)	bystь	gromъ	strašenъ	i	**zarazi**
	was-3SG.AOR	thunder-NOM	horrible-NOM	and	killed-3SG.AOR
	dvoe	**čadi**	**i**	**xraminu**	**zažže**
	two-ACC	children-ACC	and	house-ACC	set_on_fire-3SG.AOR

(*Suzdal'skaja letopis'*, year 6696 [1188])[8]

'there was a horrible thunderstorm that killed two children and set a house on fire'

It seems that Georgieva (1978: 233) claims that only the second predicate and its transitive object, namely *xraminu zažže*, are impersonal, because only this passage is italicized in her text. However, there does not seem to be any reason why the thunderstorm should function as the subject of the first predicate (*zarazi dvoe čadi*), but not of the second one (*xraminu zažže*). The slightly greater distance between the first and the second predicate is no reason to assume that the second predication is impersonal.

Things are not that easy, however, with example (17):

(17)	šelomъ	sъ	nego	sletě	i	**ščitъ**
	helmet-NOM	from	him	slid_down-3AOR	and	shield-ACC/NOM
	ottorže					
	ripped_off-3SG.AOR					

(*Suzdal'skaja letopis'*, year 6659 [1151])
'his helmet slid down and his shield was ripped off'

Georgieva (1978: 234) maintains that the second clause, *ščitъ ottorže*, is impersonal, which implies that *ščitъ* is in the accusative case. This is also in line with the analysis given in the diachronic subcorpus of the Russian National Corpus, where *ščitъ* is tagged as accusative.[9] *Ščitъ* is a masculine inanimate o-stem noun, so the accusative is identical to the nominative. The context does not give us any further clues about how to determine the syntactic structure of the phrase, either, because there is no possible nominative phrase preceding or following the passage that could function as a subject.[10] However, this does not mean that the phrase must be a transitive impersonal (that is, an EC without an instrumental phrase indicating the semantic cause of the event). Another possibility might be that the verb *otъtъrgnuti* is used intransitively rather than transitively. It is well known that transitive and intransitive verbs were not yet distinguished clearly in Old Russian; Ivanov (1995: 466), for instance, speaks of "*nečetkost' formal'nyx granic meždu perexodnymi i neperexodnymi glagolami*" [unclear formal boundaries between transitive and intransitive verbs–KS]. However, although Ivanov (1995: 466–470) indicates a number of examples of unstable valency in Old Russian, I could not find any intransitive uses of (semantically) highly transitive verbs such as *otъtъrgnuti*.

Letučij (2013) refers to verbs without a formal (in)transitivity distinction as labile verbs (*labil'nye glagoly*). The verb *otъtъrgnuti* would be a case of so-called P-lability (*P-labil'nost'*), in which the subject in the intransitive use corresponds to the object in the transitive use (ibid. 2013: 29). As Letučij (2013: 92) also notes, labile verbs of this kind were not very frequent in Old Russian. Moreover, the Old Russian subcorpus of the Russian National Corpus includes only five occurrences of the verb *otъtъrgnuti*, four of which are clearly transitive and personal, and one of which is example (17) given above. The claim that *otъtъrgnuti* is used intransitively in (17) is thus difficult to maintain.

There is yet another possible analysis that would allow for an interpretation as transitive and personal. It could be that the nominative phrase *šelomъ* 'helmet' functions as the subject of the second predicate, thus rendering 'his helmet slid down and ripped off his shield' While the intransitive analysis seems less compelling, it is impossible to determine whether the transitive impersonal or transitive personal reading is correct.

The third example given by Georgieva (1978: 234) is (18):

(18)	ozero	morozi	vъ	noščь
	lake-NOM/ACC	froze-3AOR	in	night

(NFChr, *Sinodal'nyj spisok*, year 6651[1143])[11]
'The lake froze at night.'

The analysis of (18) as a transitive impersonal has been given a number of times before and after Georgieva (1978) (e.g., Jagić 1899: 20; Ivanov 1964: 414; Borkovskij and Kuznecov 1965: 416; Stecenko 1977: 80; Cimmerling 2018: 17). The Old Russian subcorpus of the Russian National Corpus likewise tags *ozero* as accusative. But *ozero* is also a noun whose nominative and accusative forms coincide, and Bräuer (1967: 16) obviously assumes it is nominative because he analyzes the example as personal and intransitive.

Although the proponents of the interpretation of (18) as transitive and impersonal prevail, it must be noted that the example is unique. The historical subcorpus of the Russian National Corpus does not yield any more examples of this kind. Rather, the freezing of a lake or river is expressed intransitively, as in (19):

(19)	i	načja	Dněrpь	мьгъznuti
	and	began-3SG.AOR	Dnieper-NOM	freeze-INF

(NFChr, *Sinodal'nyj spisok*, year 1016 [6524])[12]
'and the Dnieper began to freeze'

Importantly, the event of freezing is not a typical context for ECs in contemporary Russian, either. As I have argued extensively in Schlund (2018), ECs are characterized by a specific causative structure: They always depict instances of external, physical and instantaneous transfer of force from an inanimate entity to another (animate or inanimate entity). The causative structure of ECs thus differs from prototypical causativity (as defined by Croft 1991: 173) only in that they do not tolerate a human agent. The process of freezing differs from the causative prototype not only because there (usually) is no human agent, but also because there is no sensually perceivable and instantaneous transfer of force. Therefore, the most natural way to express the freezing of a lake in modern Russian is not by means of an EC, but by an intransitive subject construction (*ozero zamerzlo* 'lake-NOM froze-PST.N'). Given that other instances of clearly transitive impersonals are missing in the Synodal Manuscript of the Novgorod First Chronicle, it is unlikely that the singular example of (19) was crucial for the emergence, let alone the spread, of ECs in the later sources (cf. Section 3).

There is one more case of an allegedly transitive impersonal structure that calls for critical evaluation, analyzed as impersonal by Cimmerling (2018: 17):

(20)	**zavistь**	**vъloži**	**ljudьmь**	na	arxipiskopa	Mitrofana
	envy-ACC	put-3SG.AOR	people-DAT	on	vladyka-ACC	Mitrofan-ACC

(NFChr, *Troickij spisok*, year 6719 [1210])

'envy put to people towards vladyka Mitrofan'

In a footnote inserted after the example, Cimmerling (ibid.) himself mentions the possibility of a personal interpretation of (20). I contend that this interpretation is much more likely than the impersonal one favored by Cimmerling, since the passage immediately preceding (20) includes the nominative subject *zloděi* 'devil', which is a very plausible subject also for the subsequent predicate.

(21)	isperva	ne	xotja	dobra	zloděi,	zavistь
	from_first	not	wanting-NOM.SG.M	good	devil-NOM	envy-ACC
	vъloži	ljudьmь	na	arxipiskopa	Mitrofana	
	put-3SG.AOR	people-DAT	on	vladyka	Mitrofan	

(NFChr, *Sinodal'nyj spisok*, year 1211 [6719])

'the evil-doer who from the first wished no good [to man] put envy in the people […] against vladyka Mitrofan'

(Michell and Forbes 1914: 51)

Cimmerling (ibid.) points out that *zloděi* could also be a nominative plural, yielding a reading of 'evil spirits'. This would render the second clause impersonal. Yet, there is also the participle *xotja*, which is nominative singular and masculine. There would be no subject for the participle to agree with if *zloděi* were a plural.[13]

What is more, the devil frequently occurs as a transitive subject in the Novgorod and other chronicles in very similar wording. An illustrative case in point is (22):

(22)	togo	že	leta	vstavi	dьavolъ	vraždu	iskoni
	that	same	year	put-3SG.AOR	devil-NOM	hostility-ACC	in_beginning

nenavidjaj	dobra	rodu	čelověčьskomu
hating-nom.sg.m	good-ACC	race-DAT	human-DAT

(PVL, *Lavrenťevskaja letopis'*, year 6763 [1186])[14]

'the same year, the devil, hating the good of the human race from the start, sowed hostility'

In examples (21), (22), and many similar cases, the structure is clearly transitive personal, with the devil functioning as the subject-agent of one or more predicates. Finally, (21) is not an instance of prototypical (albeit inanimate) causation, either. Transitive verbs implying a human agent, such as *vъložiti* 'put' above, are usually not accepted in ECs in modern Russian, and I have never come across such cases in historical sources. Emotional causatives such as *vъložiti zavistь* are only very marginally acceptable in ECs because they deviate too greatly from the causative prototype expressed by ECs (cf. Schlund 2018). I therefore do not see any reason to treat (21) as ambiguous, let alone as impersonal.

4. Earliest Uncontested Attestations of ECs

So far, we have only seen non-evidence or contentious instances of ECs in the town chronicles. This raises the question of how old East Slavic ECs actually are. This question was discussed intensely at the beginning of the 20th century. While some scholars have argued for an ancient, possibly even Proto-Indo-European origin of ECs (e.g., Pedersen 1907), others saw ECs as a specifically Russian innovation (e.g., Specht 1930: 280). Hofmann (1934) already provided evidence that neither of these views is correct. He showed that the earliest instances of ECs occur already in medieval town chronicles of Old Rus'; however, as we have seen in Section 2, not in the oldest town chronicle, the Novgorod First Chronicle. The oldest instance of an EC with a cause phrase in the instrumental case has been brought up many times in the literature (e.g., Jagić 1899: 20; Hofmann 1934: 211; Mrazek 1964: 170). It originates from the Pskov First Chronicle dated to the second half of the 15th century (Nasonov 1967 [1941] III):

(23) Togo že lěta […] nača naxoditi doždь silenъ […] měsjaca ijulja […], i měsjaca avgusta i sentrjabrja i oktjabrja […] i napolnišasja rěki […] aki vesně vodoju […]

a	**travu**	**vodoju**	po	rěkamъ	i	po
and	grass-ACC	water-INST	PREP	rivers	and	PREP
ručьjamъ	**otnjalo**					
streams	carried_away-3SG.N					

(PFChr, year 6976 [1468])[15]

'the same year there was heavy rain in the month of July, and in the months of August, September, and October, and the rivers filled [with water] like in spring, and the water poured the grass into the rivers and streams and carried it away with them' Lit.: 'it poured the grass with water into the rivers'

The syntactic structure of the respective forms is clear: The predicate *odnjalo* is impersonal, *travu* is a direct object in the accusative, and *vodoju* is an unambiguous instrumental case indicating the semantic cause of the event.

The Pskov First Chronicle contains many more ECs. The following passage includes two ECs, the second one of which is an EC even in the aorist:

(24) ide doždь vo vsju noščь, sъ gromomъ i sъ molnieju, i bystь predъ zautrenej, neizrečenno silno tresnu gromъ velmi i velika molnija, jako ne moščno bjaše vsjakija ploti čeloveči bezъ užasa byti, jako zemli potrjastisja i svja podnebesnaja osijala molnieju; i

toju	**molnieju**	u	svjatago	Pantelejmona	vъ		
this-INST	lightning-INST	by	Saint	Pantaleon	in		
monastyri	na	Krasnomъ	Dvorě	ne	na	vsěxъ	ikonaxъ
monastery	in	Red	Yard	not	on	all	icons
zoloto	**požglo**[…].	takože	toju	že	molnieju,		
gold-ACC	burned-PRF.N	also	this-INST	part	lightning-INST		

togo	že	utra,	**zažže**	**cerkovъ**	[...]	drevjanu
this	PART	morning	burned-3SG.AOR	church-ACC		wooden-ACC

svjatěj	Bogorodicy	[...]
holy-GEN	Mother_of_God-GEN	

(PFChr, year 6978 [1470])[16]

'it was raining all night, with thunder and with lightning, and it was before morning service that great thunder and lightning struck so unspeakably heavily that no human being could not be terrified as the ground was shaken and the whole world was illuminated by lightning; that same lightning burned the gold on almost all the icons of Saint Pantaleon in the monastery in the Red Yard [...] the same morning, that same lightning set fire to the wooden church of the holy virgin Mary'

The first clear attestations of impersonal uses of transitive verbs without an instrumental phrase indicating the cause of the event are even older. They can be found already in the Laurentian Chronicle, starting with the entry for the year 1300:

(25) Togo že lěta, sъ vesny, větri silni byša, i doždove, i gromove;

vъ	Toržku	tuča	na	odnomъ	času
in	Toržok	thunderstorm-NOM	on	one	hour
rovъ	**učinilo**	i	**xoromovъ**	**něskolko**	
ditch-ACC	created-PRF.N	and	houses-GEN	several-ACC	
sneslo	izъ	osnovanьja.			
pulled_off- PRF.N		from foundations			

(*Lavrent'evskaja letopis'*, year 6808 [1300])

'The same year, from spring on, there was strong wind, rain, and thunder; in Toržok a thunderstorm created a ditch within a single hour and several houses were pulled off their foundations.'

Importantly, example (25) is usually cited without the preceding clause introducing the weather conditions. It has also been argued that it is not clear whether the nominative phrase *tuča* 'thunderstorm' functions as the subject of the impersonal predicates *učinilo* and *sneslo* (thereby representing a transitional stage from personal to impersonal transitive, see below) because of the continuous writing (*scriptio continua*) and lack of punctuation marks of the time (Hofmann 1934: 217; Georgieva 1978: 233). Therefore, *tuča* could be the nominative subject only of a preceding, "introductory" clause with a zero copula (Hofmann 1934: 217; Georgieva 1978: 233), meaning 'there was a thunderstorm in Toržok', and followed by a transitive impersonal without a cause phrase. However, the zero copula is typical only of the present tense; in the aorist that we would expect in (25), the copula is typically expressed openly (as is the case, for instance, in examples (5), (6), (9), (12), (16), (24)). Moreover, when the clause preceding the impersonal clause is taken into account, an introductory reading of the impersonal clause becomes even more unlikely, since the weather conditions have already been mentioned in this previous clause.

Example (25) is therefore best analyzed as a hybrid, or semi-impersonal construction: although there is a nominative subject, the predicate does not agree with it but shows impersonal (default) morphology instead. Such hybrid constructions are not untypical of the chronicles, as has been noted already by Potebnja (1968 [1899]: 346). Potebnja (ibid.) and others (e.g., Peškovskij 1956 [1914]: 360; Sprinčak 1960: 93; Šaxmatov 1963 [1941]: 135 f.; Kwon 2010) have argued that ECs developed via an intermediate stage of hybrid constructions containing a nominative noun phrase and a non-agreeing predicate. A typical case in point is (26):

(26)	uxvatilo	ego	někaja	sila	aki
	caught-PRF.N	him-ACC	some-NOM	force-NOM	as_if
	větromъ				
	wind-INST				

(PFChr, year 7145 [1637])[17]

'he was caught by some force as if by wind'

The Laurentian Codex features one more EC without an instrumental phrase denoting the cause, located close to its end, and only shortly after example (25):

(27)	bystь	burja	velika,	i	mnogo	pakosti
	was-3SG.AOR	storm-NOM	big-NOM	and	a_lot_of	mischief
	bystь	po	selomъ	**dubьe**	**podralo.**	
	was-3SG.AOR	in	villages	oak_tree-ACC	uprooted-PRF.N	

(*Lavrentěvskaja letopis'*, year 6810 [1302])[18]

'there was a great storm, and a lot of mischief happened; oak trees were uprooted in the villages'

5. Conclusion

The modest goal of this short contribution was to show two things. First, the general assumptions about the earliest attestations of ECs in medieval chronicles of Old Rus' have been corroborated. The oldest example of a full-fledged EC – that is, an EC including an instrumental phrase denoting the semantic cause of the event – occurs in the Pskov First Chronicle, in the entry for the year 1468. The oldest examples of ECs without instrumental phrases denoting the cause occur towards the end of the Laurentian Codex. Some of these early examples seem to attest an intermediate stage, with a nominative noun phrase denoting the cause and a non-agreeing neuter predicate. Importantly, all the instances of ECs I have come across denote instances of external, physical causation. Other kinds of causation, such as emotional or internal causation, are missing in historical and contemporary ECs alike (cf. also Schlund 2018).

Second, there are some allegedly impersonal examples circulating in the literature whose structure is either ambiguous or, as I believe I have shown, more plausibly analyzed as personal. In some of these cases, it has been useful to include the broader context of the respective passages to determine their syntactic structure.[19] Ambiguous examples occur primarily in the aorist, since the aorist does not distinguish gender. Whether the development of the perfect tense into a multifunctional preterite helped to promote the spread of ECs, or whether these two developments were simply parallel changes, is difficult – or maybe even impossible – to tell on the basis of the data from the oldest chronicles.

Abbreviations

PSRL = Polnoe sobranie russkix letopisej
PVL = Povest' vremennyx let / Primary Chronicle
NFChr = Novgorod First Chronicle
NSChr = Novgorod Second Chronicle
PFChr = Pskov First Chronicle

Notes

1 The glosses used in this paper adhere to the Leipzig glossing rules: https://www.eva.mpg.de/lingua/resources/glossing-rules.php. Two additional glosses used here are AOR 'aorist' and EXPL 'expletive'.

2 Neither of these conditions is a precondition for the availability of an EC, since they may denote also neutral or even favorable events that do not need to be caused by forces of nature.

3 ECs with a cause phrase in the instrumental are available only in Russian, Ukrainian, Belarusian and, to a limited extent, Polish. For more information about the distribution of ECs in modern Slavic languages, cf. Junghanns, Lentertová, Fehrmann (2017) and Schlund (2020).
4 *PSRL 1.*
5 Source: http://lib.pushkinskijdom.ru/Default.aspx?tabid=4869, last access 05/25/2018.
6 The gloss EXPL stands for expletive, that is, a semantically bleached placeholder. In this case, the placeholder occupies the position of the syntactic subject.
7 German *Wasser* 'water' is a neuter noun. Therefore, anaphoric reference must be established by the personal pronoun *es* 'it', which is homonymous with the expletive *es* that would have to be used in an impersonal construction.
8 Source: http://enc.biblioclub.ru/Termin/1514048_Suzdalskaya_letopis, accessed 03/25/2020.
9 Source: http://ruscorpora.ru/new/search-old_rus.html.
10 The context is as follows:
(i) Togdy že bodoša konь podъ nimъ vъ nozdri, i konь že načatъ sovatisja podъ nimъ, i šelomъ s nego sletě i ščitъ ottorže; Božьimъ že zastuplenьemъ i molitvoju roditelь svoixъ sxranenъ bystь bezъ rany.
'Then they hit the horse beneath him into the nostrils, and the horse began rearing up beneath him, and his helmet slid down and his shield was ripped off; and by God's divine purpose and the prayer of his parents he was saved unharmed.'
11 Dietze (1971: 156).
12 Dietze (1971: 145).
13 In all fairness, it is important to point out that Cimmerling's analysis of example (20) is not crucial for his study, which does not focus on the history of ECs.
14 *PSRL 1.*
15 *PSRL 4.*
16 *PSRL 4.*
17 *PSRL 4.*
18 *PSRL 1.*
19 Moser (1998) shows the importance of considering the context with respect to some other questions of historical Russian syntax.

Bibliography

Borkovskij, Viktor I.; and Petr S. Kuznecov. 1965. *Istoričeskaja grammatika russkogo jazyka*. Izdanie vtoroe, dopolnennoe. Moskva: Nauka.

Bräuer, Herbert. 1967. Sachbezeichnungen als Subjekt im Altrussischen (in der Sprache der Novgoroder 1. Chronik in der Synodal-Handschrift). *Festschrift für Margarete Woltner zum 70. Geburtstag am 4. Dezember 1967*, ed. by Peter Brank, 13–22. Heidelberg: Carl Winter Universitätsverlag.

Cimmerling, Anton V. 2018. Impersonal'nye konstrukcii i dativno-predikativnye struktury v russkom jazyke. *Voprosy Jazykoznanija* 5. 7–33.

Croft, William. 1991. *Syntactic categories and grammatical relations. The cognitive organization of information*. Chicago; London: The University of Chicago Press.

Georgieva, V. L. 1978. Bezličnye predloženija. *Istoričeskaja grammatika russkogo jazyka*, ed. by Viktor I. Borkovskij, 230–95. Moskva: Nauka.

Hofmann, Erich. 1934. Impersonale mit Instrumental im Russischen. *Zeitschrift für Vergleichende Sprachforschung auf dem Gebiete der indogermanischen Sprachen* 61. 209–21.

Ivanov, V. V. 1964. *Istoričeskaja grammatika russkogo jazyka*. Moskva: Prosveščenie.

Ivanov, Valerij V. 1995. *Drevnerusskaja grammatika XII–XIII vv.* Moskva: Nauka.

Jagić, Vatroslav. 1899. *Beiträge zur slavischen Syntax*. Wien: Gerold.

Junghanns, Uwe; Denisa Lenertová; and Dorothee Fehrmann. 2017. Parametric variation of Slavic Accusative Impersonals. *Aspects of Slavic Linguistics. Formal grammar, lexicon and communication,* ed. by Olav Müller-Reichau and Marcel Guhl, 140–65. (Language, Context & Cognition). Berlin; Boston: de Gruyter.

Kwon, Kyongjoon. 2010. The Adversity Impersonal construction in diachrony. *Annual Workshop on Formal Approaches to Slavic Linguistics (FASL 18): The Cornell Meeting 2009,* ed. by Wayles Browne, Adam Copper, Alison Fisher, Esra Kesici, Nikola Predolac, and Draga Zec, 255–69. Ann Arbor: Michigan Slavic Publications.

Letučij, Aleksandr B. 2013. *Tipologija labil'nyx glagolov*. Moskva: Jazyki Slavjanskoj Kul'tury.

Moser, Michael. 1998. Scheinbelege in der historischen Syntax des Russischen. *Zeitschrift für Slawistik 43* (4). 401–13.

Mrazek, Roman. 1964. *Sintaksis russkogo tvoritel'nogo. Strukturno-sravitel'noe issledovanie.* (Opera Universitatis Purkynianae Brunensis, Facultats Philosophica 94). Praha: Statni Ped. Naklad.

Mustajoki, Arto, and Mixail V. Kopotev. 2005. Lodku uneslo vetrom: uslovija i konteksty upotreblenija russkoj «stixijnoj» konstruckii. *Russian Linguistics* 29 (1). 1–38.

Pedersen, Holger. 1907. Neues und nachträgliches. *Zeitschrift für Vergleichende Sprachforschung auf dem Gebiete der Indogermanischen Sprachen* XL. 129–73.

Peškovskij, A. M. 1956[7] [1914]. *Russkij sintaksis v naučnom osveščenii*. Moskva: Gosudarstvennoe učebno-pedagogičeskoe izdatel'stvo ministerstva prosveščenija RSFSR.

Potebnja, Aleksandr A. 1968 [1899]. *Iz zapisok po russkoj grammatike. Tom III. Ob izmenenii značenija zamenax suščestvitel'nogo*. Moskva: Prosveščenie.

Šaxmatov, A. A. 1963 [1941]. *Sintaksis russkogo jazyka*. (Slavistic Printings and Reprintings XLI). The Hague: Mouton & Co.

Schlund, Katrin. 2018. *The Russian "Elemental Construction" from a synchronic and diachronic perspective: An empirical contribution to the understanding of an impersonal construction in Slavic.* Unpublished post-doctoral thesis. Ruprecht-Karls-University Heidelberg, Germany.

Schlund, Katrin. 2020. Active transitive impersonals in Slavic and beyond: A parallel corpus analysis. *Russian Linguistics* 44 (1). Online: https://doi.org/10.1007/s11185-020-09221-2, last access 08/17/2021.

Specht, Franz. 1930. Lituanica. *Zeitschrift für vergleichende Sprachforschung auf dem Gebiete der Indogermanischen Sprachen* 57 (3–4). 276–96.

Sprinčak, Ja. A. 1960. *Očerk russkogo istoričeskogo sintaksisa. Prostoe predloženie*. Kiev: Učebno-Pedagogičeskoe Izdat. "Radjans'ka Škola".

Stecenko, A. N. 1977. *Istoričeskij sintaksis russkogo jazyka*. Izd. 2, ispr. i dop. Moskva: Vysšaja škola.

Sources of Chronicle Texts

Cross, Samuel H., and Sherbowitz-Wetzor, Olgerd P. 1953. *The Russian Primary Chronicle. Laurentian text.* (The Medieval Academy of America 60). Cambridge, Massachusetts: The Medieval Academy of America. Online: http://www.mgh-bibliothek.de/dokumente/a/a011458.pdf, last access 08/17/2021.

Dietze, Joachim. 1971. *Die erste Novgoroder Chronik nach ihrer ältesten Redaktion (Synodalhandschrift) 1016-1333/1353. Edition des altrussischen Textes und Faksimile der Handschrift im Nachdruck. The first Novgorod Chronicle in its oldest version (synodal transcript). Edition of the Old Russian text with facsimile of the transcript in reprint.* München: Otto Sagner.

Michell, Robert, and Forbes, Nevill (eds.). 1914. *The Chronicle of Novgorod 1016–1471*. Translated from the Russian by Robert Michell and Nevill Forbes. With an introduction by C. Raymond Beazley and an account of the text by A. A. Shakhmatov. (Camden Third Series XXV). London: Offices of the Society. Online: http://faculty.washington.edu/dwaugh/rus/texts/MF1914.pdf, last access 08/17/2021.

Nasonov, A. (1967 [1941]): *Pskovskie letopisi. Vypusk pervyj.* Unveränderter fotomechanischer Nachdruck der Originalausgabe von 1941. Moskva; Leningrad: Akad. Nauk SSSR.

Polnoe sobranie russkix" lětopisej. Tom" 1. I. i II. Lavrentievskaja i troickaja lětopisi. Sanktpeterburg". 1846. Online: http://psrl.csu.ru/index.shtml, last access 08/17/2021.

Polnoe sobranie russkix" lětopisej. Tom" 4. *IV. V. Novgorodskija pskovskija lětopisi.* Sanktpeterburg". 1848. Online: http://psrl.csu.ru/index.shtml, last access 08/17/2021.

Luka Szucsich and Karolina Zuchewicz

Incrementality and (Non)Clausal Complementation in Slavic

Abstract In this article, we discuss the notion of incrementality in Slavic languages. We build upon the standard definition of "incremental theme verbs" that take nominal objects (cf. Krifka 1989a, 1989b, 1989c, 1992 among others) and extend it to "incremental theme verbs" that take clausal complements. We follow Zuchewicz (2020) and assume that the so-called 'reveal'-type predicates ('prove'/'reveal'/'show that') imply a gradual creation of a proof for a 'that'-clause, which makes them similar to "incremental theme verbs" like 'build' or 'read'. The incrementality of this verb class is the crucial building block for the fact that perfective 'reveal'-type predicates induce a veridical interpretation of the embedded proposition. We further provide a cross-linguistic overview of incremental relations by additionally discussing data from Finnish and English.*

Keywords: Aspect, Entailment, Incrementality, Perfectivity, Polish, Slavic, Veridicality

1. Introduction

Following canonical views on Slavic verbal aspect (cf. Dickey 2000, Zaliznjak & Šmelev 2000, Gvozdanović 2012 among many others), we take the opposition perfective (pfv.) vs. imperfective (ipfv.) to be grammatical, representing what has widely been called "viewpoint aspect."[1] The grammatical nature of "viewpoint aspect" in Slavic is supported by systematic complementary behavior of verbs marked for the opposing aspect, for instance, the incompatibility of pfv. verbs with phasal verbs like Po. *zacząć*$_{\text{PFV}}$/*zaczynać*$_{\text{IPFV}}$ 'to begin', or the lack of periphrastic future forms of pfv. verbs in North Slavic languages (cf. Zaliznjak & Šmelev 2000, Zuchewicz 2020, Zuchewicz & Szucsich 2020 among others). Furthermore, we consider verbal aspect in Slavic to be morphosyntactically represented by features with semantically relevant information which, in the case of the pfv. aspect, consists in the marking of limitation (boundedness), or selection of boundaries (cf. Sonnenhauser 2008, Wiemer & Seržant 2017,

Zuchewicz 2020). Grammatical (or viewpoint) aspect can be thought of as an operator which scopes over information represented by the verbal domain or verb phrase (VP). This lexically determined information, mostly labelled "lexical aspect," interacts with grammatical aspect (cf. Filip 2012, Gvozdanović 2012, Tatevosov 2016 among many others). "Lexical aspect" is standardly assumed to comprise properties of situations expressed by verbs and their arguments, especially the internal argument, i.e., the direct objects with transitive verbs or the subject with unaccusative intransitive verbs. These properties, in turn, define different situation classes, which interact with viewpoint aspect. In the following, we will use the term "aspect" for viewpoint aspect, and "situation classes" (or just "verb classes") for lexical aspect.

One of the most prominent properties of situation classes is (a)telicity, where telic VPs express a situation containing a resultant state (also called 'goal' or 'natural endpoint'; cf. Krifka 1989b, 1992, Szucsich 2005, Filip 2012, Zuchewicz 2020). With telic verbs, and in an episodic reading, the boundary selected by a pfv. aspectual operator coincides with the left boundary of resultant states leading to a change-of-state interpretation. Another property relevant for our purpose is graduality, which results from the interplay of the fact that with certain VPs parts of objects can be mapped to parts of events and vice versa, and the fact that the uniqueness of objects holds. The latter means that there exists exactly one subobject (for instance a part of an apple) which belongs to the theme/patient of a relevant verbal predicate ('apple' in 'eat an apple') and which stands in a theme/patient relation to a particular subevent of the event represented by the verbal predicate (a subevent of eating), cf. Krifka (1989a, 1989b), and Zuchewicz (2020). The property of graduality distinguishes predicates which select so-called "incremental themes."

2. Aspectual Composition and Nominal Incremental Themes

2.1 (Non)Incremental Theme Verbs

It is a widely acknowledged assumption that there is a subgroup of verbal predicates, which combine with internal arguments in a way that nominal referential properties interact with verbal referential properties. The internal argument is commonly called an "incremental theme" (cf. Dowty 1991) and the verbal predicate an "incremental theme verb." It is assumed that with such verbs, the internal argument undergoes a gradual change over the course of the event involving parts of the denoted object, and that there is a natural endpoint of the respective event which corresponds to the totality of the object expressed by the internal argument NP. The parts of the object are mapped onto parts of events, which ultimately means that the incremental argument measures out the event (cf. Dowty 1991, Filip 1995, Krifka 1989a, 1989b, 1989c, 1992, Szucsich 2005, Zuchewicz 2020). Linguistically, this may have different effects on morphosyntactic features. In Slavic languages, ipfv. aspect marks that the event is not limited/bounded, which entails that with "incremental theme verbs," it is *not* asserted that the natural endpoint is reached. The effect on the interpretation of incremental themes is that only parts of the objects are involved in the event. With plural NPs, this effect results in a cumulative interpretation of the internal argument, whereas with pfv. verbs the internal argument is interpreted as a quantized object; cf. the contrast between (1) and (2), based on the initial observations of Wierzbicka (1967).

(1)	Ola	jadła	pierogi,	ale	część	zostawiła.
	Ola	ate.IPFV	dumpling.PL	but	part	left

'Ola was eating dumplings, but she left part of them.'

↛ (does not imply) The process of eating is completed. The amount of dumplings decreases during the process of eating.

(2)	Ola	zjadła	pierogi,	#ale	część	zostawiła.
	Ola	ate.PFV	dumpling.PL	but	part	left

'Ola ate up the dumplings, #but she left part of them.'

→ (implies) The process of eating is completed; the dumplings are not there anymore.

The examples in (1) and (2) show that the interpretation of an incremental theme depends on the aspectual marking of the verb selecting it (cf. also Zuchewicz 2018, 2020). With certain "incremental theme verbs," this interpretive dependency is particularly obvious, viz. with verbs of creation and verbs of consumption. Here, the object denoted by the internal argument gradually changes its quantity in the course of the process preceding the resultant state, which is asserted to have been reached only with verbs marked for the pfv. aspect. The pfv. operator implies a total affectedness, which, in the case of the object of *zjeść* 'eat up', translates to a complete disappearance of the object. In contrast, the ipfv. *jeść* 'eat' only implies that some parts of the object disappeared, i.e., that the object was partially affected by the process of eating (cf. Zuchewicz 2020, Zuchewicz

& Szucsich 2020); otherwise, it is neutral regarding the question of whether the event is completed after a topic time/reference time interval, or not. Additionally, linguistic and extra-linguistic contexts determine the exact interpretation of the internal argument. Several options are available: If the first clause in (1), *Ola jadła pierogi*, is considered in isolation, the internal argument *pierogi* 'dumplings' can have a weak-existential interpretation ('some'), as well as a definite referential or partitive interpretation ('some of the dumplings'). Furthermore, iterative and generic readings are available, given an appropriate context. In contrast, in the first clause containing a pfv. verb in (2), the internal argument refers to a definite group of objects (dumplings); cf. Zuchewicz (2020).

For comparison with the situation in Slavic languages, it is elucidating to take a look at Finnish which does not have a grammatical category of verbal aspect. However, with verbs of consumption and creation, the referential properties of direct objects are marked by case, which leads to similar interpretive effects as discussed for Polish above. In Finnish, the partitive signals cumulative reference with plural NPs and the accusative signals quantized reference; cf. the contrast in (3) and (4) (cf. Heinemäki 1994, Kiparsky 1998, Szucsich 2005).

(3) Mari kirjoitti kirjeitä.
Mari wrote letters.PART
'Mari was writing letters.'
↛ The process of writing is completed.

(4) Mari kirjoitti kirjeet.
Mari wrote letters.ACC
'Mari wrote the letters.'
→ The process of writing is completed.

However, with other types of "incremental theme verbs," the referential properties of the object itself need not be affected by the aspectual marking of the verb. Thus, the object of the relation *czytać*.IPFV/*przeczytać*.PFV *książkę*.ACC 'read a book' exists independently of the event, i.e., it exists as a quantized object before, during and after the *reading*-event. Thus, the internal structure of the book does not change during the process of reading. Still, the object expressed by the internal argument *książkę*.ACC 'book' is gradually subjected to the *reading*-event, i.e., the property of being read is applied to increasing parts of the object (the number of pages that were read corresponds to the realized subevents of reading; cf. Zuchewicz 2020). More precisely, we can assume that there is an ideal of 'read x', where x is read till the end, i.e., in its totality. This means that the totality interpretation of the object expressed by the internal argument *książkę*.ACC 'book' is relative to the property of being read (cf. Zuchewicz & Szucsich 2020).

Following Zuchewicz (2020), and Zuchewicz & Szucsich (2020), the achievement of the above-mentioned ideal – the natural culmination point of accomplishments – arises from a gradual disappearance of the amount of unread pages (or lines, words, letters, etc.), depending on how a particular event of reading is described or what is relevant for its description ('reading two pages in an hour', 'reading one line for the whole day', etc.). We can imagine a group of temporally ordered subevents: {e1 < e2 < e3}. Taking pages as a convenient example, the following holds for x (a book) that has 15 pages: e1: 10 unread pages, e2: 5 unread pages, e3: 0 unread pages. The gradual disappearance of unread pages leads to the completion of a *reading*-event. The fact that this completion is being achieved step-by-step confirms the incrementality of 'read' (i.e. incrementality is necessary for the reading process to progress, regardless of the properties/the quantity of an object). However, in contrast to verbs of creation and consumption, these "incremental theme verbs" allow for so-called backtracking, i.e., more than one subevent may be applied to particular parts of the object (cf. Section 2.2 for the lack of the property of uniqueness of events).

In the light of what has been said about "incremental theme verbs" which do not select for "gradually effected" or "consumed patients" (the terms were proposed in Krifka 1989a), it is revealing that, in Finnish, singular count nouns as internal arguments, although expressing a single, existing object, may be marked not only with the accusative, but also with the partitive; cf. (5) and (6).

(5) Mari luki kirjaa.
Mari read book.PART
'Mari was reading a/the book.'

(6) Mari luki kirjan.
Mari read book.ACC
'Mari read a/the book.'

The partitive in (5) indicates that the object is not totally subjected to the event. Of course, the partitive case marker does not imply that the object does not exist in its totality (cf. Heinemäki 1994, Kiparsky 1998, Szucsich 2005).

The interpretation of a direct object as a single (atomic) whole or as definite is not only dependent on the properties of the NP itself (singular count noun vs. mass noun or bare plural NP). As has been pointed out in the literature (cf. Filip 1995, 2005, Krifka 1989a, 1989b, 1989c, 1992, Szucsich 2005 among others), the question of whether the interpretation of internal arguments in the scope of aspectual operators is influenced by them depends on the semantic class a verb belongs to. There are verb classes with internal arguments which systematically do not exhibit any kind of mapping between objects and events. Transitive verbs of perception are a prominent class of verbs which select for a so-called non-gradual, simultaneous patient whose referential properties are not influenced by the aspectual operator; cf. (7) and (8).

(7)	Jan	słyszał	głosy	na	korytarzu.
	Jan	heard.IPFV	voices	on	corridor

‘Jan heard (some/the) voices in the corridor.’

(8)	Jan	usłyszał	głosy	na	korytarzu.
	Jan	heard.PFV	voices	on	corridor

‘Jan (suddenly) heard (some/the) voices in the corridor.’

In (7) and (8), the difference is not solely an aspectual one (pfv. vs. ipfv.), but also involves an aktionsart-based enrichment of the meaning of the pfv. variant (cf. Zuchewicz 2020, Zuchewicz & Szucsich 2020). The ipfv. verb in (7) denotes a state which has a cumulative reference. The internal argument may be interpreted as a cumulative object (probably the default interpretation) or as a quantized one. The pfv. counterpart in (8) receives an inchoative interpretation, i.e., prefixation with the prefix *u-* in this case introduces a left (initial) boundary of the *hearing*-event which the pfv. operator picks out as the (change-of-state) point for temporal limitation. Importantly, the interpretation of the internal argument is not affected by the aspectual operator, i.e., it again may be interpreted as a cumulative or as a quantized object.

There are other verb classes for which it has been claimed that a measuring-out analysis is not applicable. For transitive motion verbs in English as in (9),

Jackendoff (1996) claims that it is rather the directional PP which determines aspectual interpretation. Filip (2005), on the other hand, claims that in an example with a verb of motion as in (10) from Polish, the completion of an event of moving rather results from Jan's complete path-covering. She takes this to follow from the observation that the extent of a moved object does not define the extent of the event (movement to some location). The same, however, is true for the subject NP *Jan,* which may cover the path only as a whole, indivisible object.

(9) a. Bill pushed the cart to NY in/??for two days.
b. Bill pushed the cart ??in/for two days.
c. Bill pushed the cart towards the house *in/for two days.

(10) Jan przyniósł kaszę.
Jan carried.PFV porridge
'Jan brought (some/the) porridge.'

While it is certainly true that verbs of motion are peculiar regarding incrementality (cf. Krifka 1998 for a detailed discussion), there is evidence from Finnish that, at least with transitive verbal predicates such as *roll*, *push*, *carry,* etc., it is rather the internal argument which measures out the path connected to the movement; cf. (11) and (12).

(11) Janne vieritti tynnyrin talolle.
Janne rolled barrel.ACC house.ALLAT
'Janne rolled a/the barrel to the house.'
→ Endpoint reached. Continuation: #Janne got tired and left the barrel at the crossing.

(12) Janne vieritti tynnyriä talolle.
Janne rolled barrel.PART house.ALLAT
'Janne rolled a/the barrel to/towards the house.'
↛ Endpoint reached. Continuation: Janne got tired and left the barrel at the crossing.

The internal argument in (11) and (12) is a singular count noun which may be definite or indefinite. Similar to the examples in (5) and (6), the NP may be marked either with the accusative or with the partitive. The former indicates that the event is completed, which makes a continuation given below the example (*Janne got tired and left the barrel at the crossing*) contradictory. With the partitive, the sentence obviously does not imply that the event is completed, which makes the same continuation felicitous.

Additionally, at least in Slavic languages, directional PPs do not necessarily provide a natural endpoint of the movement. In any case, they certainly do not express a completion of the event by themselves; cf. the Russian examples in (13) and (14) corresponding to the Finnish examples discussed above.

(13)	Ivan	prikatil	bočku	k	domu.
	Ivan	rolled.PFV	barrel.ACC	to	house.DAT

'Ivan rolled a/the barrel to the house.'

→ Endpoint reached. Continuation: #but Ivan got tired and left it at the crossing.

(14)	Ivan	katil	bočku	k	domu.
	Janne	rolled.IPFV	barrel.ACC	to	house.DAT

'Ivan rolled a/the barrel to/towards the house.'

↛ Endpoint reached. Continuation: but Ivan got tired and left it at the crossing.

The difference between (13) and (14) lies in the successful reaching of a location by the object expressed by the internal argument. In (13) with the pfv. verb, 'the barrel' reached its destination ('house'), and the sentence cannot be continued with *but Ivan got tired and left it at the crossing*. In (14), however, it is only asserted that 'Ivan' and 'the barrel' were covering some implicit non-finite path (cf. Filip 2005, Zuchewicz 2020), but it is left open whether they have reached the destination. Therefore, the sentence can be continued with *but Ivan got tired and left it at the crossing*. The PP *k domu* 'to the house' does not imply any completion. This can be achieved only by pfv. marking of the verb as in (13).

Furthermore, one and the same directional PP in Slavic in some cases provides a natural endpoint, which may then be picked out by a pfv. operator, but in other cases it does not provide a natural endpoint for a change-of-state. Consider the examples in (15)–(17), where all the verbs involved are marked for the pfv. aspect (technically adapted from Zuchewicz 2020: 27).

(15)	Ola	weszła	do	sklepu	→Ola	jest	w	sklepie.
	Ola	**w**-went.PFV	to	store	Ola	is	in	store

'Ola entered the store. → Ola is inside the store.'

(16)	Ola	doszła	do	sklepu	→Ola	jest	przy	sklepie.
	Ola	**do**-went.PFV	to	store	Ola	is	at	store

'Ola arrived at the store. → Ola is at the store.'

(17)	Ola	wyszła	do	sklepu	↛ Ola	jest	przy	sklepie/	w	sklepie.
	Ola	**wy**-went.PFV	to	store	Ola	is	at	store/	in	store

'Ola left some location towards the store. ↛ Ola is at the store/in the store.'

In (15) and (16), the prefixes *w-* (with the allomorph *we-*) and *do-* introduce a right boundary to the event expressed by the verbal root, a lexical property which may be called "resultative". This boundary is further specified by the PP with the preposition *do* 'to', and is subsequently selected by the pfv. aspectual operator. In contrast, in (17), the prefix *wy-* introduces a left boundary to the event expressed by the verbal root resulting in an "inchoative" derivation. This boundary is not specified by the *do*-PP, but it is the left boundary which is selected by the pfv. operator.

As we have shown, the pfv. operator selects for a temporal boundary which often coincides with a culmination point (if lexically specified). With "incremental theme verbs" this implies that the internal argument is affected in its totality by the event. The ipfv. operator, on the other hand, does not mark temporal limitation. Hence, with "incremental theme verbs" this implies that the internal argument is not affected in its totality by the event. This, however, does not mean that, with "incremental theme predicates", the ipfv. allows for an interpretation that no part of the internal argument has been involved in the event. On the contrary: partial affectedness of the object is implied by ipfv. "incremental theme verbs", a phenomenon known as veridicality of the progressive; cf.

Giannakidou and Zwarts (1999), Giannakidou (2013). Consider (18), adapted from Zuchewicz and Szucsich (2020: 524).

(18)	Ola	jadła	gruszkę,	# ale	jest	ona	wciąż	cała.
	Ola	ate.IPFV	pear	but	is	she	still	whole

‘Ola was eating a pear, #but it is still in one piece.’

As soon as the dynamic process started, which, with “incremental theme verbs,” ultimately ends in an inherent culmination point (followed by a change-of-state), parts of the object expressed by the internal argument are involved in the event. In a non-generic, episodic reading, sentences containing an ipfv. verb denote the start of the process, i.e., parts of the event (subevent) took place. Since subevents of eating a pear and parts of the pear that underwent these subevents are mapped onto each other (the so-called homomorphism of (sub)objects and (sub)events), it follows that the pear cannot still be present in one piece (cf. Krifka 1989a, 1989b, 1989c, 1992).

2.2 Modelling Homomorphism

In our theoretical implementation of the homomorphism principle we build on Krifka’s (1989a, 1989b, 1989c, 1992) formalization of the aspect-dependent (partial) completion of “incremental theme verbs.” In this paper, however, we will not go into formal details (cf. Zuchewicz 2020, Zuchewicz & Szucsich 2020 for further discussion), but in Section 3 we will draw parallels between “incremental theme verbs” that take nominal and propositional complements. Our proposal, based on Zuchewicz (2020), involves a definition of partition only on the level of events, without considering parts of a direct object argument.

As we have already mentioned above, the gist of incrementality has been assumed to be that particular mapping relations have to hold between objects expressed by internal arguments and events. Krifka (1989a: 92) defines these two-way relations as mapping to objects, as in (19), and mapping to events, as in (20).

(19) $\forall R[\text{MAP-O}(R) \leftrightarrow \forall e \forall e' \forall x[R(e,x) \wedge e' \subseteq_E e \rightarrow \exists x'[x' \subseteq_O x \wedge R(e',x')]]]$

(20) $\forall R[\text{MAP-E}(R) \leftrightarrow \forall e \forall x \forall x'[R(e,x) \wedge x' \subseteq_O x \rightarrow \exists e'[e' \subseteq_E e \wedge R(e',x')]]]$

The definition of mapping to objects in (19) ensures that for every subevent e' which is part of the overall event e, there is a respective subobject x' which is part of the object x. For instance, every partial event of eating a pear can be linked to the part of a pear that disappeared during that specific subevent. The reverse case holds for the mapping to events relation given in (20). According to (20), parts of objects (x') correspond to parts of events (e'). With respect to our pear example, for every part of a pear there exists a subevent of eating, which means that this part disappears in the course of this subevent. Crucially, the presence of partial events requires the presence of partial objects that are mapped to these subevents, and the presence of partial objects implies that there are subevents that relate to these subobjects, and that have caused the affectedness of these subobjects (cf. Krifka 1989a: 92). Importantly, the lack of partial objects implies the lack of partial events and vice versa.

"Incremental theme verbs" that combine with gradual effected ('house' in 'build a house') or "gradual consumed patients" ('pear' in 'eat a pear') can be captured by an additional rule that is called "uniqueness of events" (for the terminology cf. Krifka 1989a: 92). This rule is given in (21); cf. Krifka (1989a: 92).

(21) $\forall R[\text{UNI-E}(R) \leftrightarrow \forall e \forall e' \forall x[R(e,x) \wedge R(e',x) \rightarrow e = e']]$

The rule in (21) applies to cases where there is only one event related to an object. For instance, there can be only one event of eating a particular pear, or building a particular house, etc. In contrast, the same book can be read multiple times, i.e., potentially it has an iterative reading. This means that the rule of uniqueness of events does not apply to "incremental theme verbs" that select for internal arguments which are not effected or consumed, but which have "only" the property of graduality (cf. Zuchewicz 2020 for Polish).

In Section 3 we will discuss clause-embedding "incremental theme verbs" in detail. We assume that they group with predicates like 'read', i.e., that different events may be related to a single propositional object iteratively. This means that the rule of uniqueness of events does not apply to clause-embedding "incremental theme verbs." Following Zuchewicz (2020), we will label their arguments "gradual revealed patients."

With "incremental theme verbs," the pfv. aspectual operator implies total affectedness of the object expressed by the internal argument, which excludes reference to parts of the object. This means that pfv. aspect somehow blocks the accessibility of subobjects and subevents. Krifka (1989b: 187) assumes that pfv. "incremental theme verbs" can be represented by combining the incremental relation (INC) and the maximization restriction on the object (MAX); cf. (22)

for 'Ola ate.PFV a pear.' (based on Zuchewicz 2020, Zuchewicz & Szucsich 2020). Since 'pear' appears in its totality, we cannot access its parts. We have already said that the accessibility of partial objects and partial events can only be realized as a 1:1 relationship (cf. Zuchewicz 2020, Zuchewicz & Szucsich 2020).

(22) $\lambda e \exists x[\text{eat}(e) \wedge x=\text{MAX}(\text{pear}) \wedge \text{INC}(e,x) \wedge \text{AG}(e,O)]$

Krifka's (1989a, 1989b, 1989c, 1992) analysis accounts for cases with a nominal incremental theme, where the object may easily be divided into parts. In the next section, we will move on to "incremental theme verbs" with propositional complements. With the latter, an internal argument is realized by a 'that'-clause. Crucially, a proposition described by a 'that'-clause cannot be divided into parts the way a nominal "incremental theme" can be. Therefore, based on Zuchewicz (2020), we propose the restriction of the definition of incrementality to events, without requiring the partition to be realized on the object. This enables a unified analysis for different types of incremental relations. We will elaborate our idea in the next section, without going into formal details. For the formal implementation see Zuchewicz (2020) and Zuchewicz & Szucsich (2020).

3. The Notion of 'Propositional Incremental Theme' (Based on Zuchewicz 2020)

3.1 Similarities between Nominal and Propositional Incremental Themes

Zuchewicz (2020) demonstrates that, in Polish, clause-embedding 'reveal'-type predicates[2] ('prove', 'reveal', 'show') are incremental, because their interpretation is based on a gradual, i.e., incremental formation of a proof. The object of investigation are sentences as presented in the following examples, in line with the ideas discussed in Zuchewicz (2018, 2020), and Zuchewicz & Szucsich (2020). (23) describes implications that can be drawn from ipfv. 'reveal'-type predicates in Polish, and (24) implications that apply to ipfv. verbs with a "nominal incremental theme."

(23)

Policjantka	udowadniała	/	pokazywała		/	wykazywała,	że	bank
policewoman	proved.IPFV	/	showed.IPFV		/	revealed.IPFV	that	bank
oszukuje	klientów	i	(nie)	udowodniła	/	pokazała	/	wykazała.
cheats	customers	and	NEG	proved.PFV	/	showed.PFV	/	revealed.PFV

'The policewoman was proving/showing/revealing that the bank was cheating its customers, and she has (not) proved/shown/revealed it.'

↛ The bank was cheating its customers.

↛ The bank was not cheating its customers.

→ Certain subevents of proving suggested that the bank was cheating its customers.

As Zuchewicz (2020), and Zuchewicz & Szucsich (2020) observe, the implications listed above are similar to those attested for "incremental theme verbs" with nominal complements (for the latter cf. Wierzbicka 1967).

(24)

Dziewczynka	jadła	kanapkę	i	część	zostawiła	/	i	nic	nie
girl	ate.IPFV	sandwich	and	part	left	/	and	nothing	NEG
zostawiła.									
left									

'A girl was eating a sandwich, and she left a part of it/and she did not leave anything.'

↛ A sandwich has been eaten completely.

↛ A sandwich has not been eaten completely.

→ Some parts of a sandwich have been eaten.

There is also a correlation between the respective pfv. counterparts to (23) and (24); cf. (25) and (26), based on Zuchewicz (2018), (2020), and Zuchewicz & Szucsich (2020).

(25)

Policjantka	udowodniła	/	pokazała	/	wykazała,	że	bank	oszukuje
policewoman	proved.PFV	/	showed.PFV	/	revealed.PFV	that	bank	cheats
klientów,	# ale	bank	ich	nie	oszukiwał.			
customers	but	bank	them	NEG	cheated			

'The policewoman has proved/shown/revealed that the bank was cheating its customers, #but the bank has not cheated them.'

→ The bank has cheated its customers.

(26)

Dziewczynka	zjadła	kanapkę	#i	część	zostawiła	/	#i	nic[3]	nie
girl	ate.PFV	sandwich	and	part	left	/	and	nothing	NEG
zostawiła.									
left									

'A girl has eaten up a sandwich, #and she left a part of it/#and she did not leave anything.'

→ A sandwich has been eaten completely.

Examples (25) and (26) make it clear that both an embedded proposition and a nominal "incremental theme" are totally affected by the respective verbal processes. In the former case, an investigation is completed, so the proposition receives a truth value; single pieces of evidence turn into a proof (cf. Zuchewicz 2020). Following Zuchewicz (2020), in this case, a perfective clause-embedding verb is veridical, because it entails that a proposition described by a 'that'-sentence holds, cf. Egré (2008) for the terminology. Regarding 'reveal'-type predicates, veridicality is an inherent component of perfectivity (it provides a natural way of finishing an incremental process of proving). In the latter case, the process of eating reaches its natural end point, which translates to a full disappearance of a sandwich (cf. Dowty 1991, Krifka 1989a, 1989b, 1989c, 1992 among others). According to Zuchewicz (2020), in both a propositional and a nominal case, the pfv. closes an incremental process denoted by its ipfv. twin: a gradual disappearance of a sandwich and a gradual formation of a proof. The exact realization of partition is determined by the nature of an incremental event.

3.2 The Internal Structure of a Proof

The question remains as to how to visualize the internal structure of a proof. In line with Zuchewicz (2020), we assume that a proof contains hints, single pieces of evidence, and all steps that are necessary in order to establish a truth-value of an embedded proposition. A proof is maximal evidence; if the evidence is not maximal, it does not constitute a proof.

Following Zuchewicz (2020), a 'that'-sentence embedded under a 'reveal'-type verb necessarily holds true if there is a proof for it. The difference between the pfv. and the ipfv. variant of a particular aspectual pair lies in the available amount of evidence for the proposition described by the subordinate clause. The ipfv. implies that there are some hints (that there is partial evidence) which suggest that, at the evaluation time, the proposition expressed by the 'that'-clause holds (cf. Zuchewicz 2020, Zuchewicz & Szucsich 2020 for a formal implementation). However, because the ipfv. enforces the process it relates to ('proving', 'revealing', 'showing') to be ongoing, from the semantic point of view, the evidence available is never sufficient to be automatically turned into a proof. Importantly, this does not mean that the ipfv. is not compatible with any sort of truthfulness of a 'that'-clause, which is illustrated by the implications given with the example in (23).

Now we will move on to the internal structure of a proof. Example (27) – with ipfv. 'reveal'-type predicates – confirms their incremental character.

(27)

Policjant	Rafalski	stopniowo	udowadniał	/	pokazywał	/	wykazywał
policeman	Rafalski	gradually	proved.IPFV	/	showed.IPFV	/	revealed.IPFV
że	bank	oszukuje	klientów.				
that	bank	cheats	customers				

'Policeman Rafalski was proving/showing/revealing step-by-step that the bank was cheating its customers.'

(27) says that there were some subevents of proving that provided more and more evidence towards an embedded proposition *p* ('The bank is/was cheating its customers.'). However, it is unclear whether *p* holds or not. The incremental process of collecting single pieces of evidence in the case of the ipfv. 'reveal'-type predicate can be visualized as follows (based on ideas developed in Zuchewicz 2020):

(28) **Statement**: Policeman Rafalski was gradually proving that the bank was cheating its customers.

Conclusion (to be verified): The bank was cheating its customers, henceforth *p*.

Day 1 = **evidence 1** such that the bank did not give customers enough information about credits.

Subresult: There is partial evidence towards *p*.

Day 2 = **evidence 2** such that the bank stopped answering calls.

Subresult: There is partial evidence towards *p*.

Day 3 =?

Subresult =?

General result = cannot be obtained yet; we do not know how the third subresult will be.

(Cf. Zuchewicz 2020: 180 for the imperfective variant of 'Jan proved that Anna was in Italy', with evidence (a): Anna booked a flight to Italy, and evidence (b): Anna got an Italian SIM-card. Due to the imperfective aspect marking, the proposition from the that-clause cannot be taken for granted.)

Following (28), the available single pieces of evidence are too weak to count as a proof for a 'that'-sentence. Furthermore, we do not know what the result of the third day of an investigation would be; it can happen that the bank had a system failure that caused the occurrence of evidence one and evidence two. However, due to the fact that no counterexample appeared at the evaluation time, there is no reason to assume that *p* does not hold.

As was said above, following Zuchewicz (2020), an incremental process of proving can be ended naturally by providing a proof for an embedded proposition. A proof is being delivered by the pfv. 'reveal'-type verb. (29) illustrates the internal structure of a proof – a closure of (28).

(29) **Statement**: Policeman Rafalski has proved that the bank was cheating its customers.

Conclusion (has been verified): The bank was cheating its customers, henceforth *p*.

Day 1 = **evidence 1** such that the bank did not give customers enough information about credits.

Subresult: There is partial evidence towards *p*.

Day 2 = **evidence 2** such that the bank stopped answering calls.

Subresult: There is partial evidence towards *p*.

Day 3 = **evidence 3** such that the bank has illegally raised interest rates.

Subresult = There is crucial evidence towards *p*.

General result = The bank was cheating its customers.

(Cf. Zuchewicz 2020: 179 for the perfective variant of 'Jan proved that Anna was in Italy', with evidence (a): Anna booked a flight to Italy, and evidence (b) – crucial piece of evidence – Anna was seen in Rome. The perfective aspect implies the presence of the crucial piece of evidence; the proposition from the that-clause is to be taken for granted.)

(29) demonstrates how the addition of a crucial piece of evidence turns evidence into a proof. Again, the process of the formation of a proof is similar to different stages of affectedness of a nominal object by the verbal process (for a formal implementation cf. Zuchewicz 2020, Zuchewicz & Szucsich 2020).

Finally, we would like to demonstrate that clause-embedding verbs that are not incremental do not require their objects to denote true propositions; cf. Zuchewicz (2020).

(30) Policjant Rafalski ??stopniowo mówił / oświadczał / stwierdzał, że bank oszukuje klientów.
policeman Rafalski gradually said.IPFV / declared.IPFV / stated.IPFV that bank cheats customers
'Policeman Rafalski was saying/declaring/stating step-by-step that the bank was cheating its customers.'

'Step-by-step' cannot be applied to ipfv. verbs of communication the way it was applied to 'reveal'-type predicates. Accordingly, pfv. verbs of communication do not require the presence of a proof for an embedded proposition (cf. Zuchewicz 2018, 2020).

(31)

Policjant	Rafalski	powiedział /	oświadczył /	stwierdził,	że	bank	
policeman	Rafalski	said.PFV /	declared.PFV /	stated.PFV	that	bank	
oszukuje	klientów.						
cheats	customers						

'Policeman Rafalski has said/declared/stated that the bank was cheating its customers.'

↛ The bank was cheating its customers.

These interpretive differences between 'reveal'-type verbs and verbs of communication have been also experimentally confirmed (cf. Zuchewicz 2020, Zuchewicz & Szucsich 2020 for details).

As we have argued above, the incrementality of 'reveal'-types predicates originates from the gradual creation of a proof for the proposition expressed by the 'that'-clause. According to Zuchewicz (2020), in order to establish incrementality of events of proving, revealing, or showing, we do not have to address a propositional complement directly. The interpretation of a 'that'-clause mirrors the progress of the proving-process. With the pfv., the proving-process is completed, and this is why a subordinate sentence holds true. With the ipfv., the proving-process is ongoing, and, as a result, a truth-value of an embedded proposition cannot be established yet. This works similarly to cases like 'build.PFV a house', where incrementality itself consists of a gradual process of the creation of an object. Since incremental transitive processes always require an object in order to be instantiated, single subevents of building are bound to parts of the house that already exist. The affectedness of the direct object mirrors the progress of the building event. The existence of the house suggests that the *building*-process is completed, which is only possible with the pfv. marking on the matrix verb. However, 'reveal'-type predicates selecting for clausal complements rather pattern with "incremental theme verbs" selecting for gradual patients like 'read'. Zuchewicz (2020) showed that the same proposition can be verified more than once, which implies that these predicates, although being incremental, lack the property of uniqueness of events.

4. Summary

In this article, we discussed different classes of "incremental theme verbs" selecting for nominal complements which can be distinguished mainly by the property of uniqueness of events. The common property of all "incremental theme" predicates is graduality. Based on Zuchewicz (2020), we have further shown that certain predicates taking clausal complements ('reveal'-type predicates) also exhibit the property of graduality, thus patterning with "incremental theme verbs" taking nominal internal arguments. This can be captured by assuming that incrementality is foremost a phenomenon involving the partition of events. Propositions themselves – expressed by clausal internal arguments – do not have to be split into parts ("subpropositions"). Following Zuchewicz (2020), with 'reveal'-type predicates, proofs can be thought of as consisting of pieces of evidence, i.e., they have a complex internal structure which is composed of parts. Pfv. morphology on the respective verbal predicate marks a proof as complete, which implies that all relevant parts (pieces of evidence) have been provided. This, in turn, makes the embedded proposition true, i.e., pfv. clause-embedding 'reveal'-type predicates are systematically veridical. The ipfv. counterparts do not exclude the truth of the proposition, nor do they assert a proof (a sufficient amount of evidence), although they assert that some sort of evidence has been established. Lastly, in line with Zuchewicz (2020), we have argued that clause-embedding 'reveal'-type predicates pattern with noun-selecting "incremental theme verbs" like 'read', i.e., they lack the property of uniqueness of events characteristic for verbs of consumption and creation like 'eat' and 'build'.

Notes

1 We will not discuss possible cross-Slavic differences in the exact semantics of the aspectual opposition (cf. Dickey 2000 for a prominent proposal; for an opposite view assuming a unified semantic contribution of aspectual features cf. Alvestad 2014), since these do not play a role for the purpose of this paper.
2 This term was initially used by Zuchewicz (2020).
3 This continuation is redundant because *zjadła* 'ate.PFV' implies the non-existence of the object. In contrast to the former continuation, however, it is not semantically incoherent.

Bibliography

ALVESTAD, SILJE. 2014. Fake imperfective imperatives in Slavic. *Corpus-based studies in contrastive linguistics*. ed. by Signe Ebeling, Atle Grønn, Kjetil Hauge, and Diana Santos. *Oslo Studies in Language* 6 (1). 29–42.

DICKEY, STEPHEN M. 2000. *Parameters of Slavic aspect*. Stanford: CSLI.

DOWTY, DAVID. 1991. Thematic proto-roles and argument selection. *Language* 67 (3). 547–619.

EGRÉ, PAUL. 2008. Question-embedding and factivity. *Grazer Philosophische Studien* 77 (1). 85–125.

FILIP, HANA.1995. Integrating telicity, aspect and NP semantics: The role of thematic structure. *Formal approaches to Slavic linguistics 3: The College Park meeting 1994*, ed. by Jindřich Toman, 61–96. Ann Arbor: Slavica.

FILIP, HANA. 2005. On accumulating and having it all: Perfectivity, prefixes and bare arguments. *Perspectives on aspect*, ed. by Henk Verkuyl, Henriëtte de Swart, and Angeliek van Hout, 125–48. Dordrecht: Springer.

FILIP, HANA. 2012. Lexical aspect. *The Oxford handbook of tense and aspect*. ed. by Robert Binnick, 721–51. Oxford: Oxford University Press.

GIANNAKIDOU, ANASTASIA. 2013. (Non)Veridicality, evaluation, and event actualization: Evidence from the subjunctive in relative clauses. *Nonveridicality and evaluation: Theoretical, computational and corpus approaches*, ed. by Maite Taboada and Radoslava Trnavac, 17–49. Leiden: Brill.

GIANNAKIDOU, ANASTASIA, and FRANS ZWARTS. 1999. *Temporal, aspectual operators and (non)veridicality*. Groningen: University of Groningen, MS.

GVOZDANOVIĆ, JADRANKA. 2012. Perfective and imperfective aspect. *The Oxford handbook of tense and aspect*. ed. by Robert Binnick, 781–802. Oxford: Oxford University Press.

HEINÄMÄKI, ORVOKKI. 1994. Aspect as boundedness in Finnish. *Tense, aspect, and action*, ed. by Carl Bache, Hans Basbøl, and Carl-Erik Lindberg, 207–34. Berlin – New York: Mouton de Gruyter.

JACKENDOFF, RAY. 1996. The proper treatment of measuring out, telicity, and perhaps even quantification in English. *Natural Language and Linguistic Theory* 14 (2). 305–54.

KIPARSKY, PAUL. 1998. Partitive case and aspect. *Projecting from the lexicon*, ed. by Miriam Butt and Wilhelm Geuder, 265–307. Stanford: CSLI.

KRIFKA, MANFRED. 1989a. Nominal reference, temporal constitution and quantification in event semantics. *Semantics and contextual expression*, ed. by Renate Bartsch, Johan van Benthem, and Peter von Emde Boas, 75–115. Dordrecht: Foris Publications.

Krifka, Manfred. 1989b. *Nominalreferenz und Zeitkonstitution: Zur Semantik von Massentermen, Pluraltermen und Aspektklassen*. München: Wilhelm Fink Verlag.

Krifka, Manfred. 1989c. Nominalreferenz, Zeitkonstitution, Aspekt, Aktionsart: Eine semantische Erklärung ihrer Interaktion. *Tempus – Aspekt – Modus: Die lexikalischen und grammatischen Formen in den germanischen Sprachen*, ed. by Werner Abraham and Theo Janssen, 227–58. Tübingen: Niemeyer.

Krifka, Manfred. 1992. Thematic relations as links between nominal reference and temporal constitution. *Lexical matters*, ed. by Ivan A. Sag and Anna Szabolcsi, 29–53. Stanford: CSLI.

Krifka, Manfred. 1998. The origins of telicity. *Events and grammar*, ed. by Susan Rothstein, 197–235. Dordrecht: Kluwer.

Sonnenhauser, Barbara. 2008. Aspect interpretation in Russian – a pragmatic account. *Journal of Pragmatics* 40. 2077–99.

Szucsich, Luka. 2005. Kompositionalität von Aspekt und ihre Bedingungen: Ein russisch-finnischer Vergleich. *Linguistische Beiträge zur Slavistik XII*, ed. by Monika Wingender, 171–95. München: Otto Sagner Verlag.

Tatevosov, Sergej. 2016. *Glagol'nye klassy i tipologija akcional'nosti*. Moskva: Jazyki slavjanskoj kul'tury.

Wiemer, Björn, and Ilja Seržant. 2017. Diachrony and typology of Slavic aspect: What does morphology tell us? *Unity and diversity in grammaticalization scenarios*, ed. by Walter Bisang and Andrej Malchukov, 239–307. Berlin: Language Science Press. Online: DOI 10.5281/zenodo.823246.

Wierzbicka, Anna. 1967. On the semantics of verbal aspect in Polish. *To honor Roman Jakobson: Essays on the occasion of his 70th birthday, vol. 3*, 2231–49. The Hague: Mouton.

Zaliznjak, Anna, and Aleksej Šmelëv. 2000. *Vvedenie v russkuju aspektologiju*. Moskva: Jazyki russkoj kul'tury.

Zuchewicz, Karolina. 2018. How factive is the perfective? On the relationship between perfectivity and factivity in Polish. *Advances in formal Slavic linguistics 2016*, ed. by Denisa Lenertová, Roland Meyer, Radek Šimík, and Luka Szucsich, 479–94. Berlin: Language Science Press. Online: DOI 10.5281/zenodo.2545547.

Zuchewicz, Karolina. 2020. *On the veridicality of perfective clause-embedding verbs in Polish: A unified aspect-based analysis of incremental theme verbs with nominal and propositional complements*. Berlin: HU dissertation. Online: DOI 10.18452/21887.

Zuchewicz, Karolina, and Luka Szucsich. 2020. Generalized incrementality: The truth-entailment of clause-embedding reveal-type predicates in Polish as the realization of incrementality on a propositional level. *Proceedings of Sinn und Bedeutung 24, vol. 2*, ed. by Michael Franke, Nikola Kompa, Mingya Liu, Jutta L. Mueller, and Juliane Schwab, 521–38. Osnabrück: Osnabrück University. Online: DOI https://doi.org/10.18148/sub/2020.v24i2.913. [last accessed on 16-08-2021].

Alan Timberlake

String Syntax

Abstract Syntax is strings, or forces, that link discontinuous elements and control the interpretation of constructions. There are multiple strings and they can co-exist. Examples of strings are: modality (possibility and epistemology), aspectuality (change over time), individuation and quantification.*

Keywords: Multidimensional Syntax, Individuation, Quantification, Nominative Object, Genitive Object, Independent Infinitive

1. Preliminaries

In the following, I want to suggest an approach to syntax that is more attuned to actual usage than abstract linguistic systems. The central conceptual tool is strings, a concept bowdlerized from physics. As far as I can tell from introductions to string theory in physics, the idea is that bodies are linked by multiple "strings" (such as electromagnetism or gravity), and strings allow forces to act on entities. Adapted to language, this concept suggests we think of syntax not in terms of units in fixed tree structures, but rather in terms of strings that link units, strings such as: modality, aspectuality, individuation and quantification, predicativity, location, and information.

A similar statement in a very different context was expressed by Simone Weil, who argued that the *Iliad* should be understood in terms of forces rather than heroic actors:

> The true hero, the true subject, the centre of the Iliad, is force. Force employed by man, force that enslaves man, force before which man's flesh shrinks away. In this work at all times, the human spirit is shown as modified by its relation to force, as swept away, blinded, by the very force it imagined it could handle, as deformed by the weight of the force it submits to. Ceteris paribus, so it is with language.

* I would like to dedicate this speculation to Peter Kosta, whose universal interests and nimble facility with analytic methods are an inspiration. I am grateful to my fellow editor Steven Franks for sharing his understanding of syntax.

2. Overlaid Strings, Russian Word Order

An obvious place to start is word order. Syntactic roles are maintained when constituents are ordered in different ways; as has long been known, variations in word order cannot be reduced to syntactic relations, though information operations often interact with syntactic roles.

There is another intriguing property of word order in Russian oral language which has been highlighted in Zemskaja (1981: 398–401). In speech it is possible to interweave components from two larger structures (clauses), each of which has its own internal word order and grammar (aspectual/modal values). The result of interweaving can be represented by a single line with, however, words written separated over two levels. In the example in (1), one level is written subscripted and the other superscripted.

As Zemskaja realized, the two syntactic fragments shown below have different discourse overtones. One (perhaps to be considered overarching) is modal: it is concerned with the addressee's and speaker's understanding of the possibilities of an event (*ты… догадалась*?). The other layer is narrative (here, the fact of Katia's being excluded: *Катю… за что исключили*?)

(1)		**ты**		**догадалась**?	*modality*
	Катю		**за что искючили**		*narrative*
	thematic	*thematic*	*rhematic*	*rhematic*	
	(narrative)	*(modal)*	*(narrative)*	*(modal)*	

Each of the two substrings is an utterance with its own division into theme (point of departure) and rheme (information asserted). The complex structure recorded above can then be described using the mechanism of two parallel strings which coexist in one utterance.

3. Thematic Roles and Subjects

3.1. Subjects

It will be useful to rehearse familiar properties of predicates, relying on strings. The speaker's concern with the flow of events – states and changes – can be termed "aspectual". Within the continuum of roles we need to distinguish patients, primes, and agents. Patients undergo change, at the hands of an agent. (Or more inclusively, the patient's qualities are contingent – not all patients undergo change.) An agent is held responsible for change. In between patients and agents are arguments that are the way they are without external causation. In light of their autonomy, they could be termed "prime movers", or simply "primes". (Calling this role "subject" mixes grammatical relations with the semantic arguments of aspectuality.)

I recall an argument I had years ago with a linguist friend who was scornful about the thought that the concept of subject could have any essential value, or, instead, is just a nominal convenience. That dismissive attitude persists; the subject is just the argument in a position in the syntactic tree, it is pointiness to assert that it is what the sentence is about.

It might be, however, that the subject has significance as an operator in information structure. Consider the two passive constructions in Polish. First there is the personal passive ("personal" in the sense of having a subject):

(2)	A	jak	ja	weszłam	to	ani	kanapeczek	ani	cukiereczków
	but	as	I	entered	then	not	pastries	nor	candies
	nie	było	herbata	była	wypita.				
	not	were	tea-NOM.FM.SG	been-FM.SG	drunk-PTR.FM.SG				

'And when I entered, there were neither pastries not candies, the tea had been drunk.'

In (2) the subject *herbata* 'tea' is an entity which represents the event as a whole. The fate of the subject stands for the fate of the whole. It is the most salient entity, in that finishing the tea-drinking marks a definitive end of the whole social occasion; the fact that other goodies ran out is a build-up to the definitive consumption of the tea.

Now consider an impersonal passive:

(3)	Był	piątek	i	zgodnie	ze	zwyczajem	wypito	herbatę.
	was	Friday	and	consistent	with	tradition	drunk-NT.SG	tea-ACC.SG

'It was Friday and, in accordance with tradition, tea-drinking happened.'

Here the passive is impersonal (there is no subject, agreement is then neuter singular). The impersonal passive presents the existence of a scene; what is significant is not any one entity, but the whole event as a Gestalt.

Several pieces are needed to make an account of impersonal passives in string theory. Let us assume the predicating representation involves one node (verb) and an *n*-tuple of argument positions. We can treat active and passive as a pair of almost identical *n*-tuples with the same argument positions. With a true passive, the subject of the active disappears (or was never there) and the slot is filled by the direct object. With the impersonal passive the agent position is not occupied, so the verb has no agent. Then we need to attach discourse overtones of absence of expected agent.

3.2. Case Alternations: Lithuanian Genitive Objects

In place of the expected accusative case, languages of northeastern Europe use a special case for the argument of otherwise transitive verbs: genitive in Slavic and Baltic, partitive in Finnic. In discussing genitive objects in Lithuanian, Leskien (1919:§ 225) looks at genitive objects in terms of the meaning of verbs and writes: "the object is placed in the genitive with verbs with the meaning of desire (*Begehrung*), striving (*Streben*)". His example is the verb 'seek' in *to viso*$_{\text{GEN}}$ *pagonys ieško* 'all this$_{\text{GEN}}$ gentiles seek'. Continuing from 'desire' and 'striving', he cites other verbs that take the genitive: 'request', 'call for', 'need', 'be necessary', and 'lack'. They form a group in that these verbs all involve compensating for lack. And then there are verbs of emotion: 'fear', 'pity', 'regret', 'recalling', and 'forgetting'. These are intuitively similar to each other: they all describe failure of a possible human connection. Only after these does Leskien mention the "partitive" use of the genitive – often taken to be the quintessential function of adverbal genitives – which he defines as "indeterminate group or mass"; Leskien avoids saying the usual "part of a whole".

Thus Leskien analyzes the meaning of adverbal genitives in terms of verbs (and the histories they report) rather than in terms of the nouns. The verb supplies the sense of an incomplete but potentially continuing activity. This is made explicit in his opening statement that the genitive can be construed as the goal of desire. Inasmuch as the verb is the source of meaning, we can think of the meaning of the governed genitive not as a property of the noun but as an interaction of verb and noun. There is, in other words, a relationship – a string – between the verb and the noun, with a component of modality.

3.3. Heteroclausal Case Substitution: Genitives

There is another way in which the Lithuanian genitive marking of objects involves strings. Objects that might be accusative are instead genitive when the verb is negated. In a situation in which the matrix verb is negated, and further, has a dependent infinitive with an object, the infinitival object can be genitive or accusative, depending on the degree of cohesion. The examples in (4) have been collected by Arkadiev (2016: 42–44). Those vetted with speakers are cited here with responses of native speakers (in the sequence of numbers, "genitive" /

"accusative" / "both"). Other examples without speaker responses are cited from the LKT (*Lietuvos kultūros taryba*). In the choice of case in the object of the infinitive the host verb matters a lot, the infinitive a little, and the embedded object noun, apparently, for almost nothing.

(4) Interclausal genitive of negation

a.	impersonal modal	*ne-reikia mupirkti* 'not necessary to buy x'	*(4/0/0)*
b.	personal modal	*ne-turi matyti* 'not need to see x'	LKT
c.	phasal	*ne-pradėjo rašyti* 'didn't begin to write x'	*(3/0/0)*
d.	mental	*ne-pamiršk uždaryti* 'don't forget to close x'	*(1/0/2)*
e.	demand, dative intervening	*ne-liepė Aldonai*$_{\mathrm{DAT}}$ *rašyti* 'did not order Aldona to write x'	*(3/0/0)*
f.	request, genitive intervening	*ne-prašė Aldonos*$_{\mathrm{GEN}}$ *uždaryti* 'did not ask Aldona to close x'	*(1/0/2)*
g.	demand, genitive intervening	*ne-privertė jo*$_{\mathrm{GEN}}$ *pakeisti* x 'did not force him to change x'	LKT
h.	intervening noun	*ne-turi teisėsi*$_{\mathrm{GEN}}$ *keisti* 'not have right to change x'	*(1/0/4)*

The contexts in (4), defined in terms of the semantics of head verbs, are: (a) impersonal modal, (b) personal modal, (c) phasal, (d) mental-emotional, (e) modality imposed on a dative argument of the matrix verb, to which the obligation is transferred, and (f–g) modality imposed on a matrix direct object, which itself is genitive in response to the matrix negated verb. The position of the embedded object whose case is at issue is marked as "x".

Genitive case is transmitted from the matrix clause to the embedded clause. In the most transparent situation, there are no syntactic units intervening between the negated matrix predicate and the object of the dependent predicate; that is the case in (4a–c) above. An intervening dative (target of modality in the upper clause) also does not interfere. That differs from an intervening matrix direct object as in (4 f, g), in which there is an argument in the matrix clause in addition to the object of embedded verb. Negation applies to the object of the matrix clause, so that the effect of the negation on the subordinate noun is contingent on the intermediary argument person. In (4h) the negation applies to the abstract noun in the matrix clause, thereby undercutting the force of negation in the embedded clause. In Leskien's interpretation, negation is in effect a force that flows from genitive-governing verbs (verbs of striving or frustrated striving) to possible targets; it is a string that communicates the matrix negation down into subordinate infinitive clauses. The fact that intervening syntax (partially) weakens the force of negation confirms that there is a string that transmits case from the matrix clause into the subordinate clause.

3.4. Predication, Properties

One function of syntax is to name and associate a property with a referent. In many languages the overt device for that is a special verb 'be'. That can be said of Russian, except for the familiar fact that no form of 'be' occurs in the present tense. Let's assume that a copular predication involves a predicate (call it 'be'), the subject noun, and the constituent stating the property. What are these constituents? It's not obvious. Take a standard phrase-structure tree consisting of *S > NP VP* and then *VP >V NP*. In the tree the first *NP* is of course the subject, the second (inside the *VP*) a direct object. That's standard. Where do a copula and a predicative noun go? In a copular sentence, since the copula is a kind of predicate, it would have to be a *V* inside *VP*; the *NP* that is sister to the *VP* would be the subject. Where can we attach the predicative noun or adjective? If a predicative were put inside *VP*, it would have to be some kind of direct object. And the fact is that predicatives don't have the semantics of an object or a subject. To say it another way, a predicative is not part of the aspectual gradation. It has a different kind of meaning.

This is a case where a string might be helpful. Predicatives, as a group, are not restricted to equational (copular) contexts. Predicatives can be associated with other arguments. In addition to the aspectual roles for arguments (agent, prime, patient), we could add – independent of these aspectual roles – a self-standing verb, the copula. Its function is to assign to a nominal argument a property (stated by a lexical adjective, noun, preposition, phrase, or participle). That can be done with a string attached from a source to a destination which has the force (accompanying semantics) of a property.

3.5. Individuation and Quantification

Estonian has a typologically interesting pattern of agreement and case for some intransitive verbs, for example, *kasvama* 'grow' (Nemvalts 1996; here from Hiietam 2005). In positive sentences with this verb, when the sole argument is plural, there are two possibilities for case of the object and number on the verb, depending on how the reference of the entity is understood.

(5) a. Peenral kasvasid lilled.
flowerbed-ADESSIVE grow-3PL flower-PL.NOM
'In the flowerbed there grew flowers.'
b. Peenral kasvas lilli.
flowerbed-ADESSIVE grow-3SG flower-PL.PRT
'In the flowerbed there grew some flowers.' [Hiietam 2005: 3]

It is also possible to have an infinitive subordinated to an impersonal matrix verb, such as Est *tuleb* 'be necessary', *maksab* 'be fitting' (5a) is personal – that is, it has a subject. If the sole noun is nominative plural, as in (5a), the verb will be plural, in agreement with the plural number of the subject noun phrase. In terms of the distinction personal vs. impersonal, this is a personal construction. (Recall the "personal" passive in Polish.) In the other variant, (5b), the noun is partitive (but still plural!), and because it is not nominative, the verb does not agree with it; this is an impersonal construction, so the verb must use the default singular. It is usually thought that the difference between these two sentence types is one of reference – the noun is definite (for the personal construction), as opposed to indefinite (for the impersonal construction). I would like to suggest a reformulation of the opposition, making use of a distinction suggested by the philosopher Keith Donnellan. Donnellan (1966) distinguishes two modes of reference. He defines "referential" reference thusly: "A speaker who uses a description referentially in an assertion… uses the description to enable his audience to pick out whom or what he is talking about and states something about that person or thing" (p. 46). This characterization fits (5a).

Donnellan's other type of reference (phrased in terms of the speaker) is: "a speaker who uses a description attributively in an assertion states something about whoever or whatever is the so-and-so," and a little later, "the speaker wishes to assert something about whatever or whoever fits that description." This describes the partitive noun in (5b): "in the flowerbed there is something growing that fits the definition of flowers". This, I think, is more instructive than the term "indefinite" (compare Partee 2008 for a similar approach to Russian).

Applying Donnellan's distinction to the Estonian sentences above, we have two syntagms, which can be stated in *n*-tuples as follows:

(6)

	verb number	*noun. number*	*noun case*	*agree. verb*	*noun case*	*noun reference*
a.	plural	plural	nominative	agreement	nominative	individuating
b.	singular	plural	partitive	no agreement	partitive	quantifying

A syntagm is minimally a set of values, but it is more. There is linkage between elements of the *n*-tuple. In (6) singular number in agreement (when the referent is plural) is a downgrading of the specificity of agreement. Partitive case applies to direct objects in which there is no aspectual boundary. Agreement is of course familar, but how does it get done? Quite possibly, by a string. The two kinds of reference are instantiations of more general categories. Attributive reference does not presume knowledge of the identity of the referent, but it does presume the possible existence of tokens fitting the definition. Statements of possible but not certain existence (or denial of existence) are the most general form of a general and inclusive concept of QUANTIFICATION. In quantificational predicates, the speaker is interested in how many, how numerous; one possible answer to the question could be at least one, or under negation, none. The opposing concept is one that treats the object under discussion as individuated: "the degree to which the participant is characterized as a distinct entity or individual in the narrated event" (Timberlake 1975: 124).

The opposition of individuation vs. quantification shows up in many places in the morphosyntax of the languages of northeastern Europe. Negation is a kind of quantification. (The quantity is null.) As is well-known, in much of Slavdom, negated existence leads to special case marking (genitive) and depersonalization (loss of agreement). Also, in Russian, combining a subject noun with a numeral (an obvious quantification) reduces the likelihood of agreement, depending on the quantifier. Approximate quantifiers like *mnogo* 'many' or *neskol'sko* 'several' as in (7) are thoroughly quantifying and not very specific, so a "weak existential" verb is unlikely to have plural agreement with a plural quantifier (7). In contrast, paucal numerals are individuating enough to have plural agreement (8):

(7)	Odnovremenno	pribylo	neskol'ko	èšelonov.
	simultaneously	arrived-NT.SG	several	echelons-GEN.PL.

'Simultaneously there arrived several echelons.' [Timberlake 2004: 358–59]

(8)	Na	sledujuščij	den'	javilis'	ešče	dve	sem'i.
	on	next	day	appeared-PL	still	two	families-NOM.PL

'On the next day there appeared two more families.'

To return to Donnellan, we can observe that there is interaction between reference and modality. If, in Donnellan's example, a certain Jones is already known to be the murderer of Smith, *the murderer of Smith* can be understood to refer to that unambiguously identified individual. That would be a referential operation, which I would call INDIVIDUATING. In contrast, if the legal procedure were still unresolved, it would be possible to say *the murderer of Smith is insane*, meaning by this 'whosoever fits the description of murdering Smith'. That is possible because the speaker would be referring to a modal, future time, when the identity of the murderer is still open. In a similar fashion, it used to be said with respect to Russian that the object of verbs like *ždat´* 'wait for' would be accusative if a specific vehicle was awaited (*avtobus*$_{\text{ACC}}$ 'bus') while genitive *avtobusa*$_{\text{GEN}}$ would allow any vehicle satisfying the definition of being an autobus. In both cases, realis modality patterns with individuated reference and irrealis patterns with hypothetical or still-open modality. And the certainness of past modality is correlated with individuated entity while future, open modality indicates possible existence, a kind of existential QUANTIFICATION.

3.6. Predicative Nominals

In addition to the copula, certain other verbs have the function of establishing that an entity has a property or membership in a group, with some additional flavor: *okazat'sja* 'turn out to be' is inchoative, with a modal overtone of unexpectedness; *stat'* 'become' is change of state, *sčitat'* 'consider to be' reflects perception of the speaker.

In addition, many verbs can be associated with adjectives or participles involving an individual who is named as an argument of the main verb.

(9) Oni vernulis' {uspokoennye / uspokoennymi}.
they returned {calm-NOM.PL / calmed down-INS.PL}
'They returned {calm / calmed down}.'

Predicatives such as (9) can be termed "co-predicates". Nouns can also be co-predicatives. As co-predicatives nouns often present the state as contingent on something, which is to say, modal; accordingly, the noun is therefore instrumental. In (10) the child's avoiding adults is something that happened specifically during (and as a consequence of) childhood:

(10)	Rebenkom	ja	vsegda	stremilsja	smyt´sja	ot	vzroslyx.
	as child-INS	I	always	attempted	sneak-off	from	grown-ups

'As a child I always tried to sneak-off away from grown-ups.' [Timberlake 2004: 284]

Johanna Nichols wrote this about the role of predicate nominals (1981: 15):

> In semantic structure, predicate nominals are predicates, not actants; nominal, relations are predicates, not actants; nominal relations such as agent, patient, instrument etc., do not apply to them.

On semantic grounds, Nichols shows that co-predicates are similar to the predicates of copulas. Nichol's pithy observation about the character of predicate nominals indirectly supports the concept of strings. Unlike nominal arguments, co-predicates have a wide range of hosts. At the other end of string, the co-predicate can take more than one form (noun, nominative or instrumental adjective, or participle). The rich variety of forms differs from the mode of combination seen in verb plus aspectual argument. It suggests we have *n*-tuples that hold a list of possible hosts and another *n*-tuple of possible co-predicates, with rules of combination. Those rules links the two syntactic entities; in this respect they are strings.

4. Aspectuality and Modality in Strings

4.1 Independent Impersonal Infinitives, Early Slavic

Consider one of the most famous sentences of the Slavic New Testament, which occurs in the scene in which Pontius Pilate questions Jesus about the accusations against him. Jesus does not answer; Pilate does not understand why Jesus does not respond. The evangelist summarizes (Mk 15:5):

(11)	Іс	же	к томоу	ничесоже	не отъвѣшта	ѣко	дивити-сѧ	пилатови
	Is	že	k tomu	ničesože	ne otъvěšta	ěko	diviti-sę	pilatovi
	Jesus	yet	to that	nothing	not answer	so	marveled-AOR	pilate-DAT

The Slavonic sentence translates two sentences of the Greek New Testament original. The first clause describes Jesus's failure to respond to accusations (ὁ δὲ Ἰησοῦς οὐκέτι οὐδὲν ἀπεκρίθη 'Jesus did not anything respond') and the second clause describes the subsequent effect on Pilate (…ὥστε θαυμάζειν τὸν Πιλᾶτον$_{ACC}$ '…so that marveled Pilate'). In his careful description of New Testament syntax, Gerald Stevens (1994: 293) identifies the construction of the second clause as an instance of the "accusative with infinitive", and specifically as the variant that describes a causal relation; here, Jesus's silence triggers Pilate's astonishment. Stevens cites the familiar example from Mark 15:5 as of this subtype; note that the conjunction ὥστε 'so that…' here makes the causal character overt. This shows that there are really two layers of semantics packed into one verb here. This means that, in addition to the statement of fact (or what we might call "aspectual"), there is another layer, a layer of modality. Here the aspectual level is the narrated event of Pilate's reaction and the modal layer is the hint of causation which had a result that was contrary to expectations. (Expectation is a kind of modality.) This all suggests that independent (impersonal) infinitives, in New Testament Greek and Old Slavic, harbor a hero with two hypostases, modal and aspectual. This duality is relevant to (most or perhaps all) independent infinitives. Here the hero Pilate is the focus of aspectual change (change of state): the entity whose fate is most affected by the events. The two hypostases are joined and expressed by a single morphological unit.

The dual character of autonomous (or impersonal or independent) infinitives can be illustrated by (15) below: *tъbě*-DAT / *rъže*-NOM / *svъę*-NOM / *snęti*-INF (= 'you / rye / own / must-harvest'). Here the single dative lexeme *tъbě*-DAT 'you' in the sentence has two hypostases: in the modal domain, he is given a certain task, while the aspectual level states what that task consists of. The same person is active in two domains: the activity of harvesting – that's aspectual – and the imposition of a task – that is modal. Here the aspectual layer and the modal layer are differentiated semantically into two hypostases (possibly with different properties) joined by a string with a single morphological exponent. This, I think, is a representation of dual affiliation that is more instructive than PRO.

4.2. Nominative Object with Infinitive, in Strings

In North Russian dialects, and notably in Novgorod, the medieval center of Russian commerce, objects of personal transitive verbs are marked, unremarkably, accusative, as in (12):

(12) *A: finite personal verb, matrix accusative object*

čto	oleksa	kolbinь	dalъ	poroukou	v kounaxъ
what	O	K	gave-PST.MSC.	deal-ACC.SG.FM	in pelt

'as for O. K., he made an arrangement about money' [Zaliznjak 2004, #389/G12]

Finite verbs combine with infinitives and form a kind of complex verb; an object of an infinitive will get its case from the host finite verb. In particular, if the host is a personal verb, it will pass its transitivity on to the dependent verb and its object will be accusative. In (13) the compound verb *povelě dati* takes the accusative object *opitemьju*.

(13) *Ba: finite personal matrix, dependent personal infinitive, accusative object*

i	povelě	dati	opitemьju
and	ordered	give	penance-ACC

'and (he) ordered (someone) to do penance' [VoprKir, 62]

In (14) the main verb 'show oneself' has a purpose clause 'sew a pelt':

(14) *Bb: finite personal matrix verb, dependent personal infinitive, accusative object*

a	ty	ko	mni	nь	javišisję	kouni	šiti	nošjo
and	you	to	me	not	shown	pelt-DAT	sew-INF	extension-ACC

'And you do not to come to me to sew an extension to the pelt.'
[Zaliznjak 2004, #490/G22 (XIV$_2$)]

In contrast to the verbs in (12)–(14), the matrix verb can be "independent" (not dependent on another verb). Such an infinitive is a self-sufficient verb with its own modality (as its own aspectual layer), as suggested with respect to Pilate in (11).

(15) *C: matrix impersonal infinitive, nominative object*

(mně	vyjexat′	k tobě)	tъbě	ržže	svъę	snęti
(me-DAT	travel	to you)	you-DAT	rye-NOM	own-NOM	harvest-INF

'(For me (it is necessary) to leave to go to you,) for you (it is necessary) to harvest your rye.' [Zaliznjak #142/G10]

An independent infinitive, as noted, doesn't have to be embedded in further structure. There is another rather unusual property: if the verb is transitive, then the object appears in the nominative rather than accusative case. Note the nominative in *snęti ržže*; the accusative would be *rož* or *rožь*. The fact that no further frame is needed suggests that the nominative object with independent infinitive is its oldest form.

It is also possible to have an infinitive subordinated to an impersonal matrix verb, such as the verb *dostoitь* 'be appropiate for *x*'. When *dostoitь* is attached to an infinitive, it does *not* affect the syntactic properties of the embedded affinitive. The infinitive has a dative subject and, if transitive, its direct object is nominative, as would happen with any impersonal infinitive. This fact suggests that the independent infinitive and nominative object predate the union of *dostoitь* and the infinitive. That should not be surprising; *dostoitь* is a modal. Other verbs that can host an autonomous infinitive are also modal.

(16) *D: matrix impersonal finite, impersonal infinitive, nominative object*

dostoitь	li	popou	svoje	ženě	molitva	tvoriti	vsjakaja
fit-3SG	if	priest-DAT	own	wife-DAT	prayer-NOM	do-INF	anykind-NOM.SG

'Is it fitting for a priest to say any prayer for his own wife?' [VoprKir 29]

Patterns (A) through (D) are summarized in (17).

(17)

	(A)	(B)	(C)	(D)	(E)
context	finite personal	finite personal dependent infinitive	independent infinitive	finite impersonal dependent infinitive	independent infinitive animate/ negative
personhood	personal	personal	impersonal	impersonal	personal
object	accusative	accusative	nominative	nominative	genitive
example	*dalъ poroukou*-ACC	*povelělъ dati opitemъju*-ACC	*rъže*-NOM *snęti*	*dostoit tvoriti molitva*-NOM	

There are exceptions to the use of nominative with impersonal infinitives. In particular, masculine animate nouns maintain traditional animate accusative in this context:

(18) *Ea: impersonal infinitive, animate accusative* (AN.ACC = animate accusative),

ašče	boudetь	konevyi	tatь, to	vydati	ego	knjazju	na potokъ
if	be	horse	thief then	give-INF	him-AN.ACC	prince-DAT	for detainment

'If there is a horse thief, (it is necessary) to turn him over to the prince for detainment.'

Similarly, objects of negated verbs kept their genitive case, and did not become nominative even when the verb is an independent infinitive:

(19) *Eb: impersonal infinitive, genitive of negation*

a	Ordy	mi	ne	znati,	a	Orda	znati	tobě
but	Orda-GEN.SG	for-me-DAT	not	know	but	Orda-NOM.SG	know	for-you-DAT

'and it is not for me to know the Horde but the Horde is for you to know'

The construction with nominative object is not original to Russian, but was borrowed from Finnish in northwestern dialects (Novgorod). It became a stylistic mark of official language (law) and continued to be used into the 17th century.

One could rationalize the nominative case by observing that the matrix predicate lacks a subject, leaving an empty position which could absorb an argument slot of an object. In order for that distribution to occur, there has to be communication between matrix (A) and embedded (B) and between matrix (C) and embedded (D) object and the predicates of (B) and (D).

Since nominative is normally the case of a subject, one might propose that in this instance the accusative has been changed to a nominate *subject*. In fact, the nominative fails to behave as a subject in several respects (Timberlake 1974). A nominative object does not trigger agreement for number and gender in participles (including the perfect participle) and predicate adjectives:

(20)

i	korolju	bylo	ta	ruxljadь	dati
and	prince-DAT	was-NT.SG	that	property-FM-SG-NOM	give

'and it was for the prince to give back that property' [Timberlake 1974: 52]

Animate nouns, as shown in (19), are not nominativized, when inanimate nouns would be nominativized; normally one expects rules to apply to the whole noun phrase.

Thus a nominative patient in this construction is not a subject. Nominativization can apply two levels down in the syntactic structure. All this argues that the nominatives in impersonal contexts are not subjects. How can they do what they do? Some force extends down from the matrix predicate to the subordinate infinitive. And how does that happen? The object change is confined to the level of the object, but the conditions for the change extend beyond that level. It is not clear that movement would be permitted. Sounds like strings.

Bibliography

Akt. arx. = *Akty sobrannye v biblijutekax i arxivax rossijskoj imperii arxeografičeskoju èkspedicieju IAN*, I: 1294–1598.

Arkadiev, Peter. 2016. Long-distance genitive of negation in Lithuanian, ed. by Axel Holvoet and Nicole Nau. *Argument realization in Baltic*. Amsterdam; Philadelphia: John Benjamins, 37–81.

Donnellan, Keith. 1966. Reference and definite descriptions. *The Philosophical Review* 75: 281–30.

Hiietam, Katrin. 2005. Case marking in Estonian grammatical relations. *The University of Leeds Working Papers in Linguistics and Phonetics*, vol. 10. Leeds.

Leskien, A. 1919. *Litauisches Lesebuch mit Grammatik und Wörterbuch*. Heidelberg: C. Winter.

Marianus = 1883. *Mariinskoe četveroevangelie: s primečanijami i priloženijami*, ed. by I.V. Jagič. St. Petersburg: Izd. Otd-nija russkago jazyka i slovesnosti IAN.

Nemvalts, Peep. 1996. *Case marking of subject phrases in modern Estonian*. Uppsala: Acta Universitatis Upsaliensis.

Nichols, Johanna. 1981. *Predicate nominals: A partial surface syntax of Russian*. Berkeley, CA: University of California Press.

Partee, Barbara. 2008. Negation, intensionality, and aspect: Interaction with NP semantics, ed. by Susan Rothstein, *Theoretical and crosslinguistic approaches to the semantics of aspect* V. 110, 291–317. Amsterdam; Philadelphia: John Benjamins.

Russkaja pravda = Vladimirskii-Budanov, M. 1888. *Pravda rouskaja. Ustav Velikogo Knazja Jaroslava Vladimeriča o sudiex. Russkaja pravda. Xristomatija po istorii russkago prava*, 37–82. St. Petersburg; Kiev.

Stevens, Gerald. 1994. *New testament Greek*. Lanham, Md; London: University Press of America.

Timberlake, Alan. 1974. *The nominative object in Slavic, Baltic, and West Finnic*. (Slavistische Beiträge, 82.) Munich: Otto Sagner.

Timberlake, Alan. 1975. Hierarchies in the genitive of negation. *The Slavic and East European Journal* 19.2: 123–18.

Timberlake, Alan. 2004. *A reference grammar of Russian*. Cambridge: Cambridge University Press.

VoprKir = 1908. '1130 – 1156 g. Voprosy Kirika, Savvy i Ilii, s otvetami Nifonta, episkopa novgorodskogo, i drugix ierarxičeskix lic', *Pamjatniki drevne-russkogo kanoničeskogo prava*, 1: *Pamjatniki* XI – XV, 2. 2nd ed., St. Petersburg.

Zaliznjak, Andrej A. 2004. *Drevnenovgorodskij dialekt*, 2-e izd., Moscow: Jazyki russkoj kul′tury.

Zemskaja, E.A; M.V. Kitaigorodskaja; and E.N. Shiriev. 1981. *Russkaja razgovornaja reč': obščie voprosy, slovoobrazovanie, sintaksis*. Moscow: Nauka.

Beata Trawiński

Polish *żeby* under Negation

Abstract The paper addresses two patterns in the distribution of complement clauses headed by the complementizer *żeby* in Polish related to the presence of sentential negation. It is argued that *żeby*-clauses with an obligatory negation in the matrix clause, licensed by epistemic verbs, can be treated in terms of negative polarity, with *żeby* defined as an *n*-word. Structures with *żeby*-clauses and an obligatory negation in the embedded clause, licensed by verbs of fear, are argued to be an instance of negative complementation, with *żeby* specified as a negative complementizer. A uniform lexicalist analysis within the framework of HPSG is provided, employing tools developed to account for Negative Concord in Polish.*

Keywords: Negation, *żeby*, NPI, HPSG, Polish

1. Introduction

In Polish, indicative finite complement clauses are typically introduced by the complementizer *że* 'that'. This complementizer is compatible both with affirmative and negative contexts. Thus, all of the constellations in (1) are possible: affirmative matrix predicates can combine with affirmative (1a) and negated (1b) embedded predicates, and negated matrix predicates can combine with affirmative (1c) and negated (1d) embedded predicates.

(1)	a.	Piotr	obiecywał,	że	schudnie.
		Piotr	promised	ŻE	lose-weight
		'Piotr promised that he will lose weight.'			

* I am extremely grateful to Piotr Bański, Kerstin Schwabe and the editors of this volume, Steven Franks, Alan Timberlake, and Anna Wietecka, for their helpful comments, corrections and suggestions. I am also indebted to the audience of the 14th Annual Meeting of the Slavic Linguistics Society (SLS-14), and in particular Ilse Zimmermann (†2020), for initial feedback on this work. Very special thanks go to Peter Kosta, who hosted SLS-14 in Potsdam, making it, once again, the place to exchange ideas and network. I thank Peter for inspiring discussions about and beyond (Slavic) linguistic issues. Any errors are my own.

b. Piotr obiecywał, że nie schudnie.
Piotr promised ŻE NEG lose-weight
'Piotr promised that he will not lose weight.'

c. Piotr nie obiecywał, że schudnie.
Piotr NEG promised ŻE lose-weight
'Piotr did not promise that he will lose-weight.'

d. Piotr nie obiecywał, że nie schudnie.
Piotr NEG promised ŻE NEG lose-weight
'Piotr did not promise that he will not lose weight.'

In addition to the complementizer *że*, complement clauses in Polish can be headed by the complementizer *żeby* 'that / so that' (or its variants *aby*, *ażeby*, *by*, *coby*, *iżby*), which can introduce both non-finite (2a) and finite (2b) clauses.[1] Finite *żeby*-clauses as in (2b) use the *l*-participle and are usually referred to as subjunctives, as in my gloss.

(2) a. Piotr nalegał, żeby wracać.
Piotr insisted ŻEBY return.INF
'Piotr insisted to return.'

b. Piotr nalegał, żeby Ewa wróciła.
Piotr insisted ŻEBY Ewa return.SUBJ
'Piotr insisted on Ewa to return.'

Typically, complement clauses headed by *żeby*, both non-finite (3) and finite (subjunctive) (4), are compatible with affirmative and negative contexts. Similarly to *że*-clauses, negation can occur within the matrix clause (3b, 4b), within the embedded clause (3c, 4c), or within both clauses (3d, 4d).

(3) a. Piotr nalegał, żeby wracać.
Piotr insisted ŻEBY return.INF
'Piotr insisted to return.'

b. Piotr nie nalegał, żeby wracać.
Piotr NEG insisted ŻEBY return.INF
'Piotr did not insist to return.'

	c.	Piotr	nalegał,	żeby	nie	wracać.	
		Piotr	insisted	ŻEBY	NEG	return.INF	
		'Piotr insisted not to return.'					
	d.	Piotr	nie	nalegał,	żeby	nie	wracać.
		Piotr	NEG	insisted	ŻEBY	NEG	return.INF
		'Piotr did not insist not to return.'					

(4)	a.	Piotr	nalegał,	żeby	Ewa	wracała.		
		Piotr	insisted	ŻEBY	Ewa	return.SUBJ		
		'Piotr insisted on Ewa to return.'						
	b.	Piotr	nie	nalegał,	żeby	Ewa	wracała.	
		Piotr	NEG	insisted	ŻEBY	Ewa	return.SUBJ	
		'Piotr did not insist on Ewa to return.'						
	c.	Piotr	nalegał,	żeby	Ewa	nie	wracała.	
		Piotr	insisted	ŻEBY	Ewa	NEG	return.SUBJ	
		'Piotr insisted on Ewa not to return.'						
	d.	Piotr	nie	nalegał,	żeby	Ewa	nie	wracała.
		Piotr	NEG	insisted	ŻEBY	Ewa	NEG	return.SUBJ
		'Piotr did not insist on Ewa not to return.'						

The examples in (1), (3) and (4) might suggest that there are no specific restrictions on the usage or distribution of the two complementizers with sentential negation in Polish. However, there are two phenomena which make this picture more complicated. They include cases where *żeby*-clauses are licensed only under obligatory negation either in the matrix clause or in the embedded clause. These two cases are the focus of the present paper. The goal of this contribution is to place these phenomena in the general picture related to Negative Concord and show how they can be accounted for within a unified lexicalist analysis.

In the next section, the status of the complementizer *żeby* is discussed and the distinction between the subjunctive and conditional mood in Polish is explained. Section 3 discusses the phenomena in focus: sentential structures with *żeby*-clauses and negation in the matrix clause, and structures with *żeby*-clauses and negation within the embedded clause. Section 4 suggests a unified analysis of both phenomena and presents its implementation within the framework of

Head-driven Phrase Structure Grammar. Section 5 sums up the observations and conclusions, and sketches some directions for future research.

2. Polish *żeby* and the Subjunctive versus Conditional Mood

Two usage patterns of the *że+by* combination in Polish must be distinguished. Both of them include the elements *że* and *by*, which, however, have in each case different semantic and distributional properties. In the first case, (i) *że* is optional, it can be preceded by *a*, and can be replaced – depending on the style – by other elements such as *a*, *co* or *iż* (5a), (ii) the elements *że* (and the other variants, if present) and *by* are inseparable (5b), (iii) the *że+by* combination can introduce both finite[2] as well as non-finite clauses (cf. (3) and (4) above).

(5)	a.	Piotr	nalegał,	by /	żeby /	ażeby /	aby /	coby /	iżby Ewa	wróciła.
		Piotr	insisted	BY	ŻEBY	AŻEBY	ABY	COBY	IŻBY Ewa	return.SUBJ
		'Piotr insisted on Ewa to return.'								
	b.	*Piotr	nalegał,	że	Ewa	by	wróciła /	wróciłaby.		
		Piotr	insisted	ŻE	Ewa	BY	return.SUBJ	return. PRT.BY		
		'Piotr insisted on Ewa to return.'								[intended]

In the second case, (i) *że* is obligatory and cannot be replaced by other elements except one: the rather archaic *iż* (6), (ii) the elements *że* and *by* are morphologically separate entities which need not to appear adjacently (7),[3] (iii) the *że+by* combination can only appear in finite clauses (8).

(6)	Mam	nadzieję,	że /	iż	Ewa	przyjdzie.
	have.1.SG	hope.ACC	ŻE	IŻ	Ewa	come. FUT
	'I hope that Ewa will come.'					

(7)	a	Powiedziałam,	że	Marek	zrobiłby	to.	
		said.1.SG	ŻE	Marek	do.PRT.BY	it	
	b.	Powiedziałam,	że	Marek	by	to	zrobił.
		said.1.SG	ŻE	Marek	BY	it	do.PRT
	c.	Powiedziałam,	że	to	by	Marek	zrobił.
		said.1.SG	ŻE	it	BY	Marek	do.PRT

d.	Powiedziałam,	że	by	zrobił	to	Marek.
	said.1.SG	ŻE	BY	do.PRT	it	Marek

'I said that Marek would do it.'

(8) Marek powiedział, że (może) by przyszedł / by *przyjść.
Marek said.3.SG ŻE maybe BY come.PRT BY come.INF
'Marek said that maybe he would come.' [intended]

Moreover, these two types of *że+by* combinations have different meanings. According to Tomaszewicz (2009), sentences with *że+by* combinations of the first type can refer both to hypothetical unrealized situations as well as to non-hypothetical past and present situations. By contrast, sentences with *że+by* combinations of the second type can only refer to hypothetical unrealized situations. On the basis of these semantic and distributional differences, the two usage patterns of *że+by* combinations have been captured in the literature as instances of subjunctive versus conditional mood, respectively (see also Bański 2000, Bondaruk 2004, Migdalski 2006 and Tomaszewicz 2009, among others).[4] Given this, the morpheme *by*, which is typical for many Slavic languages, can be seen as a (flexible) mood particle only in the latter case. I conclude that subjunctive clauses are introduced by the complementizer *by*, which can be facultatively prefixed by *że-*, *a-* etc., and that conditional clauses are introduced by the complementizer *że* and contain the modal particle *by*, which, as a clitic, can appear in various positions and can be realized phonologically adjacent to the complementizer *że*.

Note also that person-number markers appear on *by* in both cases (9).[5] If the markers are present (in the sense that they are phonologically realized), their attachment to *by* is obligatory both in subjunctives (9a) as well as in conditionals (9b).

(9) a. Piotr nalegał, żebym / żebyś / żebyśmy / żebyście wrócił / wrócili.
Piotr insisted ŻEBY.1.SG ŻEBY.2.SG ŻEBY.1.PL ŻEBY.2.PL return. PRT.SG return. PRT.PL
'Piotr insisted on me / you / us to return.'

b. Piotr myśli, że (ja) bym / (ty) byś / (my) byśmy / (wy)
Piotr thinks ŻE I BY.1.SG you.SG BY.2.SG we BY.1.PL you.PL
byście go odwiedził / odwiedzili.
BY.2.PL him visit.PRT.SG visit. PRT.PL
'Piotr thinks that I / you / we would visit him.'

Which type of *że+by* combination, subjunctive or conditional, is used in an embedded clause is subject to selectional restrictions of the matrix predicate. Some verbs, such as volitional or desiderative predicates, require subjunctive clauses (cf. (10a) versus (10b) and (10c)), while other verbs require indicative or conditional clauses (cf. (11a) and (11b) versus (11c)).

(10) a. Chcę, żeby Marek to zrobił.
want.1.SG ŻEBY Marek it do.PRT
'I want Marek to do it.'
b. *Chcę, że Marek by to zrobił.
want.1.SG ŻE Marek BY it do.PRT
'I want Marek to do it.' [intended]
c. *Chcę, że Marek to zrobi.
want.1.SG ŻE Marek it do.FUT
'I want Marek to do it.' [intended]

(11) a. Marek obiecał, że to zrobi.
Marek promised ŻE it do.FUT
'Marek promised to do it.'
b. Marek obiecał, że zrobiłby to
Marek promised ŻE do.BY.FUT it
'Marek promised that he would do it.'
c. *Marek obiecał, żeby to zrobił.
Marek promised ŻEBY it do.PRT
'Marek promised to do it.' [intended]

Some predicates allow both clause types, which is illustrated by (12) as opposed to (7d) above. As already indicated by the English translations in (12) and (7d), including the modals *should* versus *would*, respectively, there is a semantic difference between sentences with embedded subjunctives and sentences with the embedded modal particle *by* (cf. Tomaszewicz 2009 and the indication above).

(12)	Powiedziałam,	żeby	zrobił	to	Marek.
	said.1.SG	ŻEBY	do.PRT	it	Marek

'I said that Marek should do it.'

The phenomena addressed in this paper concern instances of subjunctive complement clauses, that is clauses introduced by *żeby* or its variants (in the following *żeby*). While it is rather uncontroversial that the two usage patterns of the *że+by* combinations, subjunctive and conditional, exist in Polish, there is no consensus on how to analyze these two structure types synchronically, and in particular, how to analyze *żeby*.[6] In this paper, I adopt a lexicalist, non-derivational approach to *żeby*, according to which this subjunctive complementizer is defined in the lexicon together with its selectional requirements, phonological realization variants, and inflectional specifications (cf. Section 4).

3. *Żeby* under Negation

In this section, two special cases of the distribution of Polish *żeby*-clauses are discussed. In both cases, *żeby*-clauses obligatorily co-occur with sentential negation. In the first case, the negation is present in the matrix clause (Section 3.1) and in the second case, it occurs within the embedded clause (Section 3.2).

3.1. Negation in the Matrix Clause

To introduce the first case, the verb *sądzić* 'think' will be used. This verb typically selects complement clauses introduced by the indicative complementizer *że*. As already indicated in the introduction, Polish *że*-clauses are compatible both with affirmative and negative contexts, thus all configurations are possible (cf. (1)). This also applies to sentences with the verb *sądzić* selecting *że*-clauses (13).

(13) a. Jan sądzi, że Ewa wróci.
Jan think.3.SG.PRES ŻE Ewa return.3.SG
'Jan thinks that Ewa will return.'

b. Jan sądzi, że Ewa nie wróci.
Jan think.3.SG.PRES ŻE Ewa NEG return.3.SG
'Jan thinks that Ewa will not return.'

c. Jan nie sądzi, że Ewa wróci.
Jan NEG think.3.SG.PRES ŻE Ewa return.3.SG
'Jan does not think that Ewa will return.'
Reading 1: It is not the case that Jan thinks Ewa will return.
Reading 2: Jan thinks that it is not the case that Ewa will return. (**Neg-Raising**)

d. Jan nie sądzi, że Ewa nie wróci.
Jan NEG think.3.SG.PRES ŻE Ewa NEG return.3.SG
'Jan does not think that Ewa will not return.'
Reading 1: It is not the case that Jan thinks Ewa will not return.
Reading 2: Jan thinks that it is not the case that Ewa will not return. (**Neg-Raising**)

Note that the verb *sądzić* is a negation raising (Neg-Raising) predicate: it can license structures where the syntactic representation of negation is (assumed to be) raised out of an embedded clause to be realized in the matrix clause. Semantically, the negation in the matrix clause is understood as negating the proposition in the complement clause.[7] Due to this property of *sądzić*, the sentencse in (13c) and (13d) have two readings: a non-Neg-Raising reading (Reading 1) and a Neg-Rasing reading (Reading 2).

In addition to indicative complement clauses introduced by *że*, a negated verb *sądzić* can combine with subjunctive complement clauses headed by the complementizer *żeby* (14). In this case, the negation in the matrix clause is obligatory; cf. (14a) and (14d) versus (14b) and (14c). A negation within the complement clause is possible but it does not constitute a licensor for a *żeby*-clause with *sądzić* (14c). In other words, *nie sądzić* can select a subjunctive or indicative complement clause, but *sądzić* only the later.

(14) a. Jan nie sądzi, żeby Ewa wróciła.
Jan NEG think.3.SG.PRES ŻEBY Ewa return.3.SG
'Jan does not think that Ewa would return.'
Reading 1: It is not the case that Jan thinks Ewa would return.
Reading 2: Jan thinks that it is not the case that Ewa would return. **(Neg-raising)**

b. *Jan sądzi, żeby Ewa wróciła.
Jan think.3.SG.PRES ŻEBY Ewa return.3.SG
'Jan thinks that Ewa would return.' [intended]

c. *Jan sądzi, żeby Ewa nie wróciła.
Jan think.3.SG.PRES ŻEBY Ewa NEG return.3.SG
'Jan thinks that Ewa would not return.' [intended]

d. Jan nie sądzi, żeby Ewa nie wróciła.
Jan NEG think.3.SG.PRES ŻEBY Ewa NEG return.3.SG
'Jan does not think that Ewa would not return.'
Reading 1: It is not the case that Jan thinks Ewa would not return.
Reading 2: Jan thinks that is not the case that Ewa would not return. **(Neg-raising)**

Similar to sentences involving *że*-clauses, the negation in the matrix clause in (14a) and (14d) can be understood as negating the proposition within the complement clause. Consequently, the sentences have two readings: a non-Neg-Raising (Reading 1) and a Neg-Raising (Reading 2) reading, respectively. However, the contrast between (13b) and (13c) on the one hand and between (14a) and (14c) on the other hand indicates that the matrix negation can be assumed to originate in the embedded clause and raise to the matrix clause only for sentences with *że*-clauses but not for sentences with *żeby*-clauses. Thus, Polish *żeby*-clauses with obligatory matrix negation provide a piece of evidence in support of the semantic-pragmatic approaches to Neg-Raising. It is also conceivable that the Neg-Raising interpretation in Polish sentences with *że*-clauses and in sentences *żeby*-clauses differ in nature. While the former is linked to some syntactic operations, the latter is not (or to different ones).

There is also a meaning difference between sentences containing a matrix negation and a *że*-clause and corresponding sentences containing a *żeby*-clause. This meaning difference, also indicated by the translations and the two readings in (13c) and (14a), goes back to the semantics of the indicative versus subjunctive mood, induced by *że* and *żeby*, respectively (see Section 2).

Besides *sądzić* 'think', the following verbs allow for *żeby*-clauses under matrix negation in Polish, while typically selecting *że*-clauses: *czuć* 'feel', *dostrzegać* 'notice', *podejrzewać* 'suspect', *przypuszczać* 'suppose', *wierzyć* 'believe', *wyobrażać sobie* 'imagine' and many others.[8] The issue of what semantic class(es) those Polish verbs constitute and in what way (if any) they correspond to the verb classes licensing similar phenomena in Romance (and other languages) exceeds the scope of this paper.[9] Essentially, epistemic predicates (or epistemic usages of predicates) would be expected to be able to select subjunctive clauses under negation (cf. also Farkas 1985, 1992 and Manzini 1994, among others). Given that epistemic predicates express the state of knowledge of a participant and that the indicative mood is selected if the "epistemic agent" is committed to the truth of the embedded proposition (the propositional attitude is veridical), while the subjunctive mood is selected if (s)he is not (the propositional attitude is non-veridical) (cf. Siegel 2009 and Giannakidou 2009, 2011 and earlier work) then the following three structure types in Polish can be assumed to encode different degrees of certainty of the truth of the embedded proposition:

uncertain ← .... → certain

NEG V [*żeby* SUBJUNCTIVE] > NEG V [*że* INDICATIVE] > V [*że* NEG INDICATIVE]

Fig. 1: Hierarchy of certainty of the truth of the embedded proposition

3.2. Negation in the Embedded Clause

The second type of structure under consideration includes sentences where *żeby*-clauses obligatorily contain sentential negation. *Żeby*-clauses with obligatory sentential negation are licensed by verbs which typically allow for other types of clausal complements without any restrictions on polarity. For illustration, the verb *obawiać się* 'be afraid' can be used, which typically combines with finite *że*-clauses and shows compatibility both with affirmative and negative contexts both within matrix and embedded clauses (15).

(15) a. Ada obawia się, że schudnie.
Ada be-afraid.3.SG REFL ŻE lose-weight
'Ada is afraid that she will lose weight.'

b. Ada nie obawia się, że schudnie.
Ada NEG be-afraid.3.SG REFL ŻE lose-weight
'Ada is not afraid that she will lose weight.'

c. Ada obawia się, że nie schudnie.
Ada be-afraid.3.SG REFL ŻE NEG lose-weight
'Ada is afraid that she will not lose weight.'

d. Ada nie obawia się, że nie schudnie.
Ada NEG be-afraid.3.SG REFL ŻE NEG lose-weight
'Ada is not afraid that she will not lose weight.'

As a subject control verb, *obawiać się* can also select complementizerless infinitival clauses with obligatory and non-obligatory control. The examples in (16) show that the compatibility with affirmative and negative contexts can also be attested here.

(16) a. Ada obawia się schudnąć.
Ada be-afraid.3.SG REFL lose-weight.INF
'Ada is afraid that she will lose weight.'

b. Ada nie obawia się schudnąć.
Ada NEG be-afraid.3.SG REFL lose-weight.INF
'Ada is not afraid that she will lose weight.'

c. Ada obawia się nie schudnąć.
Ada be-afraid.3.SG REFL NEG lose-weight.INF
'Ada is afraid that she will not lose weight.'

d. Ada nie obawia się nie schudnąć.
Ada NEG be-afraid.3.SG REFL NEG lose-weight.INF
'Ada is not afraid that she will not lose weight.'

Moreover, non-finite clauses selected by *obawiać się* can also be introduced by the complementizer *żeby* (cf. also Bondaruk 2004 and Witkoś 2008). In this case, a negative in the complement clause is obligatory (cf. (17a) versus (17c)) (see also Błaszczak 2001 and Bondaruk 2004). A negation in the matrix clause is possible (17b) but it does not provide a licensing environment for the *żeby*-clause (17d).

(17) a. Ada obawia się, żeby nie schudnąć.
Ada be-afraid.3.SG REFL ŻEBY NEG lose-weight.INF
'Ada is afraid that she will lose weight.'

b. Ada nie obawia się, żeby nie schudnąć.
Ada NEG be-afraid.3.SG. REFL ŻEBY NEG lose-weight.INF
'Ada is not afraid that she will lose weight.'

c. *Ada obawia się, żeby schudnąć.
Ada be-afraid.3.SG. REFL ŻEBY lose-weight.INF
'Ada is afraid that she will lose weight.' [intended]

d. *Ada nie obawia się, żeby schudnąć.
Ada NEG be-afraid.3.SG. REFL ŻEBY lose-weight.INF
'Ada is not afraid that she will lose weight.' [intended]

Finally, the examples in (18) show that *obawiać się* can also select finite (subjunctive) *żeby*-clauses and in this case also a negative in the complement clause is obligatory (cf. (18a) versus (18c)). As in sentences with non-finite *żeby*-clauses, a negation in the matrix clause is possible but it is not a licensing context for the *żeby*-clause (cf. (18b) versus (18d)).

(18) a. Ada obawia się, żeby jej syn nie schudł.
Ada be-afraid.3.SG REFL ŻEBY her son NEG lose-weight
'Ada is afraid that her son will lose weight.'

b. Ada nie obawia się, żeby jej syn nie schudł.
Ada NEG be-afraid.3.SG. REFL ŻEBY her son NEG lose-weight
'Ada is not afraid that her son will not lose weight.' [intended]

c. *Ada obawia się, żeby jej syn schudł.
Ada be-afraid.3.SG. REFL ŻEBY her son lose-weight
'Ada is afraid that her son will lose weight.'

d. *Ada nie obawia się, żeby jej syn schudł.
Ada NEG be-afraid.3.SG. REFL ŻEBY her son lose-weight
'Ada is not afraid that her son will lose weight.' [intended]

Similar patterns can be observed with the verbs *bać się* 'fear', *martwić się* 'worry', *niepokoić się* 'be afraid', *lękać się* 'fear', *drżeć* 'tremble', and other predicates expressing fear, often referred to as *verba timendi*. In fact, *verba timendi* can been seen as negative volitional or desiderative verbs (such as *want* or *desire*): while the former have a preference component in their semantics, the latter have a dispreference component (meaning something like "want / desire that not"). For this reason, *verba timendi* can be considered as inherently negative verbs (in a similar way as verbs such as *doubt* or *deny*; cf. Klima 1964, among others). A piece of evidence for the presence of a negation in the semantics of Polish verbs of fear can be provided by data as in (19) and (20).

(19)	a.	Politycy	bali	się	słowem	pisnąć	w	tej	kwestii.
		politicians	fear.3.PL	REFL	word. INTST.SG	screech	in	this	question
		'The politicians feared to breathe a word on this issue.'							
	b.	Politycy	*(nie)	pisnęli	słowem	w	tej	kwestii.	
		politicians	NEG	screech.3.PL	word. INTST.SG	in	this	question	
		'The politicians did not breathe a word on this issue.'							

(20)	a.	Obawiałam	się	pokazać	po	sobie	ból.	
		be-afraid.1.SG	REFL	show	on	myself	pain.ACC	
		'I was afraid to show pain.'						
	b.	*Pokazałam	po	sobie	ból.			
		show.1.SG	on	myself	pain.ACC			
		'I showed pain.'						[intended]
	c.	Nie pokazałam	po	sobie	bólu.			
		NEG show.1.SG	on	myself	pain.GEN			
		'I did not show pain.'						

The examples in (19) and (20) contain idiomatic Negative Polarity Items (NPIs) *pisnąć słowem* 'to breathe a word' and *pokazać coś po sobie* 'show something', respectively, which can only be licensed in negative contexts. This is illustrated by (19b) and by the examples in (20b) versus (20c), where the presence of the negation is obligatory. As (19a) and (20a) show, these NPIs can also be licensed by the verbs of fear *bać się* 'fear' and *obawiać się* 'be afraid'. This fact suggests that a semantic negation is available in contexts provided by those verbs. Note that the English equivalent of the Polish NPI *pisnąć słowem* 'to breathe a word' is an NPI, too, and, as the translation of (19a) demonstrates, it can also appear with a verb of fear.

Note that the negation within the *żeby*-clauses in (17a, b) and (18a, b) has no effective semantic contribution to the interpretation of the sentence. Instead, it is an instance of expletive / pleonastic negation (cf. Espinal 1992, Brown 1996, Brown and Franks 1995 for Russian, van den Wouden 1997, Tovena 1996, 1998 and Błaszczak 2001 for Polish). This is evidenced by the fact that the embedded *żeby*-clauses like in (17a, b) and (18a, b) are not able to license *n*-words (see Section 4.1), which can be illustrated by examples like (21), taken from Błaszczak (2001: 144), including the original glosses:[10]

(21) a.

Boję	się,	żeby	on	nie	przyszedł.
fear.1.SG.PRES	REFL	that+SUBJ	he	NEG	come. PAST-PART

'I am afraid he will come.'

b.

Boję	się,	żeby	*nikt /	ktoś	nie	przyszedł.
fear.1.SG.PRES	REFL	that+SUBJ	nobody	somebody	NEG	come. PAST-PART

'I am afraid that somebody will / might come.'

Given the examples above and adopting Giannakidou's approach to indicative- versus subjunctive-selection, which builds on commitment to the truth of the embedded proposition by the attitude holder or by the speaker, we can again postulate three degrees of certainty of the truth of the embedded proposition corresponding to the following three structure types with verbs of fear in Polish(cf. Fig. 2 and Fig. 1 above):

uncertain ← .... → **certain**

V [*żeby* NEG SUBJUNCTIVE] > V [INFINITIVE] > V [*że* INDICATIVE]

Fig. 2: Hierarchy of certainty of the truth of the embedded proposition

3.3. Summary of Observations

Two patterns in the distribution of complement clauses introduced by the complementizer *żeby* in conjunction with obligatory sentential negation can be observed in Polish. The first pattern is licensed by epistemic verbs and includes obligatory sentential negation in the matrix clause and a subjunctive embedded clause. The second pattern is triggered by verbs of fear and contains obligatory sentential negation within the embedded clause, which can have subjunctive or infinitival form. In both cases, the matrix clause provides a negative polarity environment. These two patterns are summarized in Tab. 1.

Tab. 1: Patterns of the distribution of *żeby*-clauses with sentential negation

Verb type	Matrix clause	COMP	Embedded clause
sądzić 'think'	*(NEG)	*żeby*	subjunctive
obawiać się 'be afraid'		*żeby*	*(NEG) infinitival *(NEG) subjunctive

4. The Proposal

I argue that the two patterns discussed in Section 3 are essentially two different phenomena, having however the same core underlying theme, namely the complementizer *żeby*. I assume that it is *żeby* that essentially licenses both types of structures due to its lexical properties (in connection with verbal selectional properties and the principles of grammar). Thus, the analysis proposed here is lexicalist in nature, and it is implemented within the paradigm of Head-driven Phrase Structure Grammar (HPSG) in the tradition of Pollard and Sag (1994). The general analytical ideas are sketched in the present section and their formalization in HPSG is provided in Section 5.

I propose to treat structures with *żeby*-clauses and an obligatory negation in the matrix clause in terms of negative polarity. More precisely, I propose that the complementizer *żeby* in such structures is an *n*-word, that is, an element that requires a negative context (similar to other *n*-words like *nikt* 'nobody', *nigdzie* 'nowhere', *nigdy* 'never' etc.). Note, however, that there is no agreement about the question whether (Polish) *n*-words are inherently negative (cf. Richter and Sailer 2004b) or non-negative (cf. Błaszczak 2001 or Richter and Sailer 1999). Here, I adopt the latter approach and treat Polish *n*-words, including *żeby*, as not being inherently negative, that is, as a kind of Negative Polarity Items (NPIs). NPIs are usually seen as entities which are semantically non-negative elements that always appear in the scope of a negation (or other licensing contexts) and get their negative import from the licensing contexts (cf. also Przepiórkowski and Kupść 1997 for Polish and Kosta 1999a, b for other Slavic languages). Moreover, the negative polarity *żeby* is a superstrong NPI in terms of the categorization put forward by Zwarts (1998) and van der Wouden (1997).[11] As a natural consequence, complement clauses introduced by the negative polarity *żeby* always co-occur with a matrix negation. Note that this proposal is in line with the analyses of corresponding phenomena – captured as *polarity subjunctives,* following Stowell 1993 – in Romance languages (cf. Quer 1998 and B-Violette 2019, among others).

I further propose to treat structures with *żeby*-clauses and an obligatory negation within the embedded clause in terms of negative complementation. In particular, I suggest that in this structure type *żeby* is a negative complementizer. Negative complementizers are attested in many different languages, such as Basque (cf. Laka 1990, 1992), English (the complementizer *lest*), Irish, Hebrew and Latin, among others (cf. Moscati 2010 for an overview), and they can be licensed (overtly or covertly) by inherently negative verbs, such as adversative predicates or verbs of fear.

Finally, selectional restrictions of verbs determine how a particular type of a *żeby*-complement clause is realized syntactically, in the same way that lexical items like *wonder* or *promise* require an interrogative or a declarative complement, respectively. Accordingly, verbs like negated *sądzić* 'think' will select complement clauses headed by the negative polarity *żeby,* while verbs like *obawiać się* 'be afraid' will select complement clauses headed by *żeby* as a negative complementizer. In the following, I present the implementation of these ideas in the framework of HPSG.

5. Formalization in HPSG

The proposal described above is, in what follows, formalized within the paradigm of HSPG in the tradition of Pollard and Sag (1994). In HPSG, linguistic expressions (signs) are represented as structured complexes of phonological, morphosyntactic, semantic, discourse, and phrase-structural information. The typical notation for these representations is the AVM (Atrribute-Value-Matrix) notation. Fig. 3 shows an example AVM of a phrasal sign, which demonstrates that all objects of the type *phrase* have the attribute PHONOLOGY, providing a representation of the phonology of a given sign, and the attribute SYN(TAX-) SEM(ANTICS), whose value has two attributes: NONLOCAL, which allows for describing unbounded dependency phenomena, and LOCAL. The value of the attribute LOCAL provides three further attributes: CONTENT and CONTEXT, providing semantic and contextual information, respectively, and the attribute CATEGORY, which has two further features: HEAD and VALENCE. The value of the HEAD attribute of a sig is its part of speech. The value of the attribute VALENCE specifies the syntactic valency of a sign. Finally, the value of the attribute DAUGHTERS describes the constituent structure of a phase.

$$\left[\begin{array}{l} \textit{phrase} \\ \text{PHONOLOGY } \textit{list(phonstring)} \\ \text{SYNSEM} \left[\begin{array}{l} \textit{synsem} \\ \text{LOCAL} \left[\begin{array}{l} \textit{local} \\ \text{CATEGORY} \left[\begin{array}{l} \textit{category} \\ \text{HEAD } \textit{head} \\ \text{VALENCE} \left[\begin{array}{l} \textit{valence} \\ \text{SUBJECT } \textit{list(synsem)} \\ \text{COMPLEMENTS } \textit{list(synsem)} \end{array}\right] \end{array}\right] \\ \text{CONTENT } \textit{content} \\ \text{CONTEXT } \textit{context} \end{array}\right] \\ \text{NONLOCAL } \textit{nonlocal} \end{array}\right] \\ \text{DAUGHTERS } \textit{constituent-structure} \end{array}\right]$$

Fig. 3: An exemplary AVM-description of a phrasal sign

I further adopt the syntactic HPSG-approach to Negative Concord (NC) in Polish put forward by Przepiórkowski and Kupść (1997). This approach is presented in Section 5.1. Section 5.2. provides the description of the relevant *żeby*-structures using the tools introduced in Section 5.1.

5.1. Negative Concord in Polish

In Polish, sentential negation is expressed by the negative element *nie*. This negation marker must precede the verb whenever any dependent of the verb (be it a subject, a direct or indirect object, or an adjunct) is a negative phrase or contains an *n*-word. This phenomenon is known as negative doubling. Moreover, Polish also exhibits negative spread, illustrated in (22) following Przepiórkowski and Kupść (1997: 3). Example (22) shows that the presence of multiple negative expressions within a clause results in a single negation meaning.

(22)	**Nikt**	**nigdy**	**nikogo**	**niczym**	*(**nie**)	uszczęśliwił.
	Nobody$_{\text{NOM}}$	never	nobody$_{\text{GEN}}$	nothing$_{\text{INS}}$	not	made happy

'Nobody has ever made anybody happy with anything.'

As further pointed out in Przepiórkowski and Kupść (1997), subordinate clauses are in general boundaries for NC in Polish. This can be illustrated by (23).

(23)	a.	Marek	(***nikomu**)	mówił,	że	**nikogo**	*(nie)	spotkał.
		Marek	nobody	said	ŻE	nobody	NEG	met

'Marek said that he didn't met anybody.'

b.	Marek	**nikomu**	nie	mówił,	że	***nikogo** /	kogoś	spotkał.
	Marek	nobody	NEG	said	ŻE	nobody	somebody	met

'Marek didn't said anybody that he met somebody.' [intended]

However, Polish NC can take place across arbitrarily many NP and PP projections / boundaries. Przepiórkowski and Kupść (1997) propose that Polish NC is a kind of Unbounded Dependency Construction (UDC). Their proposal builds on the lexical approach to UDCs put forward by Sag (1997). According to Sag (1997), words inherit SLASH values of their arguments by amalgamating them. This lexical UDC approach is applied in Przepiórkowski and Kupść (1997) to Unbounded NC in Polish. In particular, the negation requirement is assumed to be introduced lexically by *n*-words. The negation requirement is further cancelled lexically by negated verbs (cf. (23)). Lexical exceptions (in particular, the preposition *bez* 'without') can easily be modeled in this approach.

Przepiórkowski and Kupść (1997) thus introduce a new non-local attribute responsible for NC, NEGATIVE-CONCONRD, taking a boolean value (Fig. 4).

$$\begin{bmatrix} \textit{nonlocal} & \\ \text{NEG-CONC} & \text{boolean} \\ \ldots & \end{bmatrix}$$

Fig. 4: The non-local attribute NEGATIVE-CONCORD according to Przepiórkowski and Kupść (1997)

$$\begin{bmatrix} \textit{word} & \\ \text{PHON} & \langle \text{nikt} \rangle \\ \text{SYNSEM} & \begin{bmatrix} \text{LOC} \mid \text{CAT} \mid \text{HEAD} & \begin{bmatrix} \textit{noun} \\ \text{CASE nom} \end{bmatrix} \\ \text{NONLOC} \mid \text{NEG-CONC} & + \end{bmatrix} \end{bmatrix}$$

Fig. 5: The lexicon entry of the Polish *n*-word *nikt* 'nobody' according to Przepiórkowski and Kupść (1997)

The negation requirement is always provided by elements that require a negative context (typically *n*-words). This means that the NEGATIVE-CONCORD value of such elements is specified in the lexicon as positive (+) (Fig. 5).

Furthermore, the lexical items that allow percolation of negation (nouns,

$$\begin{bmatrix} \textit{word} \\ \text{SS} \mid \text{L} \mid \text{C} \begin{bmatrix} \text{HEAD noun} \lor \begin{bmatrix} \textit{verb} \\ \text{NEG} \ - \end{bmatrix} \lor \begin{bmatrix} \textit{prep} \\ \text{PFORM} \ \neg\text{bez} \end{bmatrix} \\ \text{ARG-S} \ \boxed{1} \ \text{list(argument)} \end{bmatrix} \end{bmatrix} \rightarrow \begin{bmatrix} \text{SYNSEM} \mid \text{NONLOC} \mid \text{NEG-CONC} \ \boxed{2} \end{bmatrix} \land \text{sum\_neg}(\boxed{1}, \boxed{2})$$

Fig. 6: Lexical Amalgamation of NEGATIVE-CONCORD according to Przepiórkowski and Kupść (1997)

affirmative verbs, prepositions except for *bez* 'without') specify the value of their NEGATIVE-CONCORD feature as positive (+) if at least one of their arguments is NEGATIVE-CONCORD + and as negative (–) otherwise (Fig. 6).[12]

Negation Inheritance Constraint (NIC):

$$\begin{bmatrix} \textit{phrase} \\ \text{DTRS headed-struc} \end{bmatrix} \rightarrow \begin{bmatrix} \text{SYNSEM} \mid \text{NONLOCAL} \mid \text{NEG-CONC} \ \boxed{1} \\ \text{DTRS} \mid \text{HEAD-DTR} \mid \text{SYNSEM} \mid \text{NONLOCAL} \mid \text{NEG-CONC} \ \boxed{1} \end{bmatrix}$$

Fig. 7: The NEGATION INHERINTANCE CONSTRAINT (NIC) according to Przepiórkowski and Kupść (1997)

The NEGATION INHERITANCE CONSTRAINT (NIC) ensures percolation of the NEGATIVE-CONCORD value along the head projection from a lexical item to its maximal projection (Fig. 7).

Lexical items which cancel negation percolation bear a negative NEGATIVE-CONCORD value. In Polish, those items include verbs (negated or not)[13] as

$$\begin{bmatrix} \textit{word} \\ \text{SYNSEM}|\text{LOC}|\text{CAT}|\text{HEAD verb} \end{bmatrix} \rightarrow \begin{bmatrix} \text{SYNSEM}|\text{NONLOC}|\text{NEG-CONC} \; - \end{bmatrix}$$

$$\begin{bmatrix} \textit{word} & \\ \text{SYNSEM} & \begin{bmatrix} \text{LOC}|\text{CAT}|\text{HEAD} & \begin{bmatrix} \textit{prep} \\ \text{PFORM bez} \end{bmatrix} \\ \text{NONLOC}|\text{NEG-CONC} & - \end{bmatrix} \end{bmatrix}$$

Fig. 8: Lexical items cancelling negation percolation according to Przepiórkowski and Kupść (1997)

well as the preposition *bez* 'without' (Fig. 8). If a negation percolation takes place, the total result blocks negation because of contradiction (the value of the NEGATIVE-CONCORD feature is set up as + and at the same as –).

These description tools can be used to account for the phenomena discussed in Section 3 along the proposal sketched above.

5.2. The HPSG Account of *żeby*-Structures under Negation

I propose that the Polish complementizer *żeby* bears the non-local attribute NEGATIVE-CONCORD taking boolean values and that the value of this attribute is underspecified in the lexicon. I further adopt aspects of the HPSG-analyses of *żeby* put forward by Borsley (1999) and by Kupść and Tseng (2005).[14] In particular, I treat *żeby* as a subjunctive complementizer with the following properties: (i) its morphological base is the subjunctive (not conditional) – *by*, which in turn can be optionally prefixed by *a-*, *aże-*, *co-*, *iż* and *że-*, (ii) it is a

$$\begin{bmatrix} \text{PHONOLOGY } (\textit{a} \vee \textit{aże} \vee \textit{co} \vee \textit{iż} \vee \textit{że}) + \textit{by} & \\ \text{SYNSEM} & \begin{bmatrix} \text{LOCAL} & \begin{bmatrix} \text{CAT} & \begin{bmatrix} \text{HEAD} & \begin{bmatrix} \textit{complementizer} \\ \text{CFORM } \textit{subjunctive} \end{bmatrix} \\ \text{ARGUMENT-STRUCTURE} & \left\langle \begin{bmatrix} \text{VP } \textit{infinitive} \vee \textit{l-participle} \end{bmatrix} \right\rangle \end{bmatrix} \end{bmatrix} \\ \text{NON-LOCAL} \mid \text{NEGATIVE-CONCORD } \textit{boolean} & \end{bmatrix} \end{bmatrix}$$

Fig. 9: Lexical entry of the complementizer *żeby*

syntactic head,[15] (iii) it selects for non-finite or finite saturated VPs, and (iv) it agrees with the subject of finite VPs with respect to person and number. Fig. 9 provides the relevant part of a lexicon entry of the subjunctive *żeby*.[16]

I further assume that it is a property of individual verbs selecting *żeby*-CPs to determine the value of the feature NEGATIVE-CONCORD. Accordingly, verbs like *sądzić* 'think' and other epistemic verbs select CPs headed by *żeby* with a positive valued NEGATIVE-CONCORD feature. This specification makes *żeby* an *n*-word, so that all principles responsible for negation percolation and negation cancellation (see Section 5.1) apply. It follows automatically that *żeby*-clauses are licensed with this type of verb only if those verbs are negated. Otherwise, the principles are not satisfied and a contradiction emerges (a NEGATIVE-CONCORD value + and – is required at the same time). Nothing more needs to be said in the grammar

$$\begin{bmatrix} \text{PHONOLOGY } \textit{(a} \vee \textit{aże} \vee \textit{co} \vee \textit{iż} \vee \textit{że)} + \textit{by} \\ \text{SYNSEM} \begin{bmatrix} \text{LOCAL} \begin{bmatrix} \text{CAT} \begin{bmatrix} \text{HEAD} \begin{bmatrix} \textit{complementizer} \\ \text{CFORM } \textit{subjunctive} \end{bmatrix} \\ \text{ARGUMENT-STRUCTURE} \left\langle \left[\text{VP } \textit{l-participle} \right] \right\rangle \end{bmatrix} \end{bmatrix} \\ \text{NON-LOCAL} \mid \text{NEGATIVE-CONCORD} + \end{bmatrix} \end{bmatrix}$$

Fig. 10: A description of *żeby* as selected by epistemic predicates

in order to account for structures with *żeby*-clauses and matrix negation. Fig. 10 shows a description of *żeby* as selected by *sądzić* 'think' and other epistemic verbs. Note that the verb form of the argument of *żeby* is restricted to *l*-participles.

Verbs like *obawiać się* 'be afraid' select CPs headed by *żeby* with an underspecified value of the NEGATIVE-CONCORD feature. This specification neither enforces nor forbids the presence of negation in the matrix clause. However, the verbal argument of *żeby* is specified as being negated. This makes *żeby* a negative complementizer. Moreover, the type of embedded negation is specified as *non-eventuality negation*, as opposed to *eventuality negation*. I adopt

$$\begin{bmatrix} \text{PHONOLOGY } \textit{(a} \vee \textit{aże} \vee \textit{co} \vee \textit{iż} \vee \textit{że)} + \textit{by} \\ \text{SYNSEM} \begin{bmatrix} \text{LOCAL} \begin{bmatrix} \text{CAT} \begin{bmatrix} \text{HEAD} \begin{bmatrix} \textit{complementizer} \\ \text{CFORM } \textit{subjunctive} \end{bmatrix} \\ \text{ARGUMENT-STRUCTURE} \left\langle \left[\text{VP: NEG + } \textit{(non-eventuality negation)} \right] \right\rangle \end{bmatrix} \end{bmatrix} \\ \text{NON-LOCAL} \mid \text{NEGATIVE-CONCORD } \textit{boolean} \end{bmatrix} \end{bmatrix}$$

Fig. 11: A description of *żeby* as selected by verbs of fear

this dichotomy from Przepiórkowski and Kupść (1999) to account for expletive / pleonastic negation versus negation with a semantic contribution. The relevant description of *żeby* is given in Fig. 11.

Note that except for the requirement of being negated, the verb form selected by *żeby* is underspecified. Due to this, non-finite clauses as well as *l*-participles can be licensed in this type of structure. Thus, the specifications in Fig. 9 correctly predict the properties of structures with *żeby*-clauses and embedded negation. This also includes the Genitive of Negation, which can occur within *żeby*-clauses.

6. Summary and Outlook

In this paper, I discussed two types of complement clauses in Polish introduced by the complementizer *żeby*: *żeby*-clauses with an obligatory negation in the matrix clause and *żeby*-clauses with an obligatory negation in the embedded clause. I argued that *żeby*-clauses with obligatory negation in the matrix clause can be treated in terms of negative polarity, with *żeby* defined as an *n*-word (in terms of being a superstrong NPI). I further suggested that *żeby*-clauses with an obligatory negation in the embedded clause can be treated in terms of negative complementation with *żeby* specified as a negative complementizer. I also proposed a uniform lexicalist analysis of both phenomena within the framework of HPSG. The proposed analysis employs established tools used to account for NC phenomena in Polish and does not require any further extensions or modifications of the architecture of the grammar.

The primary goal for future work would be to empirically validate the verb classes licensing *żeby*-clauses with matrix negation and embedded negation, respectively. A good starting point would be the exploration of the Polish valence dictionary Walenty and a subsequent validation of the findings using corpus data. The focus of this paper is on the syntactic aspects of the licensing of *żeby*-clauses under negation. In the next step, a closer look at the semantic aspects will be taken, in particular at the correlation between negation, mood, and verbal semantics.

Notes

1 The abbreviation SUBJ refers to subjunctive. Other abbreviations used in this paper include NEG for negation, PRT for participle, REFL for reflexive marker, PRES for present tense, 1, 2 and 3 for respectively first, second and third person, SG for singular, RM for reflexive marker, FUT for future tense, INF for infinitive, ACC for accusative, GEN for genitive.

2 Morphologically, this finite form is an active past participle, the so-called *l*-participle.
3 Note that (7d) sounds somewhat marked for prosodic reasons but grammatically, it is well-formed.
4 Bondaruk (2004) provides the following examples to show that in some cases, sentences with non-separated and separated *że+by*-combination are semantically equivalent.

(i)	a.	Nie	sądzę,	żebyś	to	zrobił.	
		not	I-think	so-that-2SG	it	do-.PRTC	
		'I don't think you would do it.'					
	b.	Nie	sądzę,	że	zrobiłbyś	to.	
		not	I-think	that	do-PRTC-BY-2SG	it	
		'I don't think you would do it.'					
	c.	Nie	sądzę,	że	to	byś	zrobił.
		not	I-think	that	it	BY-2SG	do-.PRTC
		'I don't think you would do it.'				(Bondaruk 2004, p. 97)	

On the basis of these examples (as opposed to cases in (7) versus (13)), she postulates two instances of *żeby:* an inseparable one, which introduces subjunctive clauses, and a separable one, which introduces conditional clauses. However, while the sentences in (i) can all be translated with *would* and seem to provide the same conditional meaning, a deeper examination of the modal-temporal properties of (ia) on the one hand and of (ib) and (ic) on the other hand shows that there is an important meaning difference between them. In particular, (ia) but not (ib) or (ic) can refer to a situation that presumably has already happened. This observation has been made by Tomaszewicz (2009, 2010); cf. also Migdalski (2006).

5 In Polish, 3. person singular and plural markers have no phonological realization.
6 It is also not clear whether the two types of *że+by* combinations are related historically and whether *żeby* derives from the conditional auxiliary *by*, as suggested in Borsley (1999).
7 The notion of Neg-Raising or, originally, negative transportation goes back to Fillmore (1963) and was adopted in many other approaches, such as Lakoff (1969), Ross (1973), Prince (1976) or, more recently, Collins and Postal (2014, 2017); see also Kiparsky (1970), Jackendoff (1971), Pollack (1976), Klima (1964), Lasnik (1972), Zeijlstra (2018) and others. In addition, a number of semantic-pragmatic approaches to Neg-Raising have been developed, which essentially go back to Bartsch (1973) and include Horn (1978), Horn and Bayer (1984), Tovena (2001), Sailer (2005, 2006), Gajewski (2007), Romoli (2013),

among others. See also Crowley (2019), who argues that both purely syntactic and semantic-pragmatic approaches are needed in order to account for the full range of data. For a discussion on Neg-Raising in Polish in comparison with English, see Modrzejewska (1992).

8 The Polish Valence Dictionary (Walenty, Przepiórkowski et al. 2014a, b), an electronic dictionary of subcategorisation frames for Polish verbs and quasi-verbal predicates, provides 64 such verbs.

9 For recent work on subjunctive in Romance languages, see B-Violette (2019) and the references therein.

10 But see Richter and Sailer (2004a), who point out that some speakers allow for an expletive interpretation of *nikt*. This observation also correlates with my own intuitions. In the National Corpus of Polish (NKJP, Przepiórkowski et al. (2012); http://nkjp.pl), both sentences with *nikt* as well as sentences with *ktoś* can be found (cf. (i) and (ii) found in the full version of NKJP). Clearly, further research on this phenomenon is needed.

(i) a. Rosjanie bali się, żeby ktoś nie wyniósł jakiejś
Russians feared REFL ŻEBY someone NEG take-out some.GEN
konstrukcji, nie wykradł metody.
construction.GEN NEG steal method.GEN
'Russians feared that someone might take out some construction, steal a method.'

b. Pewno obawiano się, żeby ktoś nie zwiał na inną planetę.
probably was-afraid REFL ŻEBY someone NEG scram on another planet
'It was probably afraid that someone might scram to another planet.'

c. Dyrektorzy martwią się, żeby ktoś im tych
directors worry REFL ŻEBY someone they.DAT those.GEN
komputerów [po prostu] nie ukradł.
computers.GEN just NEG steal
'Directors worry that someone might just steal those computers from them.'

(ii) a. Panicznie boję się, żeby nikt obcy jej nie skrzywdził.
panicky fear.1.SG REFL ŻEBY nobody strange her NEG hurt
'I'm panicky about making sure no stranger hurts her.'

b. Przy budowie dachu bano się, żeby nikt nie spadł [...]
during construction roof.GEN was-feared REFL ŻEBY nobody NEG fall
'During the construction of the roof, it was feared that someone might fall.'

c. I modli się, żeby nikt nie zapytał jej o godzinę.
and pray.3.SG REFL ŻEBY nobody NEG ask her about time
'And she prays that no one asks her what time it is.'

11 Zwarts (1998) and van der Wouden (1997) propose to categorize NPIs by the strength of the negation required to license them. The strength of the licensing negation can thereby be defined based on three types of contexts: (i) antimorphic contexts (property of sentential negation), (ii) anti-additive contexts (negative quantifiers like *no student*, the conjunctions *without, before*), and (iii) downward-entailing contexts (the quantifier *few*, the adverbs *seldom, hardly* etc.). These three types of contexts form a hierarchy: Antimorphism is the strongest form of negativity and downward entailment the weakest one. Antimorphic contexts constitute a proper subset of anti-additive contexts, which in turn are a proper subset of downward entailing contexts. Based on these types of contexts, three types of NPIs can be distinguished: superstrong, strong, and weak. The three categories of NPIs are defined in van der Wouden (1997) in the following way: NPIs are superstrong if they are licensed only by antimorphic contexts (overt sentential negation). NPIs are strong if they are licensed by antimorphic and anti-additive contexts. NPIs are weak if they are licensed by antimorphic, anti-additive and downward-entailing contexts. Since Polish *żeby*-clauses are licensed in the relevant structures only by an overt sentential negation, I conclude that they should be captured in terms of superstrong NPIs. In this respect, Polish *żeby*-subjunctives differ from polarity subjunctives in the Romance languages, which can be also licensed by other contexts, such as interrogatives and conditionals.

12 The relation sum_neg/2 ensures that the NEGATIVE-CONCORD value of a word is positive if at least one of the arguments is NEGATIVE-CONCORD +.

13 Assuming a negative NEGATIVE-CONCORD value for all verbs, including negated and non-negated verbs, is necessary to handle islands for NC created by non-negated verbs in Polish.

14 For configurational approaches to *żeby,* see Borsley and Rivero (1994), Bański (2000), Bondaruk (2004), Migdalski (2006), Tomaszewicz (2009) and other work cited therein.

15 In the classical HPSG approach, complementizers are markers (i.e., non-heads).

16 For the sake of simplicity, issues related to agreement and inflectional marking, which are orthogonal to the topic of this paper, are ignored here. For details and possible solutions within the HPGS framework, see Kupść and Tseng (2005).

Bibliography

Bański, Piotr. 2000. *Morphological and Prosodic Analysis of Auxiliary Clitics in Polish and English*, Institute of English Studies. Warsaw University, Ph.D. dissertation.

Bartsch, Renate. 1973. "Negative transportation" gibt es nicht. *Linguistische Berichte*, 27(7).1–7.

Błaszczak, Joanna. 2001. Investigation into the Interaction between the Indefinites and Negation. Berlin: Akademie-Verlag.

Bondaruk, Anna. 2004. *PRO and control in English, Irish and Polish. A minimalist analysis*. Lublin: Wydawnictwo KUL.

Borsley, Robert d. 1999. Weak auxiliaries, complex verbs and inflected complementizers in Polish. *Slavic in Head-driven Phrase Structure Grammar*, ed. by Robert D. Borsley and Adam Przepiórkowski, 29–59. Stanford, California: CSLI Publications.

Borsley, Robert D., and María Luisa Rivero. 1994. Clitic auxiliaries and incorporation in Polish. *Natural Language & Linguistic Theory* 12.373–422.

Brown, Sue. 1996. *The Syntax of Negation in Russian*. Indiana University, Ph.D. dissertation.

Brown, Sue; and Steven Franks. 1995. Asymmetries in the Scope of Russian Negation. *Journal of Slavic Linguistics* 3(2).239–87.

B-Violette, Laurence. 2019. *The Development of the Polarity Subjunctive in Romance Languages*. Harvard University, Graduate School of Arts & Sciences, Doctoral dissertation.

Collins, Chris; and Paul M. Postal. 2014. *Classical NEG Raising: An essay on the syntax of negation*. Cambridge, MA: MIT Press.

Collins, Chris; and Paul M. postal. 2017. Interclausal NEG raising and the scope of negation. *Glossa: A Journal of General Linguistics* 2(1):29.1–29.

Crowley, Paul. 2019. Neg-Raising and Neg movement. *Natural Language Semantics* 27.1–17.

Espinal, Teresa M. 1992. Expletive negation and logical absorption. *The Linguistic Review* 9(4). 333–58.

Farkas, Donka F. 1985. *Intensional descriptions and the romance subjunctive mood*. New York / London: Garland.

Farkas, Donka F. 1992. On the semantics of subjunctive complements. *Romance Languages and Modern Linguistic Theory*, ed. by Paul Hirschbühler and Konrad Koerner, 69–104. Amsterdam / Philadelphia: John Benjamins.

Fillmore, Charles. 1963. The position of embedding transformations in grammar. *Word* 19.208–31.

GAJEWSKI, JON. 2007. Neg-raising and polarity. *Linguistics and Philosophy* 30.298–328.

GIANNAKIDOU, ANASTASIA. 2009. The dependency of the subjunctive revisited: Temporal semantics and polarity. *Lingua* 119.1883–1908.

GIANNAKIDOU, ANASTASIA. 2011. Nonveridicality and mood choice: Subjunctive, polarity, and time. *Tense across languages*, ed. by Renate Musan und Monika Rathert, 59–90. Berlin: De Gruyter.

HORN, LAURENCE R. 1978. Remarks on neg-raising. *Pragmatics*, ed. by Peter Cole, 129–220. New York, NY: Academic Press.

HORN, LAURENCE R., and SAMUEL BAYER. 1984. Short-circuited implicature: A negative contribution. *Language and Philosophy* 7.397–414.

JACKENDOFF, RAY S. 1971. On some questionable arguments about quantifiers and negation. *Language* 47(2).282–97.KIPARSKY, PAUL. 1970. Semantic rules in grammar. *The Nordic Languages and Modern Linguistics*, ed. by Hreinn Benediktsson, 262–85. Reykjavik: Visindafelag Islendinga.

KLIMA, EDWARD S. 1964. Negation in English. *The structure of language*, ed. by Jerry A. Fodor and Jerrold J. Katz, 246–324. Englewood Cliffs, NJ: Prentice Hall.

KOSTA, PETER. 1999a. Zur Syntax und Semantik von negativen und positiven "Polaritätsanzeigern". *Slavistische Linguistik 1998: Referate des XXIV. Konstanzer Slavistischen Arbeitstreffens, Wien 15.–18.9.1998*, ed. by Renate Rathmayr and Wolfgang Weitlanger, 117–36. München: Sagner.

KOSTA, PETER. 1999b. Quantoren und Satznegation im Slavischen aus typologisch-vergleichender Sicht. *Festschrift für Klaus Trost zum 65. Geburtstag*, ed. by Ernst Hansack, Walter Koschmal, Norbert Nübler, and Radoslav Večerka, 171–87. München: Sagner. Series: Die Welt der Slaven 5.

KUPŚĆ ANNA, and JESSE TSENG. 2005. A New HPSG Approach to Polish Auxiliary Constructions. *Proceedings of the 12th international conference on head-driven phrase structure grammar*, ed. by Stefan Müller, 253–73. Stanford, CA: CSLI Publications.

LAKA, ITZIAR. 1990. *Negation in syntax. On the nature of functional categories and projections.* Cambridge, MA: Massachusetts Institute of Technology, Department of Linguistics and Philosophy, Ph.D. dissertation.

LAKA, ITZIAR. 1992. Negative complementizers: Evidence from English, Basque and Spanish. *Syntactic theory and Basque syntax,* ed. by Joseph A. Lakarra and Jon Ortiz de Urbina, 175–211. Supplements of ASJU 27.

LAKOFF, ROBIN. 1969. A syntactic argument for negative transportation. *Chicago Linguistic Society* 5. 149–57.

LASNIK HOWARD. 1972. *Analyses of negation in English.* Cambridge, MA: Massachusetts Institute of Technology, Department of Linguistics and Philosophy, Ph.D. dissertation.

MANIZNI, RITA. 1994. The Subjunctive. *Paris-8 Working Papers in Linguistics*, ed. by Léa Nash and Georges Tsoulas. Paris: Université Paris 8, Département des Sciences du Langage.

MIGDALSKI, KRZYSTOF. 2006. *The syntax of compound tenses in Slavic.* Utrecht: LOT.

MODRZEJEWSKA, EWA. 1992. *Neg-raising predicates in English and Polish. PSiCL* 13.41–52.

MOSCATI, VINCENZO. 2010. *Negation raising. Logical form and linguistic variation.* Cambridge: Cambridge Scholars Publishing.

POLLACK, JAY M. 1976. A re-analysis of neg-raising in English. *Working Papers in Linguistics* 21:189–239.

POLLARD, CARL J., and IVAN A. SAG. 1994. *Head-driven phrase structure grammar.* Chicago: The University of Chicago Press.

PRINCE, ELLEN. 1976. The syntax and semantics of neg-raising, with evidence from French. *Language* 52.404–26.

PRZEPIÓRKOWSKI, ADAM, and ANNA KUPŚĆ. 1997. Unbound negative concord in Polish. A lexicalist HPSG approach. *Computational linguistics in the Netherlands 1996. Papers form the Seventh CLIN meeting*, ed. by Jan Landsbergen, Jan Odjik, Kees van Deemter and Gert Veldhuijzen van Zanten. 129–43.

PRZEPIÓRKOWSKI, ADAM, and ANNA KUPŚĆ. 1999. Eventuality negation and negative concord in Polish and Italian. *Slavic in Head-Driven Phrase Structure Grammar*, ed. by Robert D. Borsley and Adam Przepiórkowski, 211–46. Standford, CA: CSLI Publications.

PRZEPIÓRKOWSKI, ADAM; ELŻBIETA HAJNICZ; AGNIESZKA PATEJUK; MARCIN WOLIŃSKI; FILIP SKWARSKI; and MAREK ŚWIDZIŃSKI. 2014a. Walenty. Towards a comprehensive valence dictionary of Polish. *Proceedings of the ninth international conference on language resources and evaluation, LREC 2014*, ed. by Nicoletta Calzolari, Khalid Choukri, Thierry Declerck, Hrafn Loftsson, Bente Maegaard, Joseph Mariani, Asuncion Moreno, Jan Odijk, and Stelios Piperidis, 2785–92. Reykjavík: European Language Resources Association (ELRA).

PRZEPIÓRKOWSKI, ADAM; FILIP SKWARSKI; ELŻBIETA HAJNICZ; AGNIESZKA PATEJUK; MARCIN WOLIŃSKI; and MAREK ŚWIDZIŃSKI. 2014b. Walenty. Modelowanie własności składniowych czasowniów w nowym słowniku walencyjnym języka polskiego. *Polonica XXXIII*.159–178.

Przepiórkowski, Adam; Mirosław Bańko; Rafał L. Górski; and Barbara Lewandowska-Tomaszczyk. 2012. *Narodowy Korpus Języka Polskiego.* Warszawa: Wydawnictwo Naukowe PWN.

Quer, Josep.1998. *Mood at the interface.* Utrecht: University of Utrecht, Ph.D. dissertation.

Richter, Frank, and Manfred Sailer. 1999. LF Conditions on Expressions of Ty2: An HPSG Analysis of Negative Concord in Polish. *Slavic in HPSG*, ed. by Robert D. Borsley and Adam Przepiórkowski, 247–82. Stanford, CA: CSLI Publications.

Richter, Frank, and Manfred Sailer. 2004a. Basic Concepts of Lexical Resource Semantics. *ESSLLI 2003 – Course material I*, ed. by Arnold Beckmann and Norbert Preining, 87–143. Wien: Collegium Logicum, Volume 5, Kurt Gödel Society.

Richter, Frank, and Manfred Sailer. 2004b. Polish Negation and Lexical Resource Semantics. *Electronic notes in theoretical computer science*, ed. by Lawrence S. Moss and Richard T. Oehrle, 309–21, Volume 53. Oxford: Elsevier.

Romoli, Jacopo. 2013. A scalar implicature-based approach to neg-raising. *Linguistics and Philosophy* 36.291–353.

Ross, John r. 1973. Slifting. *The formal analysis of natural languages*, ed. by Maurice Gross, Morris Halle and Marcel-Paul Schützenberger, 133–69. The Hague: Mouton.

Sag, Ivan A. 1997. English relative clause constructions. Journal of linguistics, 33(2). 431–483.

Sailer, Manfred. 2005. *NEG-raising in an underspecified semantics framework.* Paper presented at Colloque de Syntaxe et Sémantique, Paris.

Sailer, Manfred. 2006. Don't believe in underspecified semantics: Neg-raising in lexical resource semantics. *Empirical Issues in Syntax and Semantics 6*, ed. by Oliver Bonami and Patricia Cabredo Hofherr, 375–403. ISSN 1769–7158. http://www.cssp.cnrs.fr/eiss6/index_en.html

Siegel, Laura. 2009. Mood selection in Romance and Balkan. *Lingua* 119.1859–82.

Stowell, Tim. 1993. *Syntax of tense.* Los Angeles, CA: UCLA.

Tomaszewicz, Barbara M. 2009. Subjunctive Mood in Polish. *Linguistik International 21. Studies in Formal Slavic Phonology, Morphology, Syntax, Semantics and Information Structure, Proceedings of FDSL 7, Leipzig 2007,* ed. by Gerhild Zybatow, Uwe Junghanns, Denisa Lenertova, and Petr Biskup, 221–34. Frankfurt am Main: Peter Lang.

Tomaszewicz, Barbara M. 2010. Subjunctive Mood in Polish and the Clause Typing Hypothesis. *Formal studies in slavic linguistics*, ed. by Anastasia

Smirnova, Vedrana Mihaliček, and Lauren Ressue, 121–42. Newcastle upon Tyne: Cambridge Scholars Publishing.

Tovena, Lucia M. 1996. Negative concord, events and negative chains. *Proceedings of the 13th Eastern States conference on linguistics*, ed. by Anthony D. Green, and Virginia Motapanyane, 313–22. Ithaca: Cascadilla Press.

Tovena, Lucia M. 1998. *The fine structure of polarity sensitivity*. New York: Garland Publishing.

Tovena, Lucia M. 2001. Neg-raising: Negation as failure. *Perspectives on negation and polarity items*, ed. by Jack Hoeksema, Hotze Rullmann, Victor Sanchez-Valencia and Ton van der Wouden, 331–56. Amsterdam: John Benjamins.

van der Wouden, Ton. 1997. N*egative contexts. Collocations, polarity and multiple negations*. London/New York: Routledge.

Witkoś, Jacek. 2008. CP-infinitives in Polish and two theories of control: A reply to the analysis by Anna Bondaruk. *Research in Language* 6.217–59.

Zeijlstra, Hedde. 2018. Does neg-raising involve negraising? *Topoi* 37(3).417–33.

Zwarts, Frans. 1998. Three types of polarity. *Plurality and quantification*, ed. by Fritz Hamm and Erhard W. Hinrichs, 177–238. Dordrecht: Springer.

Mladen Uhlik and Andreja Žele

Reflexive Possessive Pronouns in Slovene: A Contrastive Analysis with Russian[1]

Abstract This article is concerned with the use of the Slovene reflexive possessive pronoun *svoj*. The properties are contrasted with those of its Russian counterpart, the anaphoric pronoun *svoj*. Various syntactic environments as well as the question of coreference between the pronoun and the antecedent are considered. Laying bare the rules governing the use of reflexive possessive pronouns in both languages sheds light on the connection between the syntactic contexts they function in and the various meanings they express.*

Keywords: Reflexive Pronoun, Possession, Coreference, Slovene, Russian

1. Introduction

In the present discussion of the Slovene[2] reflexive possessive pronoun *svoj* and its Russian counterpart *svoj*,[3] we consider the syntactic, semantic and to some extent pragmatic aspects of its usage. Both pronouns, the Slovene *svoj* and the Russian *svoj*, are typically used as anaphors and so in most cases require an antecedent. The antecedent is an argument in the same clause which binds *svoj* and semantically enters into a possession relationship with the NP hosting *svoj* (1). For a regular possessive pronouns in the vast majority of cases the nominative antecedent must be outside of the same clause (2).[4]

(1) Slvn.

Martin$_i$	je	našel	svojo$_i$	uro.
Martin-NOM	AUX.PRS.3SG	found-SG.M	one's own	watch-F.ACC.SG

'Martin$_i$ found his$_i$ watch.'

* The authors would like to thank Oliver Currie, David Erschler and Mikhail V. Oslon for their comments and suggestions that helped us to improve the article. All faults and shortcomings in the analysis are ours.

(2) Slvn.

Martin$_i$	je	našel	njegovo$_{j/*i}$	uro.
Martin-NOM	AUX.PRS.3SG	found-SG.M	his	watch-F.ACC.SG

'Martin$_i$ found his$_{j/*i}$ watch.'

We analyze the various functions of *svoj* in Slovene and Russian and show how they are connected in both languages with syntactic contexts in which the pronoun is used.

The first part of the paper focuses on the relationship between a reflexive possessive pronoun and its antecedent within a simple sentence. In the second part, we analyze the various meanings in which *svoj* can be used in Russian and Slovene. In the third part, we discuss how *svoj* is used in infinitival complements. The fourth and final part focused on the cases in Slovene where the non-reflexive possessive pronoun is preferred to the reflexive possessive *svoj* due to contextual and pragmatic factors. To compare the properties of the Slovene and Russian reflexive possessive pronouns, we provide translations of the Slovene examples into Russian.

2. The Use and Reference of *svoj* in a Simple Sentence

The prototypical meaning of the reflexive possessive pronoun *svoj* in Slovene is the possessive form of the reflexive personal pronoun *sebe* as well as its supplementary genitive form.

Whereas in (3) the reflexive personal pronoun *sebe* is used to establish coreference between the subject and the pronominal object, in (4) the reflexive possessive pronoun functions as the modifier in an NP and is coreferential to the antecedent NP that denotes the possessor.

Thus, in (3) the reflexive possessive *svoj* is coreferential with the NP which functions as the subject within the same clause.

(3) Slvn.

a.

Martin$_i$	je	v	ogledalu	zagledal	**sebe**$_i$.
Martin-NOM	AUX.PRS.3SG	in	mirror	saw-SG.M	himself

Ru. Martin v zerkale uvidel sebja.

'Martin saw himself in the mirror.'

b.	Martin$_i$	**se**$_i$	je	v	ogledalu	**zagledal**.
	Martin-NOM	REFL	AUX. PRS.3SG	in	mirror	saw-SG.M

Ru. Martin v zerkale uvidel sebja.

'Martin saw himself in the mirror.'

In Slovene, but not in Russian, the coreference between the subject and the object in (3b) may be also expressed with a reflexive verb *zagledati se* 'to see oneself'.[5]

(4) Slvn.

Martin$_i$	je	v	ogledalu
Martin-NOM	AUX.PRS.3SG	in	mirror
zagledal	**svoj**$_i$	odsev.	
saw-SG.M	one's own	reflection-M.ACC.SG	

Ru. Martin v zerkale uvidel svoe otraženie.

'Martin saw his own reflection in a mirror.'

Henceforth, we shall specify for each example the syntactic context in which the relationship between the anaphoric pronoun and its antecedent is realized.

Every NP containing *svoj* expresses a possessor and typically has an antecedent with which it is coreferential. This antecedent, which is usually animate, is typically realized in Slovene by a nominative subject (5). In other words, the most typical cases of true possession are those where a nominative subject c-commands a non-nominative NP within the same clause containing *svoj*:

(5) Slvn.

Martin$_i$	je	izgubil	**svojo**$_i$	uro.
Martin-NOM	AUX.PRS.3SG	lost-SG.M	one's own	watch-F.ACC.SG

Ru. Martin poterjal svoi časy.

'Martin lost his watch.'

In cases with psych-predicates where there is no nominative antecedent, the NP containing *svoj* may be bound by a dative NP (6, 7) or an accusative NP (8), in both cases expressing the experiencer:[6]

(6) Slvn.

Iskreno	**mi**$_i$	je	žal
sincerely	me-DAT	AUX.PRS.3SG	sorry
za	**svoje**$_i$	neodgovorno	ravnanje.
for	one's own	irresponsible	behaviour-N.ACC.SG

Ru. Ja iskrenne prošu proščenija za svoë bezotvetstvennoe povedenie.

'I am really sorry for my irresponsible behaviour.'

(7) Slvn.

Žal	**mu**$_i$	je	**svojega**$_i$	prijatelja.
sorry	him-DAT	AUX.PRS.3SG	one's own	friend-M.GEN.SG

Ru. Emu žal' svoego druga.

'He feels sorry for his friend.'

(8) Slvn.

Sram	**me**$_i$	je	pred	**svojimi**$_i$	starši.
Shame	me-ACC	AUX.PRS.3SG	in front of	one's own	parents-M.INS.PL

Ru. Mne stydno pered svoimi roditeljami.

'I feel embarrassed to face my parents.'

In examples (6–8) where the non-nominative argument functioning as its antecedent binds the reflexive possessive pronoun, non-reflexive possessive pronouns may be used in place of *svoj*: *Iskreno mi je žal za moje neodgovorno ravnanje* 'I am terribly sorry for my irresponsible actions.' *Sram me je pred mojimi starši.* 'I feel embarrassed to face my parents.'

Indeed, an experiencer in the dative or the accusative case may bind a hierarchically lower NP containing a reflexive possessive pronoun, if there is no nominative agent present: *mi* (DAT) VS *za svoje neodgovorno ravnanje* (ACC), *mi* (DAT) VS *svojega prijatelja* (GEN), *me* (ACC) VS *pred svojimi starši* (INS). However, it is important to note that a non-nominative experiencer cannot bind a nominative NP containing *svoj*. For this reason, examples such as (10) do not work in Slovene:

(9) Slvn.

Skrbi	**ga**$_i$	za	**svojo**$_i$	službo.
be worried-3.SG	him-ACC	for	one's own	job-F.ACC.SG

Ru. On bespokoitsja za svoju rabotu.

'He is worried about his job.'

(10)

*Skrbi	ga	*svoja	služba.
worry-3SG	him-ACC	one's own	job-F.NOM.SG

Ru.??Ego bespokoit svoja rabota.

This rule which renders ungrammatical the use of nominative NPs containing reflexive possessive pronouns, also blocks the use of nominative *svoj* as a stimulus in predicative constructions (see (11)):

(11)

*Martinu	so	všeč	svoje	razvade.
Martin-DAT	are.3PL	like	one's own	bad habits-F.NOM.PL

Ru. *Martinu nravjatsja svoi durnye privyčki.

'Martin likes his bad habits.'

However, examples such as (12) show that a dative experiencer may bind the reflexive possessive pronoun in a nominative-dative predicative construction (*všeč mi je* + NOM 'like + NOM') if and only if the pronoun modifies the possessor of the NP (*svojih prijateljev* 'of his friends') rather than directly the NP itself (*razvade*$_{\text{NOM}}$ 'bad habits').

(12) Slvn.

Martinu$_i$	so	všeč	razvade	svojih$_i$	prijateljev.
Martin-DAT	are.3PL	like	bad habits-F.NOM.PL	one's own	friends-M.GEN.PL

Ru.??Martinu nravjatsja durnye privyčki svoix druzej.

'Martin likes the bad habits of his friends.'

We show below that Russian tolerates more readily the cases of nominative *svoj* where it is used in a sense which is less directly connected to its prototypical meaning of possession, as in (13):

(13) Ru.

Mne$_i$	tol'ko	**svoi**$_i$	pirogi	nravjatsja.
me-DAT	only	one's own	cake-M.NOM.PL	like-3PL

Slvn. Všeč so mi samo domači pirogi.

'I only like homemade cakes.'

Apart from cases in which the antecedent is in the dative or the accusative, we note that in Slovene, genitive antecedents may bind an NP containing *svoj* as well. Yet this use is marginal compared to the others and is mostly restricted to a specific type of antecedents, namely negated genitival forms of the subject in locative clauses containing the fixed expression *X ni na svojem mestu* 'X is not in its usual position' (see Chapter 2.6 for this type of use of *svoj*).

(14) Slvn.

Vratarja	**Damjana**	**Goloba**	ni
goalkeeper-M.GEN.SG	Damjan-M.GEN.SG	Golob-M.GEN.SG	NEG.3SG
bilo	na	**svojem**	mestu (Gigafida 2.0).
was-SG.N	on	one's own.	place-N.LOC.SG

Ru. Vratarja Damiana Goloba ne bylo na ~~svoëm~~ meste.[7]

'The goalkeeper Damjan Golob was found out of position.'

(15) Slvn.

Mežnar	je	ponovno	opazil,	da
sexton-M.NOM.SG	AUX.PRS.3SG	again	noticed-SG.M	that
kipa	ni	na	**svojem**	mestu.
statue-M.GEN.SG	is.NEG.3SG	on	one's own	place-N.LOC.SG

Ru. Cerkovnyj storož snova zametil, čto statui net na ~~svoëm~~ meste.

'The sexton noticed again that the statue is not in its usual position.'

The exceptions in which *svoj* is bound by the object will be analyzed in depth in 2.4 where we discuss the distributive meaning of *svoj*.

3. The Semantic Diversity of *svoj*

The various syntactic environments allow for various meanings[8] of the reflexive possessive pronoun *svoj*. We will show that in some uses the pronoun *svoj* does not even require an antecedent and may conceivably constitute a separate lexeme.

3.1. True Possession

The NP containing *svoj* functions as the antecedent's possessed. The object participant is typically an item of personal property.

(16) Slvn.

Martin$_i$	je	prodal	svoj$_i$	klobuk.
Martin-NOM	AUX.PRS.3SG	sold-SG.M	one's own	hat-M.ACC.SG

Ru. Martin$_i$ prodal svoju$_i$ šljapu.

'Martin sold his hat.'

3.2. Relational possession.

The NP containing *svoj* typically includes nouns of relationship (such as *sister*, *brother*, *neighbour*, *classmate* or *friend*).

(17) Slvn.

Martin$_i$	je	jezen	na	(svojo)	sestro.
Martin-NOM	is.3SG	angry	on	one's own	sister-F.ACC.SG

Ru. Martin zlitsja na (svoju) sestru.

'Martin is angry with his sister.'

(18) Slvn.

Martin$_i$	je	pripeljal	tudi	(svojega)	prijatelja.
Martin-NOM	AUX.PRS.3SG	drove-SG.M	too	one's own	friend-M.ACC.SG

Ru. Martin privël takže svoego druga.

'Martin brought his friend along.'

Using a relational noun usually implies a possessor. Thus, *sestra* 'sister' is necessarily a sister of someone else. The absence of *svoj* with relational nouns contextually implies that the possessor is one participants in the situation. The use of the reflexive possessive pronoun is not obligatory in sentences such as (17) and (18): *Martin je jezen na sestro* 'Martin is angry with his sister.' *Pripeljal je tudi prijatelja*. 'He brought along a friend.'

3.3. Possession where *svoj* Carries the Meaning of 'one's Own, that of Home, Non-alien, Belonging to X as Exclusively their Property'

Such use is closely connected to the type of use described in 2.1 and differs from it only in the fact that it emphasises the contrast between one's own and somebody else's possession (see Timberlake 2004: 244, Testelec 2015). Example (19) contains *svoj* in its nominalised use.

(19) Slvn.

pro	Tujega	nočemo,	
	anyone else's	want-NEG.1PL	
pro$_i$	svojega$_i$	ne	damo.
	one's own	NEG	give-1PL

Ru. Čužogo ne nado, svoë ne otdadim.

'We don't want anyone else's, and we're not giving up our own.'

There is a formal difference between Russian and Slovene regarding this type of use: in some constructions Russian tolerates NPs containing *svoj* in the nominative, which is ungrammatical in Slovene.

Expressions with *svoj* in the nominative are typical in Russian for denoting the possessed with the construction *U A est' B*$_{NOM}$ (*U menja est' svoja kvartira* 'I have my own apartment'). In Slovene, the corresponding structure is *imeti* + NP$_{ACC}$ where the possessed is expressed with an accusative NP (*Imam svoje stanovanje* 'I have my own apartment.')

(20) Ru.

Ty	vzjal	mašinu	naprokat.	
you-NOM	took-SG.M	car-F.ACC.SG	for rent	
Net,	u	menja$_i$	svoja$_i$	mašina.
No	at	me-GEN	one's own	car-F.NOM.SG

Slvn. (A) Si najel avto? – Ne, imam svoj avto$_{ACC}$.

'Did you rent a car? – No, I have my own car.'

Svoj may also be used generally in Russian in the nominative within subject complements. In cases such as (21) the possessor is left unexpressed, yet it is clear and deictically unambiguous that it must be the speaker whenever the syntactic environment is a subject complement construction. In Slovene, this type of nominative *svoj* cannot be used in subject complements, which is why this type of possession is typically expressed with the adjective *domač* 'homemade, that which belongs to the home'.

(21) Ru.

Xleb	**svoj**.	My	ego	doma	pečëm.
bread-M.NOM.SG	one's own	we-NOM	him-ACC	at home	bake-1PL

Slvn. Kruh je **domač**. Pečemo ga doma.

'The bread is homemade. We bake it at home.'

It is also possible in Russian to use the nominative *svoj* meaning 'one's own' for denoting an unexpressed arbitrary possessor (the unexpressed antecedent). Rappaport (1986: 114) notes that such use with an implied possessor is typically idiomatic, that is, restricted to a limited configurational context (see example (22)). As this use is typically found primarily in proverbs, the possessive object is considered to be non-referential and is comparable to a distributive meaning (*svoja rubaška* ≅ 'every shirt').

(22) Ru.

Svoja	rubaška	bliže	k	telu.
one's own	shirt-F.NOM.SG	closer	to	body-N.DAT.SG

Slvn. Še Bog je najprej sebi brado ustvaril.

'Self comes first.'

3.4. Distributive Meaning

NPs containing *svoj* with the quantifier *vsak* 'each, every' as antecedent indicating a distributive possession and multiple possessors.

(23) Slvn.

Vsak$_i$	je	dobil	svoj$_i$	delež.
Every-M.NOM.SG	AUX.PRS.3SG	got-SG.M	one's own	part-M.ACC.SG

Ru. Každyj polučil svoju dolju.

'Everybody got their share.'

The NP expressing the possessed has a distributive meaning when its antecedent is the NP containing the quantifier *vsak*.

Curiously, this use licenses nominative use of *svoj* both in Slovene and in Russian. Thus, in examples (24) and (25) the quantifier *vsakemu* (*vsak* in dative) binds the NP with the nominalized pronoun *svoj*:

(24) Slvn.

Vsakemu$_i$	gre	svoje$_i$.
every-M.DAT.SG	go-3SG	one's own

Ru. Každomu svoë.

'To each his own.'

(25) Slvn.

Popolnosti	tako	ali	tako	ni,
Perfection-F.GEN.SG	so	or	so	NEG.3SG
vsakemu$_i$	je	všeč	svoje$_i$.	
every-M.DAT.SG	is.3SG	like	one's own	

Ru. Soveršenstva v ljubom slučae net, každomu nravitsja čto-to svoë.

'There is no such thing as perfection anyway, everyone likes something different.'

In (26) where the antecedent of *svoj* is not the quantifier, the nominative use of *svoj* meaning 'the possessed' is disqualified.

(26)

*Martinu	je	všeč	svoje.
Martin-DAT	is.3SG	like	one's own

Ru. *Martinu nravitsja svoë.

In Slovene there's an exceptional situation when the direct or indirect object can serve as the antecedent of *svoj*. It happens when the object is the universal quantifier *vsak*. To serve as the antecedent, the quantifier must precede the pronoun:

(27) Slvn.

Martin	je	vsakemu$_j$	dal
Martin-NOM	AUX.PRS.3SG	everyone-M.DAT.SG	gave-SG.M
svoj$_j$	delež.		
one's own	part- M.ACC.SG		

Ru.[?]Martin každomu dal svoju dolju deneg.

'Martin$_i$ gave everyone$_j$ his$_j$ share.'

The distributive meaning is impossible if the word order is reversed and the reflexive possessive pronoun is used before the quantifier *vsak*. In such examples, the possessed is no longer distributed but rather is the exclusive property of e.g. Martin:

(28) Slvn.

Martin$_i$	je	dal	svoj$_i$	delež
Martin-NOM	AUX.PRS.3SG	gave-SG.M	one's own	part-M.ACC.SG
vsakemu$_j$				
everyone-M.DAT.SG				

Ru. Martin razdal svoju dolju vsem.

'Martin$_i$ gave his$_i$ share to everyone$_j$.'

3.5. Cases where the Possessive Reflexive Pronoun is Used in the Meaning of 'special, unique, unlike any other'

As the distributive meaning as such can also imply specificity, i.e. 'each possessor gets their own special part; each part is special', the quantifier *vsak* may be used with this type of *svoj* as well.

(29) Slvn.

Vsaka	tekma	je	svoja	zgodba.
every	match	is.3SG	one's own	story-F.NOM.SG

Ru. Każdyj matč – èto osob' stat'ja.

'Every match is its own tale.'

It is typical of this type of use of *svoj* in both languages that the pronoun may take as its antecedent an inanimate denotatum, especially when metonymic shift is involved:

(30) Slvn.

Restavracija$_i$	je	znana	po
restaurant-F.NOM.SG	is.3SG	known-F.NOM.SG	on
svoji$_i$	izjemno	bogati	ponudbi.
one's own.	exceptionally	rich	offer-F.LOC.SG

Ru. Restoran slavitsja svoim isključitel'no bogatym menju.

'The restaurant is renowned for its exceptionally rich choice of menu.'

As indicated by the Slovene translations of examples (31) and (32), this type of use of *svoj* is much more restricted in Slovene than it is in Russian. The antecedent in Russian examples is a non-nominative thematic argument.

(31) Ru.

V	takix	delax	nužny	svoi	metody.
In	such	matters	necessary-M.NOM.PL	one's own	methods-M.NOM.PL

Slvn. Pri tovrstnih zadevah so potrebne posebne metode.

'Matters of this kind require special procedures.'

(32) Ru.

Infinitivu$_i$	svojstvenny	svoi$_i$	funkcii.
Infinitive-M.DAT.SG	inherent-F.NOM.PL	one's own	function-F.NOM.PL

Slvn. Za nedoločnik so značilne posebne vloge.

'The infinitive is used in specific roles.'

On the other hand, in Slovene, *svoj* can mean 'typical of someone'. This type of use is a subtype of the one from 2.5 but restricted by the syntactic rule mentioned earlier, which states that *svoj* may be used only in non-nominative forms.

(33) Slvn.

Martin$_i$	vedno	pride	s	svojimi$_i$	pripombami.
Martin-NOM	always	come-3SG	with	one's own	comments-F.INS.PL

Ru. U Martina večno est' ~~svoi~~ zamečanija.

'Martin is always complaining.'

(34) Slvn.

Ta	trener$_i$	ima	svoje$_i$	prijeme.
This-M.NOM.SG	coach-M.NOM.SG	have-3SG	one's own	tricks-M.ACC.PL

Ru. U ètogo trenera svoi priëmy.

'This coach works in his own way.'

3.6. Cases where the Reflexive Possessive Pronoun is Used in the Meaning of 'appropriate'

This type of use of *svoj* can be considered distant from the pronoun's prototypical meaning and restricted to idiomatic use in fixed expressions such as *postaviti na svoje mesto* 'to put sbd/sth in his/its place; to put sth back where it belongs'. See (35–37):

(35) Slvn.

Vse	zahteva	svoj	čas.
Everything-N.NOM	demand-3SG	one's own	time-M.ACC.SG

Ru. Vsemu svoë vremja.

'Everything takes time.'

(36) Slvn.

pro	Postavili	so	stvari$_i$	na	svoje$_i$	mesto.
	put-PL.M	AUX.PRS.3PL	things-F.ACC.PL	on	one's own	place-N.ACC.SG

Ru. Oni vernuli vešči na svoë mesto.

'They put things back in order.'

As we have already mentioned, for this type of use, it is possible to find a genitive-NP subject as the antecedent of *svoj* in the fixed expression *na svojem mestu*: see examples (14) and (15). However, in such use, *svoj* may also take an antecedent functioning as the object (see example (37)), which is again indicative of the shift away from the prototypical meaning. Our informants, all native speakers of Russian, have shown that such use is not typical in Russian.

(37) Slvn.

Martin$_i$	je	postavil	stol$_j$	na	svoje$_j$	mesto.
Martin-NOM	AUX.PRS.3SG	put-SG.M	chair-M.ACC.SG	on	one's own	place-N.ACC.SG

Ru. Martin postavil stul na ~~svoë~~ mesto.

'Martin put the chair in its usual place.'

3.7. Cases where the Implied Antecedent of the Reflexive Possessive Pronoun is a Relative or a Close Person

In Slovene, non-nominative use of *svoj* is typical of this type of use, as in *med svoje ljudi* 'to his own people' nominalized as *med svoje* in (38):

(38) Slvn.

Martin$_i$	se	je	vrnil	med	svoje$_i$.
Martin-NOM	REFL	AUX.PRS.3SG	came-SG.M	among	one's own-M.ACC.PL

Ru. Martin vernulsja k svoim.

'Martin returned home/to his family.'

(39) Slvn.

pro$_i$	Martina	so	sprejeli	kot	svojega$_i$.
	Martin-ACC	AUX.PRS.3PL	accepted-PL.M	like	one's own-M.ACC.SG

Ru. Martina prinjali kak svoego.

'They accepted Martin as one of their own (kind).'

This type of use of *svoj* is much more widespread in Russian than in Slovene. As can be seen in examples (40) and (41), Russian also permits its nominative form here, which Slovene prohibits. Nominative use in Russian, however, only implies the antecedent. Actual coreference between the antecedent and *svoj* with the sense of "closeness" is largely context-dependent.

In (40), the closeness is based on the speaker and the addressee (*svoi* 'ours') whereas in (41), it is based on the group to which the object-patient (*Vasja*) belongs. When translating Russian examples into Slovene we must therefore consider the specific circumstances of the context.

(40) Ru.

Stoj,	kto	idët?	Ne	streljaj,	svoi.
stop	who	go-3SG	NEG	shoot-2SG	one's own

Slvn. Stoj, kdo gre? – Ne streljaj, naši smo.

'Halt, who goes there? – Friends! Don't shoot!'

(41) Ru.

$Vasju_i$	ubili	$svoi_i$.
Vasja-ACC	killed-PL.M	one's own

Slvn. Vasjo so ubili njegovi.

'It was his own people that killed Vasja.'

There is a class of set expressions (*svoj čelovek*, *svoj narod*, *svoi ljudi*) in Russian in which this type of use of *svoj* – meaning close to the possessor, usually the speaker, through belonging to the common group – is present as well. If reference is established between the speaker and the addressee, as is the case in (40) and (42), Slovene speakers use the possessive pronoun *naš* instead of the reflexive possessive.

(42) Ru.

Martin	svoj	čelovek.
Martin-NOM	one's own	man-M.NOM.SG

Slvn. Martin je naš človek.

'Martin is our man.'

The set expression *svoj človek* used as the subject complement in (43) carries an entirely different meaning in Slovene: it denotes not belonging but being an independent, autonomous person.

(43) Slvn.

Ne	Skrbi,	Martin	je	svoj	človek.
NEG	worry	Martin-NOM	is.3SG	one's own	man-M.NOM.SG

Ru. Ne volnujsja, Martin samostojatel'nyj čelovek.

'Don't worry. Martin is his own man.'

4. *Svoj*-Binding in Infinitival Complements

One of the basic rules regarding locality constraints states that the reflexive possessive pronoun *svoj* has a limited scope of coreference: it has to be bound by a prior argument within a clause. In finite clauses, this argument is typically a nominative participant.

This brings us to the question concerning the reference of *svoj* in infinitival clauses. Those appear in Slovene as complements to various semantic classes of predicates.[9] In infinitival clauses, the implied antecedent is not expressed on the surface level.

4.1. *Svoj*-Binding in Subject-Controlled Infinitival Clauses

In subject-controlled infinitival clauses where the subject of the matrix clause controls the understood subject in the infinitival clause, there is little trouble involved in describing the nature of *svoj*-binding as *svoj* refers in those cases to the null subject of the infinitive (see examples (44–46)), which is coreferential with the nominative, dative or accusative prior participant from the matrix clause.

Subject-controlled infinitival clauses are typically complements to modal verbs (44), several types of modal predicates (45) or conative verbs (45).[10]

(44) Slvn.

Martin$_1$	noče	[**PRO**$_1$	srečati	svojega$_1$	učitelja.]
Martin-NOM	want-NEG.3SG		meet	one's own	teacher-M.GEN.SG

Ru. Martin ne xočet vstrečat'sja so svoim učitelem.

'Martin does not want to encounter his teacher.'

(45) Slvn.

Martina$_i$	je	sram	[**PRO**$_i$	misliti
Martin-ACC	is.3SG	shame		think
na	svoje$_i$	probleme.]		
on	one's own	problems-M.ACC.PL		

Ru. Martinu stydno dumat' o svoix problemax.

'Martin is ashamed to only be concerned with his own problems.'

(46) Slvn.

Martin$_i$	se	trudi	[**PRO**$_i$	manj
Martin-NOM	REFL	strive-3SG		less
misliti	na	svoje$_i$	probleme.]	
think	on	one's own	problems-M.ACC.PL	

Ru. Martin staraetsja men'še dumat' o svoix problemax.

'Martin tries to think less about his problems.'

4.2. *Svoj*-Binding in Object-Controlled Infinitival Clauses

In object-controlled infinitival clauses where the unexpressed subject is coreferential with the object of the matrix clause with a transitive predicates, the reference of *svoj* is sometimes ambiguous.[11] According to Rappaport (1986: 104), "a reflexive pronoun in [such a] context can take either its PRO clause subject or the matrix clause subject as its antecedent".

In the following sections we describe the semantic classes of predicates selecting infinitival complements. First we list those semantic classes where *svoj* may be used to refer either to the matrix-clause subject or the unexpressed subject of the infinitival clause: verbs of permission (*dopustiti* 'allow'), verbs of perception (*videti* 'see', *slišati* 'hear') and imagination (*predstavljati si* 'imagine'). We then list the semantic classes where *svoj* typically refers to the unexpressed subject in the infinitival clause: *pomagati* 'help' and verbs of saying with a directive semantic component (such as *ukazati* 'order', *prepričati* 'convince'). The understood subject is coreferential with the object of the matrix clause in all the above classes.

4.3. Verbs of Permission (*dovoliti* 'permit', *dopustiti* 'allow') with Infinitival Complements

It is typical of this class of verbs that they allow *svoj* to be bound either by the unexpressed subject of the infinitival clause (47) or the subject of the matrix clause (48, 49). Both options appear with similar frequencies in Gigafida 2.0, the currently available corpus. The crucial factor in identifying the antecedent of *svoj* is the type of verb used in the infinitival clause and the arguments it selects.

(47) Slvn.

Mednarodni	olimpijski	komite$_i$	ne	bo	dovolil
international	olympic	committee	NEG	AUX.FUT.3SG	allowed-SG.M
Rusiji$_j$	[**PRO**$_j$	nastopiti	pod	vojo$_j$	zastavo.]
Russia-DAT		compete	under	one's own	flag-F.ACC.SG

Ru. Meždunarodnyj olimpijskij komitet ne razrešit Rossii vystupat' pod svoim flagom.

'The International Olympic Committee will not permit Russia to fly its own flag at the Olympics.'

(48) Slvn.

Poljska$_i$	ne	bo	dovolila	Rusiji	[**PRO**$_j$
Poland-NOM	NEG	AUX.FUT.3SG	allowed-SG.F	Russia	
zgraditi	plinovoda	čez	svoje$_i$	ozemlje.]	
construct	gas pipeline	across	one's own	territory-N.ACC.SG	

Ru. Pol'ša ne razrešit Rossii stroit' gazoprovod na svoej territorii.

'Poland will not allow Russia to construct a gas pipeline over its territory.'

(49) Slvn.

In	nanjo	je	bila	besna,	ker
And	on her	AUX. PRS.3SG	was-SG.F	furious	because
je **pro**$_i$	dopustila	tako	arogantnemu	moškemu	
AUX. PRS.3SG	allowed-SG.F	so	arrogant	man	
[**PRO**$_j$	stopiti	v	svoje$_i$	življenje.]	
	enter	in	one's own.	life-N.ACC.SG	

Ru. I ona tak zlilas' na nee, potomu čto ta pozvolila takomu vysokomernomu mužčine vojti v svoju/eë žizn'.

'And she was mad at her for allowing such an arrogant man to enter her life.'

4.4. Verbs of Perception (*videti* 'See', *slišati* 'Hear') and Imagination (*predstavljati si* 'Imagine') with Infinitival Complements

Unlike Russian, Slovene allows infinitival complements with verbs of perception:

(50) Slvn.

Martin$_i$	je	slišal	Petro$_j$
Martin-NOM	AUX.PRS.3SG	heard-SG.M	Petra-F.ACC
[**PRO**$_j$	peti	svojo$_{i/j}$	pesem.]
	sing	one's own	territory-F.ACC.SG

Ru. Martin slyšal, kak Petra poet ego/svoju pesnju.

'Martin heard Petra sing his/her song.'

The antecedent of *svoj* in (50) may be either the null subject of the infinitive – which is coreferential with its most proximal participant, the object of the matrix clause – or the subject of the matrix finite clause.[12] In the Russian translation of (50) the antecedent of *svoj* is unambiguous: since the subordinate clause is finite, the only possible referent of *svoj* is the subject (*ona* 'she').

Identifying the antecedent of *svoj* is also dependent on the event in the infinitival clause, which is usually determined by the verb in its predicate and the arguments which this verb selects. Because the verb *slačiti* 'undress, take off' is used in (49), the null subject of the infinitive, which is coreferential with the object of the matrix clause (Petra$_{jACC}$), will typically be selected as the antecedent:

(51) Slvn.

Martin$_i$	si	predstavlja	Petro$_j$
Martin-NOM	REFL.DAT	imagine-3SG	Petra-F.ACC
[**PRO**$_j$	slačiti	svoj$_j$	plašč.]
	take off	one's own.	coat-M.ACC.SG

Ru. Martin predstavljaet sebe, kak Petra snimaet (svoë) pal'to.

'Martin imagines Petra taking off her coat.'

4.5. The Verb *pomagati* 'Help' with Infinitival Complements

The outward-oriented intention of the verb *pomagati* 'help' is a key feature of its use as a matrix verb: the action performed by the subject of the matrix clause is directed towards another participant which is coreferential with the subject of the infinitival clause. Our corpus analysis showed that the event described by the infinitival clause is always related to the action performed by this second participant. For this reason, *svoj* used in such cases is always coreferential with the unexpressed subject of the infinitival clause.[13]

(52) Slvn.

Martina	namreč	**pro**	nismo	ugrabili
Martin-ACC	namely		are-NEG.1PL	kidnap-PL.M
zato,	da	bi	nam	dal
so	that	PART	us-DAT	gave-SG.M
milijon	mark,	temveč	da	
million	deutschmarks	but	that	
bi	**pro**	pomagali	Petelinu$_j$	
PART	helped-PL.M	Petelin-M.DAT		
[**PRO**$_j$	priti	nazaj		
	come	back		
do	svojega$_j$	premoženja.]		
to	one's own	property-N.GEN.SG		

Ru. My poxitili Martina ne zatem, čtoby on dal nam million marok, a čtoby pomoč' Petelinu vernut' svoë imuščestvo.

'It is not the case that we kidnapped Martin in order to get a million marks from him, but rather to help Petelin get back what is rightfully his.'

(53) Slvn.

Različnosti$_i$	usod$_i$ …	so	pomagale	Avstriji$_j$	[**PRO**$_j$
diversities	destiny	AUX.PRS.3PL	helped-PL.F	Austria-DAT	
utrjevati	svojo$_j$	identiteto	nasproti	Nemčiji.]	
strengthen	one's own	identity-F.ACC.SG	opposite	Germany	

Ru. Raznye sud'by […] sposobstvovali tomu, čtoby v Avstrii zakrepilas' svoja, otličnaja ot nemeckoj, identičnost'.

'The ways in which their destinies diverged […] helped Austria consolidate its identity in opposition to Germany's.'

4.6. Directive Verbs of Saying (*ukazati* 'order', *prositi* 'ask, request', *prepričati* 'convince', *svetovati* 'advise') with Infinitival Complements

Using infinitival complements with verbs of saying with a directive semantic component (*prositi* 'ask, request', *predlagati* 'suggest', *svetovati* 'advise', *prepričati* 'convince', *nagovarjati* 'urge') is much rarer in contemporary Slovene than it is in Russian as their function is typically carried out by subordinate clauses with *da* and *naj* as conjunctions of purpose, which take finite clauses. This is demonstrated by the Slovene translation of (54) where the Russian infinitival complement to the verb *predložit'* 'suggest' is translated as a subordinate clause with *naj* where *svoj* can only be bound by the unexpressed subject **pro**, thus ruling out any ambiguity.

(54) Ru.

Ja	imel	besedu	so	svjaščennikom	Štajnom$_i$
I	had	conversation	with	priest	Stein-INS
i	predložil	emu$_j$	[**PRO**$_j$	izložit'	v
And	proposed	him-M.DAT.SG		explain	in
pis'mennom	vide	svoi$_j$	soobraženija	po	povodu
written	form	one's own	consideration-N. ACC.PL	by	reason-M.DAT.SG
služenija	na	ivrite.] (Ulickaja 2006)			

service-N.GEN.SG	on	hebrew

Slvn. Pogovoril sem se s patrom Steinom in mu predlagal, naj $_{pro(on)}$ pisno razloži svoja stališča o maševanju v hebrejščini. (Ulicka 2009).

'I talked to Father Stein and suggested that he should give a written explanation of his views on divine service in Hebrew.' (Ulicka 2009)

The Gigafida 2.0 corpus shows that of all the verbs of saying mentioned above, only *ukazati*/*ukazovati* 'order' takes the infinitival clauses as the complement.

As can be seen from example (55), the unexpressed object is typically identified as the antecedent of *svoj*.[14]

(55) Slvn.

Znan	je	samo	en	primer,	ko
Known	is.3SG	only	one	example-M.NOM.SG	when
je	sodišče$_i$	ukazalo	zasebni	družbi$_j$	
AUX.PRS.3SG	court-N.NOM.SG	ordered-SG.N	private-F.DAT.SG	company-F.DAT.SG	
[**PRO**$_j$	izplačati	odškodnino	družini	svojega$_j$	zaposlenega.]
	pay off	compensation-F.ACC.SG	family-F.DAT.SG	one's own	employed-M.GEN.SG

Ru. Izvesten tol'ko odin primer, kogda sud prikazal častnoj kompanii vyplatit' vozmeščenie sem'e svoego sotrudnika.

'There is only one known case where the court ruled that a company is to compensate their employee's family for damages.'

Our discussion shows that using *svoj* in infinitival complements and identifying its antecedent depends on various factors. The matrix verb determines whether the null subject of the infinitival clause is coreferential with the subject or the object of the matrix clause. In object-controlled infinitival clauses where the unexpressed subject is coreferential with the object of the matrix clause, identifying the antecedent of *svoj* depends not only on the matrix verb but also the event described in the infinitival clause, which is in turn determined by the verb in the infinitival clause and consequently the arguments it selects.

5. Contextually Determined Variation between the Possessive and the Reflexive Possessive Pronoun

In this final section we would like to focus our attention on how using the reflexive possessive pronoun depends on pragmatic and situational factors. More specifically, we discuss two environments in which the non-reflexive possessive pronoun is used instead of the expected reflexive possessive *svoj*.

To start with, standard Slovene speakers observe the difference in the 1st and 2nd person between the possessive *moj* "my, mine", *tvoj* "your, yours" and the reflexive possessive *svoj* much more rigorously than Russian speakers. When the agent and the possessor are coreferential, *svoj* will be used in the 1st and 2nd person in Slovene with much greater regularity than in Russian.

(56) Slvn.

pro$_i$	Predstavil	bom	svoje$_i$	primere.
	presented-SG.M	AUX.FUT.3SG	one's own.	examples-M.ACC.PL

Ru. Ja predstavlju moi/svoi primery (Padučeva 1983).
'I will present my examples.'

There are two noteworthy cases in contemporary standard Slovene where, in spite of the agent and the possessor being coreferential, non-reflexive possessive pronouns are regularly used, especially in the 1st and 2nd person. This competition between *svoj* and the 1st-person plural possessive pronoun *naš* is typically connected to the difference between inclusive and exclusive possession whenever the possessed is an institution, a company or an establishment. See (57):

(57) Slvn.

S	projektom	**pro**	predstavljamo	dejavnosti
with	project-M.INS.SG		present-1PL	activity-F.ACC.PL
naše	šole	mladim,	ki	nas
our-F.GEN.SG	school-F.GEN.SG	young-M.DAT.PL	who	us
še	ne	poznajo.		
yet	NEG	know-3PL		

Ru. Posredstvom proekta my predstavljaem našu školu molodëži, eščë ne znakomoj s nami.
'The project allows those young people who are not yet familiar with us to learn about the activities we organize at our school.'

The speaker in (57) shares the public institution (a school) with other people as a common possessed. They emphasise the communal activities, too. For those reasons, using the reflexive possessive pronoun (**predstavljamo dejavnosti svoje šole* "allows [...] to learn about the activities we [i.e. exclusively the speaker] organize at our school") would indicate emphasising the exclusive nature of the possession.

It is also worth mentioning that in the domain of commerce, using the non-reflexive possessive pronoun instead of the reflexive possessive *svoj* in contemporary Slovene has become widespread in recent years when it comes to imperative sentences in which the speaker addresses their clients. See (58):

(58) Slvn.

pro$_i$	Vzemite	Vašo	kartico!
	take-2PL	your-F.ACC.SG	card-F.ACC.SG

Ru. Zaberite kartu!

'Please take your card.'

This can be interpreted as the following. When a particular construction, i.e. the honorific *Vaš* 'your' in (58), takes over the pragmatic function of polite instructions or requests, another construction, i.e. *svoj* in *Vzemite svojo kartico!* 'Take your card!' adds an additional layer of pragmatic meaning on the existing function. Using the reflexive possessive *svoj* thus works as a (rather forceful) command in *Vzemite svojo kartico!* 'Take your card!'[15]

6. Conclusion

We have discussed the syntactic and semantic properties of the reflexive possessive pronoun *svoj* in Slovene and Russian. Besides morphosyntactic and semantic properties, we also discussed some situational and pragmatic factors influencing the use of *svoj*. In both languages, the primary function of the reflexive possessive pronoun is establishing coreference between the modifier of the NP and its antecedent (possessor), which is a prior participant within the same clause. In a finite clause, the reflexive possessive pronoun most typically refers to the nominative subject. If the subject is absent, the role of the antecedent may be taken over by various non-nominative arguments in the roles of experiencers. Cases where *svoj* refers to a genitive antecedent in negated locative clause are more common in Slovene than in Russian.

It needs to be said that the most important rule governing the use of *svoj* in Slovene is that it either has to be in its non-nominative form or in a form which is, syntactically speaking, on a lower hierarchical position than the antecedent. Few examples deviate from this rule, and those exhibit a digression from the prototypical meaning of *svoj*, namely true possession. In particular, the nominative form of *svoj* may be part of a subject complement in several fixed expressions, e.g. *On je svoj človek* 'He is his own man' and in cases where the antecedent of *svoj* is an NP containing the universal quantifier *vsak* used before *svoj* in a sentence, e.g. *Vsakemu je všeč svoj stil* 'Everybody has their own style'. The universal quantifier may also be its antecedent when it functions as a direct or indirect object, but only if it is used before the reflexive possessive pronoun: *Vsakemu je dal svoj delež* 'Everyone got their share' (antecedent = *vsakemu*) as opposed to *Martin je dal svoj delež vsakemu* 'Martin gave his share to everyone' (antecedent = *Martin*).

Our contrastive analysis of Slovene and Russian showed there are numerous contexts in Russian that permit using the nominative *svoj*. The pronoun is most frequently used to denote the possessed in the construction *U A est' svoj B* 'Somebody has their own X' but may also be used in various other cases where nominative *svoj* would be ungrammatical in Slovene (*Xleb svoj* 'The bread is homemade', *Svoja rubaška bliže k telu* litt. One's own shirt is closer to body, 'Self comes first'). These Russian examples do not contain an overt antecedent, which is an indication of *svoj* diverging from the anaphoric pronoun expressing possession only.

We also show that identifying the antecedent of *svoj* in Slovenian infinitival clauses depends on many factors, among which the choice of matrix verb and its infinitival complement is the most prominent.

Notes

1 This article has been supported by ARRS (program P6-0038).
2 For the role of the reflexive possessive pronoun in Slovene, see M. Bolta (1988, 1990), J. Orešnik (1992) and A. Stopar (2001). These works also note the specific properties of coreference with *svoj*, especially as part of contrastive analysis with English. For an analysis from the point of view of Slovene linguistics, see J. Toporišič (2000) and A. Žele (2020).
3 The use of the Russian anaphoric *svoj* is most extensively described in E. V. Padučeva (1983), A. Timberlake (1980, 1996, 2004), G. Rappaport (1986) and Y. Testelec (2001). For general properties of the reference of *svoj* in Slavic languages see S. Franks (1995, 2013).

4 In this matter, there is a complementary distribution within a clause between a reflexive pronoun (*svoj*) and a non-reflexive possessive pronoun (*njegov*) (Timberlake 2004:240). Some exceptions will be adressed in section 5.
5 For the position of a reflexive clitic *se* in Slovene and the South Slavic languages, see Franks, Hooloway King 2000, Kosta 2002.
6 For the dative NP in the function of the antecedent in Russian experiential predicates, see Franks 1995:253, Timberlake 2004:245.
7 Speakers of Russian diverge in their opinion on the use of *свой* in negated locative clauses. Cases such as (11) are rare but do exist in the corpora. If the antecedent is in the nominative, e.g. *Vratar byl na svoëm meste* 'The goalkeeper was in his position', *Statuja na svoëm meste* 'The statue is in its usual position', the examples are completely grammatical.
8 We base the typology of the types of use of *svoj* proposed here on Padučeva 1983 and the contrastive study of Czech and Russian Nedoluzhko 2016.
9 For semantic classes of predicates with infinitival complements in connection with the use of *svoj* in Croatian, see M. Batinić Angster (2019:279–297).
10 For the use of reflexive pronoun in subject-controlled Russian infinitive-clauses, see Timberlake (2004:248–248).
11 Timberlake (2004:249) draws attention to the complexity of the issue of Russian reflexive pronoun antecedents in constructions with object-controlled infinitives.
12 In the beginning of 2020 the authors carried out a survey of fifteen native speakers of Slovene. We asked them what participant *svoj* refers to in (50). Understanding the sentence as containing a long-distance anaphor proved to be much more frequent than the strict-anaphor interpretation as fourteen participants selected the subject of the finite clause as the antecedent of *svoj*, with only one selecting the unexpressed subject of the infinitival clause.
13 As Timberlake (2004:252) has noted, the issue of the pronoun antecedent is also a matter of the cohesion between the matrix predicate and infinitive clause: if the cohesion decreases, the possibility of using reflexives to refer to the infinitival subject increases.
14 P. Kosta (1992:227) quotes the Russian example *Ona*$_i$ *zastavila ix*$_j$ [**PRO**$_j$ *otredaktirovat' svoju*$_i$ *stat'ju.*], in which he attributes the role of the antecedent of the reflexive pronoun to the subject of the matrix clause (ona 'she'). As far as Slovenian data are concerned, we have not found this type of long distance anaphora in the complements of the directive verbs of saying.
15 For cases where *svoj* carries the meaning of an order, see O. T. Yokoyama and E. Klenin 1976: 266.

Bibliography

Batinić Angster, Mia. 2019. Može li hrvatska anafora *svoj* biti dalekometna? Odgovor na temelju analize infinitivnih dopuna. *Rasprave: Časopis Instituta za hrvatski jezik i jezikoslovlje* 45/2. 279–97.

Bolta, Marija. 1988. *Navezovanje povratnih zaimkov v slovenski in angleški skladnji*. Poročilo o raziskovalni nalogi. Maribor: Pedagoška fakulteta.

Bolta, Marija. 1990. Slovenski in angleški povratni zaimki v vezalno-navezovalni teoriji. *Anthropos* 3–4. 333–49.

Franks, Steven. 1995. *Parameters of Slavic Morphosyntax*. Oxford, New York: Oxford University Press.

Franks, Steven. 2013. Binding and morphology revisited. *Current Studies in Slavic Linguistics,* ed. by Chahine, Irina Kor, 25–42. Amsterdam, Philadelphia: John Benjamins.

Franks, Steven, and Holloway King, Tracy. 2000. *A Handbook of Slavic Clitics*. New York, Oxford: Oxford University Press.

Kosta, Peter. 1992. *Leere Kategorien in den nordslavischen Sprachen. Zur Analyse leerer Subjekte und Objekte in der Rektions-Bindungs-Theorie*. Frankfurt am Main (unveröffentlichte Habilitationsschrift). Online: http://www.uni-potsdam.de/u/slavistik/wsw/habil/habil.htm. Accessed January 2020.

Kosta, Peter. 2002. Klitika im Slavischen: Sind sie immer optimal? *Zeitschrift für Slawistik* 47/2. 127–46.

Nedoluzhko, Anna. 2016. A new look at possessive reflexivization: A comparative study between Czech and Russian. *Proceedings of the Workshop on Grammar and Lexicon: Interactions and Interfaces*. Osaka: The COLING 2016 Organizing Committee. 110–19.

Orešnik, Janez. 1992. *Udeleženske vloge v slovenščini*. Dela 37. Ljubljana: SAZU.

Padučeva, Elena V. 1983. Vozvratnoe mestoimenie s kosvennym antecedentom i semantika refleksivnosti. *Semiotika i informatika* 21. 3–32.

Rappaport, Gilbert. 1986. On Anaphor Binding in Russian. *Natural Language and Linguistic Theory* 4. 97–120.

Stopar, Andrej. 2001. Aspects of Binding theory in English, Slovenian and Chinese. *Vestnik* 35/1–2. 323–29.

Testelec, Yakov G. 2001. *Vvedenie v obščij sintaksis*. Moskva: Rossijskij gosudarstvennyj universitet.

Testelec, Yakov G. 2015. Svoj i čužoj: polunaforičeskie èlementy v russkom jazyke. Doklad v Institute lingvisticheskix issledovanij. Online: https://www.academia.edu/16839546_Свой_и_чужой_полуанафорические_элементы_в_русском_языке. Accessed January 2020.

Timberlake, Alan. 1980. Conditions on Russian Reflexivization. *Language* 56/4. 777–96.

Timberlake, Alan. 1996. Reflexives with Object Antecedent. *International Journal of Slavic Linguistics and Poetics* 39/40. 261–78.

Timberlake, Alan. 2004. *A Reference Grammar of Russian*. Cambridge, New York: Cambridge University Press.

Toporišič, Jože. 2000. *Slovenska slovnica* (*SS*). Četrta prenovljena in razširjena izdaja. Maribor: Obzorja.

Ulickaja, Ljudmila E. 2006. *Danièl' Štajn, perevodčik*. Moskva: Èksmo.

Ulickaja, Ljudmila E. 2009. *Daniel Stein, prevajalec*. Maribor: Litera.

Yokoyama, Olga T., and Emily Klenin. 1976. The Semantics of Optional Rules: Russian Personal Possessives. *Sound, Sign, and Meaning*, ed. by Ladislav Matejka, 249–70. Ann Arbor: University of Michigan.

Žele, Andreja. 2020. Izražanje povratnosti v slovenščini. *Pogled v jezik in iz jezika: Adi Vidovič Muha ob jubileju*, ed. by Krajnc Ivič, Mira and Andreja Žele, 148–62. Maribor: Zora.

Vladislava Warditz[1]

Structural Variation in Heritage Russian in Germany: Language Usage or Language Change?

Abstract This paper examines transgenerational language changes in heritage Russian in Germany by describing the system-linguistic processes behind the observed diversity in heritage language usage. Because of the wide variation of individual language usages, the paper presents heritage languages as language systems within a set of sociolinguistic variables. Building on established theoretical concepts and the author's previous work, this paper focuses on structural borrowings and variations in word-formation. From a methodological point of view, the study uses a mixed approach, combining observations in an experimental setting with corpus data collected during field work.

Keywords: Heritage Russian, Transgenerational Language Changes, Structural Borrowings in Word-Formation

> *What can happen if the speaking habits of Russian speakers in Germany become systematic devices of a new Russian urban style abroad?* (Kosta 2015: 126)

1. Introduction

This paper presents my ongoing research into transgenerational language changes in heritage Russian in Germany (Ždanova 2012, Warditz 2016, Warditz 2017), and discusses their dynamics in multilingual contexts from a diachronic perspective. In doing so, I diverge from the synchronic perspective in mainstream studies of Slavic heritage languages and (re)connect to the pleas made by Dauzat (Dauzat 1927: 49–55) and later Weinreich in favor of a (dia)chronological interpretation of transference phenomena:

> The synchronic slant has been so dominant in descriptive linguistics that students of interference have generally over-looked the possibility of studying of the contact-induced progressive changes in a language against the time dimension. Yet an attractive opportunity for short term diachronic observation is offered by languages freshly brought into contact, as through migration. (Weinreich 1953: 103)

In fact, migration-affected heritage languages offer a fertile ground for examining language changes because of their often unconventional usage and modelling of noncanonical structures in their grammatical system. In my previous work, I demonstrated that certain language changes in heritage languages can already be observed after a relatively short time of language contact, especially in sensitive language areas, such as verbal or nominal rection (Warditz 2014, 2016). Building on these theoretical and methodical concepts, I will focus on structural borrowings and variations in word-formation. In doing so, I also want to connect to the existing research on language variation and change in multilingual settings, cf. Chamoreau & Léglise 2012, Léglise & Moreano 2017, Johannessen 2018 and Grant 2020.

I study heritage languages as migration-affected contact varieties that can be described within the paradigm of contact linguistics, next to other contact varieties, such as historical contact-affected dialects, pidgins and creoles (Ždanova 2009). Apart from that, I understand *heritage languages* as varieties of their corresponding baseline languages. Accordingly, e.g. heritage Russian can be seen as an oral contact variety of Russian within its variety system, next to other standard and non-standard varieties.[2] Consequently, in my research the corresponding baseline languages are used as a comparison etalon in the description and evaluation of the variation phenomena in the contact varieties.

Furthermore, I assume that like other language varieties, heritage languages can be described as a language system ("langue") behind the varying language usage ("parole") of individual speakers. Despite their wide sociolinguistic variation and asymmetric functional distribution, from the system-linguistic point of view, heritage languages have predictable vectors of variation and change. These, in turn, are affected by the character of the language contact (e.g. duration, intensity), the interaction of individual socio- and psycho-linguistic factors, and can be observed, to a greater or lesser extent, in resistant and sensitive fragments of the language system. Precisely because of the wide variation spectrum of individual languages usages, heritage languages should be described as language systems within a set of sociolinguistic variables.

Whereas the existing studies on multilingualism in Slavic heritage speakers in Germany focus on the diverse, mainly extra-linguistic factors that determine language acquisition and attrition in individual heritage speakers (Anstatt 2013, Brehmer & Kurbangulova 2017), I investigate variation and change from a systemic point of view, describing the system-linguistic processes behind the observed diversity in language usage. From a methodological point of view, I use a mixed approach, combining observations in an experimental setting with corpus data collected during field work (cf. Chamoreau & Léglise 2012). The insights derived from my research can be relevant for contact linguistics, as well as for linguistic typology (Kosta 2015: 128).

Additionally, it needs stressing that the observed dynamics of heritage languages are not only contact-induced, but also comply with the linguistic laws of oral communication, i.e. the special pragmatics of oral communication and transgenerational changes (even in a monolingual environment).

Building on this theoretical framework, in this study, I want to examine the relationship between individual language usage(s) and language system changes on the example of structural variations in word-formation in heritage Russian.

2. Language Usage and Language Change: The Case of Heritage Languages

I define HERITAGE LANGUAGES as languages emerging in families with an migrant background (Fishman 2001: 81). The term HERITAGE SPEAKERS typically refers to second generation migrants, living in a bilingual environment from an early age:

> A heritage speaker is an early bilingual who grew up hearing and speaking the heritage language (L1) and the majority language (L2) either simultaneously or sequentially in early childhood, but whose L2 became their primary language at some point during childhood (typically after the onset of schooling). (Elabbas et al. 2013: 130)

Therefore, the status of heritage languages within the study of language acquisition and didactics is quite complicated. The reason for this is that a heritage language is neither L1 nor L2 in the classical meaning, cf. the terminological overview in Polinsky & Kagan 2007. This unsettled issue is also relevant for my study, as it implies the co-existence of two mental grammars and lexicons in the same heritage language speaker; on top of that, these two systems are not organized and hierarchized in a straightforward, simplistic manner, but in a differentiated way, depending on the linguistic category under scrutiny (syntax, morphology, word-formation, lexis). Moreover, the organization and hierarchization in heritage language speakers is different from that in L1 speakers and L2 speakers. The co-existence of two mental grammars and lexicons – and, also, two cultural-pragmatic frames of language usage – generates (or affects) contact-induced variations in their own right, and that at all language levels (phonetics/ phonology, lexis, semantics, grammar, syntax). Therefore, for the description of heritage languages, I adhere to the sociolinguistic concept of language variation as a polylingual variation which can comprise (single) varieties within the same language as well as two or more typologically different languages (Franceschini 1998, Léglise & Moreano 2017).

Contact-induced variations can be qualified as a distinctive linguistic feature of heritage languages. This linguistic feature, however, is in turn defined by the social environment of heritage languages, characterized by the inequality of languages in a multilingual setting:

i. As a primarily oral contact language variety, acquired and mainly used in a family context, a heritage language is reduced in its communicative spectrum whereas the dominant (official) language is fully operational in all spheres of communication, official as well as unofficial.
ii. Due to this reduced functionality, a heritage language has no prestige and, consequently, is often branded as marginal or even stigmatized by the dominant language group.
iii. In a functionally unbalanced, multilingual environment, individual multilingualism is ubiquitous, with the individual's heritage language being affected by (contacts with) the majority language.
iv. As a result, functionally reduced usage and permanent language contact with the socially prestigious and functionally unreduced majority language provoke transfers, variations and convergences on all linguistic and pragmatic levels, and finally cause a language change.

Following Mattheier (1984) and Leiss (1998), I understand concrete manifestations of language variation as a preparatory stage of language change or as an indication of beginning language change.

How do these language changes present themselves in the individual language usage in a heterogenous sociolinguistic group of heritage speakers? Previously, I have demonstrated that although concrete linguistic manifestations of language contact are conditioned by the speaker's socio- and psycho-linguistical situation, they nevertheless can be categorized and set out in the following scale dynamics and establishment of variations (Warditz 2016: 107–109):[3]

i. transfers in the prosody, as a rule, in L2 toponyms or proper names and in intonation patterns:

K[œ]ln	M[ʏ]nchen	Bre[ç]t
'Köln	München	Brecht'

ii. transfers in the lexis, beginning with the transfer of L2 realia (social organization, toponymy of the urban space etc.), that set off processes of morphological adaptation (a) or (derivational) word-formation (b):

a. Zavtra pridët otvet **s financamta**.
s financamta-M.SING.GEN.
'Tomorrow, the answer from the financial department German: *Finanzamt* will arrive.'

b. U nas problemy **s socialom**
s socialom-M.SING.INSTR.
'We have problems with the social welfare services German: *Sozialhilfe*.'

iii. transfers in the grammar and syntax:

My dolžny sosredotočit'sja **na učëbu**
na učëbu-F.SING.ACC. instead of PREP.: *na učëbe*.
'We have to concentrate on our studies.'

The aforementioned variations can eventually lead to the formation of a mixed code as the final stage of language convergence through multilingual variation, including thematically conditioned code-mixing (Auer 1999: 309). Variation, mixing and convergence in heritage languages, whether described as systemic or as individual utterances, follow the same logic, cf. Thomason & Kaufman 1988: 74. Undoubtedly, prosody and lexis are the most susceptible to changes, both at the systemic and individual level. However, a lexical transfer can induce word-formation and morphological processes; these morphosyntactic variations, in turn, represent the most advanced stage of language variation and change.

In this study, I focus on structural borrowings and variations in word-formation as a trigger for morphosyntactic variations in heritage languages. I also investigate how morphology and lexis influence each other through word-formation strategies (Otsuka 2012). Moreover, the comparison of the first and second generations of heritage speakers in Germany can also provide evidence for language change in the multilingual settings and shed light on the theoretical question, how do two concurrent / coexistent linguistic systems influence each other.

3. Structural Borrowing and Variation in Word-Formation: A Hypothesis

Accordingly to Renner, structural borrowing in word-formation is defined here as "the increase or decrease in frequency of use of a word-formation pattern caused by language contact and includes the new availability of a virtually unknown pattern." (Renner 2018: 2) Although there is a substantial amount of research available on heritage language lexis and morphology, it is not so easy to find studies related to word-formation in heritage languages. Obviously, this is not restricted to Slavic linguistics (Gardani 2015):

> Structural borrowing in word-formation seems to have been a relatively under-researched area within contact linguistics. Studies on morphological borrowing are numerous, but specific discussions on the borrowing of abstract morphological schemata, or morphostructural borrowing, are noticeably rarer. This is especially so in the case of word-formation, a domain in which relevant examples and analyses are sparsely scattered in the linguistic literature. (Renner 2018: 2)

The existing literature on Russian heritage language provides quite contradictory views with regard to word-formation. Whereas Zemskaja asserts that word-formation is hardly affected by language contacts (Zemskaja 2001: 128–129), Osipova shows that the word-formation system is clearly weakened as of the second generation (Osipova 2001: 448–464). Others, such as Glovinskaja (2001) and Ždanova (2012) deal with word-formation while describing lexis or grammar. This lack of interest may be explained by the intermediate status of the word-formation in linguistics in general and in contact linguistics in particular (Jarceva 1990).

However, from my earlier work it transpires that next to lexicon, word-formation constitutes a major linguistic characteristic of heritage Russian, and, for that matter, of any other heritage language. Moreover, my observations also show that samples of word-formation occur very frequently in everyday, oral migrant communication. Moreover, word-formation is a language area that is very useful for word-creation; compare, for instance, in Russian oral speech, (a) the spontaneous naming of non-conventionally named objects as *ėta štuka* ('this thing') or *ėto delo* ('this thing') or semantic condensation, such as *kurilka* from *komnata dlja kurenija* ('smoking room or lounge'), or *čitalka* from *čital'nyj zal* ('reading room'), (b) or the frequent use in word-formation of borrowed morphemes, such as *super-* or *post-*, and how they provoke language changes.

Building on the theoretical concept outlined above, my hypothesis runs as follows: The language resources of heritage speakers are organized in a different way than those of monolingual speakers, because they use two language systems as one language repertoire. In diverse communicative situations, they have to choose or create a device for expressing themselves in an appropriate functional, social, and pragmatic way. In doing so, heritage speakers resort to a number of different strategies based on German or Russian language patterns or on their own creativity. This results in a number of not only different occasional variants, but also variations with a systemic character (i.e., modelling of noncanonical structures in grammar system of heritage language). In other words, the more variations are used in everyday language, the more likely it becomes that they become part of the speakers' linguistic repertoire and lead to changes in the heritage language.

4. Database

The present study is based on a corpus of linguistic data obtained by means of different elicitation tasks (picture and process descriptions, storytelling and interviews). In addition, I also used data from my previous research on the communication of heritage speakers, collected through participatory monitoring (Ždanova & Trubtschaninov 2001, Ždanova 2007).

These are the main characteristics of my corpus:

a. area: 8 Federal States of the Federal Republic of Germany, i.e. Baden-Württemberg, Berlin, Brandenburg, Bremen, Hamburg, Nordrhein-Westfalen, Rheinland-Pfalz, Thüringen
b. period: 1999–2019
c. number of participants: 135.

The samples presented below refer to the first and second generations of heritage speakers, of which the first is defined as an immigrant generation in the narrow sense, with the following sociolinguistic characteristics:

a. country of birth: Russia or GUS-States
b. date of birth: 1970–1980
c. time of immigration: 1990–1996
d. age at time of immigration: 17–20
e. language distribution and acquisition: L1 Russian, L2 German, consecutive bilingualism
f. formal education: primary and secondary education in Russia or GUS-States; partial secondary education (Gymnasium) and/or higher education in Germany.

The second generation are effectively heritage speakers, and has the following sociolinguistic characteristics:

a. country of birth: Germany
b. language distribution and acquisition: Russian heritage language, L1 German, simultaneous bilingualism
c. formal education: primary, secondary and higher education in Germany.

Both groups of respondents were on average between 22 and 25 years old at the moment of the data collecting.

I use data from my whole corpus "across time and space", in accordance with the aim of this study, i.e. to illustrate the multiformity of word-formation processes in variation and change in heritage Russian. In this instance, the focus will be on the qualitative approach (the samples collected in the database), whereas in the future I intend to verify these data quantitatively.

5. Word-Formation Processes and Functions in Heritage Russian

In this section, I present an illustrative sample of cases compiled in my main and additional corpora. I thereby focus in the first place on the multiformity of the structural changes and their distribution over the two generations.

As a matter of fact, we can observe a wide spectrum of derivation processes in heritage Russian, ranging from the central, concatenative processes, i.e. affixation and compounding, to the peripheral, non-concatenative types of structure, i.e. clipping.

The most frequently observed process, affixation, is used in diverse variations and functions, so as to create either a word-form or a new word.

In the first place, affixation is used for the morphological adaptation of borrowed words, and serves as a connecting link between the transferred lexis and the target language morphology, cf., for instance, the usage of Russian endings indicating genus in the adaptation of borrowed German words (1), where the genus of the same words can vary, especially between the first and second generation (2a and 2b):

(1) German: *Kneipe*-F. 'pub, bar' – heritage Russian: *knajp****a***-F.

pošli **v knajpu** [F.SING.ACC.]

'[we] went to a pub'

(2) German: *Heizung*, F. 'heating, radiator' – heritage Russian: *hajcunk* F. or M., cf.

a. u nas v bade **heicunk slomannaja** [F.SING.]

'the radiator in our bathroom is broken'

b. **vmesto haicunga** [M.SING.GEN.] tam ofen…

'instead of heating there [was] a stove'

The comparison of both corpora shows that the second generation generally tends to transfer the genus of borrowed words into their heritage Russian, whereas the first generation adapts them accordingly to the Russian grammar rules. So, the affixation here functions as an indicator of variations already on the grammatical level, i.e. in the grammatical category of genus.

Conversely, the endings can be also transferred from German into heritage Russian; cf., for instance, the transfer of plural forms of the borrowed substantives (3) or the transfer of substantives including their grammatical attributes (4):

(3) u nich sejčas sdelali desjat' **juniorprofessur-en** [F.PL.ACC.]
'[at their place] were created ten junior professorships'

(4) pokupajte … cede-**s**, video-**s**, defaude-**s** [N.PL.ACC.]
'buy [IMPERATIVE] … CDs, video CDs, DVDs…'

In this way, these structural borrowings expand the repertoire of plurality forms in heritage Russian, cf. more complicated hybrid forms with borrowings of German suffixes in combination with Russian endings (5), and sometimes by Russian suffixes as well (6):

(5) portug-**iz**-**y** (from German *Portug-ies-en*)
'Portuguese'

(6) brazil'jan-**c**-**y** (from German *Brasilian-er*)
'Brazilians'

Moreover, affixation operates in the morphological adaptation of German verbs through Russian word-formation processes, in which the borrowed German verbs receive a Russian aspect category by attaching an appropriate suffix such as *-ova-* (7–8):

(7) kritizir-**ova-t'** (cf. German *kritisier-en* and Russian *kritik-ova-t'*)
'to criticize'

(8) propagir-**ova-t'** (cf. German *propagier-en* and Russian *propagandir-ova-t'*)

'to propagate'

The usage of hybrid forms as parallel variants is indicative of the next – advanced – stage of language variation and change and can be observed especially in the second generation of heritage speakers.[4] This is the case particularly in variations of the past tense. Next to the usage of the German past forms, namely of the participle II with ellipted copula – cf. (9), (10) and (11) – heritage speakers use hybrid forms built from the Russian past tense participles (so-called *l*-forms) and German affix *ge-*, which functions as a derivational device in the building of Germans past tense's participles, cf. (12):

(9) Ty uže **gešpaichert**? (cf. German PAST PART. *hast gespeichert* from *speichern*)

'have you already saved [something on the PC]?'

(10) Esli opazdaeš' – ty uže **durchgefalen**. (cf. German PAST PART. *bist durchgefallen* from *durchfallen*)

'if you come later, you have already failed.'

(11) On sejčas **ferlipt**. (cf. German PAST PART. *ist verliebt* from *sich verlieben*)

'now he is in love.'

(12) Ty uže **gekušala**? (cf. Russian PAST PART. *kušala* from *kušat'*)

'have you already eaten?'

Thus, word-formation used in heritage Russian is based on the repertoire of derivations from both languages, with the second generation preferring German derivational patterns and devices, even as an additional – and effectively superfluous – derivational formant attached to the appropriate Russian form (12).

These differentiated tendencies can be observed not only in the building of the past tense, but in other derivational patterns as well. In line with what we have demonstrated above, the second generation uses German derivational patterns with Russian words or stem morphemes, whereas the first generation uses diverse Russian formants productively for the morphological adaptation of borrowed German words, simultaneously giving them additional semantic meanings (cf. the examples below). To illustrate this tendency, we can refer to the following examples:

The creation of verb action types, i.e. the iterative-diminutive meaning for expressing a chronologically split and interruptedly realized action from the German verb *putzen* 'to clean' by attaching the Russian prefix *po-* and suffix *-yva-*:

(13) Po pjatnicam ona **po-putc-yva-et** v odnoj firme.

'Fridays, she cleans in an firm.'

The formation of the Russian adverb participle form from the German verb *verbieten* 'to forbid' by attaching the Russian prefix *za-* and suffix *-eno*:

(14) My zdes' ne priparkujemsja: zdes' **za-ferboč-eno**.

'We cannot park here, it's forbidden.'

Or the formation of the Russian adjective participle form from the German noun *Zoll* 'customs duty' by attaching the Russian prefixes *ne-* and *ot-* and the suffix *-enn-*:

(15) prodajut **ne-ot-col-enn-yje** sigarety…

'they sell undeclared cigarettes…'

As far as other word-formation processes are concerned, we are confronted with a rather paradoxical situation. In our corpora, clipping as an peripherical process is more often observed than compounding, although in German, and to a lesser extent in Russian, compounding is the one of the main processes of word-formation. Compounds in heritage Russian are usually transferred from German and as a rule morphologically adapted to the Russian declination paradigms (as shown above):

(16) Mne nado **štojerkartu** [F.SING.ACC.] sdelat'. (German: *Steuerkarte*)

'I have to get an income tax declaration.'

(17) **Grafikkarta** [F.SING.NOM.] nakrylas'. (German: *Grafikkarte*)

'The graphics card is broken.'

In the majority of the cases, however, the borrowed nominal compounds are clipped (cf. 18). The result of clipping in (19) additionally receives a Russian plural ending, obviously by analogy with the Russian semantic equivalent of the borrowed compound *kursy* (courses):

(18) social [M.SING.NOM.] (from the German *Sozialhilfe*)

'social welfare'

(19) šprachi [PL., GENUS UNDEFINABLE, NOM.] (from the German *Sprachkurs*)

'language course'

As such, clipping results are often not only morphologically adapted, but also receive certain semantic connotations, e.g. the creation of diminutive forms by attaching of the suffix *-k-*, cf.:

(20) frjuš-**k**-a [F.SING.NOM.] (from the German *Frühschicht*)

'morning shift'

(21) špet-**k**-a [F.SING.NOM.] (from the German *Spätschicht*)

'evening shift'

(22) špjul'-**k**-a [F.SING.NOM.] (from the German *Spülmaschine*)

'dishwasher'

The remarkable productivity of clipping in heritage Russian can be explained by the linguistic laws of Russian oral speech. Clipping is a very productive word-formation process in Russian oral speech in a monolingual setting as well, and heritage Russian as a primarily oral variety is liable to the linguistic laws of oral communication, even in a multilingual setting. In this case, structural variations of the borrowed compounds mark the pragmatically conditioned change according to the language economy of oral communication.

6. Conclusion

By examining word-formation in heritage Russian, we can draw some conclusions about the relationship between individual language usage(s) and language system changes.

First of all, by sampling individual usages in a longitudinal perspective, we can identify certain systemic tendencies. Secondly, these tendencies differ between the first and second generations of heritage speakers: in the first generation it mainly operates with Russian derivational patterns and formants for morphological adaptation or semantic extension of the borrowing lexis; the second generation actively uses German patterns and/ or formants. Moreover, the increased frequency of certain types of variation is indicative of a change in the language skeleton, usually understood as a more resistant area than the lexis or prosody. Thus, the observed preference for structural patterns of the majority language as of the second generation of Russian heritage speakers suggests at least a transgenerational language change in certain language areas.

By documenting the multiformity of contact-affected word-formation we can identify areas of potential language shifting and sensitivity vs resistance of certain structures. These insights may apply to other contact situations as well and serve as basis for further quantitative research.

Last but not least, the present study has shown that word-formation connects morphology, semantics, pragmatics and lexis, and, next to the lexis, is a sensitive area in oral speech, in mono- as well as in multilingual settings. Therefore, the documentation and exploration of word-formation in heritage speakers can provide new insights into the special dynamics of language variation and change in contact situations and give new impulses for the investigation of heritage languages in general.

Abbreviations

ACC.	– accusative (case)
F.	– feminine (genus)
GEN.	– genitive (case)
INSTR.	– instrumental (case)
M.	– masculine (genus)
N.	– neuter (genus)

NOM.	– nominative (case)
PAST PART.	– past participle (verb form)
PL.	– plural (number)
PREP.	– prepositional (case)
SING.	– singular (number)

Notes

1 Until 2012, I published under my former name Ždanova resp. Zhdanova.

2 The status of migrant or heritage languages as varieties of the corresponding baseline languages is still controversial. Whereas Polish linguistics includes Polish contact-affected varieties and even Polish historical contact-affected dialects in the varieties' system of Polish (cf. Gaida 2001: 212), the Russian linguistic paradigm places Russian migrant languages outside the language system, cf. details in Zhdanova 2009.

3 See also *Duration of Contact, Crystallization of New Languages*, and *Language Shifts* in (Weinreich 1953: 103, 105, 107).

4 For details, see my papers presented at the 13th Slavistentag (23-26.9.2019, University of Trier) and at the University of Innsbruck (3.3.2020). Publications are forthcoming.

Bibliography

ANSTATT, TANJA. 2013. Polnisch als Herkunftssprache: Sprachspezifische grammatische Kategorien bei bilingualen Jugendlichen. *Deutsche Beiträge zum 15. Internationalen Slavistenkongress, Minsk 2013,* ed. by Sebastian Kempgen, Monika Wingender, Norbert Franz, and Miranda Jakiša, 15–25. München: Otto Sagner.

AUER, PETER. 1999. From Code-switching via Language Mixing to Fused Lects: Toward a Dynamic Typology of Bilingual Speech. *International Journal of Bilingualism 3(4)*. 309–32.

BREHMER, BERNHARD, and TATJANA KURBANGULOVA. 2017. Family language input and its role for the development of Russian as a heritage language in Germany. *Integration, Identity and Language Maintenance in Young Immigrants: Russian Germans or German Russians* (Impact 44), ed. by Ludmila Isurin and Claudia Maria Riehl, 225–68. Amsterdam, Philadelphia: John Benjamins Publishing Company.

CHAMOREAU, CLAUDINE, and ISABELLE LÉGLISE (eds.). 2012. *A Multi-Model Approach to Contact-Induced Language Change. Dynamics of Contact-Induced Language Change*. Berlin & Boston: De Gruyter.

Dauzat, Albert. 1927. *Les patois,* 49–55. Paris: Librairie Delagrave.

Elabbas, Benmamoun; Silvina Montrul; and Maria Polinsky. 2013. Heritage Languages and Their Speakers: Opportunities and Challenges for Linguistics. *Theoretical Linguistics 39, 3–4.* 129–81.

Fishman, Joshua. 2001. 300-plus years of heritage language education in the United States. *Heritage Languages in America: Preserving a National Resource,* ed. by Joy Kreeft Peyton, 81–89. Washington: DC: Center for Applied Linguistics – Delta Systems.

Franceschini, Rita. 1998. Varianz innerhalb zweier Sprachsysteme: eine Handlungswahl? *Sprachvarianz als Ergebnis von Handlungswahl,* ed. by Beate Henn-Memmesheimer, 11–26. Tübingen: Niemeyer.

Gaida, Stanisław (ed.). 2001. *Język polski.* Opole: Uniwersytet Opolski – Institut Filologii Polskiej.

Gardani, Francesco; Peter Arkadiev; and Nino Amiridze. 2015. Borrowed morphology: An overview. *Borrowed Morphology,* ed. by Francesco Gardani, Peter Arkadiev, and Nino Amiridze, 1–23. Berlin: De Gruyter.

Glovinskaja, Marina. 2001. Obščie i specifičeskie processy v jazyke metropolii i ėmigracii. *Jazyk russkogo zarubež'ja: Obščie processy i rečevye portrety,* ed. by Elena A. Zemskaja, 341–492. Moskau – Wien: Jazyki slavjanskoj kul'tury.

Grant, Antony (ed.). 2020. *Contact-Induced Linguistic Change: An Introduction. The Oxford Handbook of Language Contact.* Oxford: Oxford University Press.

Jarceva, Viktorija. 1990. Tipologičeskie universalii i kreolizacija jazyka. *Izvestija AN SSSR, Serija literatury i jazyka, 49/6,* 483–93.

Johannessen, Janne Bondi. 2018. Factors of variation, maintenance and change in Scandinavian heritage languages. *International Journal of Bilingualism, 22/ 4.* 447–65.

Kosta, Peter. 2015. Code-switching and Code-mixing Revisited in Urban and Ethnic Styles: A Brief Sketch on Variation and Language Shift. *Multilingualism and Translation. Studies on Slavonic and Non-Slavonic Languages in Contact,* ed. by Vladislava Warditz and Beatrix Kreß, 111–29. Frankfurt am Main, Berlin, Bern, Bruxelles, New York, Oxford, Wien: Peter Lang.

Léglise, Isabelle, and Santiago Sánchez Moreano. 2017. From varieties in contact to the selection of linguistic resources in multilingual settings. *Identity and Dialect Performance: A Study of Communities and Dialects,* ed. by Reem Bassiouney, 143–59. London: Routledge.

Leiss, Elisabeth. 1998. Ansätze zu einer Theorie des Sprachwandels auf morphologischer und syntaktischer Ebene. *Sprachgeschichte. Ein Handbuch zur Geschichte der deutschen Sprache und ihrer Erforschung.* Bd.2, ed.

by Werner Besch, Anne Betten, and Oskar Reichmann, 850–60. Berlin, New York: De Gruyter.

Mattheier, Klaus. 1984. Sprachwandel und Variation. *Sprachgeschichte: ein Handbuch zur Geschichte der deutschen Sprache und ihrer Erforschung.* Bd. 1, ed. by Werner Besch, Anne Betten, and Oskar Reichmann, 768–79. Berlin, New York: De Gruyter.

Osipova, Marina A. 2001. Razgovornyj russkij jazyk immigrantov v SŠA. Leksika i slooobrazovanie. *Slavjanskaja jazykovaja i ėtnojazykovaja sistemy v kontakte s neslavjanskim okruženiem,* ed. by Tat'ana M. Nikolaeva, 448–64. Moskau – Wien: Jazyki slavjanskoj kul'tury.

Otsuka, Hitomi; Thomas Stolz; Aina Urdze; and Martine Vanhove (eds.). 2012. *Morphologies in Contact.* Berlin: Akademie Verlag.

Polinsky, Maria, and Olga Kagan. 2007. Heritage Languages: In the 'Wild' and in the Classroom. *Language and Linguistics Compass, I, 2007, 5.* 368–95.

Renner, Vincent. 2018. Structural borrowing in word-formation: An exploratory overview. *SKASE Journal of Theoretical Linguistics. 2018, 15/2.* 2–12.

Thomason, Sarah Grey, and Terence Kaufman. 1988. *Language Contact, Creolization, and Genetic Linguistics.* Berkeley: University of California Press.

Warditz, Vladislava. 2014. Zum Status syntaktischer Variationen in Sprachkontaktsituationen: Eine Fallstudie zum Polnischen in Deutschland. *Zeitschrift für Slawistik. 2014/ 59(*1). 1–20.

Warditz, Vladislava. 2016. Slavische Migrationssprachen in Deutschland: Zur Erklärungskraft von Sprachwandelfaktoren in Kontaktsituationen. *Gegenwärtige Sprachkontakte im Kontext der Migration,* ed. by Stefania Ptashnyk, Ronny Beckert, Patrick Wolf-Farré, and Matthias Wolny, 99–118. Heidelberg: Winterverlag.

Warditz, Vladislava. 2017. Russisch als Migrationssprache in Deutschland: Zur Typologie des Mikrosprachwandels (Eine systemlinguistische Studie). *Handbuch des Russischen in Deutschland,* ed. by Kai Witzlack-Makarevich and Nadja Wulff, 267–85. Berlin: Frank & Timme.

Weinreich, Uriel. 1953. *Languages in Contact: Findings and Problems.* New York: Linguistic Circle of New York.

Ždanova, Vladislava. 2007. Zum Problem der Sprachkompetenz bilingualer Migranten mit Russisch als Erstsprache. *Beiträge der Europäischen Slavistischen Linguistik (POLYSLAV).* (=Die Welt der Slaven. Sammelbände/ Sborniki, Bd. 10), ed. by Bernhard Brehmer, Vladislava Ždanova, and Rafał Zimny, 188–98. München: Otto Sagner.

Ždanova, Vladislava. 2009. K probleme lingvističeskogo statusa jazyka russkoj diaspory. *Russkij jazyk v uslovijach kul'turnoj i jazykovoj polifonii.* (= Die Welt der Slaven. Sammelbände / Сборники, Bd. 38), ed. by Vladislava Ždanova, 89–101. München: Otto Sagner.

Ždanova, Vladislava. 2012. Jazyk russkoj diaspory: K probleme tipologii morfologičeskich i sintaksičeskich charakteristik. *Meaning, Texts and other Exciting Things. A Festschrift to Commemorate the 80th Anniversary of Professor Igor A. Mel'čuk,* ed. by Jurij Apresjan, Igor' Boguslavskij, Leonid Iomdin, Marie-Claude L'Homme, Jasmina Milićević, Alain Polguère, and Leo Wanner, 682–95. Moskva: Jazyki slavjanskoj kul'tury.

Ždanova, Vladislava, and Dmitrij Trubtschaninov. 2001. Nekotorye osobennosti rečevogo povedenija russkojazyčnoj diaspory v Germanii. *Beiträge der Europäischen Slavistischen Linguistik (POLYSLAV)* (=Die Welt der Slaven. Sammelbände / Sborniki, Bd. 4), ed. by Katharina Böttger, Sabine Dönninghaus, and Robert Marzari, 274–85. München: Otto Sagner.

Zemskaja, Ęlena A. 2001. Obščie jazykovye processy i individual'nye rečevye portrety. *Jazyk russkogo zarubež'ja: Obščie processy i rečevye portrety*. Jazyki slavjanskoj kul'tury, ed. by Zemskaja, Elena A., 25–277. Moskau – Wien: Jazyki slavjanskoj kul'tury.

Jacek Witkoś

On Some Aspects of Agree, Move and Bind in the Nominal Domain

Abstract This contribution focuses on reflexive binding in the nominal domain in Polish. In particular, it applies a theory of reflexive binding based on Agree and (covert) Move developed for the clausal domain in Witkoś et al. (2020), to the domain of nominal phrases. It offers a detailed account of ambiguous cross-nominal binding of the reflexive possessive; a case where the role of the binder is fulfilled either by the nominal/pronominal specifier or the clausal subject, which is placed outside the nominal projection. A formulation is proposed for a correlation holding between the position of the binder, the position of the covertly moved bindee and its lexicalisation as either a reflexive possessive or pronominal possessive.*

Keywords: Binding, Reflexives, Nominals, Reflexive Possessives, Move, Agree

1. Introduction

Witkoś et al. 2020 and Witkoś & Łęska 2020 present a descriptively adequate account of reflexive binding in Polish which draws from both the Agree-based and Move-inspired theories, with an addition of a competition-based element. It is closely related to a proposal developed for Russian in Nikolaeva (2014), with a number of significant modifications. The two sources concerned with Polish mentioned above chiefly deal with various aspects of the distribution and licensing of reflexive pronouns and reflexive possessives in the clausal domain. In this brief contribution I would like to show how this account fares with respect to cases where a reflexive element is placed in the complement position within a nominal projection and its antecedent is placed either within the nominal projection or outside it.

* I am grateful to the reviewers for this volume for their constructive critical comments which helped me improve the original version of this material. I claim full responsibility for any shortcomings of this text.

2. An Outline of the Theory of the Distribution of Reflexives

Nikolaeva (2014) defines A-binding in a very conservative manner, as the sharing of the index between an antecedent and an anaphoric pronoun. Building on Chomsky (1986), Hestvik (1992), and Avrutin (1994), she proposes that the ability to bind anaphors depends on the relative configuration of the DP antecedent and the pronoun/anaphor, wherein pronouns and anaphors are indices that covertly raise as heads to the positions of v and T. The gist of Nikolaeva's system is as follows, (Nikolaeva 2014: 68):

(1) a. Movement: an index must undergo covert Index Raising unless it is at a Reflexivization site or movement is no longer possible.

b. Reflexivization site: an index is a sister to a node with label D/v/T and is c-commanded by a specifier.

c. Co-argumental Reflexivization: if an index is at a reflexivization site and is coindexed with a specifier which is its co-argument, the index has to be realized as reflexive.

d. Reflexivization at spell-out: when the sentence is sent to spell-out, if an index is coindexed with a specifier of the projection to which it is adjoined, the index has to be realized as reflexive.

e. Pronominal is an elsewhere condition: if an index has not been realized as reflexive, it is realized as pronominal.

In this system VP is not a reflexivisation site by definition and the overt position of the index (pronoun or anaphor) is mostly ignored in the calculation of its binding domain.

A related set of ideas is presented in Safir (2014), who underscores the fact that an element which is most dependent in terms of interpretation may be spelled out either as a reflexive or as a pronoun, depending on the morphological resources available in a given language.[1] Safir submits that, generally, an indexically-dependent element (his D-bound) in a local, phase-internal c-command relation with its antecedent, takes on the morphological form of an anaphor, while a D-bound element further removed from the antecedent spells out as a pronoun. Yet, the phase internal procedures of Spell-out depend on morphological choices available to particular languages.

2.1. The Core Data Set

Core properties of the distribution of reflexives in Polish are shown below:

(2)	a.	Jan$_1$	opowiedział	Marii$_2$	[o sobie$_{1,*2}$/?niej$_2$ (samej)/*nim$_1$].	
		Jan-NOM	told	Maria-DAT	about self/her (alone)/him	
		'Jan told Maria about himself/her.'				
	b.	Jan$_1$	pokazał	Marii$_2$	[swoje$_{1,*2}$/jej$_2$/*jego$_1$	zdjęcie].
		Jan-NOM	showed	Maria-DAT	self/her/his	picture-ACC
		'Jan showed Maria his/her picture.'				

(3)	Maria$_1$	kazała	Piotrowi$_2$	pozdrowić	swoich$_{1,2}$/jego$_2$/jej$_1$	przyjaciół.
	Maria-NOM	told	Piotr-DAT	greet-INF	self's/his/her	friends
	'Maria told Piotr to greet his/her friends.'					

(4)	a.	Marii$_1$	było	żal	siebie$_1$/*?jej$_1$ (samej).	
		Maria-DAT	was-3.N.SG	sorrow	self-GEN/*?her-GEN (alone)	
		'Maria felt sorry for herself.'				
	b.	Marii$_1$	było	żal	swojej$_1$/jej$_1$	koleżanki.
		Maria-DAT	was-3.N.SG	sorrow	self's-GEN/her-GEN	friend-3.F.SG.GEN
		'Maria felt sorry for her female friend.'				

The general picture emerging from these data is as follows:

(5) Anaphoric binding in Polish:

a. the nominative subject serves as an antecedent for (i) reflexive pronouns and (ii) reflexive possessives

b. the object (either dative or accusative) asymmetrically c-commanding the other object cannot serve as an antecedent for a reflexive pronoun/reflexive possessive in the lower object

c. the superior object acts as an antecedent for a pronominal possessive in the other object

d. dative object experiencers acts as antecedents for: (i) reflexive pronouns; (ii) reflexive possessives, and (iii) pronominal possessives

e. dative object experiencers can marginally act as antecedents for reflexive possessives embedded in nominative constituents.

The examples in (4) display an intriguing property of dative object experiencers in Polish: they function as antecedents to both reflexive and pronominal possessives which are indexically dependent on them. In terms of the classical Binding Theory of Chomsky (1981, 1986; Manzini and Wexler 1987; Rappaport 1986 and Reinders-Machowska 1991) they "bind" both reflexive and pronominal possessives in the same syntactic domain.[2]

2.2. Engineering Details

The account of A-binding addressing the empirical issues raised by examples (2–4) above rests on four pillars. First, Witkoś et al. (2020) and Witkoś and Łęska (2020) propose that the LF-relevant aspect of A-binding (traditionally captured through coindexation) is based on Agree for the feature [var:_] (variable), interpretable and valued on R-expressions and pronouns ([var: x]) and unvalued on anaphors (D-bound/index), as proposed in Hicks (2008, 2009). Second, it is proposed that what Nikolavea takes to be Index Raising, (1a), has a near overt equivalent in Polish in the distribution of the clitic/weak pronoun, which leaves the VP and moves into the functional domain of the clause. The clitic/weak pronoun also optionally climbs into the main clause out of the domain of the infinitive. Thus the movement mentioned in (1a) receives independent empirical justification. Third, in contrast to clitics/weak pronouns, the chain of D-bound/index movement shows copy pronunciation, that is, the head of the chain is never pronounced, although the landing site of its movement directly determines the pronunciation of the bottom copy. Fourth, because the D-bound/index bears two relevant features (one that drives its movement and the other, relevant for its interpretation in the form of [var:_]), either can be valued/satisfied first, prior to the other, so it leads to the "Agree first/Move next" or "Move first/Agree next" options.

Hicks (2009) submits that binding relations require the sharing of φ-features between the antecedent and the dependent but they are not limited only to sharing these features.[3] Particular types of nominal phrases bear the following sets of features:

(6) a. name var: [+int, +val]
 b. pronoun var: [+int, +val]
 c. reflexive var: [+int, -val]

For Hicks, indexically dependent elements show the following structure:

(7) $[_{DP}\ [_{D[\varphi][var\_]}$ him] $[_{NP}$ self]]

Let me adopt this structure for English and take this syntactic object to be equivalent to the D-bound of Safir (2014) and the Index of Nikolaeva (2014). The feature [var:_] acts as a probe. It cannot find any matching goal in its c-domain and so it probes upwards within the immediate derivational phase, in line with Rezac (2004), Béjar and Rezac (2009), and Zeijlstra (2012):[4]

(8) Upward Agree: α can Agree with β iff:
 a. α carries at least one unvalued feature and β carries a matching valued feature;
 b. β c-commands α;
 c. β is the closest goal to α.

In the English example below upward Agree operates as follows:

(9) $[_{TP}$ John$_{[var:1]}$ $[_{vP}$ <John$_{[var:1]}$> likes $[_{VP}\ [_{DP}\ [_{D[\varphi][var:1]}$ him] $[_{NP}$ self]]]]]

The unvalued feature [var:_] serves as a probe, searches upwards for a matching goal with a valued [var:x] feature and finds it in the DP *John* in [spec,vP]. Thus a minimalist relation of Agree for [var:x] replaces index sharing of the GB vintage. I take the Polish reflexive pronoun and the reflexive possessive to have analogous representations:

(10) a. $[_{DP}\ [_{[\varphi][var\_]}\ D]\ [_{NP}$ siebie]]
self

b. $[_{NP}\ [_{DP}\ [_{[\varphi][var\_]}\ D]\ [_{NP}$ swój]]$[_{NP}$ dom]]
self's house

Let me point out that the D-bound/Index in Polish shares an important property with the clitic/weak pronoun: they both leave the VP and move into the functional domain of the clause. In Polish, domains for both A-binding and clitic/weak pronoun (hence CL/WP) distribution overlap (up to the application of the Tensed Sentence Condition, Chomsky (1981)):

(11) a. Jan$_1$ (**go**$_2$) kazał (**go**$_2$) Marii$_3$ [PRO$_3$ (**go**$_2$) pokazać (**go**$_2$) w lustrze ***go**$_2$] CL
Jan-NOM him-CL.ACC told Maria-DAT show-INF in mirror
'Jan told Maria to show him in the mirror.'

b. Jan$_1$ (**się**$_{1/2}$) kazał (**się**$_{1/2}$) Marii$_2$ [PRO$_2$ (**się**$_{1/2}$) obejrzeć **się**$_{1/2}$ w lustrze] SELF
Jan-NOM refl-CL.ACC told Maria-DAT watch-INF in mirror
'Jan told Maria to show him in the mirror.'

(12) Maria$_1$ • kazała • Piotrowi$_2$ [PRO$_2$ • pozdrowić • swoich$_{1,2}$ przyjaciół]. BIND
Maria-NOM told Piotr-DAT greet-INF self's friends
'Maria told Piotr to greet his/her friends.'

In (11a) the clitic/weak pronoun in Polish can occupy a variety of positions in the clause but the right-most one must be right-adjacent to the lexical verb, see Witkoś (1998). I take this position to be v. The clitic/weak pronoun cannot be lexicalised within VP, the lexical projection of the verb. It can climb out of the infinitive into the main clause; in the process, it typically occupies positions corresponding to v or T. Crucially for my parallel treatment of A-binding and clitic/weak pronoun distribution, the clitic form of the reflexive pronoun shows the same distribution pattern in example (11b). Example (12) shows that the same domain allows for long distance binding, where the reflexive can be bound either locally, by an object-controlled PRO, or non-locally, by the main clause subject. I propose that syntactic movement similar to that of the clitic/weak pronoun is relevant for A-binding (the D-bound/Index moves to the positions marked with bullets in (12)), thus the local domains for both phenomena overlap.[5] In terms of the engineering details, clitic/weak pronouns are impoverished in their sets of φ-features: only the [number] and [gender] features are both interpretable and valued in them but not the [person] feature, which is interpretable but unvalued (see Franks 2017 or Stegovec 2016 for an analysis of clitics/weak pronouns along these lines):

(13)	clitic/weak pronoun:	gender	[+int, + val]
		number	[+int, + val]
		person	[+int, - val]

For lack of value of the person feature the clitic/ weak pronoun cannot express its φ-features in situ and moves to a position of v (and T), where the valuation of the [person] feature takes place, in line with upward Agree and the following principle (Béjar and Rezac 2003: 53; Franks 2018):

(14) Person as Probe: an interpretable person feature must be licensed by entering into an Agree relation with a functional category.

These authors assume that the head v is equipped with the person [- int, + val] feature and some form of the [+EPP], either as an independent property or a sub-feature of the [person] feature, as in Pesetsky and Torrego (2001), to generate displacement. The clitic/weak pronoun moves to this head position to become φ-complete. Its further movement to T and onwards into a higher clause receives an account equivalent to clitic climbing.

I submit that the D-bound/index follows a similar derivational path but, unlike the clitic/weak pronoun, it carries no valued phi-features at all. Its φ-feature valuation "piggy-backs" on the valuation of the [var:_] feature; indexically dependent elements end up carrying φ-features of their antecedents, which produces the effect of antecedent-agreement highlighted by Safir (2014). The D-bound/ Index shows the following features in its VP-internal position:

(15)	D-bound/Index: φ-features:	gender	[+int, - val]
		number	[+int, - val]
		person	[+int, - val]

I assume that in constructions with the D-bound/Index, the relevant functional category from definition (14), namely v, carries an unvalued person feature

([-int,-val]) which is nevertheless equipped with the [+EPP] property.[6] Thus, crucially, it attracts the D-bound/Index just like it attracts clitics/weak pronouns. Analogously, the head $[_{[\varphi][var\_]}$ D] is able to move further to v/T within the domain determined by the Tensed S-Condition of Chomsky (1981) according to the scenario sketched out in Roberts (2009).[7]

So far the similarity between the $[_{[\varphi][var\_]}$ D] head and the clitic/weak pronoun was crucial: they share the deficiency in [person] feature licensing. Yet, there is one respect in which they are different from each other. Franks (2017) postulates that clitic/weak pronouns are deficient in three dimensions: the semantic one, the structural one, and the phonological one. This property distinguishes the $[_{[\varphi][var\_]}$ D] head from the clitic/weak pronoun. In example (12) below, the D head of $[_{DP}$ $[_{[\varphi][var\_]}$ D] $[_{NP}$ …]] moves from its thematic/case position to the head v (T) where its underspecified person feature is compensated for, but it is not phonologically impoverished the way clitics are. This is why its movement forms a chain in which the copy is pronounced (see the positions of *się* 'self' in example (11b) vs. *swój* 'self's' in example (12)).

Subsequent to valuation, the φ-features of $[_{[\varphi][var:1]}$ D] undergo deletion under identity with the φ-features of the NP as they are fully recoverable from them, as postulated in Reuland (2011).[8] The bottom of the chain of the D-bound/Index spells out as *siebie* 'self', a form morphologically devoid of any person, number, or gender distinctions in Polish.[9]

Considering the discussion thus far, the Lexicalisation Rule now reads as follows:

(16) The Lexicalisation Rule:

The (bottom copy in the chain of the) D-bound/index contributes to its lexicalisation as reflexive when (i) $[_{[\varphi][var\_]}$ D] is adjoined to v/T and (ii) the [var:_] feature of the $[_{[\varphi][var\_]}$ D] is involved in Agree with the [var:x] feature of the NP in [spec, vP/TP]. The antecedent must occupy its case position. Otherwise the D-bound/index is lexicalised as a pronoun.[10]

So the lexicalisation of the D-bound/Index as reflexive or pronominal depends on its relative positioning with respect to the antecedent.[11]

The key properties of the distribution of reflexives stem from the probing procedures in which two features of the $[_{[\varphi][var\_]}$ D] head are involved: the [var_] feature probing for a c-commanding goal (an NP/DP) with a valued [var:1/2, etc.] feature and the [-val person] features. The latter matches and is attracted by the [-val person] feature on a functional head of v/T. This Agree and feature sharing relation forces movement of the $[_{[\varphi][var\_]}$ D] head to v. While the valuation of the [var:_] feature is relevant for the LF-interpretation of the D-bound/index, the Agree and feature sharing of the [person] feature, the movement of the [$_{[\varphi]}$ $_{[var\_]}$ D] head to v/T (and its further clitic-climbing style movement) is relevant for the PF-interpretation. In principle, either feature can be accessed first in the derivation, with distinct consequences. Analogous cases with English reflexives are illustrated in Hicks (2009: 158):[12]

(17) a. John$_1$ wondered [which pictures of himself$_{1/2/3}$] Bill$_2$ claimed Paul$_3$ had bought.

b. John$_1$ wondered [$_{CP}$ [$_{DP}$ which pictures of himself$_{1/2/3}$] Bill$_2$ claimed [$_{CP}$ <[$_{DP}$ which pictures of himself$_{1/2/3}$]> Paul$_3$ had bought <[$_{DP}$ which pictures of himself$_{1/2/3}$]>

Hicks assumes that the ambiguity of binding in the English case of (17) stems from the interplay between the copy theory of movement and probing for the [var:_] feature on the part of the reflexive, shown in (17b). Following Belletti and Rizzi (1988) and Lebeaux (2009), he allows for a certain derivational lag in the valuation of this feature: so either [var:_] starts probing early in the derivation and probes from its original position receiving interpretation marked as [val:3] here, or it probes later, after the constituent including *himself*$_{[var\_:]}$ has been moved in the derivation to tend to the needs of the *wh*-feature. The latter tactics results in the interpretations marked as [var:2] or [var:3]. Thus the *wh*-feature drives movement, while the [var:_] feature drives the setting up of an indexical dependency and either feature can be satisfied first.

3. A-Binding within and across the DP/NP

An interesting empirical challenge appears in constructions with NP-internal reflexives. Here the similarity between clitic/weak pronoun placement in the verbal domain breaks down, as clitics/weak pronouns are not allowed to leave the nominal domain but a reflexive can be bound outside the NP in which it is embedded, see example (18b):[13]

(18)	a.	Wierni	obserwowali	[wyniesienie	go	na ołtarze].
		congregation	watched	raising	him-CL.ACC	onto altars

'The congregation watched his raising onto the altars.'

b.	*Wierni	go	obserwowali	[wyniesienie	~~go~~ na ołtarze].
	congregation	him-CL.ACC	watched	raising	~~him~~ onto altars

At the same time, Polish allows for phrasal movement out of the nominal phrase in the form of Left Branch Extraction (for details see, among others, Willim 1989; Tajsner 1990; Author 5; Przepiórkowski 1999; Bošković 2005, 2012, 2013, 2014; Pereltsvaig 2007; Cegłowski 2017; Author 6). Consider the following illustrative examples from Cegłowski (2017: 71):

(19)	a.	Czyje$_i$	znalazł [t$_i$	klucze]?
		whose	found-3.M.SG.PST	keys
		'Whose keys did he find?'		
	b.	Ciekawe$_i$	czytał [t$_i$	książki].
		interesting	read-3.M.SG.PST	books
		'He read interesting books.'		

I therefore need to concede that for an empirically tenable account of the escape from the nominal projection, a step of phrasal (XP) movement is required. Caution is necessary, as the successful account must predict that examples similar to (20) are correct but it cannot overgenerate by allowing the phrasal step of movement to cross a tensed CP phase boundary, as clitic/weak pronouns and reflexives abide by the Tensed Sentence Condition.

(20)	Jan$_1$	czytał	[książkę	Marii$_2$	o swoim$_{1,2}$	ojcu/o jej$_2$ ojcu/o jego$_1$ ojcu].
	Jan	read	book-ACC	Maria-GEN	about self's	father/about her father/about his father

'Jan read Maria's book about her father/his father.'

Jan can be coindexed with both a reflexive and a pronominal possessor and *Maria* can also be coindexed with the reflexive and the prononominal possessor:

(21)	a.	Jan$_1$	→	swoim$_1$/jego$_1$
	b.	Marii$_2$	→	swoim$_2$/jej$_2$

How does the derivation provided for by this system produce these options for LF- and PF-relevant interpretations? I have assumed throughout that the covert movement of the head [$_{[\varphi][\text{var:\_}]}$ D] is driven by Agree and [-val, person] feature sharing between a designated functional head v/T and Poss within the projection of the nominal. There is evidence that [$_{[\varphi][\text{var:1}]}$D] cannot be PF-interpreted in situ in complex NPs/DPs (just like in a ditransitive VP in example (2)). If it could, the reflexive form might be coindexed with a dependant of the nominal head which is not the Agent. Thus we could expect the example below to be acceptable with *swojego* 'self's' coindexed with *Tomek*$_{\text{DAT}}$. But this option is very marginal, at best:[14]

(22)	pokazanie	przez	Jana$_1$	Tomkowi$_2$	[swojego$_{1/*?2}$/jego$_{*?1/2}$	zdjęcia]
	showing	by	Jan$_1$-ACC	Tomek$_2$-DAT	[self's$_{1,*?2}$/his$_{*?1,2}$	picture]

'the showing of his picture to Tom by Jan'

I take the Agent-orientation of the reflexive to mean that within nominal projections the D-bound/Index must (covertly) move to a functional head and cannot be spelled out in situ, analogously to its VP-internal copy.

So one interpretive option (the one where the D-bound/Index is bound within the nominal phrase) arises when the [-val person] feature is placed on the head Poss in (23). In order to facilitate two PF forms of the D-bound/Index in example (20) I propose that the placement of the [-val, person] feature on Poss is optional. Should it be present on Poss, the head [$_{[\varphi][\text{var:1}]}$D] is raised to this position and remains here to trigger Spell-Out as a reflexive, in line with the Lexicalisation Rule in (16). I propose that the structure of the nominal includes the following representation with two functional projections, whose role becomes clear as we proceed:

(23) [$_{\text{FP}}$ … F [$_{\text{PossP}}$ …Poss [$_{\text{NP}}$ …N …]]]

(24) [$_{\text{vP}}$ Jan$_{[\text{var:1}]}$ read-v [$_{\text{VP}}$ V [$_{\text{FP}}$ book [$_{\text{F'}}$ F [$_{\text{PossP}}$ Maria$_{[\text{var:2}]}$-GEN [$_{\text{Poss'}}$ [$_{[\varphi][\text{var:2}]}$D]-Poss [$_{\text{NP}}$ [$_{\text{NP}}$ ~~book~~] [$_{\text{PP}}$ about [$_{[*\varphi][\text{var:2}]}$D] father]]]]]]]

(25) a. upward Agree: Maria$_{[\text{var:2}]}$-GEN > [$_{[\varphi][\text{var:2}]}$D]

b. Move [$_{[\varphi][\text{var:2}]}$D] to Poss driven by Agree for [-val, person] feature on Poss

c. Spell-out of the reflexive form, in line with (16); (*Maria*$_2$ vs. *swoim*$_2$ 'self's).

Another interpretive option is obtained when the D-bound/Index first has its [var:_] feature valued in situ via upward probing against *Maria* but next it moves as a maximal projection outside the nominal phrase. This is possible when the [-val, person] feature is absent from Poss.[15] Assuming that the intuition expressed in Bosković (2012, 2013, 2014) is correct and every maximal projection capping the nominal projection constitutes a derivational phase, movement through the edge of this nominal projection is mandatory. Then a process similar to the Indirect Feature-Driven Movement (IFM) of Chomsky (1995, 2000, 2001), takes place: the nominal phase head, marked F in (24–25), is equipped with an [+EPP] property which attracts the entire possessive DP ([$_{\text{DP}}$ [$_{[\varphi^*][\text{var\_}]}$ D] [$_{\text{NP}}$ …]]) to its edge. At this stage of the derivation, the projection of DP does not benefit from the movement but it opens up a possibility for valuation of its features outside the nominal phase within which it remains. From the phrasal position at the edge of the nominal phase the [$_{[\varphi][\text{var\_}]}$ D] head is free to search upwards for a goal for its [var:_] feature if one is still required, as well as move on as a head (copies are marked in grey):

(26) [$_{\text{NP}}$ [$_{\text{DP}}$ [$_{[\varphi^*][\text{var\_}]}$ D] [$_{\text{NP}}$ … (swoja/jego)]][$_{\text{NP}}$ książka]]
self's/his book

(27) [$_{\text{vP}}$ Jan$_{[\text{var:1}]}$ read-v [$_{\text{VP}}$ V [$_{\text{FP}}$ [$_{\text{DP}}$ [$_{[\varphi][\text{var:2}]}$ D] [$_{\text{NP}}$ …] [$_{\text{F'}}$ book [$_{\text{F'}}$ F [$_{\text{PossP}}$ Maria$_{[\text{var:2}]}$-GEN [$_{\text{Poss'}}$ Poss [$_{\text{NP}}$ [$_{\text{NP}}$ book] [$_{\text{PP}}$ about [$_{\text{NP}}$ [$_{\text{DP}}$ [$_{[*\varphi^*][\text{var:2}]}$ D] [$_{\text{NP}}$ …]] [$_{\text{NP}}$ father]]]]]]]

Subsequently the D-bound/Index moves up and adjoins to v, which bears the [-val person] feature by assumption. This leads to the lexicalisation of the D-bound/Index as a pronominal, in line with (16):[16]

(28) [$_{\text{vP}}$ Jan$_{[\text{var:1}]}$-NOM[$_{[\varphi][\text{var:2}]}$ D]-v [$_{\text{VP}}$ V [$_{\text{FP}}$ [$_{\text{DP}}$ [$_{[\varphi][\text{var:2}]}$ D] [$_{\text{NP}}$ …] [$_{\text{F'}}$ book [$_{\text{F'}}$ F [$_{\text{PossP}}$ Maria$_{[\text{var:2}]}$-GEN [$_{\text{Poss'}}$ Poss [$_{\text{NP}}$ [$_{\text{NP}}$ book] [$_{\text{PP}}$ about [$_{\text{NP}}$ [$_{\text{DP}}$ [$_{[\varphi^*][\text{var:2}]}$ D] [$_{\text{NP}}$ …]][$_{\text{NP}}$ father]]]]]]]

(29) a. upward Agree: Maria$_{[\text{var:2}]}$-GEN > [$_{[\varphi][\text{var:2}]}$ D];
b. Move the whole DP ([$_{\text{DP}}$ [$_{[\varphi][\text{var:2}]}$ D] [$_{\text{NP}}$ …]) to [spec, FP] as the edge of the nominal derivational phase, this is a covert analogue to Left Branch Extraction;

c. Move the head [$_{\text{[}\varphi\text{*][var:2]}}$ D] to v, to satisfy its [-val, person] feature;

d. Spell out the pronominal form, in line with (16); (*Maria*$_2$ vs. *jej*$_2$ 'her').

Another interpretive option to be accounted for is the one where the D-bound/Index has its [var:_] feature valued against *Jan*, the main clause subject, and spells out as a reflexive possessor. This derivation is very similar to the one in (28–29) above but for one difference, the [var:_] feature of the D-bound/Index does not participate in upward Agree before movement but rather after it has moved to the edge of the nominal phase:

(30) [$_{\text{vP}}$ Jan$_{\text{[var:1]}}$-NOM[$_{\text{[}\varphi\text{][var:1]}}$ D]-v [$_{\text{VP}}$ V [$_{\text{FP}}$ [$_{\text{DP}}$ [$_{\text{[}\varphi\text{*][var:\_]}}$ D] [$_{\text{NP}}$ …] [$_{\text{F'}}$ book [$_{\text{F'}}$ F [$_{\text{PossP}}$ Maria$_{\text{[var:2]}}$-GEN [$_{\text{Poss'}}$ Poss [$_{\text{NP}}$ [$_{\text{NP}}$ book] [$_{\text{PP}}$ about [$_{\text{NP}}$ [$_{\text{DP}}$ [$_{\text{[}\varphi\text{*][var:\_]}}$ D] [$_{\text{NP}}$ …]] [$_{\text{NP}}$ father]]]]]]]

(31) a. Move the whole DP ([$_{\text{DP}}$ [$_{\text{[}\varphi\text{*][var:\_]}}$ D] [$_{\text{NP}}$ …]) to [spec, FP] as the edge of the nominal derivational phase;

b. value the [var:_] feature of the D-bound/Index via upward Agree against the [var:1] feature of *Jan*; Jan$_{\text{[var:1]}}$-NOM > [$_{\text{[}\varphi\text{][var:1]}}$ D].

c. Move the head [$_{\text{[}\varphi\text{][var:1]}}$ D] to v, driven by its [-val, person] feature;

d. Spell-out the reflexive possessor, in line with (16); (*Jan*$_1$ vs. *swoim*$_1$ 'self's').

The final option to be considered is the most demanding one: the D-bound/Index has its [var:_] feature valued against *Jan* but it spells out as a pronominal possessor. Here, I need to fall back on the Principle of Minimal Compliance.[17] This derivation does not involve the presence of the [-val, person] feature on Poss but requires its presence on one head above it, that is, on F. The D-bound/Index moves as a head to F and thus places itself at the edge of the nominal derivational phase, which renders it accessible to relations with probes/goals in the vP phase (the head F belongs to the left edge of the FP phase). From this position the head [$_{\text{[}\varphi\text{*][var:\_]}}$ D] probes upward and reaches the [var:_] feature of *Jan*. In the context of the PMC, this relation is facilitated by a less complex and more local relation of Agree/valuation for case on FP and φ-features on v. Finally, the D-bound/Index spells out as a pronominal possessor, in line with (16):

(32) [$_{\text{vP}}$ Jan$_{\text{[var:1]}}$-NOM read-v [$_{\text{VP}}$ V [$_{\text{FP}}$ book [$_{\text{F'}}$ [$_{\text{[}\varphi\text{][var:1]}}$ D]-F [$_{\text{PossP}}$ Maria$_{\text{[var:2]}}$-GEN [$_{\text{Poss'}}$ Poss [$_{\text{NP}}$ [$_{\text{NP}}$ book] [$_{\text{PP}}$ about [$_{\text{NP}}$ [$_{\text{DP}}$ [$_{\text{[}\varphi\text{*][var:\_]}}$ D] [$_{\text{NP}}$ …]][$_{\text{NP}}$ father]]]]]]]

(33) a. Move the head $[_{[*\varphi][var:\_]}$ D] to head F as Agree for [-val, person] feature on F, this position is at the edge of the nominal derivational phase;

b. value the [var:_] feature of the D-bound/Index via upward Agree against the [var:1] feature of *Jan*; $Jan_{[var:1]}$-NOM > $[_{[\varphi][var:1]}$ D].

c. Spell-out the pronominal possessor, in line with (16); (*Jan*$_1$ vs. *jego*$_1$ 'his').

To sum up, the derivations above result from a conspiracy of conditions and circumstances, such as presence or lack of optional [-val, person] feature on the Poss/F heads, the order of upward Agree for the [var:_] feature vs. movement for the satisfaction of the [+EPP] property on the head F, and the Principle of Minimal Compliance.

Two further remarks are in order in the context of the derivational options mentioned above. First, the presence of the [-val, person] feature is optional on the heads Poss/F as long as they license nominal specifiers. Yet, apparently, this feature must be prohibited from appearing on Poss/F when no nominal specifiers are present in the nominal projection. Otherwise the possessors could be moved and adjoined to these projections and lead to the lexicalisation of pronominal possessors rather than the expected reflexive possessors:

(34)	Jan_1	czytał	książkę	o $sobie_1$/ ?nim_1/	o $swoim_1$ ojcu/	o ?$jego_1$	ojcu.
	Jan	read	book	about self/ him/	about self's father/	about his	father.

'Jan read a book about himself/his father.'

The correlation between lack of the [-val, person] feature on the heads Poss/F and lack of lexical nominal specifiers is easy to capture in the broader picture of nominal projections we are pursuing here. If the nominal projections can be of varying categorical status, depending on their size (NP, PossP, FP, QP, as proposed in Bošković 2012, 2013, 2014 and Despić 2013, 2015), lack of nominal specifiers implies that these nominal categories are only NPs:

(35) $[_{NP}$ $[_{NP}$ book$]$$[_{PP}$ about self$]]$

Let me assume that the structure of our example without any lexical specifier is (35). If so, this structure is too small to harbour nominal specifiers and there is no functional head to carry the [-val, person] feature, as we consistently claim that this feature is borne only by functional heads. Now, the pronominal versions of the possessor are (somewhat marginally) allowed in example (34) as well, but then the interpretation clearly involves an implicit, lexically unexpressed Agent, the author if the book. But if so, the internal structure of the nominal phrase is larger, it includes at least PossP, so the structural conditions for nominal-internal adjunction of the head [$_{[\varphi][\text{var:\_}]}$ D] are met:

(36) a. [$_{\text{PossP}}$ PRO [$_{\text{Poss'}}$ Poss [$_{\text{NP}}$ [$_{\text{NP}}$ book][$_{\text{PP}}$ about self]]
PRO book about self

b. [$_{\text{vP}}$ Jan$_{[\text{var:1}]}$-NOM read-v [$_{\text{VP}}$ V [$_{\text{PossP}}$ PRO$_{[\text{var:2}]}$ [$_{\text{Poss'}}$ [$_{[\varphi][\text{var:1}]}$ D] Poss [$_{\text{NP}}$ [$_{\text{NP}}$ book] [$_{\text{PP}}$ about [$_{\text{NP}}$ [$_{\text{DP}}$ [$_{[\varphi^*][\text{var:\_}]}$ D] [$_{\text{NP}}$ …]][$_{\text{NP}}$ father]]]]]]]

The specifier of the head to which it adjoins bears a different value for the [var:_] feature, assuming that the derivation runs along the lines analogous to (32–33) above and the PMC allows for a controlled violation of the MLC (the local case licensing relation between v and PossP allows for the nonlocal relation of upward Agree between [$_{[\varphi][\text{var:1}]}$ D] and *Jan* in [spec, vP], crossing over PRO in [spec, PossP]). The Lexicalisation Rule in (16) applies and returns a pronominal possessor.

Another question is how this system predicts that although the D-bound/Index can move out of the nominal projection, it cannot leave the clause, that is while the nominal phase boundary can be negotiated a finite CP boundary cannot. I submit that the movement resulting from Agree for [-val, person] feature is always as minimal as possible, so a (covert) head movement. Now, I consistently assume that within the extended projection of the verb in the finite clause either the head v or the head T must obligatorily carry the feature [-val, person]. So one of these heads must become involved in Agree with [$_{[\varphi][\text{var:1}]}$ D], share its [-val, person] feature and cause the (covert) movement of [$_{[\varphi][\text{var:1}]}$ D] to it (v/T). These are the positions where the head [$_{[\varphi][\text{var:1}]}$ D] is potentially lexicalised. Consider example (30) again:

(30) [$_{\text{vP}}$ Jan$_{[\text{var:1}]}$-NOM [$_{[\varphi][\text{var:1}]}$ D]-v [$_{\text{VP}}$ V [$_{\text{FP}}$ [$_{\text{DP}}$ [$_{[\varphi][\text{var:\_}]}$ D] [$_{\text{NP}}$ …] [$_{\text{F'}}$ book [$_{\text{F'}}$ F [$_{\text{PossP}}$ Maria$_{[\text{var:2}]}$-GEN [$_{\text{Poss'}}$ Poss [$_{\text{NP}}$ [$_{\text{NP}}$ book] [$_{\text{PP}}$ about [$_{\text{NP}}$ [$_{\text{DP}}$ [$_{[\varphi^*][\text{var:\_}]}$ D] [$_{\text{NP}}$ …]][$_{\text{NP}}$ father]]]]]]]

Once the movement of [$_{[\varphi][\text{var\_}]}$ D] to v/T takes place, the head [$_{[\varphi][\text{var:1}]}$ D] cannot re-project and resort to moving as a maximal projection. So the derivation allows for the PIC-compatible escape from the nominal phase and further head-movement from this DP constituent but it disallows a reverse process. This effectively means that the head [$_{[\varphi][\text{var:1}]}$ D] can leave only the nominal domain but never the finite clausal domain (CP): while the optional presence/absence of the [-val, person] feature on Poss/F within the nominal projection does not block phrasal DP movement to the edge, v or T must obligatorily carry the [-val, person] feature, which forces (covert) head movement of $[_{[\varphi][var:1]}$ D] and prohibits its movement to [spec,CP] as a maximal projection.[18]

4. Conclusions and Open Questions

It must be acknowledged that, as always, certain open questions remain. Let me mention at least two.

Marciniak (1999: 131) observes that Polish allows for binding relations with reflexives which are embedded quite deep in a sequence of NPs:

(37)	Jan_i	pokazał	$Piotrowi_j$	[dom	[córki	[brata [$swojego_{i/*j}$/ $jego_{*i/j}$ kolegi]]]]
	John	showed	Peter	house of	daughter of	brother self's/his colleague

'John showed Peter the house of a daughter of a brother of his colleague.'

Such examples are quite challenging to any theory involving movement, because the launch site is embedded deep in a number of NP projections. Here, a mitigating element concerns performance factors; native speakers I have consulted tend to disagree with Marciniak's original judgments given for example (37) in the sense that they also accept the pronominal possessor as able to be coindexed with the subject *Jan*. This indicates that the depth of embedding nullifies the effects of both Binding Condition A and Binding Condition B but still such an example is a considerable challenge to any account of A-binding.[19] I leave this problem for further study.

Zubkov (2018: 40–42) makes an interesting and novel observation concerning intervention effects in binding within more complex nominals in Russian. It is known that the nominative binder can reach a reflexive embedded inside a nominal phrase across a local antecedent in the genitive. So no intervention from the genitive antecedent is detectable here. But he observes that a very strong intervention effect arises when the more distant antecedent is not nominative but genitive as well. Here is a Polish equivalent of his example, which shows exactly the same strong intervention effect:[20]

(38) [opinia $Jana_1$ $[_{PP}$ o jej_2 stosunku do $siebie_{*1/2}$/$niego_1$/[$swojej_{*1/2}$/$jego_1$ siostry]]]

opinion-NOM Jan-GEN about her attitude to self/him-GEN/[self's/his sister]-GEN

'Jan's opinion about her attitude towards herself/him [her/his sister].'

Jana cannot be the antecedent for *siebie* 'self' or *swojej*'self's' but *jej* 'her' can, as it is close and more local with respect to the reflexives. Interestingly, when the complex NP becomes embedded in a structure with a prominent nominative-marked antecedent, it can access the embedded reflexive:

(39)	[oni$_3$ poznali	[opinię	Jana$_1$ [$_{PP}$	o jej$_2$ stosunku	do
	they got to know	opinion-ACC	Jan-GEN	about her attitude	to
	siebie$_{*1/2/3}$/niego$_1$/	ich$_3$/[	swojej$_{*1/2,3}$/	jego$_1$/	ich$_3$ siostry]]
	self/	him-GEN/	them[self's/	his/	their sister]-GEN

'They got to know Jan's opinion about her attitude towards herself/him/them/ [her/his/their sister].'

It seems that a dative Object Experiencer (DAT OE) can also function as the antecedent to the reflexive but this option is more marginal:

(40)	im$_3$	było	wstyd za [opinię	Jana$_1$ [$_{PP}$	o	jej$_2$ stosunku	do
	they-DAT	was	shame for opinion-ACC	Jan-GEN	about	her attitude	to
	siebie$_{*1/2,??3}$/	swojej$_{*1/2,?3}$	siostry]]				
	self/him-GEN/	[self's/his	sister]-GEN				

'They were ashamed with Jan's opinion about her attitude towards herself/ him/themselves [her/his/their sister].'

Thus relevant data from Polish confirm the "super-strong" nominative subject orientation of reflexives embedded deep in complex NPs. Zubkov captures this fact by claiming that the [+person, +number] probe (corresponding to T) overpowers the more local [+number] probe within the NP.[21]

A movement-inspired account like the one here needs to treat (38) as a challenge, as it is not immediately clear why the longer movement of the D-bound/ Index to T should be more feasible and successful than the more local movement to the next NP up. This issue deserves being taken up in future research but one possibility may be dismissed right away. If example (40) with a dative antecedent is acceptable, specifically with the reflexive possessive, then Zubkov's 'super-strong' effect of the [+person] probe does not explain the full set of facts either, because in his account this kind of probe should be coupled only with an antecedent in the nominative. Certainly, this aspect of the data set requires further study, including an extensive empirical analysis.

Notes

1 Safir (2014: 91–92) defines properties of D-bound in the following way:

(i) Always a variable: D-bound is the same object in SEM (the syntactic input to semantic interpretation) in all cases; it is interpreted as a bound variable regardless of its φ-features.

(ii) Always A-bound: the binder of D-bound (its antecedent) must c-command it from an A-position; that is, the D-bound form is A-bound.

(iii) Always feature compatible: D-bound must be feature compatible with its antecedent (informally, this property may be termed antecedent agreement).

(iv) Spell-Out of the morphological shape of D-bound is potentially sensitive to whether A-binding is phase internal.

(v) Agreement compatible with morphological shape may be determined by phase internal factors locally distinct from antecedent agreement.

(vi) Anywhere phase-internal shape is not required, D-bound receives default pronominal shape.

This view of Spell-out is related to the competition-based approaches of Burzio (1991) and Safir (2004).

2 There is a split between psychological predicates with dative object experiencers licensing another argument in the genitive (usually these are non-verbal predicates) and ones licensing an argument in the nominative (typically verbal predicates). The typical verbal psychological predicate *podobać się* 'appeal to, like' shows that the possessive pronoun in the nominative argument is strongly preferred to the possessive reflexive, when bound as in (i). Yet, Witkoś (2008) shows that a preverbal dative experiencer can bind a reflexive bearing case different from nominative, although embedded in the nominative-marked constituent, as in (ii):

(i)	Marii$_1$	spodobała się	?*swoja$_1$/jej$_1$	nowa	sukienka.	
	Maria-DAT	liked SE	?*self's/her	new	dress-NOM	
	'Maria liked her new dress.'					
(ii)	[Nowakom$_2$]	spodobała		się [nowa	książka (Kowalskich$_1$)	o sobie$_{1,2}$]
	Nowaks-DAT	liked		SE new	book-NOM (Kowalskis')	about self
	'The Nowaks liked the new book (by the Kowalskis) about themselves/them.'					

Witkoś et al. (2020) credits the difference between (i) and (ii) to Rizzi's (1990a) Anaphor Agreement Effect.

3 "What is at stake in anaphor binding is referential dependency, not simply a φ-feature dependency",(Hicks 2009: 112).

4 Zeijlstra's original definition uses the term uninterpretable, rather than unvalued, as he basically follows Chomsky (2000, 2001, 2008), where uninterpretable features are unvalued. This distinction is irrelevant to the discussion in the paper.

5 The analogy between index raising and clitic movement is forcefully argued in Chomsky (1986) and Hestvik (1992).

6 Pesetsky and Torrego (2007) allow for Agree (and movement relations) involving probes/goals sharing unvalued features which later obtain a value at a further stage of the derivation.

7 Roberts (2009) devises an account of successive-cyclic head movement and excorporation, compatible with both the Empty category Principle and Minimal Link Condition. I believe that Polish clitic/weak pronoun movement follows such trajectory.

8 As deletion operations apply at the end of each cycle determined by phase-based Spell-Out (Chomsky 1995, 2000, 2001, 2008), we take φ-feature deletion on $[_{D[\varphi][var\_]}$ 0] to apply after the clitic climbing operations it participates in.

9 A similar idea of an element raising (to the edge of the vP Phase) and having its copy pronounced as reflexive is applied in an analysis of binding in German in Safir (2004) and in Lee-Schoenfeld (2008: 291).

10 I keep the distinction between co-argument reflexivisation and non-co-argument reflexivisation, Nikolaeva's (1d).

11 This account predicts that the difference between languages where the object can function as an antecedent to a reflexive pronoun and ones showing subject orientation depends on whether or not the reflexive element can remain in situ to express its φ-features. This is possible in English but not in Polish. See Franks (this volume) for a comparison between binding in English and Bulgarian based on different modes of movement.

12 Franks (this volume) shows that English is very special in the sense that it disrespects the Tensed Sentence Condition in this case and allows for the binding of the anaphor in the intermediate position within the wh-chain; Slavic languages do not allow for this option despite allowing for long-distance binding into infinitive clauses.
13 As observed by a reviewer the internal structure of (18) must include a deverbal noun with some VP structure plus a functional domain, probably clause-like, that blocks clitic climbing.
14 In terms of Nikolaeva's claim for Russian, the *by*-phrase *przez Jana* in example (22) should count as/be equivalent to a specifier. I leave the issue of the internal structure of this example for further research, but see Rozwadowska (1995) and Cetnarowska (2005) for relevant proposals.
15 A reviewer for this volume points out that a similar effect for Condition A satisfaction can be obtained if any c-commanding DP/NP were taken far a potential antecedent; then the movement of the D-bound/Index would be superfluous. Yet, in the account I am outlining, binding is taken to result from Agree for the [var:_] feature, which should ideally be unambiguous and subject to minimality constraints. Movement of the D-bound/Index (or a constituent containing it, as in the English example (17)) helps to create such unambiguous configurations. Plus this movement is necessary to satisfy the Lexicalization Rule (16).
16 This representation does not involve the necessary step of escape movement of PP and remnantmovement of NP *książka* 'book' prior to its raising to [spec, FP].
17 Richards (1998) argues for the Principle of Minimal Compliance, whose central claim is that an initial legitimate local relation involving a particular head (probe) in domain D 'pays the derivational tax' and opens the way to a less local relation which would otherwise violate a constraint on minimality or locality in the same domain D.
18 I leave for further research the question of why the finite CP domain as well as the nominal domain in our account do not allow for PIC-compatible head movement outside.
19 I am grateful to a reviewer of this volume for pointing out to me the unsuitability of both Binding Conditions A and B in this construction.
20 Zubkov's Russian example looks as follows, Zubkov (2018:41):

(i) mnenie Vani$_i$ o ee$_j$ otnošenii
opinion Vania-GEN about her attitude-LOC
k sebe$_{*i,j,*k}$/nemu$_{i,k}$/[svoej$_{*i,j,*k}$/ego$_{i,k}$ sestre].
to self/him-DAT/[self's/his sister]-DAT
'Vanya's opinion about her attitude towards herself/him [her/his sister].'

21 The idea that the [+person] probe can act across the [+number] probe (but not vice versa) is reminiscent of the key idea in Progovac (1992, 1993) based on the concept of Relativised Minimality in Rizzi (1990a). Russian has reflexives which can be either XP or X° reflexives. As such they are sensitive to both XP antecedents (nominal specifiers) and X° antecedents T(AGR). Minimality effects do not apply across the types, so an XP-antecedent does not interfere with an X° reflexive. In effect, the nominative subject can always bind into the complex DP, across a closer nominal specifier. Although attractive, this account cannot deal with examples such as (4b), where the dative experiencer acts as antecedent for either a reflexive or pronominal possessive. The nominative antecedent, agreeing with T(AGR), functions as antecedent only for reflexive possessives.

Bibliography

Avrutin, Sergey. 1994. The structural position of bound variables in Russian. *Linguistic Inquiry* 25.709–27.

Béjar, Susana, and Milan Rezac. 2003. Person licensing and the derivation of PCC effects. *Romance Linguistics: Theory and Acquisition*, ed. by Ana T. Perez-Leroux and Yves Roberge, 49–62. Amsterdam: John Benjamins.

Béjar, Susana, and Milan Rezac. 2009. Cyclic agree. *Linguistic Inquiry* 40. 35–73.

Belletti, Adriana, and Luigi Rizzi. 1988. Psych-verbs and theta theory. *Natural Language and Linguistic Theory* 6.291–352.

Bošković, Željko. 2005. On the locality of left branch extraction and the structure of NP. *Studia Linguistica* 59.1–45.

Bošković, Željko. 2012. Phases in NPs and DPs. *Phases: Developing the Framework*, ed. by Ángel J. Gallego, 343–83. Berlin: Mouton de Gruyer.

Bošković, Željko. 2013. Phases beyond clauses. *The Nominal Structure in Slavic and Beyond*, ed. by Lilia Schürcks, Anastasia Giannakidou and Urtzi Etxeberria, 75–128. Berlin: De Gruyter Mouton.

Bruening, Benjamin. 2014. Precede-and command revisited. *Language* 90.342–88.

Burzio, Luigi. 1991. The morphological basis of anaphora. *Journal of Linguistics* 27.81–105.

Cegłowski, Piotr. 2017. *The Internal Structure of Nominal Expressions: Reflections on Extractability, Fronting and Phasehood.* Poznań: Wydawnictwo Naukowe UAM.

Cetnarowska, Bożena. 2005, *Passive Nominals in English and Polish: An Optimality-Theoretic Analysis.* Katowice: Wydawnictwo Uniwersytetu Śląskiego.

Chomsky, Noam. 1981. *Lectures on Government and Binding.* Dordrecht: Foris.

Chomsky, Noam. 1986. *Knowledge of Language: Its Nature, Origin and Use.* New York: Praeger.

Chomsky, Noam. 1995. *The Minimalist Program.* Cambridge, MA: The MIT Press.

Chomsky, Noam. 2000. Minimalist inquiries: The framework. *Step by Step. Essays on Minimalist Syntax in Honor of Howard Lasnik,* ed. by Roger Martin, David Michaels and Juan Uriagereka, 89–155. Cambridge, MA: MIT Press.

Chomsky, Noam. 2001. Beyond explanatory adequacy. MIT occasional papers in linguistics 20. [Published 2004 in Belletti, A. (ed.), *Structures and Beyond – The Cartography of Syntactic Structure.* Vol. 3, 104–31. Oxford: Oxford University Press.]

Chomsky, Noam. 2008. On phases. *Foundational Issues in Linguistic Theory,* ed. by Robert Freidin, Caroline Otero and Maria-Luiza Zubizarreta, 133–66. Cambridge, MA: MIT Press.

Despić, Miloje, 2013, Binding and the structure of NP in Serbo-Croatian. *Linguistic Inquiry* 44.239–70.

Despić, Miloje. 2015. Phases, reflexives and definiteness. *Syntax* 18.201–34.

Franks, Steven. 2017. *Syntax and Spell-Out in Slavic.* Bloomington, IN: Slavica Publishers.

Franks, Steven. 2018. PCC Violations and Their Resolutions. *Formal Approaches to Slavic Linguistics: The Urbana-Champaign Meeting,* ed. by Tania Ionin and Jonathan MacDonald, 93–111. Ann Arbor, MI: Michigan Slavic Publications.

Franks, Steven. (This volume). Reflexive Typology, Movement, and the Structure of NP.

Hestvik, Arild. 1992. LF movement of pronouns and anti-subject orientation. *Linguistic Inquiry* 23.557–94.

Hicks, Glyn. 2008. Why the binding theory doesn't apply at LF. *Syntax* 11.255–80.

Hicks, Glyn. 2009. *The Derivation of Anaphoric Relations.* Amsterdam: John Benjamins.

Lebeaux, David. 2009. *Where Does Binding Theory Apply?* Cambridge, MA: MIT Press.

Lee-Schoenfeld, Vera. 2008. Binding, phases and locality. *Syntax* 11.281–98.

Manzini, Rita, and Kenneth Wexler. 1987. Parameters, binding theory and learnability. *Linguistic Inquiry* 18.413–44.

Marciniak, Małgorzata. 1999. Towards a binding theory for Polish. *Slavic in Head-Driven Phrase Structure Grammar*, ed. by Robert Borsley and Adam Przepiórkowski, 125–48. Stanford, CA: Center for the Study of Language and Information, Leland Stanford Junior University.

Nikolaeva, Ludmila. 2014. The secret life of pronouns. Doctoral dissertation, MIT, Cambridge, MA.

Pereltsvaig, Asya. 2007. The universality of DP: A view from Russian. *Studia Linguistica* 61.59–94.

Pesetsky, David, and Esther Torrego. 2007. The syntax of valuation and the interpretability of features. *Phrasal and clausal architecture: Syntactic derivation and interpretation. In honour of Joseph Emonds*, ed. by Simin Karimi, Vida Samiian and Wendy K. Wilkins, 262–94. Amsterdam and Philadelphia: John Benjamins.

Progovac, Ljiljana. 1992. Long-distance reflexives without movement. *Linguistic Inquiry* 23.671–80.

Progovac, Ljiljana. 1993. Long-distance reflexives: Movement to INFL versus Relativized SUBJECT. *Linguistic Inquiry* 24.755–72.

Przepiórkowski, Adam. 1999. Case assignment and the complement/adjunct dichotomy. A non-configurational constraint-based approach. Doctoral dissertation, University of Tuebingen.

Rappaport, Gilbert. 1986. On anaphor binding in Russian. *Natural Language and Linguistic Theory* 4.97–120.

Reinders-Machowska, Ewa. 1991. Binding in Polish. *Long-distance Anaphora*, ed. by Jan Koster and Eric Reuland, 137–50. Cambridge: Cambridge University Press.

Reuland, Eric. 2011. *Anaphora and Language Design*. Cambridge, MA: MIT Press.

Rezac, Milan. 2004. Elements of cyclic syntax: Agree and Merge. Doctoral dissertation: University of Toronto.

Richards, Norvin. 1998. The principle of minimal compliance. *Linguistic Inquiry* 29.599–629.

Roberts, Ian. 2009. *Agreement and head movement*. Cambridge, MA: MIT Press.

Rozwadowska, Bożena. 1995. Configurational hypothesis and Polish NPs. *Papers and Studies in Contrastive Linguistics* 30.131–44.

Safir, Ken. 2004. *The syntax of anaphora*. Oxford: Oxford University Press.

Safir, Ken. 2014. One true anaphor. *Linguistic Inquiry* 45.91–124.

Stegovec, Adrian. 2016. *A person case constraint without case*. University of Connecticut, ms.

Tajsner, Przemysław. 1990. Case marking in English and Polish: A government and binding study. Adam Mickiewicz University, Poznań, Doctoral dissertation.

Willim, Ewa. 1989. *On word-order: A government-binding study of English and Polish*. Kraków: Wydawnictwo Uniwersytetu Jagiellońskiego.

Witkoś, Jacek. 1998. *The syntax of clitics. Steps towards a minimalist account*. Poznań: Motivex.

Witkoś, Jacek. 2008. On the correlation between A-type scrambling and Weak Crossover Effects. *Studia Anglica Posnaniensia* 44. 297–328.

Witkoś, Jacek, and Paulina Łęska. 2020. Dative antecedents for reflexives and pronouns. *Acta Linguistica Academica,* DOI: ALING-2020.00014.

Witkoś, Jacek; Paulina Łęska; Aleksandra Gogłoza; and Dominika Dziubała-Szrejbrowska. 2020. *Bind me tender bind me do! Dative and accusative arguments as antecedents for reflexives in Polish*. Frankfurt am Main: Peter Lang.

Zeijlstra, Hedde. 2012. *There is only one way to Agree*. Utrecht: University of Utrecht, ms.

Zubkov, Petr. 2018. The grammar of binding. A study with reference to Russian. University of Utrecht, Doctoral dissertation.

Ilse Zimmermann†

On Pronouns Relating to Clauses

Abstract The present contribution deals with Russian anaphoric and cataphoric, interrogative and relative pronouns relating to root and embedded clauses. The analysis takes into account the semantic flexibility and vagueness of constructions with these pronouns. It includes parameters in their grammatically determined Semantic Form, which are specified on the level of Conceptual Structure depending on the context and knowledge of the interlocutors. It will be shown why embedded clauses in many cases function as modifiers and where they are complements. Within the presupposed minimalist framework, lexical entries of the anaphor *èto*, of the cataphoric pronoun *to* and its zero-correspondent, and of the interrogative and relative pronoun *čto* play a basic role in the correlation of their phonological, morphosyntactic, and semantic properties. In addition to their structural capacities, semantic type shifts are at work in relating the pronouns and their clausal dependents.*

Keywords: Pronouns Relating to Clauses, Embedded Clauses, Complements versus Modifiers, Zero Constituents, Type Shifts, Lexical Entries for Determiners and Complementizers

1. Introduction

1.1. The Issue

In a language like Russian, without definite and nonspecific indefinite articles, it will be clarified which morphosyntactic and semantic status the pronouns *to*, *èto*, and *čto* have relating to clauses, whether they are multifunctional, and what the nature of their relation to clauses is. It is discussed what it means to supply embedded clauses with nominal character and to give them the status of modifiers, at least in many cases.

Examples (1–5) illustrate occurrences of the pronouns in typical functions. *To* is shown as a cataphoric correlate introducing an embedded clause. In (3) and (4), it is placed together with its clausal dependent at the left periphery. In (4), it

---

* This study is dedicated to Peter Kosta. I hope he will enjoy the present contribution. I have profited from talks and discussions in the syntax and semantics seminars of Leibniz-ZAS in Berlin, in the Slavic colloquium of Humboldt-University Berlin, and in the semantics-syntax colloquium at Potsdam University. I am grateful to Kerstin Morrison for assistance with English.

needs the help of *èto* as a resumptive pronoun in order to realize the prepositional governing by the matrix verb of its object. In (1), *èto* functions as an anaphoric pronoun, relating to the preceding clause. The pronoun *čto* shows its multifunctional character as a relative pronoun in (2) and as an interrogative pronoun in (5B). In all these examples except for (5A), the matrix-verb *somnevat'sja* 'doubt' embeds its object with a governed preposition. In (5A) it is invisible, together with the dependent DP. The embedded clause by itself cannot be put into a question. The silent embedding PP comes to light in the echo question (5B).[1]

(1)	Zemlja	kruglaja.	V	**ètom**	nikto	ne	somnevaetsja.
	earth	round	in	this	nobody	not	doubts

'The Earth is round. About this nobody is in doubt.'

(2) Zemlja kruglaja, v **čëm** nikto ne somnevaetsja.

(3) V **tom**, čto Zemlja kruglaja, nikto ne somnevaetsja.

(4) (To,) čto Zemlja kruglaja, *(v **ètom**) nikto ne somnevaetsja.

(5) A: Nikto ne somnevaetsja, čto Zemlja kruglaja.

B:	V	**ČËM**	nikto	ne	somnevaetsja?
	in	WHAT	nobody	not	doubts

'About WHAT is nobody in doubt?'

The combinatory capacities of *somnevat'sja* 'doubt' also allow for an embedded yes–no question like *zemlja li krugla* 'whether the Earth is round' or for a nonsentential object like *ego dostovernost'* 'his credibility'. Thus, we must take into account several types of possible complements of a predicate expression. The following question arises: What are the morphosyntactic features and the semantic types of the pronouns under consideration when they relate to root or embedded clauses as in (1–5)? Evidently, the clauses are of different types. Nevertheless, the pronouns do combine with them and seem to be multifunctional.[2]

1.2. Theoretical Assumptions

My considerations are built on a conception of minimalism (Chomsky 1995) and on the central role of the lexicon as the interface of different levels (Zimmermann 1987). As to the interpretation of linguistic utterances, I distinguish between grammatically determined Semantic Form (SF) and Conceptual Structure (CS) (Bierwisch and Lang (eds.) 1987, 1989, Bierwisch 2007, Lang and Maienborn 2011, Dölling 1997). Unbound variables are parameters which are specified or appropriately bound in CS. In the semantic amalgamation of constituents, semantic type shifts apply where necessary (Partee 1987). They do not have any morphosyntactic reflex. In contrast, zero-formatives occur where they can be legitimized for paradigmatic reasons (Zimmermann 1990, 2018b). As regards morphology, I adhere to an approach according to which the lexicon brings in fully derived and inflected word forms (Wunderlich 1997, 2012).

2. The Analysis

2.1. Semantics

Semantic representations consist of operators, constants, and variables. Semantic types can be reduced to <e> for individuals, <t> for propositions, <s> for worlds, and <a> for illocutionary acts, plus combinations thereof.[3] Sortal differentiations will be expressed by predicates like HUMAN, PROCESS, TIME, DEGREE, etc.

2.2 Syntax

For syntactic representations of clauses and DPs, I assume the following hierarchical domains:

(6) (ForceP) (PP) CP (GivenP*) MoodP TenseP AspP PolP (vP*) VP

(7) $([_{DP})\alpha\ [_{DP}\ [_{D'}D\ (NP)](CP)]\ (YP])\alpha$

ForceP is absent in embedded clauses. Many adverbial clauses are PPs. CPs are complements or relative clauses and characterize the various sentence types (Brandt et al. 1992). GivenP marks possible positions for given XPs and clitics. MoodP, TP, and AspP serve to specify the reference of finite clauses to worlds and time. PolP is where the decision between affirmation and negation takes place (Pollock 1989). DPs can be reduced to their functional head D. Complements of D are predicate expressions. Adjuncts of DP and CP are appositions.

The pronoun *to* in its role as functional head D and as introducer of embedded clauses deserves special mention (Knjazev 2016, Zimmermann 1967, 1983, 1993, 2016a, 2016b, 2018a, 2018b, 2021).[4] These clauses are governed by the pertinent matrix predicate as to their c– and s–selectional properties. Therefore, they are placed in SpecD, from where they can easily be extraposed.

2.3. Lexicon

Lexical entries correlate three types of structural information (Jackendoff and Audring 2019): (i) the phonological form of the item, (ii) the morphosyntactic categorization, and (iii) the grammatically determined SF. (8–10) show the entries for the pronouns *to*, *èto*, and *čto*.[5]

(8) a. /{to, ∅}/

b. $+D_{(i)}\beta$ +def βgiven –I –II –pl –fem –masc γR –P –U

c. $(\lambda P_1)(\lambda Q)\lambda P_2. [P_2 (\iota x ([)\beta[[P_1 (x)] (\wedge [Q (x)])] (\wedge [(x) = g(i)]])\beta)]$

$Q, P_1, P_2 \in \{<et>, <\alpha t>\}$[6]

The pronoun *to* 'that' and its zero partner are generalized quantifiers with three predicates. P_1 is the restrictor and P_2 the nuclear scope. In addition, the predicate Q is introduced as a possible modifier of P_1. The proposition $[(x) = g(i)]$ is present if the functional head D has the reference index i. This is the case when the external argument of the DP is given. If Q in the modifier proposition [Q (x)] is specified by an embedded clause, then *to* functions as correlate. The restrictor can be realized by an NP or be left unspecified. In this case, one has to do with a parameter which is interpreted on the level of CS.

The morphosyntactic features in (8b) characterize the pronoun *to* as a definite, possibly given formative in the third person singular neuter nominative or accusative.[7]

(9) a. /èto/

b. $+D_i$ +def +given –I –II –pl –fem –masc γR –P –U

c. $(\lambda P_1)(\lambda Q)\lambda P_2. [P_2 (\iota x [[[P_1 (x)] (\wedge [Q (x)])] \wedge [x = g(i)]]])]$

$Q, P_1, P_2 \in \{<et>, <\alpha t>\}$

The pronoun *èto* 'this' differs from *to* in not having a zero partner and in referring to a given entity.[8]

(10) a. /ʃto/

b. +D +wh αrel −I −II −pl −fem −masc γR −P −U

c. $\lambda P_2. [[Q (x)] \wedge [P_2 (x)]]$

$Q, P_2 \in \{<\beta t>\}$

The pronoun *čto* 'what' belongs to the wh-words, which are characterized by the parameter Q (Zimmermann 2020). The pronoun can be used with the features +wh +rel as a relative pronoun or with the features +wh −rel as an interrogative pronoun. Both items are semantically interpreted in situ as generalized quantifiers. The complementizer of their clause attracts them in PF to SpecC by its features +E(dge)F(eature), +wh, αrel. Semantically, the MoodP of the pertinent clause undergoes lambda abstraction in order to combine with the semantics of the complementizer. This is represented in (12) and (13). In (11), the unmarked complementizer *čto* 'that', which is homophonous with the pronoun *čto*, is provided for comparison.[9]

(11) a. /ʃto/

b. +C

c. $\lambda p. [p]$

This complementizer takes a proposition as its argument and preserves its status, in contrast to zero complementizers.

(12) a. /Ø/

b. +C +wh +rel +EF

c. $\lambda P \lambda x. [P (x)]$

This complementizer s-selects a predicate and results in a predicate, a possible candidate for a modifier. In order to be an appropriate argument for this C, the SF of MoodP undergoes lambda abstraction. The same is true with respect to the following empty C.

(13) a. /Ø/

b. +C +wh −rel +EF

c. $\lambda P \lambda y. [(y) \in \lambda x. [P (x)]]$

Wh-questions are composed of a background predicate λx, [P (x)], and an open position y to be specified by an appropriate answer, the focus (Krifka 2001a, Zimmermann 2009). This treatment of relative and interrogative pronouns and their semantic partners in C allows for a uniform analysis of apparently homophonous wh-elements (Zimmermann 2000, 2020). Their semantic differentiations take place via C-representants.

So far, the three pronouns to be examined here are characterized as representants of DPs, which are governed by predicate expressions.

3. On Multifunctionality

Now we must draw attention to the problems of what types of clausal arguments take matrix predicates, how the pronouns considered here fulfill the selectional requirements of the matrix predicates, and of what nature the related clauses are. Although the focus of the present paper is on coreference of pronouns with clauses, I will try to delimit reference to clauses and reference to eventualities. In many cases, pronouns and matrix predicates are multifunctional in this respect.

In connection with these questions, it is useful to look at some components of sentences. According to my view, what is called THE PROPOSITIONAL CONTENT of a sentence is represented by CP, whose SF is often identical with the meaning of MoodP. In MoodP, the referential eventuality argument of verbs is bound and related to the world of a modal subject (Zimmermann 2015). Very often, the meaning of CP is referred to by a pronoun, such as *èto* 'this' in (1), the relative pronoun *čto* in (2), or the interrogative pronoun *čto* in the echo question in (5B). And when a yes-no question is involved, as in (14), *èto* also refers to the CP where the interrogative meaning is represented.

(14)	A:	Zemlja	li	kruglaja?	B:	Èto	mne	tože	ne	jasno.
		earth	PART	round		this	me.DAT	ALSO	not	clear
		'Is the Earth round?'				'This is for me also not clear.'				

This means that the pronouns in these examples do not refer to the meaning of the ForceP but only to the content of CP, which can be of type <t> or, as in 14, of type <tt<t>>.[10]

In examples with nominalizations like (15a), the type of the object phrase is <e>, while in (15b) the non-nominalized variant is of type <t>. This multifunctionality is characteristic of the matrix verb and the object variants fulfill its selectional requirements in either case.

(15) a. A:

Nikto	ne	somnevaetsja	v	dostovernosti	Petra.
nobody	not	doubts	in	reliability	Peter.GEN

'Nobody is in doubt about Peter's reliability.'

B:

V	**ČËM**	nikto	ne	somnevaetsja?
in	WHAT	nobody	not	doubts

'About WHAT is nobody in doubt?'

b. A:

Nikto	ne	somnevaetsja	(v tom),	čto	Pëtr	dostoveren.
nobody	not	doubts	in that	that	Peter	reliable

'Nobody is in doubt (about it) that Peter is reliable'

B:

V	**ČËM**	nikto	ne	somnevaetsja?
in	WHAT	nobody	not	doubts

'About WHAT is nobody in doubt?'

There is a fundamental difference between reference to an eventuality e of type <e> as in (15a) and to a clausal entity of type <t> as in (15b), where mood, tense, and aspect are expressed. Furthermore, example (15b) raises the question of the interrelation between the correlate *to* and the dependent embedded clause, which by itself is of type <t>. The question is also to be answered with respect to the examples in (3) and (4).

Many researchers assume that there are no complemen clauses. Instead, these are considered to be relative clauses (Krtzer 2006, 2014, Moulton 2014, 2015, 2017, Bogal-Allbritten and Moulton 2019, Caponigro and Polinsky 2011, Arsenijević 2009, 2021). My analyses choose a more flexible approach (Zimmermann 2016a, 2016b, 2018a, 2018b, 2019a, 2019b, 2021). There are constructions with matrix predicates which select prepositional complements or complements with so-called lexical cases. Under these circumstances, the embedding of a clause must proceed via a PP or a DP. But this is not the case with matrix predicates governing structural cases. Here, the embedding of a clause is possible without the help of a PP or DP. In contrast to *somnevat'sja* 'doubt', *ubedit'(sja)* 'convince (oneself)', *osvedomit'(sja)* 'inquire', *zaviset'* 'depend', *soglasit'sja* 'agree', *dovol'stvovat 'sja* 'content', *radovat'sja* 'enjoy', *želat'* 'wish', *trebovat'* 'demand', *prosit'* 'beg', and so forth, the verbs *predpolagat'* 'presume', *dumat'* 'think', *znat'* 'know', *zabyt'* 'forget', *vspomnit'* 'remember', and *sprosit'* 'ask' can embed clausal complements directly. The same is true for the pronouns examined here.[11]

If there is a mediating PP or DP it introduces the clause as a modifier, Q in (8) and (9). But the clause by itself is not an appropriate modifier. For this function it must be adapted to a predicate. This can be done in two ways, the simplest of which is by a type shift, TS_{PM1}, that preserves the type of the clause and delivers a predicate by identifying the clause with another one. The other way is connected with so-called content nouns like *fakt* 'fact', *obstojatel'stvo* 'circumstance', *sovet* 'advice', *trebovanie* 'demand', *somnenie* 'doubt', *utverždenie* 'assertion', *lož'* 'lie', etc. in the NP position of (8) and (9). Here, the type shift TS_{PM2} applied to the embedded clause serves as predicate maker for an argument of type <e> (Zimmermann 2019a, 2019b).

(16) TS_{PM1}: $\lambda q \lambda p\ [p =_{<t<tt>>} q]$

(17) TS_{PM2}: $\lambda p \lambda x.\ [CONSIST\_IN_{<\alpha_{<et>>}}\ p\ x]$

After the application of these predicate makers to an embedded clause, the result is a modifier that can function as a dependant of the correlate. (18) illustrates the SF of example (3) with the correlate *to*.[12]

(18) ||V tom, čto Zemlja kruglaja, nikto ne somnevaetsja.|| =
DECL ∃e [[IN ($w_{sp)}$ (e)] ∧ ¬∃x [[HUMAN (x)] ∧ [(e) INST [BE_IN_DOUBT_ABOUT
(ι**p** [[P_1 p] ∧ [p = ∃e'[[IN w_x e'] ∧ [e' INST [ROUND ιy [y = EARTH]]]]]])
(x)]]]]

While in (18) the object NP is not realized and P_1 in the SF is represented as a parameter, example (19) shows the correlate *to* together with an NP and the dependent embedded clause to which TS_{PM2} is applied.

(19) ||Studenty učityvajut to obstojatel'stvo, čto professor ploxo slyšit.||[13] =
DECL ∃e [[IN ($w_{sp)}$ (e)] ∧ ∃!z [[STUDENTS (z)] [(e) INST [TAKE_INTO_ACCOUNT (ι**x**
[[CIRCUMSTANCE (x)] ∧ [CONSIST_IN (∃e' [[IN (w_{sp}) (e')] ∧ [(e) INST
[HARD_OF_HEARING (ιy [PROFESSOR (y)])]]]])]]) (x)]] (z)]]

Here, the type shift in (17) delivers a predicate of type <et>, which allows for the conjunct [Q (x)] in (8) to function as a modifying proposition to

[CIRCUMSTANCE$_{\langle et\rangle}$ (x)]. Constructions like (19) have been analyzed by Fabricius-Hansen and von Stechow (1989), without the adaptation (17) proposed here. This amounts to saying that the nouns are considered as being of type <tt>, taking a propositional argument without the mediation of a template. Although I regard this as a matter of discussion, it seems to me that we are dealing here with abstract objects of type <e>.

One specific component in the SF of clauses and their nominalizations deserves attention, the constant INST(ance) (Bierwisch and Lang (eds.) 1987, 1989). This relates propositions of type <t> to eventualities of type <e> and in this way makes propositions capable of referring to times and worlds. Only verbs and certain deverbal and deadjectival nouns have this component. Without it, propositions like [HOUSE (x)] or [READ (y) (x)] describe objects. The orientation to eventualities of different types leads to states of affairs as a special object.[14] It assembles other objects with their properties and in their relations, and we can refer to this special object by combining it with various modifiers or by treating it as a complement. Only if this entity is related to time and worlds do we have finite clauses of type <t> or <αt>. Matrix predicates like *proizojti* 'occur', *slučit'sja* 'occur', *dlit'sja* 'last', *zakončit'* 'finish', or *prodolžat'(sja)* 'continue' have eventualities as arguments, whereas *kazat'sja* 'seem', *dumat'* 'think', and *utverdit'* 'assert' take propositions, and predicates like *nabljudat'* 'observe' or *videt'* 'see' allow for eventualities or propositions.

Some interesting examples are given in (20–22), which differ in the relation of the anaphoric pronoun *èto* to its antecedent.

(20)	Včera	stolknulis'	dva	avtobusa.	Naš	sosed	èto	videl.
	yesterday	collided	two	busses	our	neighbor	this	saw

'Yesterday two busses collided. Our neighbor saw it.'

Neither the first clause in (20) nor the anaphoric pronoun in the second one gives a hint about whether *èto* refers to the proposition ‖CP‖ in the first clause or to the incident. The linguistic substitution of *èto* would be as in (21) and (22).

(21) Naš sosed videl, čto včera stolknulis' dva avtobusa.

(22) Naš sosed videl, kak včera stolknulis' dva avtobusa.

In the interpretation in (21), the speaker has in mind the expressed proposition which he presents as being true in his world. By contrast, in the interpretation in (22), he concentrates on the eventuality by using the wh-formative *kak* 'how' pointing to properties of the event. In this case, the clause substituted for *èto* in CS would have the representation in (23) (Zimmermann 2020).

(23) λz. ∃e'[[IN (w_u) (e')] ∧ ∃x [[TWO_BUSSES (x)] ∧ [[(e') INST [COLLIDE (x)]] ∧ [[Q (z) ∧ [R (z) (e')]]]]]

With a silent determiner, the argument z will be bound and the result can serve as an appropriate complement of the matrix predicate *videt′* 'see' of type <e>. The parameter Q leaves room for inserting PROCESS or INCIDENT and R can be substantiated as IN. But at the level of SF, the grammatically determined meaning of the anaphor *èto* is underdetermined: both interpretations as in (21) and (22) are possible. I do not assume any substitution for pronouns at the level of SF. (23) is based on the TS_{MOD} (24) (Zimmermann 1992), which unifies the SF of PolP with the meaning of the formative *kak*, λzλe'. [[Q (z)] ∧ [R (z) (e')]]. In contrast to adverbs like *gde* 'where' or *kogda* 'when', *kak* is anonymous as regards its adverbial type. The parameter Q can be specified in various ways, as we will see also below. In any case, the formative *kak* is integrated into its clause as a modifier, Q_2, as in (24). The modifiee Q_1 is the SF of PolP with the referential argument e'.

(24) TS_{MOD}: $\lambda Q_2 \lambda Q_1 \lambda x. [[Q_1\ x] \wedge [Q_2\ x]]$

Below, adverbial clauses will be inspected. The constructions contain the pronouns we are dealing with in connection with adverbial prepositions or with adverbial cases.

(25)

Tem,	čto	Anna	reguljarno	zanimaetsja	sportom,
that.INSTR	that	Anna	regularly	occupies	sports
ona	ulučšaet	svoë	zdorov′e.		
she	improves	her	health		

'By regularly doing sports Anna improves her health.'

In (25), the adverbial instrumental of the cataphoric pronoun *to*, together with its dependent clause, expresses the means by which Anna improves her health. This meaning is brought about by a silent preposition, as in (26), which governs the dependent DP and the clause embedded in SpecD.

(26) a. /Ø/

b. −V −N +adv

c. $\lambda z_{<-_{R+P}-_{U>}} \lambda e.\ [R_{<e<et>>}\ (z)\ (e)]$

The internal argument z of (26) is required to be in the instrumental case, which has the marked feature +P(eriphery). Together with the pronoun *to* in the instrumental and the type shift (17), applied to the embedded clause, the following configuration will result:[15]

(27) $\|Ø \text{ tem } TS_{PM2}\ CP\| =$

$\lambda e.\ \exists! z\ [[[P_1\ (z)] \wedge [CONSIST\_IN\ (\|CP\|)\ (z)]] \wedge [R\ (z)\ (e)]]$

The proposition [R (z) (e)] is the adverb maker (Zimmermann 2020). The parameters P_1 and R can be specified in CS by MEANS and BY, respectively. And the whole representation in (27) is an adverbial modifier to be combined with the matrix clause by predicate unification in (24).

Now let us try to analyze example (28) with an appositive relative clause semantically relating to the clause to which it is adjoined at the level of CP, like the one in (2).[16]

(28) Anna reguljarno zanimaetsja sportom, čem ona ulučšaet svoë zdorov′e.

The relative clause is introduced by the relative pronoun *čto* in the adverbial instrumental case and can be translated as 'by (means of) which she improves her health'. It does not seem wrong to have the SF in (29) for the relative clause.

(29) $\lambda p.\ \exists e'\ [[IN\ (w_{sp})\ (e')] \wedge [[(e')\ INST\ [IMPROVE\ (\iota y\ [HEALTH\ (x_i)\ (y)])\ (x_i)]]$
$\wedge\ \exists! z$

$[[P_1\ (z)] \wedge [CONSIST\_IN\ (p)\ (z)]] \wedge [R\ (z)\ (e')]]] \in <tt>$

This predicate combines with the main clause at its level of CP, where it is of the appropriate type <t> and can be amalgamated with its appositive modifier. But it is evident that (29) contains more semantic components than have been introduced by corresponding formatives so far. The meaning of the silent adverbial preposition in (26) is enriched here with additional parts, i.e., with the SF of the correlate and the type shift in (17):

(26') a. /Ø/

b. −V −N +adv

c. $\lambda z_{<-R+P\ -U>} \lambda e.\ [R_{<e<et>>} (z)\ (e)]\ (\lambda p \lambda P_2.\ \exists! z'\ [[[P_1\ (z')] \wedge [CONSIST\_IN\ (p)\ (z')]] \wedge [P_2\ z']]) \equiv$
$\lambda p \lambda e.\ \exists! z'\ [[[P_1\ (z')] \wedge [CONSIST\_IN\ (p)\ (z')]] \wedge [R\ (z')\ (e)]]$

This representation is amalgamated by the TS_{MOD} in (24) with the SF of PolP and results in ModP as in (29).

If the two involved clauses are not combined into one speech act under ForceP as in (28), but rather represent two autonomous declarative speech acts as in (30), then the adverbial anaphoric phrase *ètim* 'by (means of) this' will be treated in an analogous way.

(30) Anna reguljarno zanimaetsja sportom. Ètim ona ulučšaet svoë zdorov′e.

According to (9), the anaphoric pronoun *èto* is a generalized quantifier coindexed with its antecedent with the SF $\lambda P_2.\ \exists! x\ [[[P_1\ (x)] \wedge [(x) = g(i)]] \wedge [P_2\ (x)]]$. The coreferent XP_i is a CP of type <t> of the preceding sentence. Thus, the adverbial phrase *ètim* in the second sentence of (30) will get the SF $\lambda e'.\ \exists! x\ [[[P_1\ (x)] \wedge [(x) = g(i)]] \wedge \exists! z'\ [[[P_1\ (z)] \wedge [CONSIST\_IN\ (x)\ (z)]] \wedge [R\ (z)\ (e')]]]$, with $x \in$<t>. This modifier is unified by the type shift in (24) with the SF of PolP, and their common external argument e is existentially bound in ModP.

To summarize so far, adverbial pronouns relating to clauses are combined with a zero preposition which is enriched by semantic components allowing for the embedding of clauses or, in parallel, for the use of pronouns relating to clauses. Predicates like MEANS, GOAL, and so forth are possible specifications of the parameter P_1, and Q and can be combined with the component CONSIST_IN, which allows for a clausal internal argument (see (17)).

Let us discuss further adverbial examples.

(31)	a.	Mal′čik	včera	otsutstvoval,	po	tomu	čto	mat′
		boy	yesterday	was.absent	PREP	that.DAT	that	mother
		zabolela.						
		fell.ill						
		'The boy was absent yesterday because his mother fell ill.'						
	b.	Mal′čik	včera	otsutstvoval	po	toj	pričine,	čto
		boy	yesterday	was.absent	PREP	that	reason.DAT	that

mat′	zabolela.
mother	fell.ill

'The boy was absent yesterday for the reason that his mother fell ill.'

In both variants, the preposition *po* governing the dative introduces the causal adverbial. In (31a), the dependent DP consists of the correlate and an embedded clause in SpecD. In (31b), the correlate is accompanied by an NP in the governed dative, *pričine* 'reason', explicating the adverbial type. Here, the causal PP is freely construed. In (31a), the causal connector *po tomu čto* 'because' comes from the lexicon, where it has the following representation (Zimmermann 2019b):

(32) a. $[_{PP}\,[_{P}\,/\mathrm{po}/_{1}][_{DP}\,[_{D'}[_{D}\,/\mathrm{tomu}/_{2}]][_{CP}\,[_{C}\,/\int\!\mathrm{to}/_{3}]/\_\_\mathrm{ModP}]]]]$

b. $-V\ -N\ +adv_{1};\ +D\ +def\ \beta given\ -I\ -II\ -pl\ -fem\ -masc\ +R\ +P\ -U_{2};\ +C_{3}$

c. $\lambda z \lambda e'.\ [R\,(z)\,(e')]_{1};\ \lambda P_{1} \lambda Q \lambda P_{2}.\ [P_{2}\,(\iota x\,[[P_{1}\,(x)] \wedge [Q\,(x))]]]_{2}\,(CAUSA_{<et>})_{2};$
$\lambda p \lambda x.$

$[CONSIST\_IN_{<}\alpha_{<et>>}\ p\ x]\ (\lambda p.[p]_{3})$

This proposal to represent phrases in the lexicon and to correlate corresponding lexical information by coindexing follows suggestions made by Jackendoff and Audring (2020). The entry in (32) illustrates that the preposition *po* is semantically underdetermined. Therefore, the causal specification comes from the predicate CAUSA introduced here as specification of the variable P_1 of the correlate *to*. Furthermore, it can be seen that the semantic interpretation of the entry involves the type shift in (17) in order to coerce the dependent clause. In the same way, adverbial connectors like *s tem čtoby* 'in order to' with the predicate GOAL will be represented in the lexicon. For semantically transparent cases like (31b) and (33), this is not necessary.

(33)	Posle	togo	kak	Pëtr	vyzdorovel,	on	poexal	na	more.
	after	that	how	Peter	recovered	he	went	to	sea

'After Peter had recovered he went to the sea.'

In contrast to the uninformative prepositions *po* in the causal connective *po tomu čto*, or in the causal adverbials *po ètomu* 'therefore' or *po čemu* 'why', the temporal preposition *posle* 'after' as in (33) refers to time spans of eventualities. The dependent clause is introduced by the multifunctional formative *kak* 'how'. In Russian temporal clauses, it prepares them for functioning as a modifier. Here, it can be looked upon as an adverb maker (Grønn and von Stechow 2013a, 2013b, Zimmermann 2018a, 2020). (34) shows the semantic composition of (33).

(34) ‖Posle togo kak Pëtr vyzdorovel, on poexal na more.‖ =

DECL ∃e [[IN w_u e] ∧ [[e INST [DRIVE_TO THE SEA x_i]] ∧ ∃!z [[P_1 z] ∧ ∃e' [[IN w_u e'] ∧

[[e' INST [RECOVER $peter_i$]] ∧ [R z e']]] ∧ [e > z]]]] ≡

‖$Ø_{Force}$‖ (‖$Ø_C$‖ (‖$Ø_{Mod}$‖ (TS_{MOD} (TS_{ASA} (‖posle‖ (‖togo‖ (‖$Ø_{C +rel +EP}$‖ (‖$Ø_{Mod}$‖ (TS_{MOD} (‖$Ø_{POL}$‖ (‖kak‖) (‖Pëtr vyzdorovel‖)))))))) (‖on poexal na more‖))))

The temporal relation between the root and the embedded clause, [e > z], is introduced by the preposition *posle*. It takes the cataphoric pronoun *to* with the embedded clause as internal argument. The pronoun binds the argument z and delivers the parameter P_1, which can be left unspecified in the given context in view of a meaning postulate connected with the meaning of the preposition *posle* specifying z as a time span of an eventuality. The second parameter in (34) is R, introduced by the formative *kak*. It is attracted to the left *edge* of the embedded clause by its empty complementizer with the morphosyntactic features +wh and +EF. Semantically, the formative *kak* contributes the component [R z e'] in situ with the help of TS_{MOD} in (24). Its arguments e' and z get bound by Mood and *to*, respectively. The parameter R in the SF of *kak* can be specified by the relator IN. (35) demonstrates these steps for the adverbial clause.

(35) ‖ $[_{P'}$ posle $[_{DP}$ $[_{D'}$ $[_D$ togo]]$[_{CP}$ kak …]]] ‖ =

λe. ∃!z [[[P_1 z] ∧ ∃e' [[IN w_u e'] … ∧ [R z e']]] ∧ [e > z]] ≡

TS_{ASA} (‖posle‖ (‖togo‖ (TS_{LA} (… ‖kak‖))))

It deserves mention that in the adverbial clauses in (25), (31), and (34), the cataphoric pronoun *to* binds entities of type <e> and leaves them anonymous at the level of SF. The parameter P_1 gets substantiated at the level of CS. Second, it is important to observe at which level of syntactic structure the respective embedded clauses are combined with the matrix clause. Appositives as in (28) are adjoined to CP, causal and final clauses to MoodP, where the eventuality argument e of the matrix clause is bound, and temporal adverbials to TP, where e is still unbound.

But why does it seem that adverbial prepositions combined with the anaphoric pronoun *èto* or with the interrogative pronoun *čto* refer to propositions, not to objects? What does it mean when Letuchiy (2011, 2019a, 2019b) relates the anaphor *èto* to situations? Example (36) demonstrates the problem: Is *èto* coreferent with the preceding proposition of type <t> or with the eventuality described by the proposition?

(36)	Pëtr	vyzdorovel.	Posle	ètogo	on	poexal	na	more.
	Peter	recover.PF.PRET	after	this	he	go.PF.PRET	to	sea

'Peter recovered. Afterwards he went to the sea.'

Since the preposition *posle* does not embed propositions, the anaphoric pronoun *èto* is related to the eventuality e' described in the preceding clause. The temporal adverbial *posle ètogo* has the following SF:

(37) ||posle ètogo|| =

$$\lambda e.\ \exists ! e'\ [[[[P_1\ (e')] \wedge [Q\ (e')]] \wedge [e' = g(i)]] \wedge [e > e']]$$

This modifier combines with the SF of TP by predicate unification, i.e., by TS_{MOD} in (24). It contains two parameters brought in by *èto* (see (9)), which can be specified in CS on the basis of the context, that is, for P_1 to become a predicate relating to time, $\lambda e'.\ \exists ! z\ [[TIME\ (z)] \wedge [R\ (z)\ (e')]]$. TIME, in contrast to CAUSA and GOAL, is not a content noun which could be related to a proposition by the TS_{PM2}. This is a decisive difference.

As complements of predicates of saying and thinking, the reference of the pronouns studied here to propositions is in many cases unequivocal.

(38)	A:	Vse	znajut	(èto),	čto	klimat	izmenjaetsja.
		all	know	this	that	climate	change.IPF.PRES

'All know (it) that the climate is changing.'

B: ČTO vse znajut?

(39) Klimat izmenjaetsja, čto vse znajut.

In (38) and (39), the pronouns refer to the proposition that the climate is changing. And in questions as in (40) and (41), the pronouns also refer to this type of clause, not to situations.

(40)	A:	Kak	bistro	izmenjaetsja	klimat,	(èto)	my	točno	ne	znaem.
		how	quick	change.IPF.PRES	climate	this	we	exactly	not	know

'How quickly the climate is changing, (this) we do not know exactly.'

	B:	ČTO	my	točno	ne	znaem?

'WHAT do we not know exactly?'

(41)	Odin	učenik	osvedomilsja	(o tom),	kto	otkryl
	a	pupil	inquire.PF.PRET	about that	who	discover.PF.PRT
	(èto),	čto	Zemlja	kruglaja.		
	this	that	Earth	round		

'A pupil inquired (about it) who discovered (it) that the Earth is round.'

The verb *osvedomit'sja* 'inquire' embeds a clausal argument of type <αt> and the verb *otkryt'* 'discover' of type <t>. The mediation by the correlate *to* preserves these types by applying the type shift in (16) to the clause. In both cases, the pronoun refers to the embedded clauses, not to situations.

On the other hand, predicates like *byvat'* 'used to occur' and *slučit'sja* 'occur' have eventualities as their argument. And pronouns like the anaphor *èto* in (42) or the cataphor *to* in (43) refer to an eventuality, despite the presence of a proposition.

(42)	Zdes'	včera	stolknulis'	dva	avtobusa.	Èto	zdes'	ne
	here	yesterday	collide.PRET	two	busses	this	here	not
	slučilos'	v	pervyj	raz.				
	occur.PRET	in	first	time				

'Yesterday two busses collided here. This is not the first time this has occurred here.'

(43)	To,	čto	zdes′	včera	stolknulis′	dva	avtobusa,	ne
	that	that	here	yesterday	collid.PRET	two	busses	not
	slučilos′	v	pervyj	raz.				
	occur.PRET	in	first	time				

'That two busses collided here yesterday did not occur for the first time.'

That the pronouns in these examples refer to the eventuality described in the accompanying proposition is predetermined by the verb *slučit′sja* 'occur' and by the multifunctionality of the pronouns (see (8) and (9)). Here, the restrictor of these pronominal determiners P_1, its modifier Q, and the nuclear scope predicate P_2 all are of type <et>. For the involved clauses – the embedded CP in (43) and the CP to which the anaphor *èto* in (42) is related – this means that they are understood as predicates to an event, an incident, a fact, or a state of affairs consisting in the content of the proposition.

4. Summary

This study argues for multifunctional determiners in Russian. Three pronominal representants of determiners – *to, èto,* and *čto* in its function as relative and interrogative pronoun – have been characterized with respect to their morphosyntactic and semantic properties. They are differentiated as cataphoric and anaphoric items, respectively, and are shown to relate to clauses of various types as well as to eventualities. Like the entities to which they relate, they fulfill the selectional requirements of the respective predicates.

As far as root clauses are involved, the pronouns refer to their CP domain, not to the ForceP. Argument clauses are CPs by themselves, to which the pronouns can relate. When these clauses are embedded by the cataphoric pronoun *to* or *èto,* then the clause must be adapted to a modifier. This is done by two type shifts functioning as predicate makers. One of them, $\lambda q \lambda p\ [p =_{<t<tt>>} q]$, is conservative in preserving the semantic type of the clause, <t> or <αt>. The other, $\lambda p \lambda x.$ $[\text{CONSIST\_IN}_{<t<et>>}\ (p)\ (x)]$, changes the type of the clause to <et> in delivering an appropriate modifier of content nouns. In both cases, the cataphoric pronouns introduce the clause they relate to as modifiers. In a sense, they bring in a definite binder, an external head with its modifier, and the nuclear scope.

As to the nuclear scope, various types of predicates have been inspected with respect to their affinity to propositional and/or e-type arguments. With regard to the pronouns analyzed here, coreference with clauses was contrasted to coreference with eventualities. It turned out that the pronouns are flexible as regards to this contrast and thereby can satisfy the selectional requirements of various types of matrix predicates, as do their respective coreferents.

A general theoretical issue is the role of parameters in the SF of pronouns. Here, the two levels of semantic interpretation, Semantic Form and Conceptual Structure, come into play. Parameters, that is unbound variables, in SF give room for explication depending on context and on the respective knowledge and convictions of the interlocutors. Thus, pronouns with open variables partially mirror the flexibility and vagueness of natural languages in their sound–meaning correlation.

Last but not least, precise semantic typing and morphosyntactic categorization of all involved components proved to be a welcome precondition for insights, fruitful discussion, and progress.

Notes

1 On the specific conditions of usage for echo questions, see Beck and Reis (2018).

2 The most far-reaching multifunctional pronoun I found is Spanish *lo* (see Fernández López 2020). In Zimmermann (2016a), it is shown that the pronoun *es* 'it' and its suppletive forms can refer to entities of various semantic types.

3 On the semantics of ForceP, see Krifka (2001, 2020).

4 Cf. also Pütz (1986), Sudhoff (2003, 2016), Schwabe (2013), Schwabe, Frey and Meinunger (2016), Mollica (2010), and Willer-Gold (2013). On correlates and clause integration in the history of German see Axel (2009).

5 Greek letters represent variables over values of features and can be correlated to indices of brackets where they are variables for the presence vs. absence of the expression within the brackets.

6 The type <αt> in 8–10 takes into account the different types of embedded *čto(by)*-clauses and interrogative clauses. Infinitival constructions will be neglected.

7 According to Jakobson (1936, 1958), the Russian cases are differentiated by the features R(ichtung)/napravlenie 'direction', U(mfang)/ob″ëm 'extent', P(eripherie)/periferija 'periphery'.

8 Letuchiy (2011, 2019a, b) gives a comprehensive analysis of the structural properties of *èto*. As for the semantics of pronouns, see Padučeva (1985).

9 The complementizer *čtoby* is the result of clitic movement of the subjunctive particle *by* from Mood to C (Zimmermann 2015).

10 Yes-no questions denote predicates of validity and have the SF in (i) (Zimmermann 2009).

(i) $\lambda p \lambda y. [y \in \lambda G. [G(p)]]$
$y, G \in$ <tt>

11 For various restrictions, see Letuchiy (2019a)
12 I omit here the representation of tense and aspect.
13 Example (19) is glossed and translated as follows:

(i) Studenty učityvajut to obstojatel'stvo, čto professor ploxo slyšit.
students account that circumstance that professor badly hears
'The students take into account the fact that the professor is hard of hearing.'
Observe throughout the paper that the generalized quantifiers in (ii) are equivalent.

(ii) $\lambda P_1 \lambda P_2. \exists! x [[P_1(x)] \wedge [P_2(x)]] \equiv \lambda P_1 \lambda P_2. [P_2(\iota x [P_1(x)])]$

14 On different sorts of eventualities, see Dölling (2014).
15 In (27), the Semantic Forms of the silent preposition and of its DP complement are combined with the help of the template in (i), which is an adaptation of the argument structure of a predicate in order to integrate a generalized quantifier of type <et<t>>.

(i) $TS_{ASA}: \lambda \wp_{<et<t>>} \lambda x_{n-1} \ldots \lambda \in x_1. [\wp \lambda x_n. [\ldots x_n \ldots x_1 \ldots]]$

16 In the text of Willer-Gold's 2013 dissertation on Croatian, I found many continuative appositives like ***što*** *umogućuje da …*,'which makes possible that … ', *na* ***što*** *ukazuje …* 'to which points …', ***što*** *je u skladu s …*'which is in harmony with …', ***što*** *znači da …*'which means that … ', *iz* ***čega*** *izlazi …*' from which follows … ', *zbog* ***čega*** … 'because of which …', *nakon* ***čega*** … ' after which … ', and so forth.

Bibliography

Arsenijević, Boban. 2009. Clausal complementation as relativization. *Lingua* 119, 39–50.

Arsenijević, Boban. 2021. Situation relatives: Deriving causation, concession, counterfactuality, condition and purpose. *Advances in Formal Slavic Linguistics 2018*. Online: https://langsci-press.org/catalog/book/280.

Axel, Katrin. 2009. Die Entstehung des *dass*-Satzes – ein neues Szenario. *Linguistische Berichte*, Sonderheft 16, 21–41.

Beck, Sigrid, and Marga Reis. 2018. On the form and interpretation of echo wh-questions. *Journal of Semantics* 35.3, 369–408.

Bierwisch, Manfred, and Ewald Lang (eds.). 1987. *Grammatische und konzeptuelle Aspekte von Dimensionsadjektiven*. Berlin: Akademie-Verlag.

Bierwisch, Manfred, and Ewald Lang (eds.). 1989. *Dimensional Adjectives: Grammatical Structure and Conceptual Interpretation*. Berlin: Springer-Verlag.

Bierwisch, Manfred. 2007. Semantic Form as interface. *Interfaces and Interface Conditions* (Language, Context, and Cognition 6), ed. by Andreas Späth, 1–32. Berlin, New York: de Gruyter.

Bogal-Allbritten, Elizabeth, and Keir Moulton. 2019. Nominalized clauses and reference to propositional content. *Proceedings of Sinn und Bedeutung* 21, ed. by Robert Trusswell, Chris Cummins, Caroline Heycock, Brian Rabert, and Hannah Rode. Edinburgh: University of Edinburgh.

Brandt, Margareta; Marga Reis; Inger Rosengren; and Ilse Zimmermann.1992. Satztyp, Satzmodus und Illokution. *Satz und Illokution* (Linguistische Arbeiten 278), Band 1, ed. by Inger Rosengren 1992/1993, 1–90. Tübingen: Niemeyer.

Caponigro, Ivano, and Maria Polinsky. 2011. Relative embeddings: a Circassian puzzle for the syntax/semantics interface. *Natural Language and Linguistic Theory* 29, 71–122.

Chomsky, Noam. 1995. *The Minimalist Program*. Cambridge, MA: MIT Press.

Dölling, Johannes. 1997. Semantic form and abductive fixation of parameters. *From Underspecification to Interpretation. Working Papers of the Institute of Logic and Linguistics*, ed. by Rob van der Sandt, Reinhard Blutner, and Manfred Bierwisch, 113–39. Heidelberg.

Dölling, Johannes. 2014. Aspectual coercion and eventuality structure. *Aspects, Phases, and Arguments: Topics in the Semantics of Verbs* (Studies in Language Companion Series 152), ed. by Klaus Robering, 189–226. Amsterdam: Benjamins.

Fabricius-Hansen, Cathrine, and Arnim von Stechow. 1989. Explikative und implikative Nominalerweiterungen im Deutschen. *Zeitschrift für Sprachwissenschaft* 8.2, 173–205.

Fernández López, Justo. 2020. Die verschiedenen Funktionen des Artikels lo. Online: www.hispanoteca.eu/Gramáticas/Gramatika im PDF accessed: 15.11.2018

Grønn, Atle, and Arnim von Stechow. 2013a. Tense in adjuncts. Part I: Relative clauses. *Language and Linguistics Compass* 7.5, 295–310.

Grønn, Atle, and Arnim von Stechow. 2013b. Tense in adjuncts. Part II: Temporal adverbial clauses. *Language and Linguistics Compass* 7.5, 311–27.

JACKENDOFF, RAY, and JENNY AUDRING. 2019. *The Texture of the Lexicon: Relational Morphology and the Parallel Architecture.* Oxford: Oxford University Press.

JACKENDOFF, RAY, and JENNY AUDRING. 2020. Relational Morphology: A cousin of Construction Grammar. Frontiers in Psychology 11. Online: https://doi.org/10.3389/fpsyg.2020.02241.

JAKOBSON, ROMAN. 1936. Beiträge zur allgemeinen Kasuslehre. Gesamtbedeutungen der russischen Kasus. *TLCP* VI, 240–88.

JAKOBSON, ROMAN. 1958. Morfologičeskie nabljudenija nad slavjanskim skloneniem (Sostav russkix padežnyx form). *American Contributions to the Fourth International Congress of Slavicists* (Moscow), 127–56. 's-Gravenhage: Mouton.

KNJAZEV, MIKHAIL. 2016. Licensing clausal complements. The case of Russian *čto*-clauses. University of Utrecht. Published by LOT, Utrecht, PhD dissertation.

KRATZER, ANGELIKA. 2006. Decomposing Attitude Verbs, The Hebrew University of Jerusalem. Honoring Anita Mittwoch on her 80th birthday. Online: https://works.bepress.com/angelika_kratzer/15/.

KRATZER, ANGELIKA. 2014. Semantics of Embedding and the Syntax of the Left Periphery. Plenary speaker, Annual Meeting of the Linguistics Association of Great Britain 2014. Ouline: http://www.lagb.org.uk/lagb2014/semantics.

KRIFKA, MANFRED. 2001a. Quantifying into question acts. *Natural Language.*

KRIFKA, MANFRED. 2001b. For a structured meaning account of questions and answers. *Audiatur vox sapientiae. A Festschrift for Arnim von Stechow,* ed. by Caroline Féry and Wolfgang Sternefeld, 287–319. Berlin: Akademie Verlag.

KRIFKA, MANFRED. 2020. Layers of assertive clauses: Propositions, judgements, commitments, acts. *Propositionale Argumente im Sprachvergleich: Theorie und Empirie* (Studien zur deutschen Sprache), ed. by Jutta M. Hartmann and Angelika Wöllstein. Tübingen: Narr, to appear.

LANG, EWALD, and CLAUDIA MAIENBORN. 2011. Two-level semantics: Semantic form and conceptual structure. *Semantics*, ed. by Claudia Maienborn, Klaus von Heusinger, and Paul Portner, 709–40. Berlin: de Gruyter.

LETUCHIY, ALEXANDER B. 2011. Pronominalizacija sentencial'nogo aktanta v russkom jazyke. Kompjuternaja lingvistika i intellektual'nye texnologii. Moskva: RSUH.

LETUCHIY, ALEXANDER B. 2019a. Mestoimenie *èto* kak pokazatel' anafory k situacii: semantika i sočetaemost'. *Sbornik statej k 85-letiju V. S. Xrakovskogo,* ed. by Dmitrij V. Gerasimov, Natalja M. Zaika, and Sergej Ju. Dmitrenko, 237–79. Moskva: Jazyki slavjanskoj kul'tury.

LETUCHIY, ALEXANDER B. 2019b. Pronominalization of argument clauses in Russian. Manuscript. Moscow.

Mollica, Fabio. 2010. *Korrelate im Deutschen und Italienischen* (Deutsche Sprachwissenschaft international 9). Frankfurt am Main: Peter Lang.

Moulton, Keir. 2014. Simple event nominalizations. Roots and their interpretation. *Cross-Linguistic Investigations of Nominalization Patterns*, ed. by Ileana Paul, 119–44. Amsterdam: Benjamins.

Moulton, Keir. 2015. CPs: Copies and compositionality. *Linguistic Inquiry* 46.2, 305–42.

Moulton, Keir. 2017. Nouny propositions. Handout. Selection Fest, Berlin, ZAS.

Padučeva, Elena. V. 1985. *Vyskazyvanie i eë sootnesënnost' s dejstvitel'-nost'ju; referencial'nye aspekty semantiki mestoimenij.* Moskva: Nauka.

Partee, Barbara. 1987. Noun phrase interpretation and type-shifting principles. *Studies in Discourse Representation Theory and the Theory of Generalized Quantifiers*, ed. by Jeroen Groenendijk, Dick de Jongh, and Martin Stokhof, 115–43. Dordrecht: Foris.

Pollock, Jean_Yves. 1989. Verb movement. Universal Grammar and the structure of IP. *Linguistic Inquiry* 20.3, 365–424.

Pütz. Herbert. 1986. *Über die Syntax der Pronominalform* ***es*** *im modernen Deutsch.* 2., durchgesehene Auflage (Studien zur deutschen Grammatik 3). Tübingen: Gunter Narr.

Schwabe, Kerstin. 2013. Eine uniforme Analyse sententialer Proformen im Deutschen. *Deutsche Sprache* 41, 142–64.

Sudhoff, Stefan. 2003. *Argumentsätze und* es-*Korrelate. Zur syntaktischen Struktur von Nebensatzeinbettungen im Deutschen.* Berlin: Wissenschaftlicher Verlag Berlin.

Sudhoff, Stefan. 2016. Correlates of object clauses in German and Dutch. *Inner-Sentential Propositional Proforms: Syntactic Properties and Interpretative Effects*, ed. by Werner Frey, André Meinunger, and Kerstin Schwabe, 23–48. Amsterdam: Benjamins.

Willer-Gold, Jana. 2013. Minimalistički pristup strukturi glagolskih skupina sa složenom dopunom u hrvatskome jeziku. Zagreb, PhD dissertation.

Wunderlich, Dieter. 1997. A minimalist model of inflectional morphology. *The role of Economy Principles in Linguistic Theory* (Studia grammatica 40), ed. by Chris Wilder, Hans-Martin Gärtner, and Manfred Bierwisch, 267–98. Berlin: Akademie Verlag.

Wunderlich, Dieter. 2012. Polarity and constraints on paradigmatic distinctness. *The Morphology and Phonology of Exponence*, ed. by Jochen Trommer, 160–94. Oxford: Oxford University Press.

Zimmermann, Ilse. 1967. Der Parallelismus verbaler und substantivischer Konstruktionen in der russischen Sprache der Gegenwart. *Zeitschrift für Slawistik* 112.5, 744–55.

Zimmermann, Ilse. 1983. Untersuchungen zum Verhältnis von Substantivgruppe und Nebensatz. *Untersuchungen zur Semantik* (Studia grammatica 22), ed. by Rudolf Růžička and Wolfgang Motsch, 201–42. Berlin: Akademie-Verlag.

Zimmermann, Ilse. 1987. Die Rolle des Lexikons in der Laut-Bedeutungs-Zuordnung. *Das Lexikon als autonome Komponente der Grammatik* (LS/ ZISW/A 163), ed. by Wolfgang Motsch and Ilse Zimmermann, 1–27. Berlin.

Zimmermann, Ilse. 1990. Zur Legitimierung leerer Köpfe. *Syntaktische Repräsentationen mit leeren Kategorien oder Proformen und ihre semantischen Interpretationen* (LS/ZISW/A 206), ed. by Anita Steube, 75–90. Berlin.

Zimmermann, Ilse. 1992. Der Skopus von Modifikatoren. *Fügungspotenzen. Zum 60. Geburtstag von Manfred Bierwisch* (Studia grammatica 34), ed. by Ilse Zimmermann and Anatoli Strigin, 251–79. Berlin: Akademie Verlag.

Zimmermann, Ilse. 1993. Zur Syntax und Semantik der Satzeinbettung. *Satz und Illokution* (Linguistische Arbeiten 278), Band 2, ed. by Inger Rosengren 1992/1993, 231–51. Tübingen: Niemeyer.

Zimmermann, Ilse. 2000. Die Analysierbarkeit von Pronomen und Proadverbialia. *Angemessene Strukturen: Systemorganisation in Phonologie, Morphologie und Syntax*, ed. by Andreas Bittner, Dagmar Bittner, and Klaus-Michael Köpcke, 261–82. Hildesheim, Zürich, New York: Olms.

Zimmermann, Ilse. 2009. Satzmodus. *Die slavischen Sprachen. Ein internationales Handbuch zu ihrer Struktur, ihrer Geschichte und ihrer Erforschung* (HSK 32.1), ed. by Sebastian Kempgen, Peter Kosta, Tilman Berger, and Karl Gutschmidt, 484–505. Berlin, New York: de Gruyter.

Zimmermann, Ilse. 2015. The Russian subjunctive. *Slavic grammar from a formal perspective.* The 10th anniversary FDSL conference, Leipzig 2013 (Linguistik International 35), ed. by Gerhild Zybytow, Petr Biskup, Marcel Guhl, Claudia Hurtig, Olav Mueller-Reichau, and Maria Yastrebova, 579–94. Frankfurt am Main: Peter Lang.

Zimmermann, Ilse. 2016a. Phonological, morphosyntactic and semantic properties of *es*. *Inner-Sententialpropositional Proforms: Syntactic Properties and Interpretative Effects*, ed. by Werner Frey, André Meinunger, and Kerstin Schwabe, 147–69. Amsterdam: Benjamins.

Zimmermann, Ilse. 2016b. Nebensatzeinbettungen mit Korrelat im Deutschen und Russischen. *Germanistik in der Ukraine* 11, 149–58.

Zimmermann, Ilse. 2018a. Das Korrelat in temporalen Nebensätzen. *Linguistische Berichte* 253, 37–57.

Zimmermann, Ilse. 2018b. Was nicht alles in leeren Köpfen ist. Vortrag am Leibniz-Zentrum Allgemeine Sprachwissenschaft, 16. Juli 2018. *Germanistik in der Ukraine* 13, 50–62.

Zimmermann, Ilse. 2019a. Nominalisierungen zu intensionalen Verben. *Linguistische Berichte* 259, 319–47.

Zimmermann, Ilse. 2019b. Zur Analysierbarkeit adverbieller Konnektive. *Of trees and birds. A festschrift for Gisbert Fanselow*, ed. by J.M.M. Brown, Andreas Schmidt, and Marta Wierzba, 37–59. Potsdam: Universitätsverlag Potsdam.

Zimmermann, Ilse. 2020. Mit *WIE* bzw. *KAK* eingeleitete Nebensätze. Submitted to *Zeitschrift für Sprachwissenschaft*.

Zimmermann, Ilse. 2021. The role of the correlate in clause-embedding. *Advances in Formal Slavic Linguistics 2018*. Online: https://langsci-press.org/catalog/book/280.

Potsdam Linguistic Investigations
Potsdamer Linguistische Untersuchungen
Recherches Linguistique à Potsdam

Edited by / Herausgegeben von / Edité par
Peter Kosta, Gerda Haßler, Teodora Radeva-Bork, Lilia Schürcks,
Nadine Thielemann and / und / et Vladislava Maria Warditz

Band 1 Peter Kosta / Lilia Schürcks (eds.): Linguistics Investigations into Formal Description of Slavic Languages. Contributions of the Sixth European Conference held at Potsdam University, November 30–December 02, 2005. 2007.

Band 2 Lilia Schürcks: Binding and Discourse. Where Syntax and Pragmatics Meet. 2008.

Band 3 Christiane Hümmer: Synonymie bei phraseologischen Einheiten. Eine korpusbasierte Untersuchung. 2009.

Band 4 Svetlana Friedrich: Definitheit im Russischen. 2009.

Band 5 Matthias Guttke: Strategien der Persuasion in der schriftkonstituierten politischen Kommunikation. Dargestellt an Parteiprogrammen der Neuen Rechten in Polen. 2010.

Band 6 Peter Kosta / Lilia Schürcks (eds.): Formalization of Grammar in Slavic Languages. Contributions of the Eighth International Conference on Formal Description of Slavic Languages – FDSL VIII 2009. University of Potsdam, December 2–5, 2009. 2011.

Band 7 Roman Sukač (ed.): From Present to Past and Back. Papers on Baltic and Slavic Accentology. 2011.

Band 8 Diego Gabriel Krivochen: The Syntax and Semantics of Nominal Construction. A Radically Minimalist Perspective. 2012.

Band 9 Teodora Radeva-Bork: Single and Double Clitics in Adult and Child Grammar. 2012.

Band 10 Anja Hennemann: A Context-sensitive and Functional Approach to Evidentiality in Spanish or Why Evidentiality needs a Superordinate Category. 2013.

Band 11 Diego Gabriel Krivochen / Peter Kosta: Eliminating Empty Categories. A Radically Minimalist View on Their Ontology and Justification. 2013.

Band 12 Christina Behme: Evaluating Cartesian Linguistics. From Historical Antecedents to Computational Modeling. 2014.

Band 13 Kathleen Plötner: Raum und Zeit im Kontext der Metapher. Korpuslinguistische Studien zu französischen und spanischen Raum-Zeit-Lexemen und Raum-Zeit-Lokutionen. 2014.

Band 14 Marion Eva Ernst: Produktnamen der Lebensmittelindustrie. Eine empirisch-strukturelle Untersuchung. 2014.

Band 15 Stefanie Wagner: Eine „unbekannte" Sprache lesen *oder* Von der Entdeckung des Nissart durch Interkomprehension. 2015.

Band 16 Nataša Todorović: The Indicative and Subjunctive da-complements in Serbian: A Syntactic-Semantic Approach. 2015.

Band 17 Vladislava Warditz / Beatrix Kreß (eds.): Multilingualism and Translation. Studies on Slavonic and Non-Slavonic Languages in Contact. 2015.

Band 18 Nadia Varley: Optionality and overgeneralization patterns in second language acquisition: Where has the expletive ensconced *it*self? 2015.

Band 19 Verónica Böhm: La imperfectividad en la prensa española y su relación con las categorías semánticas de modalidad y evidencialidad. 2016.

Band 20 Roland Wagner: Reflexivität im tschechisch-deutschen Sprachvergleich. Möglichkeiten und Grenzen einer Prognose. 2016.

Band 21 Ray C. H. Leung: Institutional Construction of Gamblers' Identities. A Critical Multi-method Discourse Study. 2017.

Band 22 Markéta Ziková: Licensing of Vowel Length in Czech. The Syntax-Phonology Interface. 2018.

Band 23 Ludmila Veselovská: Noun Phrases in Czech. Their Structure and Agreements. 2018.

Band 24 Carmen Conti Jiménez: Complejidad lingüística. Orígenes y revisión crítica del concepto de lengua compleja. 2018.

Band 25 Nadine Thielemann / Nicole Richter (eds.): Urban Voices: The Sociolinguistics, Grammar and Pragmatics of Spoken Russian. 2019.

Band 26 Udo Mai: La modalité et ses réalisations en français. 2019.

Band 27 Davide Fanciullo: Temporal expression in nominals: tripartite deictics in the Bulgarian Rhodope dialects. 2019.

Band 28 Olga Flug: Russisch und Ukrainisch im Wandel. Eine korpusbasierte Untersuchung zur Destandardisierung am Beispiel der Anglisierung in der Werbesprache nach 1985. 2019.

Band 29 Teodora Radeva-Bork / Peter Kosta (eds.): Current Developments in Slavic Linguistics. Twenty Years After (*based on selected papers from FDSL 11*). 2019.

Band 30 Anja Hennemann: Topic and Focus Markers in Spanish, Portuguese and French. 2020.

Band 31 Peter Kosta: The Syntax of Meaning and the Meaning of Syntax. Minimal Computations and Maximal Derivations in a Label-/Phase-Driven Generative Grammar of Radical Minimalism. 2020.

Band 32 Magdalena Lipinski: Wortbildung Polnisch und Deutsch: Integrative Darstellung ausgewählter Wortbildungsprozesse. Mit einem Anhang von Hans-Heinrich Lieb. 2020.

Band 33 Peter Kosta / Katrin Schlund (eds.): Keynotes from the International Conference on Explanation and Prediction in Linguistics (CEP): Formalist and Functionalist Approaches. Heidelberg, February 13th and 14th, 2019. 2021.

Band 34 Steven L. Franks / Alan H. Timberlake / Anna W. Wietecka (eds.): Selected Proceedings of the 14th Meeting of the Slavic Linguistics Society. In Honor of Peter Kosta. 2021.

www.peterlang.com

www.ingramcontent.com/pod-product-compliance
Ingram Content Group UK Ltd.
Pitfield, Milton Keynes, MK11 3LW, UK
UKHW021420091026
15624UKWH00010B/270

9 783631 811603